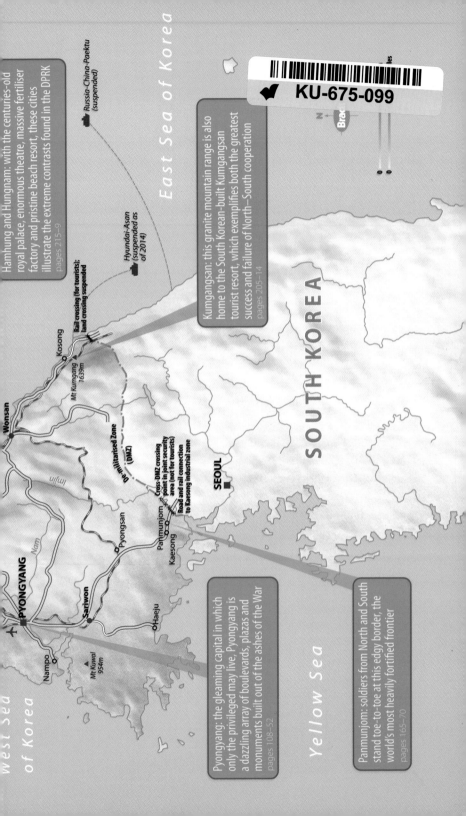

West Sea of Korea

East Sea of Korea

Yellow Sea

SOUTH KOREA

Russia-China-Paektu (suspended)

Hamhung and Hungnam: with the centuries-old royal palace, enormous theatre, massive fertiliser factory and pristine beach resort, these cities illustrate the extreme contrasts found in the DPRK
pages 215–9

Hyundai-Asan (suspended as of 2014)

Kumgangsan: this granite mountain range is also home to the South Korean-built Kumgangsan tourist resort, which exemplifies both the greatest success and failure of North–South cooperation
pages 205–14

Rail crossing (for tourists); land crossing suspended

Wonsan

Kosong

Mt Kumgang 1639m

De-militarised Zone (DMZ)

Cross-DMZ crossing point in joint security area (not for tourists)

Road and rail connection to Kaesong industrial zone

PYONGYANG

Nampo

Sariwon

Namm

Pyongsan

Panmunjom

Kaesong

Haeju

Mt Kuwol 954m

SEOUL

Pyongyang: the gleaming capital in which only the privileged may live, Pyongyang is a dazzling array of boulevards, plazas and monuments built out of the ashes of the War
pages 108–52

Panmunjom: soldiers from North and South stand toe-to-toe at this edgy border, the world's most heavily fortified frontier
pages 165–70

North Korea
Don't miss...

Monuments and palaces
A young pioneer places flowers
outside the Mansudae Art Studio
in Pyongyang — the capital is
filled with monuments and statues
depicting the Kims (EL) page 131

Chongjin
The second-largest industrial
city in the DPRK, Chongjin is now
beginning to open up and become a
regular tourist site (EvdB) page 226

Pyongyang
Every visitor will spend time in the
DPRK's capital, which plays host
to the epic Arirang Mass Games,
with around 100,000 participants,
including thousands of children

(EL) pages 138–9

North Korea

the Bradt Travel Guide

Robert Willoughby

edition
3

www.bradtguides.com

Bradt 1
The Glo

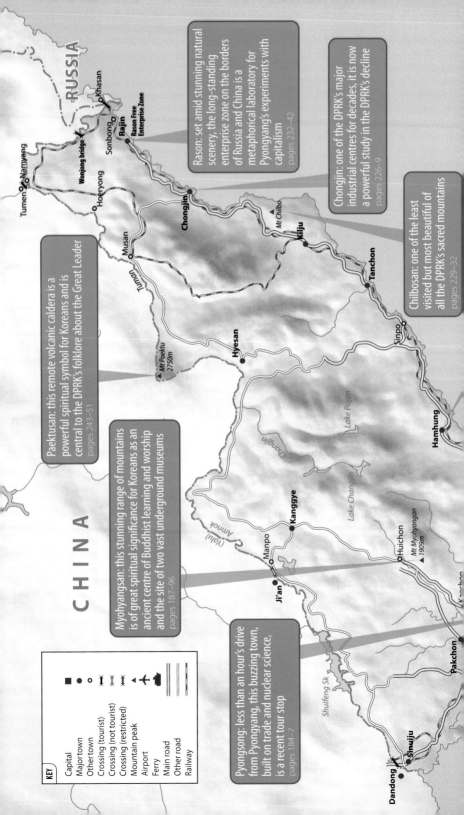

KEY

- ■ Capital
- ● Major town
- ○ Other town
- ⤬ Crossing (tourist)
- ⤫ Crossing (not tourist)
- ⤫ Crossing (restricted)
- ▲ Mountain peak
- ✈ Airport
- ⛴ Ferry
- ═══ Main road
- ─── Other road
- ┼┼┼ Railway

RUSSIA

CHINA

Rason: set amid stunning natural scenery, the long-standing enterprise zone on the borders of Russia and China is a metaphorical laboratory for Pyongyang's experiments with capitalism
pages 232–42

Chongjin: one of the DPRK's major industrial centres for decades, it is now a powerful study in the DPRK's decline
pages 226–9

Chilbosan: one of the least visited but most beautiful of all the DPRK's sacred mountains
pages 229–32

Paektusan: this remote volcanic caldera is a powerful spiritual symbol for Koreans and is central to the DPRK's folklore about the Great Leader
pages 243–51

Myohyangsan: this stunning range of mountains is of great spiritual significance for Koreans as an ancient centre of Buddhist learning and worship and the site of two vast underground museums
pages 187–96

Pyongsong: less than an hour's drive from Pyongyang, this buzzing town, built on trade and nuclear science, is a recent tour stop
pages 184–7

Tumen • Namyong
Khasan
Wonjong bridge
Sonbong
Rajin
Rason Free Enterprise Zone
Hoeryong
Chongjin
Musan
Mt Chilbo ▲
Kiju
Tanchon
▲ Mt Paektu 2750m
Hyesan
Sinpo
Lake Pujon
Changjin
Hamhung
Lake Changjin
Kanggye
Huichon
Mt Myohyangan ▲ 1909m
(Yalu) Amnok
Manpo
Ji'an
Shuifeng Sk
Pakchon
Dandong
Sinuiju

Panmunjom and the DMZ
Visit the heavily militarised DMZ, marking the border between North and uth Korea, and learn about the armistice in Panmunjom
(RW) page 165

Chilbosan
The remote area of Chilbosan offers stunning mountain scenery as well as beautiful stretches of coastline
(EL) page 229

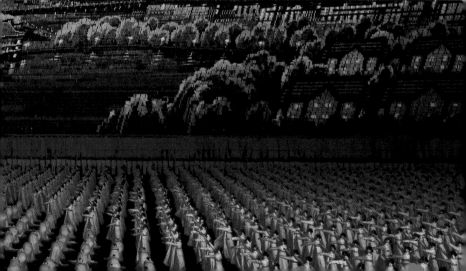

North Korea in colour

above   Pyongyang's most famous site, the Grand Monument on Mansu Hill has two 20m-tall bronze statues of Kim Il Sung and Kim Jong Il standing in front of a 70m-wide mosaic of sacred Mount Paektu (BCT) page 131

above left   Although the exterior has now been glazed, the Ryugyong Hotel in Pyongyang may end up taking as long as the pyramids to complete (NL/AWL) page 141

left   Residential and office buildings in Pyongyang surround the Monument to the Foundation of the Korea Workers' Party Foundation (EL) page 146

below   Women in brightly coloured traditional dresses engage in a mass dance in front of a mosaic of Kim Il Sung next to Pyongyang's Arch of Triumph – the mosaic depicts Kim Il Sung's triumphant return to Pyongyang in 1945 (RW) page 132

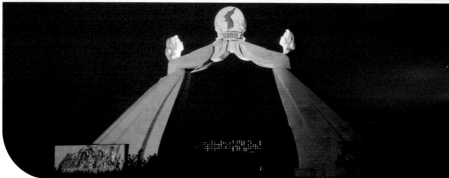

top **Kim Il Sung Square** (EL) page 128

above **The monument to the Reunification of Korea in southern Pyongyang, lit up in the evening** (EL)

right **The Socialist Revolution statue that flanks the Grand Monument on Mansu Hill, Pyongyang** (BCT) page 131

below **The Arch of Triumph in Pyongyang in the early evening** (SS) page 132

We're **40**...
how did that happen?

How did it all happen?
George (my then
husband) and I wrote the
first Bradt guide – about
hiking in Peru and Bolivia
– on an Amazon river
barge, and typed it up on
a borrowed typewriter.
We had no money for the next two books so
George went to work for a printer and was paid
in books rather than money.

Forty years on, Bradt publishes over 200 titles
that sell all over the world. I still suffer from
Imposter Syndrome – how did it all happen?
I hadn't even worked in an office before!
Well, I've been extraordinarily lucky with the
people around me. George provided the belief
to get us started (and the mother to run our
US office). Then, in 1977, I recruited a helper,
Janet Mears, who is still working for us. She and
the many dedicated staff who followed have
been the foundations on which the company
is built. But the bricks and mortar have been
our authors and readers. Without them there
would be no Bradt Travel Guides. Thank you all
for making it happen.

Hilary Bradt

Celebrate our anniversary and get a **40%** discount
on all titles with the code BRADT40.

Available from www.bradtguides.com

AUTHOR

Robert Willoughby was born in London, where he is based as a freelance journalist and author. Realising conventional university would be the death of him, he went to work selling ice cream in Chicago in the summer of 1995, whereupon he became smitten with the absolute thrill and education of living and working abroad – something he thinks he inherited from his father. He qualified as a TEFL teacher and started an Open University degree, while working in Moscow and Hanoi and travelling across southeast Asia before moving to Beijing, where he moved into journalism. In late 2001 he crossed the final frontier into North Korea, then returned to London to hire out his soul reporting on commodity markets in order to buy a place in Deptford. As well as Bradt's truly pioneering *North Korea*, he has also written about conspiracy theories and global surveillance. Since 2001, he's also been working on a novel about selling ice cream in Chicago.

CONTRIBUTOR

Robin Paxton, a Bangalore-based journalist for Reuters (and formerly in Singapore, Moscow and Almaty), contributed sections on the parts of the DPRK other travellers haven't reached, which in this volume comprise the *East Coast to Tanchon* chapter. Robin Paxton can be contacted at robinpen@hotmail.com.

HOW TO USE THIS GUIDE

NON-TOURIST HOTELS AND RESTAURANTS There are a number of hotels and restaurants (mainly in Pyongyang) that are not accessible to tourists. They're listed in the guide without any contact details and marked on the map as points of interest.

LISTING CONTACT DETAILS AND INFORMATION As North Korea is a country in which all tourists must be accompanied by a guide(s) and independent travel is not allowed, many hotel, restaurant and bar listings in this guide (particularly outside Pyongyang) do not have comprehensive contact details such as addresses, telephone numbers and email addresses. Where possible, the author has included websites and other relevant details.

MAPS
Keys and symbols Maps include alphabetical keys covering the locations of those places to stay, eat or drink that are featured in the book. Note that regional maps may not show all hotels and restaurants in the area: other establishments may be located in towns shown on the map. Not all listings in text are included on the maps.

Grids and grid references Several maps use gridlines to allow easy location of sites. Map grid references are listed in square brackets after the name of the place or sight of interest in the text, with page number followed by grid number, eg: [103 C3].

PUBLISHER'S FOREWORD   *Hilary Bradt*

We're incredibly proud to be taking this book – still the only major standalone tourist guide to North Korea – into its third edition. It just goes to show travellers are continuing to visit this strictly controlled country without letting red tape hinder its merits. A feedback letter we received from a reader sums up its importance perfectly: 'I found [this guide] very useful to have with me. And I was not the only one: on the train back from Pyongyang we shared a compartment with the Indian ambassador for North Korea. He was surprised to discover we had a guidebook about the country; he didn't know it existed. He spent most of the journey writing down notes from the guidebook!'

Reprinted April 2016
Third edition published August 2014
First published 2003

Bradt Travel Guides Ltd
IDC House, The Vale, Chalfont St Peter, Bucks SL9 9RZ, England
www.bradtguides.com
Print edition published in the USA by The Globe Pequot Press Inc,
PO Box 480, Guilford, Connecticut 06437-0480

ISBN: 978 1 84162 476 1 (print)
e-ISBN: 978 1 84162 784 7 (e-pub)
e-ISBN: 978 1 84162 685 7 (mobi)

British Library Cataloguing in Publication Data
A catalogue record for this book is available from the British Library

Photographs AWL Images: Gavin Hellier (GH/AWL), Nick Ledger (NL/AWL); Bjørn Christian Tørrissen, www.bjornfree.com (BCT); Edwin van den Bergh (EvdB); Eric Lafforgue (EL); hemis.fr: Patrick Frilet (PF/h); Robert Willoughby (RW); Shutterstock: Anton Ivanov (AI/S), Astrelok (A/S), Maxim Tupikov (MT/S); SuperStock (SS)
Front cover Schoolgirls on their way home, near Mount Kumgang (PF/h)
Back cover A cyclist in front of Pyongyang's skyline (EL)
Title page Grand Monument on Mansu Hill, Pyongyang (BCT); Arirang Mass Games, Pyongyang (EL); tomb of King Kong Min (EL)

Maps David McCutcheon FBCart.S

Typeset from the author's disc by Wakewing
Production managed by Jellyfish Print Solutions; printed in India
Digital conversion by the Firsty Group

Acknowledgements

For the first two editions of this book, in 2002 and 2007, it was rarely possible to gather information by straightforward question and answer; instead I had to learn and apply the black arts of inference, deduction and logic puzzles. That's also been true for this third edition, because one of the DPRK's most notable attributes is that, in the main, so little is known about the place. The country is continuing to open up, and of late, at a greater rate, but we're talking about an acceleration in the 'melt speed' of a glacier.

The North Korean state is possibly best known as a surveillance state that knows everything about its citizens, but tells neither them nor the outside world anything about itself. And into this vacuum of knowledge the Western media, and journalists of usually great repute, unfortunately produce a surprising amount of hackneyed, recycled tosh about the land and its people, with news agencies straying between sensationalism and naivety as they unquestioningly carry stories simply made up by Pyongyang's numerous enemies.

But there are many people who work with, visit, live in and/or study the DPRK, who've accrued incredible expertise and insights about the land, often presenting truths that are at great odds with mainstream beliefs. The emergence of social media has enabled many of them to regularly share their incredible knowledge with the world and with each other, and to engage in often vigorous debate. Everybody with anything to do with the DPRK knows everybody else, making for a richly diverse yet peculiarly exclusive crowd, and I must thank many of them for changing the writing and updating of this book from a laborious sifting of a million Post-it notes into a labour of love. One contact has led to another and it has been personally incalculably enriching for me to have met, online or in person, so many interesting people who have proven so generous with their time and knowledge. I am forever indebted to them.

This guide could not have been written without the following people. First and foremost, I have to thank the ebullient Nick Bonner, whose knowledge and infectious enthusiasm he so generously imparted, and Simon Cockerell, for his unique insights and very patient assistance with maps. I must thank Robin Paxton for his section on the northern parts of the DPRK, and in both London and Pyongyang, Dr Jim Hoare and Susan Pares donated their time and knowledge of the DPRK from decades of working with and in the country, with insights ranging from the country's place in history to where's good to eat in Pyongyang.

I must also thank Roger Barrett for his enthusiastic support and introductions and for imparting his pioneering spirit, and Paul White for information he shared with me. I also thank Keith Bennett, who smoothed off a surprising number of corners in the original draft. Jon Cannon so enthusiastically shared his views and experiences of the DPRK and gave generously regarding the view of the DPRK from China, especially Dandong, and the various capers one can get up to on the Chinese side of the fence. For that I also thank Bryan Schmuland, and the anonymous contributors of Dandong Expat.

Curtis Melvin of the brilliant North Korea Economy Watch (*www.nkeconwatch.com*) was instrumental in pointing satellite searches in the right direction, and I must thank Hannah Barraclough and Amanda Carr of Koryo Tours, and Carl Meadows of Regent Holidays, for their assistance in answering my multiple enquiries and pedantries as well as sharing their own insights. Jos Emmerik and Kees van Galen of VNL Travel also provided answers to nitty bits and pieces.

For the third edition, often via Facebook and Twitter, I've also benefited enormously from debating and nattering with the following. To that end I thank Nigel Cowie, Felix Abt, Matthew Reichel, Charles Park, Michael Bassett, Leonid Petrov, Christopher Graper and Daniel Levitsky, and Chad O'Carroll and Oliver Hotham – but I must stress that how the information is presented in this book, and the views of the author, are the responsibility of the author alone! As for the first edition, which remains the bulk of the book, I still have to thank Neil Taylor, then of Regent Holidays, who clarified parts and suggested further leads. Thanks also to Pyongyang resident Joanne Richardson and frequent Pyongyang visitor Paul White for their snippets of life in the city. I must also thank Dermot Boyd-Hudson for explaining Juche; Dr Philip Edwards, Hall Healy and Angela Choe for their help with the wildlife and DMZ Peace Park project; and Guy Horne for his Pyongyang Marathon information. Andrea Godfrey and Rachel Russell brought forth further information and assistance, and Veronica Malykh and Richard Hunt were invaluable in getting me those itsy bits of info beyond my linguistic reach. Many thanks to Steve and Rowena Samuels for housing me in Beijing during my foray into the DPRK in 2001 and 2002, for which I also thank Michelle Gamelin for generously lending me her apartment. Peter Hare and Tiffany You helped organise the first DPRK visit. Amanda Cooper and Chris Bland read the finished manuscript and gave very valuable comments and questions, Jorinde Chang helped with translations, and Colin Tudge, Matt Milton, Jerry Goodman and James McConnachie were very helpful with the first edition. I must also thank Laetitia Antonowicz for her unending support and asking the right questions when and where I couldn't throughout the writing of the book, especially those five days when the wheels came off of the whole adventure. Thanks to my Ma for putting me up during the nuclear winter of my earning ability and to all my friends and family who listened to me talk of little else until spring finally arrived. Great thanks to Dawn and Ben for being lovely, and to Robin Tudge, whose help can't be put into words.

Foreword

The Democratic People's Republic of Korea, generally known as North Korea, is by no means an ordinary tourist destination. Not only has its government been traditionally wary of the outside world but the long-lasting state of tension on the Korean peninsula has tended to put off visitors. Yet the country has much to offer. There are spectacular mountain scenes, fast-flowing rivers, waterfalls and fine beaches. The sea is clear and unpolluted. Whatever view one may have of the country's political system, the monuments and vistas of Pyongyang, the capital, are like no others in the world.

All of this is covered in Robert Willoughby's most welcome guidebook, which should meet the needs both of the visitor and of the growing number of longer-term foreign residents. Hitherto, it has been hard to find an adequate guidebook to North Korea. At best, the country has attracted a chapter or two tacked on to much fuller accounts of the Republic of Korea or South Korea. It is true that, once in North Korea, the visitor may find quite good locally produced guidebooks. But even the best of these assume that all visitors will be part of a guided tour, with no free time. They are far from comprehensive and usually fail to deal with practical matters such as where to eat or how to get around. And they are not always available, even in the bigger hotel bookshops. So to have gathered together in one place both descriptive and practical information is a great benefit. In addition, the reader will find sufficient background material to make any visit enjoyable and more rewarding.

Unless there is some major change in the country's circumstances, visiting North Korea will always be something for only a few. Those few will in future have the benefit of this useful and informative work.

J E Hoare
Chargé d'Affaires, British Embassy, Pyongyang 2001–2

Contents

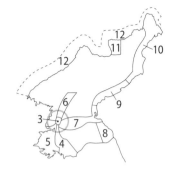

LIST OF MAPS

Introduction

The first time I flew from Beijing to Pyongyang, in the late 1990s, I became aware of going somewhere else, somewhere different, before even getting on the plane. It was a compact Air Koryo Ilyushin-62 with an unusually well-glazed cockpit, parked at the farthest, darkest end of a Beijing terminal wing. It didn't look like a Boeing or Airbus or anything built to fly this last decade; it had engines at the back and a particular swoop to its design. The Koreans waiting to board wore quality suits of sombre-coloured cloth of an oddly uniform, timelessly stylish cut. They talked to each other, not on mobiles, and not to me. I spoke with the other foreigners, all strangers to one another but bound by the common interest and thrill of having any business in North Korea.

Boarding the plane, I saw that in the interior, the colours, shapes, seats, knobs and dials were all stylish in a conservative, '70s kind of way. The in-flight magazine and free copy of the *Pyongyang Times* newspaper wrote of the brilliance and world-encompassing influence of people and ideas I hadn't heard of, with current affairs dominated by wars and empires I thought were finished 50 years ago. The air hostess wheeled the drinks trolley along, laden with beer, cider and mineral water, all North Korean brands, none that I recognised.

Pyongyang airport looked like any other, except for Kim Il Sung's portrait hanging over it. I and the other passengers went through passport control, with the passport officer notably high up in his cubicle. The other side, everyone was met by a driver and car. No throng of taxi men hassling and haggling, no buses. No advertising! I and some other strangers who quickly befriended one another on our joint adventure (of being in North Korea) were whisked away in a large car, with driver and guide, around empty hills, through road checkpoints dotted along empty roads. Everything seemed straight out of the opening scenes in Tintin's *Destination Moon*.

Soon, a clean, tall city unfolded before us, and unfold is the word. Many cities unravel, their layouts like random bits of string flung in a box, but Pyongyang's vistas and boulevards of sharp-sided buildings pan out so neatly, as definable sections on a vast plan of the city. We arrived at the hotel, a soaring metallic gantry tower on an island, and entered its cavernous foyer, with its steel-frame roof and a glass elevator zooming up and down through it. Here I met everyone I'd met waiting for the plane. You're here too? My my! This wasn't Tintin, but Orwell, and any second, Bond. A Korean Blofeld would appear in the lift, guffawing over the tannoy, 'Ho ho ho! So, Mr Willoughby … or should I say, Mr Smith?', whereupon the roof would open like a massive steel flower and we would all disappear in a shower of sparks and rocket fumes.

It's easy for the imagination to run riot about North Korea (or as they prefer to call it in Pyongyang, the Democratic People's Republic of Korea). I first became interested in the place while working in China, itself a country abounding in frontiers for foreigners convinced they're the first to set foot anywhere. It was at Beijing's airport that I noticed flights to Pyongyang on the departures board. So there was a way into the land on the edge of the world, that small pocket of mountains that the Western press was forever wailing to be a worry and a menace, this secretive, hermetic state referred to as Stalinist on the good days, that final bastion of high ideals and base deeds. I got my chance to go as part of a larger delegation, and while I remember every single moment, the trip as a whole confirmed some rumours and debunked other myths. A lot of things I had read about the place before going didn't seem true while there, or was I being brilliantly hoodwinked? I realised I didn't really know anything at all worth knowing. So when the grapevine sent a memo that Bradt wanted someone to write a guidebook about the DPRK, I jumped at the chance, to find out as much for myself as to try and flash a bit of torchlight into this dark corner of the world.

That said, it hasn't been easy to research. A massive amount of the information in print is incomplete and out of date, and it's an uphill climb to stay on top of recent changes. In the country, a lot of basic information about places, like opening times, prices and phone numbers, was refused. I learnt this was because if the person I was asking actually knew, and I was definitely asking the right person, they still wouldn't tell me because they didn't feel entitled to tell me. It was not up to them to decide what I could and couldn't be told, and that rule applies to everything. On a wider note, there are few objective sources about the country, and literature ranges between the extremes of veneration and vitriol.

That has not changed in the decade plus since first visiting and writing this book, and nor has the country. There are many more cars in Pyongyang now, there are even traffic jams, but many of the trams and trolleybuses are at death's door. You see many more people out and about, many with mobile phones, but their phone networks are entirely shut off from those used by foreigners. People in Pyongyang seem relaxed and buoyant in a way that they were not in 2002, when still staggering out of the famine, and they smile and wave. But they keep their distance. There are more new buildings and lights that stay on at night, but they still lack any hoardings or adverts for goods or any reference to the outside world whatsoever, and the astonishingly monothematic presence of all things Kim still dominates every facet of life, education, the media, history, tourism, imagery, etc. And the military are everywhere. For all the changes around the edges, it remains fundamentally the same.

There are more sights to see and the list is growing all the time, but it's as true that the bulk of the country remains off-limits. One learns that restrictions on what people can see in different areas depends on the conservatism of the local authorities, and their mystification in many ways at what could possibly be of interest to outsiders. The outlook of the Korean International Travel Company (KITC, one of the DPRK's three tourism units) varies from location to location, with the Pyongyang division being the most receptive in their approach to visitors and to ideas and new stops, like Pyongsong, while the Chilbosan division is still very restrictive. They can handle the opening up of beauty spots but not major cities. Hence Chongjin, one of the DPRK's largest cities, has just a handful of sights to see. The further one goes from the capital, the less there is that one's allowed to see. A lot of that comes from trust, relations, knowledge and communications. Traditionally people have not visited Chilbosan, for one because it's so far and difficult to get to with old buses battering along terrible roads, and they don't know what's there, so the locals don't cater for them. There haven't been tourists so there isn't the infrastructure to deal with them, although that is supposedly changing by decree of Kim Jong Un. There is also a town and country divide; guides from Pyongyang can seem as if they're in the Wild West.

I've tried to write this book as much for those people who go in with a guide (mainly tourists) as for those who live there or are visitors for other reasons. There are omissions of basic information and broad issues. On the first point, for tourists, questions about times, prices and numbers are largely irrelevant because they're with guides at all times and their itineraries are planned so that museums and whatnot can be opened especially for one tour group. Non-tourists are still barred from visiting grand public buildings or museums without guides to take them round, which must be arranged, but parks, the right restaurants and shops can all be visited relatively freely, as can a few outlying temples and museums in outer places – but don't rely on just turning up. There are also quite a few subject areas that cannot be readily discussed in a guidebook that is only of use if it's allowed into the country. For what's not explicitly written about, I've included many links to further sources – but bear in mind the motives of whoever writes anything about this most mysterious of lands. Pyongyang has as many real enemies as imaginary. I promise I've done my best to provide as much information as possible; to anyone who can plug the obvious gaps, snippets of prices, numbers, times, who can prove something is wrong or something is no longer true, I and Bradt will be exceedingly grateful for your input.

Keep your eyes and mind open, smiles wide and hands waving high – when not shaking the hands of Koreans.

FEEDBACK REQUEST AND UPDATES WEBSITE

At Bradt Travel Guides we're aware that guidebooks start to go out of date on the day they're published – and that you, our readers, are out there in the field doing research of your own. You'll find out before us when a fine new family-run hotel opens or a favourite restaurant changes hands and goes downhill. So why not write and tell us about your experiences? Contact us on ☎ 01753 893444 or e info@bradtguides.com. We will forward emails to the author who may post updates on the Bradt website at www.bradtupdates.com/northkorea. Alternatively you can add a review of the book to www.bradtguides.com or Amazon.

FOLLOW BRADT

For the latest news, special offers and competitions, subscribe to the Bradt newsletter via the website www.bradtguides.com and follow Bradt on:

- ⓕ www.facebook.com/BradtTravelGuides
- 🐦 @BradtGuides
- 📷 @bradtguides
- ⓟ pinterest.com/bradtguides

Part One

GENERAL INFORMATION

Location Northeast Asia: China and Russia are along the northern borders; South Korea (the Republic of Korea, ROK) to the south; Japan to the east

Area 120,540km²

Climate Long, cold winters; short, hot, humid and rainy summers

Population 22,225,000

Capital Pyongyang

Main towns Kaesong, Wonsan, Hamhung, Nampo, Chongjin, Kangye, Sinuiju

Currency Won; North Korean Won is referred to as KPW (1 won = 100 chon)

Exchange rate £1 = 218KPW, €1 = 179KPW, US$1 = 129KPW, 1 CNY = 21KPW (May 2014); for up-to-date rates, see www.xe.com.

Official language Korean

Religion Atheist

Ethnic divisions Racially homogeneous; there is a very small Chinese community.

Type of government Authoritarian socialist dictatorship

International telephone code +850

Time GMT +9

Weights and measures Metric

Electricity 220v, 60Hz

Flag Three horizontal bands, blue–red–blue, with thin white lines dividing them; off-centre-left of the red band is a white circle with a red, five-pointed star.

Public holidays 1 January (New Year's Day), 16 February (Kim Jong Il's birthday), 15 April (Kim Il Sung's birthday), 25 April (Army Day), 1 May (May Day), 8 July (Memorial day to Kim Il Sung's death), 27 July (Victory Day), 15 August (Independence from Japan Day), 9 September (Republic Foundation Day), 10 October (Korean Workers' Party Foundation Day), 27 December (Constitution Day)

Important commemoration days 20 February (Machine Workers' Day), 5 March (Farmers' Day), 8 March (International Women's Day), 22 March (Fishermen's Day), 5 April (Public Health Day), 6 April (Reforestation Day), 8 April (Communications Day), 11 May (Railway Day), 15 May (Geological Survey Day), 21 May (Builders' Day), 1 June (International Children's Day), 6 June (Day of the Foundation of Korean Children's Union), 7 June (Local Industry Day), 1 July (Miners' Day), 7 July (Coal-Miners' Day), 10 August (Forestry Workers' Day), 20 August (Air Force Day), 28 August (Navy Day and Youth Day), 5 September (City Administration Day), 15 September (Commerce Day), 9 October (Metal Workers' Day), 14 October (Broadcasting Workers' Day), 15 October (Textile Industry Day), 1 November (Press Day), 16 November (Land and Marine Transport Day), 6 December (Chemical Industry Day).

1

Background Information

GEOGRAPHY

The Korean peninsula protrudes about 1,000km southwards from northeast Asia, a mountainous outcrop centred squarely between China, Russia and Japan, the last cupping the peninsula in shelter from the Pacific. The peninsula runs from 43° 00'N, south down towards the East China Sea at 33° 06'N, and its 222,209 km² area was, up to 1945, a land mass where lived one homogeneous people in one country: Korea. However, since that time, this country has been bitterly divided into north (the Democratic People's Republic of Korea, DPRK) and south (the Republic of Korea, ROK), with their mutual border being a 238km-long demarcation line going from the east coast to the west more or less along the 38th line of latitude. This border is coated by a 4km-thick zone of restricted military activity, namely the De-Militarised Zone or DMZ, although it is really the most heavily fortified border in the world. But maps from both sides show the DMZ as a faint detail across one country, as both states still consider Korea as one country divided into two states – one being run by the rightful government of the whole peninsula, and the other not. Maps from the DPRK show Pyongyang as the only capital and Seoul is just a village. This is reciprocated on maps made in the ROK. This can be confusing, for at least in northern publications, figures exclusively for the northern area slip amid figures for the whole peninsula. For example, the figure for Korea's borders totalling 1,369km in the Korean International Travel Company's *Korea's Tourist Map* excludes the DMZ and the same book states Korea's total area as 222,209.31km², which is true, but doesn't distinguish that the DPRK's territory is only 120,540km² of that (*CIA Factbook*). For this section, unless stated as relating to the entire peninsula, all figures pertain only to the DPRK.

Besides the DMZ, the DPRK has a 1,425km-long northern border with China and a 19km one with Russia. Both borders are 'natural'. The Chinese border follows the River Amnok (or Yalu by its Chinese name) southwest between Sinuiju and Dandong cities to the West Sea and the Tuman River that flows northeast to the Korean East Sea (also called the Sea of Japan), the Tuman's final section comprising the Russian border at Rajin-Songbun. These rivers source approximately two-thirds north along the Chinese border at the volcanic crown that is Mount Paektu and the mighty Lake Chon within. From the lake's opposing shores Chinese and Koreans holler at one another in this forum amid a formidable range of mountains, so Korea's northern border is a natural border of river-sized moats and igneous walls. The DPRK has the monopoly on the peninsula's mountains, which with highlands constitute 80% of the DPRK's land area. The DPRK has over 50 mountains above 2,000m, many grouped in the Hamgyong range that tapers into the wedge shape of the country's northeast. The highest mountain on the peninsula is Mount Paektu

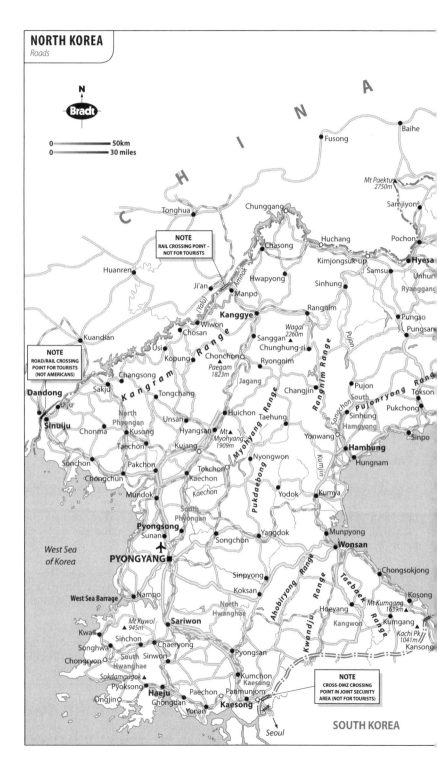

NORTH KOREA
Roads

N

Bradt

| 0 | 50km |
| 0 | 30 miles |

C H I N A

Fusong

Mt Paektu
2750m

Tonghua

Chunggang

Samjiyon

NOTE
RAIL CROSSING POINT –
NOT FOR TOURISTS

Chasong

Huchang

Pochon

Kimjongsuk-up

Hyesa

Huanren

Hwapyong

Samsu

Unhur

Ji'an

Manpo

Sinhung

Ryanggang

Kanggye

Wiwon

*Wagal
2260m*

Rangnim

Pungso

Chosan

Sanggan

Pungsan

Kuandian

Usi

Chonchon

Chunghung-ri

NOTE
ROAD/RAIL CROSSING
POINT FOR TOURISTS
(NOT AMERICANS)

Kopung

*Paegam
1823m*

Ryongnim

Pujon

Tokson

Changsong

Jagang

Changjin

Pukchong

Dandong

Sakju

Tongchang

South

Uiju

Unsan

Huichon

Taehung

Sinhung

Sinpo

Sinuiju

Chonma

Kusong

Hyangsan

*Mt
Myohyang
1909m*

Yonwang

Hamhung

Taechon

Kujang

Nyongwon

Hungnam

Sonchon

Pakchon

Tokchon

Yodok

Kumya

Chongchun

Kaechon

Kaechon

Mundok

South
Phyongan

Pyongsong

Sunan

Songchon

Yangdok

Munpyong

PYONGYANG

Wonsan

*West Sea
of Korea*

Sinpyong

Chongsokjong

West Sea Barrage

Nampo

Koksan

Kosong

North
Hwanghae

Hoeyang

Mt Kumgang
1639m

*Mt Kuwol
945m*

Sariwon

Kangwon

Kumgang

Kwall

Sinchon

Chaeryong

Kachi Pk
1041m

Songhwa

South
Hwanghae

Sinwon

Pyongsan

Kansong

Chongryon

Sokdamgugok

Kumchon

Kaesong

NOTE
CROSS-DMZ CROSSING
POINT IN JOINT SECURITY
AREA (NOT FOR TOURISTS)

Pyoksong

Paechon

Panmunjom

Ongjin

Haeju

Chongdan

Kaesong

Yonan

Seoul

SOUTH KOREA

Kangram Range

Myohyang Range

Rangnim Range

Pujonryong Rang

Songchon

Hamgyong

Pukdaebong

Kumjin

Ahobiryong Range

Kwandiu Range

Taebaek Range

(Yalu)

Amnok

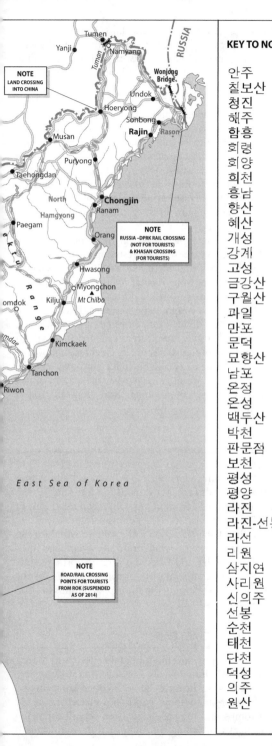

KEY TO NORTH KOREAN NAMES

안주	Anju
칠보산	Chilbo san
청진	Chongjin
해주	Haeju
함흥	Hamhung
회령	Hoeryong
회양	Hoeyang
희천	Huichon
흥남	Hungnam
향산	Hyangsan
혜산	Hyesan
개성	Kaesong
강계	Kanggye
고성	Kosong
금강산	Kumgang san
구월산	Kuwol san
과일	Kwail
만포	Manpo
문덕	Mundok
묘향산	Myohyang san
남포	Nampo
온정	Onjong
온성	Onsong
백두산	Paektusan
박천	Pakchon
판문점	Panmunjom
보천	Pochon
평성	Pyongsong
평양	Pyongyang
라진	Rajin
라진-선봉	Rajin-Sonbong
라선	Rason
리원	Riwon
삼지연	Samjiyon
사리원	Sariwon
신의주	Sinuiju
선봉	Sonbong
순천	Sunchon
태천	Taechon
단천	Tanchon
덕성	Toksong
의주	Uiju
원산	Wonsan

at 2,750m. In the DPRK's north are the higher and drier hills and plains spiked with needle-leaf and spruce trees. Only faint traces of farmland tuck into the gaps between the hills. The lowland, fertile plains in the southwest and scattered along the island-free east coast hold most of the arable land (and most of the country's 24.05 million people, according to the 2008 census), tended by the orderly groups of houses in collective or co-operative farms. These neat one-storey brick houses with traditional roofs, or multi-storey concrete cubes, stand in the centre of vast paddyfields that roll floor-flat to the horizon. The elaborate hillside terracing seen in southern Asia isn't here, as the water in these thin, muddy strips would quickly freeze in winter and destroy the paddies' delicate structure. Instead, the hillsides are covered with whichever crop can grow that season, as is every spare strip of earth; in the cities as out in the country, foodstuffs protrude from every possible surface. Rice and maize are harvested around October, so spring is for the secondary crops of barley, wheat and potatoes. Soya beans, pumpkins, eggplant, red peppers and ginseng are also important.

The seasonal droughts and floods that have always blighted the peninsula's agriculture have worsened partly through extensive deforestation of the lowlands' mixed forests of pine and broad leaf, oak and birch. Afforestation is visible in many of the DPRK's nine provinces (Kangwon, Jagang, Ryanggang, North and South Pyongan, North and South Hamgyong, North and South Hwanghae), and around its four 'special cities' (Pyongyang, Nampo, Rajin-Sonbong, Kaesong) that are under central authority. Provinces are divided into cities (*si*) and counties. A county is further subdivided into smaller geographic areas called *ri* (towns) and *dong* (districts), while smaller *dongs* (as boroughs) also make up cities and towns.

Under the ground, the country's mineral wealth includes soft coal, copper, tungsten, gold and uranium. Place names are suffixed by what the feature is, like Panmun-ri, Taedong-gang (*gang* = river), Potong-dong, Kumgang-san (*san* = mountain), Moranbong (*bong* = hill).

CLIMATE

The DPRK's warm, temperate climate divides into four seasons: spring (March to May), summer (June to August), autumn (September to November) and winter (December to February). The seasons are dry except the monsoon-like rainy season of summer; that over half of Pyongyang's 916mm of annual precipitation falls in July and August is very typical. Typhoons also tour the peninsula's coasts, causing floods and wind damage. The southeast coastal region is the wettest, with Wonsan averaging 1,400mm in annual rainfall. Westerly winds from the Asian land mass make winters cold and dry, getting colder and drier the further north you go. High humidity besides, the DPRK's July temperatures can run up to 25°C in the southwest round Nampo to Pyongyang, while winter in the capital plumbs to –8°C and atop Mount Paektu plummets below –20°C.

NATURAL HISTORY AND CONSERVATION

The DPRK has a few national parks, mainly around mountain sites, as in Mount Chilbo, Mount Paektu, Mount Kuwol, Mount Myohyang and Mount Kumgang, which have varying degrees of religious and historic significance and are sprinkled with temple sites, ruined and restored. In these parks and elsewhere, many cultural sites, particularly old tombs and temples, have been rebuilt following the ravages of war, looting, neglect and falling into official ill-favour. Though

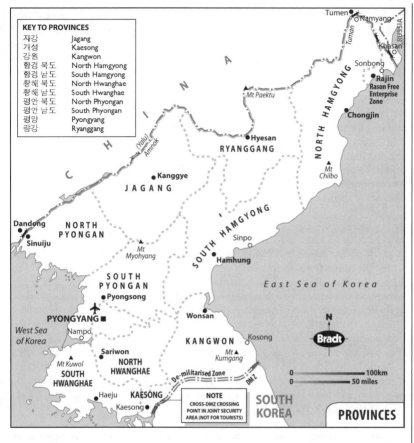

KEY TO PROVINCES

자강	Jagang
개성	Kaesong
강원	Kangwon
함경 북도	North Hamgyong
함경 남도	South Hamgyong
황해 북도	North Hwanghae
황해 남도	South Hwanghae
평안 북도	North Phyongan
평안 남도	South Phyongan
평양	Pyongyang
량강	Ryanggang

PROVINCES

NOTE
CROSS-DMZ CROSSING
POINT IN JOINT SECURITY
AREA (NOT FOR TOURISTS)

the parks and other sites accumulatively cover thousands of square kilometres, the country overall has only around 580km² of protected land, and the national proportion of pristine land is less than 1% of the total area. Pollution from heavy industry has turned some local ecosystems into alien worlds, and respite has come not by decree but through economic contraction that has cut the output of the polluting factories. However, areas of extreme human impact contrast with areas of extremely sparse human inhabitation, as around Mount Paektu and the mountains leading into the DPRK's northeast.

The DPRK altitude, long latitude and climatic range make it home to a wide variety of flora and fauna found in temperate evergreen forests through to broadleafed deciduous forests and up to tundra meadows. Amongst those species indigenous to Korea and to the northern area specifically are wildlife found in Japan, China and Russia, while the DPRK is a grand roosting place for migrating birds. Across Korea can be found black and brown bear, tiger, sable and deer, and often seen soaring over the peninsula are Baikal teal, white-naped crane and white-bellied black woodpecker, while maple and azalea dowse the land in colour. Wildlife-oriented trips can be arranged through tour operators.

The DPRK has for some time realised the potential benefits of tourism, mainly in the form of increasingly large tours from cash-rich China and Russia and more direct investments by ROK firms (above all else, from Hyundai-Asan), as well as a growing number of much smaller, but nonetheless significant tours organised with Western companies. The financial and infrastructural benefits have to be weighed against the losses in terms of pristine, or near-pristine, wildlife cover and the erosions and despoliation brought by inflows of booted feet and the places required to transport and accommodate them. But it also means that areas without much hope for economic rejuvenation and means of income become viable again, and environmental sites possibly at risk for want of any other value become protected by their intrinsic value. In addition, historical sites of forts and temples receive funding for restoration and protection, and sometimes total reconstruction (if not fabrication). In the early years of this century, the DPRK government opened up the possibilities wrought by having sites recognised and listed for their natural and cultural worth with organisations like UNESCO, and this appears to be a growing field of interest in the country; however, there are doubts as to how many of these sites are genuinely 'old'.

HISTORY

A stock phrase found everywhere in Korean literature is '5,000 years of Korean history'. It comes from the following tale. In the beginning, there was the God Hwan In and his son Hwan Ung, who wanted to govern the earth's people. His father consented and sent him earthwards into the Korean peninsula where he established agriculture and the laws of humanity. A bear and a tiger prayed to Ung to be human. Ung gave them garlic and cloves and told them to avoid sunlight for 100 days. The bear succeeded and transformed into a woman, and later married Ung. In 2333BC they had a son, Tangun Wanggom, who set up his capital at Pyongyang and called his kingdom Choson (Morning Freshness). So was born Korea, and they ruled it for a millennium and a half. This story denotes a Chinese influence: 'Morning Freshness' indicates the peninsula's location relative to ancient China, east where the sun rises, while Wang in Chinese means 'king'.

The more modern alternative history of Korea begins with the first human habitation originating from east and northeast Asia. Remains of 'Ryonggok man' of some 400,000 years of age have been found near Pyongyang, as have the remains of man from 40,000 years ago. Culture sites date back to 30000BC, with evidence of ancient Mongolian and Manchurian tribes.

From 6000BC 'combed' pottery and other evidence in unearthed villages suggests sedentary agricultural lives, with domesticated farm animals, and huts sunk into the earth. The first dolmens, large graves of slabs of stone laid flat across upright stones, possibly also used for ritual sacrifice, with agricultural stone implements found buried around them, started to appear from 3000BC. Bronze mirrors and daggers date from 1500BC, and mirrors, knives, bells and other ceremonial trinkets with heavy Chinese influence in their design have also been found.

Early records say that by 300BC there were five tribes controlling distinct areas of the Korean peninsula and the adjacent mainland. The largest, most powerful tribe was the Choson, with its capital Wang-hsien-ch'eng near today's Pyongyang. Trade was conducted with the Chinese state of Yan, one of China's many warring states, and it was a Yan warlord that took over the Choson. The Choson expanded their territory from around the Taedong northwards, to the east coast and south to the Han River, building forts all the way. In China, the Han were ascendant and sought to move on from just trading with the peninsula to demanding tribute and subservience. In 109BC, Han emperor Wu sent land and sea forces to destroy the Choson, sweeping down the peninsula, leaving only the southernmost area free.

Wu's gains were absorbed into the Han Empire and, combined with Manchurian areas beyond the Yalu and Tuman rivers, were divided into four 'commanderies' under Chinese administration. The biggest commandery, with a population of 400,000, was Lo-lang (with Pyongyang the capital).

Rice cultivation was introduced, mainly in the south, and a greater variety of sophisticated tools and weapons in iron and bronze was imported. The tombs of Chinese officials, large mounds dotted around modern Pyongyang, have been found to contain many sophisticated paintings and artefacts from Han culture.

Chinese rule continued for four centuries. Individual tribes could be brought to order, their chieftains sometimes given 'official' status with bronze seals to prove it as their tribes were exploited for labour and goods. There was generally more subservience than resistance, and divided tribes located near to commanderies were controllable. But the hardy Koguryo people, hunters and warriors, were spread across the mountains of northern Korea and eastern Manchuria. Their numerous tribes combined under one 'king' who was thus empowered to resist commandery rule and invade Chinese and northeast Korean regions for food, materials and slaves.

By 37BC, the Koguryo had developed a powerful state, with influence from far into Manchuria to the southern Han River. As China was debilitated by dynastic infighting and barbarian invasions, the country's grip on the peninsula faltered and, by the 3rd century AD, its commanderies were facing sustained tribal resistance. As China imploded, the Lo-Lang and Tai-Feng commanderies were cut off, and the Koguryo absorbed the Lo-Lang in AD313. Meanwhile, two states were forming from the tribes in the peninsula's deepest south. The Ma Han tribes in the southwest combined to form the Paekche state and abolished Tai-Feng soon after the Koguryo victory. In the southeast, the Chin Han tribes united to create the Silla state. Wedged between Silla and Paekche lay the small Pyon Han states (also called Kaya) that were dominated by Japan, but it was Silla, Paekche and Koguryo who made up the 'Three Kingdoms Period' that lasted 700 years.

ANCIENT STATES: THE THREE KINGDOMS PERIOD The Koguryo was the biggest of the three kingdoms, covering the peninsula's northern half and beyond the rivers Yalu and Tuman. Its expansion west into China halted when the Yen warrior-state raided and ransacked Koguryo in the mid 4th century. So, for easier pickings, Koguryo forces went south, jabbing and clawing territory from Silla and Paekche. Tens of thousands of Koguryo's population were conquered people, including many former officials of Lo-Lang, so a strong, military-based government was needed to run the expanding Koguryo state. A large fort in Pyongyang, Koguryo's capital since 427, was among many built, while those who the Koguryo defeated in battle or surrendered were executed. The administrative and military chiefs in Pyongyang were former tribal chiefs who became Koguryo nobility. Their sons were schooled in Confucian teachings derived from China to administer the land by regular taxation in grain from the peasants and labour from the slaves, and to codify the nation's laws in the adopted Chinese written language, which made Chinese texts accessible. From China also came Buddhism in the 4th century AD, with all its glories of architecture and arts, and China remained a regional player who alternately allied with the three kingdoms as they warred among themselves. Hence Chinese culture permeated the three kingdoms throughout their existence.

Paekche's Sino connections saw it more imbued with Buddhism earlier than the other kingdoms. Paekche's foreign policy was, like those of the Silla and Koguryo, essentially a continual series of alliances made to attack or defend the aggressor of the day, but Paekche endured more unwelcome interest from the other two. From the mid 4th to the late 7th century, Koguryo forces compressed Paekche into the peninsula's corner, and Paekche's Puyo royal family took the capital south from Hansong to Ungjin to Sabi, leaving behind slain troops and offering tributes of live slaves to appease Koguryo. But the Puyo were outsiders trying to rule a large area populated by Paekche's indigenous Ma Han, who had unfortunately been suppressed very effectively under commandery rule. Hence, their governance was not based on any great loyalty nor had they learned much from Chinese ways of governance. Paekche's main asset was the peninsula's best agricultural land, which the kingdom's slaves cultivated well, but the land was all the more alluring to jealous neighbours.

Silla was the kingdom with the smallest population and land area, and was clamped between Koguryo and Kaya. From its tribes, the Silla had developed governance from a council of tribal chieftains, a *hwabaek* that discussed great matters of state. Conquered tribes were not made hwabaek; that was only for the victors who chose their joint leader. Therein began the division of power based on clan, developing into a multi-layered social structure of rights and privileges based on kinship, rank and status, ascribed through a hereditary caste system, the bone-rank system. The ruling royal clan was the *songgol* rank (the top) and affiliates of the *chingol* ranks. Regulations dictated the size of one's house and stables, cut of dress and cloth used, and other distinctive ornamentation. This regimented caste system would continue throughout the Silla's existence.

Silla also developed an administrative system of state based on Chinese practice, with the monarch overseeing numerous controlling boards with their own remits over finance, war, personnel, etc. This centralised government drew taxes, labour and troops from the local level through an administrative chain breaking the country down into province, district and county levels. This efficient form of governance, with a stable royal household at its heart, was able to organise Silla's warring so effectively that it averted being totally lost to its neighbours. In the early 600s, the Tang of China were able to refocus on the peninsula, and when taking on Koguryo, Silla allied with the Tang to conclusively quash the Koguryo and Paekche threats.

Paekche collapsed, and in 668 Koguryo was pacified – but the Tang emperor then sought total Tang hegemony, and the Silla hadn't fought long and hard just to be robbed of the spoils by their erstwhile ally. Remaining Koguryo aristocrats and their forces were generously welcomed by the Silla in a new front to oust the Tang. A reformed alliance of Silla, Paekche and Koguryo forces, each in distinctive uniforms, set off north, countering Tang attacks with their own crippling assaults, and by the late 670s, the Tang were out.

Unified Silla ... and Palhae The Silla dominated from the Taedong southwards, but Koguryo's aristocracy were not spent as a group capable of command and rule. With the Malgal tribes, the state of Palhae was formed straddling the Yalu River and could access the sea on both the east and west sides, and so could forge substantial trade links with the Chinese and Japanese. It thus grew westwards and northwards, placing its capital in Dunhua in today's Jilin Province. For two centuries the state existed and traded, reaching 2,000km across, until the unity of the tribes succumbed to the nuances of internal conflict that makes tribes tribal, and the state couldn't resist the encroaching Qidan from China in the 10th century.

Meanwhile, the Silla ran their kingdom for many fortuitous years, albeit with a good deal of Chinese influence politically and culturally. A half-century after the Tang were ousted, Chinese suzerainty over the peninsula was re-established. Silla students had already been sent to study Tang governance administration, bringing back further developments in the ethics of Confucianism and its wisdom on the structures and working relations of administration.

Chinese culture permeated Korea through trade, and was carried on through Korean trade into Japan. Trade with China developed links as far away as Iran, and India became a mine of knowledge for Silla's burgeoning love of Buddhism. Buddhism became the national religion and was lavished with gifts of land, slaves and money in the hope that it would protect the state in return. Woodcut prints of the Buddhist scriptures were housed in magnificent temples built in the royal city and taken across the country high into the fabulous mountain temples and monasteries. A rising tide of literary works from this time was permeated with Buddhist thoughts, and the importing of the religion also brought its associated literature, architecture and paintings across the new territories in what is now looked upon as a golden age of arts.

Silla's territory and population had both more than trebled in size, with the territory then redistributed among the nobles of the victorious side and magnanimously given back to the surrendering tribal chiefs; those chiefs who had professional skills and scholarly understanding were employed in government. As such, the 8th century was marked by a period of relative peace in the kingdom, affording both the time and prosperity to promote the arts and sciences. Departments of medicine, mathematics and astronomy were established, as was a department of translation for the Silla's growing trade network. Goods ranging from textiles, furs, pottery and instruments through to advanced iron weapons, silver and gold jewellery were exported.

The population of the capital Kjongju grew to over a million and streets 10km in length were built, with dozens of immense private estates, palaces, monasteries and government buildings, staffed by a ruling class whose provincial lands were tilled by slaves. The Tang had carted off 200,000 into slavery, and slavery continued under the Silla. In the counties, many peasants had their own life-tenancies on land but were still subject to tax and labour service, of which their rulers kept account on continually updated registers. These dues were collected and concentrated in the provincial capitals delegated to run the regions outside the state capital, and became concentrations of power away from the Silla court.

The capital and county distinction grew as the families of the elite moved to the capital, and the Silla kings became more autocratic and determined to distinguish between themselves and their underlings. The hwabaek was finally replaced by Chinese style of administration, and by the late 700s, civil examinations allowed a few commoners to attain position through ability, threatening the aristocrats' long-standing system of position through birth.

For the aristocracy however, their own allegiance of bone-clan kin-ties to the dynasty became of less value than material wealth, and with peace and prosperity came decadence. Provincial revolts broke out with increasing frequency, starting in King Hyegong's reign (765–79), which ended in his assassination. A succession of coups and massacres marred the reigns of the next 20 kings in the 150 years from 784, marking the Silla's accelerating decline. While the aristocrats connived and conspired, the people on their lands tired of the rising taxation on their toils, so they upped sticks and and left, roaming the counties as destitute migrants, forming their own popular rebellions or turning to banditry. A plague of banditry inland accompanied a plague of piracy that afflicted Korea's coasts, exacerbating regional instabilities and power struggles ever more focused on the throne. The bandits themselves accrued land and slaves and became powerful factions in their own right, such that one bandit, Kungbok, became a king-maker, helping Kim Ujing take the throne. Subsequently, Kungbok's desire to take the throne for himself led to his death in 846.

As the Sillan state began to break down in the late 800s and early 900s Paekche re-emerged, and a formidable general called Wang Kon from the former Koguryo region led from 918 a new state around the Taedong, later called Koryo, from which the name Korea derives. These states formed with the Silla the 'Later Three Kingdoms' Period' marked by intense inter-state warfare, from which the Koryo came out supreme.

Koryo Wang Kon, crowned King Taejo in 935, magnanimously welcomed the fallen Sillan king and his nobles into his court, giving them land and positions in government. Over the next couple of decades, from his new Songak capital (today's Kaesong) near to his realm's northern border, he launched a systematic offensive of gifts and privileges and later caste titles to bring the provincial barons and castle towns on side. Regional leaders gave familial 'hostages' or kin to the court to ensure loyalty, and Koryo soon spanned all the peninsula up to the Yalu's mouth, whence its border stretched across to near today's Wonsan. This fortified border was supported by two provinces under military command, connected to Kaesong and the other provinces through new roads and a postal system.

King Taejo's successors developed new government boards, and expanded government-owned factories of raw materials. The career routes into government were subject to more civil service examinations taken by students of new Confucian academies, meaning more 'commoners' could attain positions of power and privilege. Privilege principally was the dispensation of land to officials (that returned to the state upon their death), eroding the divine rights of the old aristocracy. Nonetheless, Koryo's social structure was still as regimented as its predecessors and ancestry counted for a great deal, as one new government board dealt with genealogical records. At the top were the royal caste, then the military and civil officials' class, called the *yangban*. Below them were more grades of profession, down to the *yangmin*, or commoners of peasants, and below them, the 'untouchables'. At least eight generations clean of untouchable status had to be proved by would-be officials.

Buddhism was further encouraged with lavish gifts of land, slaves and tax exemptions, until the temples and monasteries became grand concentrations of wealth within a tight hierarchical structure of considerable political and economic power, and its leaders of high aristocratic stock. Monasteries provided welfare for the poor and usurious loans for others, and it was a Buddhist monk that persuaded his brother King Sukchong (1082–96) to scrap barter for a standard coinage. Woodblock printing also revived with a great number of Chinese texts.

Foreign affairs were as usual dominated by events in China. To be safe, from 1033 a grand wall was built connecting the dozen fortified towns along Koryo's northern border. Paying tribute to whichever dynasty held the other side of the wall seemed a sure route to peace, and over the following years there were only a few incursions from the Sung, the Jurchen, the Liao and the Chin.

Then in the early 13th century, the Mongols (also known as the Yuan) came. They'd stormed out of the Gobi Desert, smashed the Chin from power, taking China and Manchuria, then looked south on to the peninsula. Years of battling the Jurchen hadn't prepared the Koryo armies for the Mongols, who washed over the country in a tide of blood. Fortunately the Mongols were poor navy men and the Koryo court, with the Choe family at the front, sailed with every official and jewel their boats could carry to safe exile on Kanghwa Island. There they lived and prospered for nearly three decades, while the mainland people were enslaved or just massacred. The court used this unreal time to build great palaces and pavilions and recarve the woodblocks for the Tripitika, which the original the Mongols had burnt in their invasion. Slowly the Choe realised that their great service to Buddha wasn't going to remove the Mongols, and in 1258 a little bloody coup won a new leader, who led the return to the mainland, and through apology, tribute, marriage and familial hostage-taking by the Mongols, re-established Koryo as a Mongol vassal state.

Now, through the Mongols, Koryo could prove its heartfelt loyalty to its rulers by pouring all its resources into invading Japan. In 1274 and 1281, hundreds of thousands of soldiers and hundreds of ships and crews were put up for two massive invasions of Japan. Neither succeeded. Notwithstanding the huge economic drain this had on the peninsula, Koryo was totally subjugated and sucked drier by the Mongols, who took what they wanted. But the Mongols were not entirely parasitical, being partly responsible for the influx of neo-Confucian texts, and the Confucian study of King Chungson (1309–13) at the Mongol capital. This helped end Buddhism's dominance, as it became broadly apparent that Buddhism was useless at protecting the state from troubles external and internal. By the mid 14th century, Japanese pirates, or Wako, were touring and pillaging Koryo shores. Also in the same century, the Mongols were losing control of China as the Ming resurged from the south towards Korea. One insurrectionist group fighting the Yuan were known as the Red Turbans, and from 1360 and 1361 they forayed into China's vassal Korea, taking Pyongyang and wrecking Kaesong. Meanwhile the Koryo court buckled under factional fights and usurpations, while one general, Ri Songgye, made a name for himself battling the Wako. Sent by pro-Mongol King U to fight the Ming, Ri Songgye considered it to be a futile exercise. Indeed, he decided instead that they would surely be an improvement on the Mongols. So Ri turned his forces on U and deposed him in 1389. An efficient purge followed and, with Ming relations affirmed, Ri Songgye became undisputed Ri Taejo, in 1392.

RI (ALSO KNOWN AS THE CHOSEN OR YI) 1392–1910

Ri Taejo moved the capital from Kaesong to the city of Hanyang, renaming it Seoul, or 'capital'. He gave the land of Koryo loyalists to his followers after having all the old land registry records burnt, creating a clean slate for him to distribute lands as he liked. However, as under the Koryo, dual governance came through military and civil officials, run by Yangban atop a rigid social pyramid of caste and substrata of professions, yangmin commoners, and still the untouchables at the bottom, who now included sorcerers and actors!

During the reigns of Taejo, Taejong and Sejong, Korea expanded northwards until all the area south of the Yalu and Tuman rivers was theirs, the land being cultivated and claimed by migrants from the south as the population boomed. Foreign policy was *sadae*, or 'serving the great', as in continuing to pay tribute to the Ming Emperor of China. With the Mongol shackles thrown off, and no distracting Ming–Mongol warring, the Ri could deal with pirates by sending boats to destroy their ships and settlements, and by 1420 the threat was curtailed. Then the forts and outposts of the northern frontier could be bolstered.

The capital was fortified and built up. With peace came greater scholarship and the sowon schools of Confucianism, needed for the examination system, flourished about the country. The Hangul alphabet was completed in the mid-1440s, along with movable type printing. Korean and Chinese influences led to a rebirth of the arts and sciences, with advancements from arms to poetry.

Although Buddhism again had a hand in the arts, the power of the monasteries was curbed. Over the centuries the monasteries had acquired huge tracts of land

and through tax exemption had the wealth to defend them, depriving others to their inevitable discontent. The monks were perceived to have become too powerful, too corrupt and were too collusive with suspicious elements, so they were evicted from the court and cities and stripped of their wealth, albeit slowly so as not to provoke insurrection. King Taejo finished their tax exemption and King Taejong limited their ownership of land and slaves, which his successor King Sejong reduced further. King Sejo (1455–68) was a practising Buddhist and he supported a brief revival, but he was an anomaly as his successors went with the tide of Confucianism.

Copper-type cast printing allowed Confucian texts to be spread among the new Confucian schools set up in the prefectures and counties, and the schools achieved a similar build-up of power and privileges that the Buddhists were stripped of. The schools' alumni formed groups for mutual advancement and further ensnaring of the youth. They competed, of course, at court for power and offices, as did the members of the royal families, so all Ri dynasty officials were Confucian scholars.

But their professed veneration of learning and authority was not manifest from the late 1400s, and departments of differing Confucian doctrine stifled their monarchs' wishes so they could concentrate on settling their own scores. The zealous reformers of the Sallim school, a puritan lot, incurred much resentment. To be fired was to get off lightly. Four bloody purges of the 'literati' occurred from 1498 to 1545, so bitter that the bones of dead scholars were dug up and scattered. The ruler Yonsangun was deposed by his own officials in the first purges and the battles became aristocratic feuds, which would mar the functioning of the court thereafter.

These feuds did not affect society as a whole. The comprehensive genealogical records founded under the Koryo were continued. There was a degree of social fluidity: slaves did become tenant farmers as Yangban fell earthwards. Some records were lost, some burnt, some doctored as fallen Yangban sold their status, but the class system remained largely intact, and Korea had slaves right up until the 19th century. The real threat came from beyond Korea's shores.

JAPAN AND THE IMJIN WAR The anti-pirate war and the success in holding off the Mongols made for about two centuries of peace for Korea. Trade routes were established with the Ming and Japan, whose people were allowed to set up trading settlements in the south of the peninsula.

But feudal infighting in Japan in the 15th century meant piracy resumed as Japan's worst export. The Ashikaga military government curtailed piracy and peaceful trade was set up in the late 1400s. But from the mid-1500s the Wako resumed piracy as the Ashikaga declined, now in greater force and sacking whole cities. A new leader, Hideyoshi Toyotomi, brought order and restored peaceful trade with Korea, but this wasn't all he had in mind, for Hideyoshi's imperial plans stretched to India, taking in China on the way. Korea, of course, was the most convenient land route into China, and Hideyoshi set about persuading the Ri from 1587 to join him against Ming China before taking on all Asia. But the only coherent response from the Ri court, torn between tribute-loyalty to the Ming, profiting from Hideyoshi's scheme and aversion to any involvement, was 'thanks, but maybe we'll just sit this one out'. Hideyoshi responded by invading Korea in early 1592 and, within a month, his 158,000-strong force had taken the capital as the stagnated Ri military went to bits. The court fled to the Yalu and tremulously persuaded the Ming that these invaders were dangerous. A Ming army attacked down to Pyongyang but was repelled, only for another force to charge Kaesong in early 1593. Meanwhile, however much face the Ri had lost on land they won back at sea under the brilliant admiral Ri Sunsin, with his cannon-firing, iron-decked 'turtle boats' that sunk Hideyoshi's supply ships. Hideyoshi's debilitated land forces were then kept pinned down by Korean guerrilla attacks, and he sued for peace.

But the peace was just a lull. Many Japanese stayed on in Korea, eking a living amid the post-battle chaos, until Hideyoshi attacked again with 140,000 troops in 1597. Toughened Chinese and Korean forces were ready, and, aided by winter, held up Hideyoshi's forces until he declared on his deathbed in 1598 that this time enough really was enough.

Still, Japanese forces didn't do too badly out of it, returning back to the islands reasonably unscathed with the priceless booty of many skilled artisans. The Toyotomi family were replaced by the Tokugawam, who resumed simple trade as before, after a few thousand captives were negotiated back to the Koreans. On the peninsula, the wars' taxation and devastation compounded the land's material exhaustion. Local rebellions during the conflict preceded passionate factional fighting at court in a series of coups in the 1600s, including the Injo faction of 1624 that briefly installed a new royal family.

Further north, the war had emptied the coffers of the Ming, who faced growing threats from the Manchus in northeast Asia. Ming–Manchu fights stumbled into Korea until the Manchus stood victorious on Korea's borders, with Ming China shoved westwards. Now the Manchus demanded suzerainty from their 'younger brother', Korea, a fraternal love the Manchus marked by a punitive invasion in 1627. Korea conspired to have the Ming return, until the Manchus, styling themselves as the Qing, rumbled the plan and invaded Korea again in late 1637. Korea's misery would only cease, seethed the Manchus, upon payment of food, troops and the handing over of 'hostage' envoys. They did, and relative peace was Korea's prize for 200 years.

But not in the court. The literati purges had opened a can of worms. Ancestor worship, the importance of filial piety, familial and old clan ties, academic alumni and regional relationships meant that the fights of the forebears were carried on by their successors. From the 1550s until the late 1700s, factions fought and splintered into 'westerners', 'northerners', 'greater' and 'lesser northerners', 'southerners', and so on and on, in a maelstrom of fights, coups and burning buildings.

So no-one really saw the real aliens turn up in the 1700s, in the form of Europeans. There had been some brief, isolated contact with Europeans over the years. Jesuits reached Japan in the late 1500s. Some Dutch washed ashore in 1627, and one became prominent in the Korean army for his cannon-casting skills. Yet in practical terms, Korea's foreign relations had only ever involved jostling between China and Japan.

Meanwhile, however, European missionaries had been spreading the Gospel across Asia, and Catholic missionaries were having great success in China by the 1790s. Already from the late 18th century the Catholic Church had been spying Korea as the next great congregation. A Chinese priest smuggled himself into Seoul and began converting peasants by the thousand. Bad enough, but Catholicism forbade ancestral worship and therefore threatened the entire social structure in the country, as Christianity obviated the legitimacy of the ruling family. News filtered to the court of the Peking government's sufferance of Christian subterfuge, and Korea's Christians were thus pre-emptively persecuted, but the Church already had friends in very high places. In 1801 court official Hwang Sa Yong appealed to the French bishop in Peking to send in armies to purge the Korean government of its anti-Catholicism, but the message was intercepted and the suspicions harboured by Korea's rulers were proved, and mightily alarmed they were by the extent of these Catholics' reach and conspiracy. Mass 'martyring' of Catholics ensued.

THE GREAT POWERS COME The appeal for the Western nations of spreading the word of Christ wasn't just born out of the altruistic belief that every soul needed saving; there was also the idea, held mainly by the French, Russians, British and Americans, that wanted the locals converted to Christ because Christians were easier to trade with than the average Asian. Business followed the Cross, and despite the great feats and dire fates of missionaries in Korea, trade ships began arriving. At first they came alone, with an English merchant ship anchoring off the Chongchung Province coast in 1832, but more and more came and prospected. Still, more often than not they went away empty-handed, having been (usually) politely turned away by the Koreans, who preferred the devils they knew in China and Japan.

But these foreign powers were not used to being rebuffed, however politely; China's ports had been jemmied for trade following the Opium War in 1842, and Japan's doors were blown open in 1854. Lonely Korea had no right not to trade with the West, and if it couldn't be reasoned with, then it would be forced. Trading ships arriving off Korea's coast started sporting more arms, then it was French, Russian and British warships that began turning up ever more frequently.

And in the early 19th century the country wasn't doing so well. A ruinous drought from 1812 had apparently killed millions. Rice riots occurred in Seoul in 1833. The Tonghak 'religion' fused Eastern and Western religions, yet promoted the interests of the poor and not the usual deference to the rich. Its creator Choe Cheu was executed for 'confusing society' in 1862, but his death apparently sparked uprisings by destitute farmers of all classes in the southern provinces. Many merchants and officials were killed before this burgeoning insurrection was put down. More unrest followed in 1864, so all in all the Ri were in less genial mood to receive anyone. But things were precarious. King Kojong was a minor and the country was under the regent Taewongun, who concentrated on rebuilding fortifications and who also reformed the military. The Ri worried that these increasingly aggressive Western traders were the external force of destruction, while Western religion would destroy Korea from within, and they weren't going away. The Koreans were going to have to react with the violence that these foreigners understood.

Russian pressure to trade was aggressive, but the French priests' offers to mediate with them in 1866 made the Taewongun suspect a broader foreign plot, and so nine priests were interrogated and executed before a bloody purge of tens of thousands of converts. The French took great exception to their priests falling to the sword, and their navy invaded Kanghwa Island in retaliation, but were routed by Korean forces. That same year, the armed American missionary trader *General Sherman* arrived in Pyongyang, but was beached and burnt in the shallow waters of the Taedong River. A punitive occupation by American forces of Kanghwa Island in 1871 was as successful as the French occupation. American admiral Rogers was dispatched to organise the protection of US vessels from Korean 'tiger hunters' along Korea's shores, but Taewongun took heart: his reforms had enabled his country to repel all boarders.

There were other tacky incursions. In 1867, a priest, a German and an American adventurer, bent on raiding royal tombs, sailed from Shanghai to extort concessions from the king for trade and missionary work. Another rumour that circulated Beijing's diplomatic circle was that Korea was volunteering to help expel all foreigners from China. Bolstered by military success, the Taewongun kept Korea closed and belligerent. His belief that the only thing that worked with these barbarians was violence was borne out, and he had stelae erected round the country to remind the people how awful foreigners were, and how terrifying would be the fate of any collaborators with them.

THE JAPANESE Plenty of outsiders presumed to know better than Korea itself what the Koreans needed. Since the 1860s Meiji restoration in Japan, the imperial government had reformed itself and the economy along Western lines, and sent emissaries to Korea to show them how progressive it was to trade with the West. But King Kojong, enthroned since coming of age in 1873, was as suspicious of outsiders as his father Taewongun, and his courtiers were not interested in reforms that would put them out of work. They were convinced that these Japanese were simply Eastern conveyors of Western subversion, using trickery to smokescreen more base motives. In 1875 the Japanese warship *Unyo* sailed passed Kanghwa Island, which the Koreans took as a hostile act and shelled it from land batteries. The *Unyo* was arguably a classic case of gunboat diplomacy, sending in a ship not to quell things but as a trigger to execute a far bigger plan. Hence the Japanese retaliated to this ill-mannered action with an armed expedition to Korea, demanding unprecedented trade concessions, including residence rights in three Korean ports and a legation in Seoul, in the 1876 Treaty of Kanghwa. The treaty also secured 'independence' for Korea from China. This gun-muzzle diplomacy gained a major foothold in what was a long, profitable relationship for Japan, with Korean rice poured out to Japan as Japanese goods and ideas trickled in.

But it only led to more factionalism in the court. Queen Min and her family favoured Japanese-style reforms, but Taewongun still skulked in the court's shadows and, as some feared, reforms disposed and made malcontents of government and army men alike, who flocked to Taewongun's conspiring. In 1882, they rebelled against the queen, killing her, her family and ministers, burnt down the Japanese legation and caused its minister and staff to flee to sea in a junk. Only the intervention of the Qing saved the day for King Kojong, with 2,000 troops sent to Seoul to suppress the rebellion and restore Min – for, joyously, the 'slain' queen was actually alive and well, as an impersonator had gamely taken the blade for her.

The Qing intervention brought Korea back under Chinese suzerainty and they pressed for Korea to broaden its relations with the outside world, arguing this was inevitable, and enticing a mix of competing influences could prevent any one foreign nation from dominating (namely Japan). Commercial treaties quickly followed with the US, Germany, UK, France, Russia and Italy, with investment inflows into mining, railways, universities and hospitals, and Western-style banking, customs and communications in post and telegraph being set up.

But these rapid advances led not to peace at the court, which divided into pro-Chinese conservatives and pro-Japanese modernisers, with the arguments over how to secure Korea's future becoming more twisted and no less cloak-and-dagger. The pro-Japanese faction advocated ending Korea's vassal status to China, as by definition Korea was not the equal of any outside power, and they also sought industrialisation. Distracted Chinese military forces led to the modernisers attempting a Japanese-supported coup in 1884, as bloody as the 1882 incident, and as successful. Again, the Japanese legation was burnt; again, Japanese nationals were killed, and some thought the Chinese might at last prevail. But they were becoming yesterday's empire. Into the power vacuum came the Russians, expanding their empire from Siberia, their envoys busily laying diplomatic and commercial ties with Korea. Only the British, seeking to check the Russians' expansion, stepped in and blocked a Russian sea route. This 'saved' Korea for a while but made one fact glaringly obvious: the last people to control Korea's destiny were the Koreans.

While Korea's diplomatic strategy involved many foreign powers cancelling out each other's aims, a neat power-balance trick, the country's autonomy and stability were being undermined by economic forces. Taxation for the court's expenditure increased to help sustain the unwieldy bureaucracy, procure foreign arms and establish diplomatic missions in those countries whose cheap goods flooded Korea and destroyed the local cottage industries. This trade demanded money, not barter, and farmers became tied into exporting their grain to where most of the imports originated: Japan.

Peasants lost their subsistence living to usury and penury as the state's taxes escalated. Uprisings and banditry grew. Yangban joined forces with peasants and in the southwest the Tonghak resurrected, beginning a serious rebellion in February 1894. Japan ignored Korean claims about dealing with the crisis and, with the Taewongun in tow, sent troops over in July 1894, sinking the Chinese fleet on the way to driving the Chinese army from Korea altogether and establishing themselves at the heart of the Korean court.

The Japanese brought reforms that at this point weren't all terrible, making the Yangban and commoners equal before the law, abolishing slavery and the practice of whole families being punished for the crimes of one member, as well as standardising the currency.

But they had yet to secure Korea from trouble outside and within. Russian, French and German concerns about anyone except themselves controlling the region led them to gang up and deliver a 'Three Powers Intervention', which demanded from Japan swingeing concessions in Korea (and further north saw China smashed open for the last time). Queen Min, possibly seeing salvation with Russia, was now leaning their way, but the pro-Japanese faction in the Korean court launched their own coup against the queen, finally killing her and sending the king to hide in the Russian legation for a year, only for the coup to collapse and the Japanese find themselves being driven out yet again in early 1895.

In a flamboyant, fanciful assertion of Korean sovereignty, King Kojong then pronounced himself the emperor of Taehan Cheguk, Empire of the Han, with envoys sent out from the nation with its own flag and anthem and now the equal of China and Japan. But grandly empty gestures aside, Kojong's confidence in his empire was demonstrated by his move into the Kyongun palace, which had escape doors into each of the surrounding foreign legations.

A more realistic attempt to galvanise independence for Korea came with So Chaep Il (also called Philip Jaisohn), a Korean educated in the US who founded the Independence Club, believing that Korea's structure and fate should be decided by Koreans, with a new covenant of civil rights and independence. Students, intellectuals, workers, urban dwellers and government officials of all ranks rallied to the cause. The court aligned with those profiting from the unbalanced trade regime to form the Imperial Association, and following pitched battles with the Independence Club, had the latter outlawed. The only reform was the modernising of the army.

The last gasps of Korea for Koreans were drowned out as the century turned, for Russia, the UK, Japan and others whipped up a tornado of treaties, diplomatic and military manoeuvres, checking, bluffing, suspecting and counter-checking each others' imperial plans into east Asia. China's implosion changed it from player to prey. Finally, tiring of the frenetic hoo-ha, Russia and Japan decided all-out war would reach a conclusion of sorts. Japan set troops in Incheon in February 1904 that led to a Korean–Japanese protocol, with the Japanese guaranteed real powers. They then went off and squarely beat up the Russians, who exited Korea and left the Japanese unquestionably in charge. They were the only game in town, in force, with the papers to prove it.

Shortly after, in 1905, Japan and Korea signed the Japan–Korea Protectorate Treaty (with 'protect' in the racket sense of the word), with Japanese troops surrounding the imperial palace by way of persuading Kojong to sign the treaty. A Japanese resident-general was installed in Seoul to direct the country's foreign affairs as an *in situ* extension of the Tokyo Foreign Office, directing Korea for Japan's ends, to 'protect' Korea against further foreign interference. The diplomatic agencies of those other countries that battled to be in Korea were abolished along with 'Korea's' foreign policy. To all geopolitical purposes, Korea had lost its autonomous national entity. It would soon lose its domestic autonomy as well, with the 1907 Japan–Korea treaty taking all powers of lawmaking, reforms and appointments to government and putting it all under the approval of the resident-general. The army was disbanded; the administration of justice and prisons came unto Japanese hands, as did the police. King Kojong, still vainly protesting the 1905 treaty to the deaf ears of the great Russian and European empires, was forced to abdicate and be replaced by the puppet king Sunjong, 'Emperor of Korea' in name only. Ownership of the land, particularly by the peasants, was difficult to prove to the Japanese authorities who were taking it over en masse, and resistance was met with execution.

Resistance groups, poorly armed and poorly led, sprung up across the country, carrying out guerrilla attacks on Japanese positions, but the guerrillas' dispersal and the randomness of their attacks achieved nothing but the accelerated drafting in of more Japanese forces of repression. There were, though, thousands of recorded disturbances by individuals and crowds demanding independence. Two of the most spectacular included two Koreans assassinating the Resident-General Ito Hirobumi at Harbin railway station in October 1909, and in December, the pro-Japanese Prime Minister Ri Wanyong was stabbed. But these only served to convince the Japanese that total domination was necessary. In August 1910 the protectorate was formalised in a treaty of annexation, with the Korean government dissolved two months later. Emperor Sunjong was deposed and Korea came under Japan's Meiji rulers. All political organisations were banned, and all foreign intervention finished. As a sovereign state, Korea was gone.

KOREA UNDER THE JAPANESE The Japanese were the masters of the region. They'd taken Manchuria, flattened the Chinese, ousted the Russians in presence and power, and with the exception of Christian churches and hospitals they'd booted all Western interests from Korea. Korea was theirs to do with as they wanted.

The resident-general was replaced by a governor-general, a retired Japanese admiral or general appointed by the emperor in Tokyo, to whom the governor-general answered and to no-one else. With this autonomy the governor-general could appoint the provincial governors, senior judicial members and high civil service positions, ostensibly to be shared between Koreans and Japanese, but in practice any job with any seniority went to the Japanese. The plan was for Korea to be Japanised by every measure. They banned Korean-language newspapers and any 'large' meetings of Koreans. Grass-roots control came through the ever-increasing police force that had numerous summary powers, from flogging and fining to imprisonment. The fact that educators and non-military officials wore Japanese-style uniforms and swords proved beyond doubt the nature of Japan's rule. While Japan considered Korean culture to be backward and worthy of eradication, they still looted thousands of historical artefacts and antiques back to the islands.

Now that the Koreans and their culture mattered little beyond how they could best serve Japan, the colonisers set about reforming the country's economy. From 1912, a comprehensive land registration programme was carried out over six years, establishing nationwide the rights (and restrictions) of the nation's farmers. Many Yangban peasants lost their pre-existent claims, were ruined or made de facto registered tenant farmers on enlarged estates that were regularly taxed by the authorities.

Japan's own industrialisation needed increased Korean rice production to allow its cities to swell with factory workers – like the rest of the world, Japan had seen in Russia's cities how the want for bread could bring down the rulers, and Japan itself had suffered rice riots in 1918. Investment from the landlords and Japan's ministries poured into agriculture to increase rice output, and rice exports to Japan indeed went up significantly. However, the exports outweighed actual production gains, and the Koreans were forced to import millet.

Investment in Korean agriculture went into new planting techniques, irrigation and crop varieties but mainly into the use of chemical fertilisers, the production of which underpinned Korea's own industrialisation. Chemical plants for fertilisers were powered by Japanese-built hydro-electric systems. The Japanese also invested in mining, producing the raw ores for Japan's manufacturing industries and steel mills, and manufacturing plants came on stream, connected by a new network of roads and rail. Most of the industrial growth, operated by the cheap labour of former farmers, was concentrated in the peninsula's north as the south held more and better-quality farming land.

This was all development of sorts, that wasn't always unbeneficial, but Japan's wants in the region and the world were becoming increasingly rapacious, acutely so when the country was dragged into the pit of global depression following the 1929 Wall Street crash. Vigorous imperial adventures in East Asia and the Pacific would galvanise Japan's political economy back into rude health, a plan that started with a bang. In 1931, a bomb of unknown origin blew up the Japanese railway near China's Shenyang in the 'Manchurian Incident' (otherwise known as the 'Mukden Incident', Shenyang having been renamed by Japan), which pretexted the Japanese military occupation of southern Manchuria. The war machine was unleashed, and in order to feed and build it investment poured into Korea. Chemicals and food processing became the major industries, accounting for over half of the yen value of Korea's output, with their own spin-offs in affiliated industries. Iron and steel output increased dramatically, as did ceramics and light industries, like machine tools. The peninsula was being built as a great staging-post for Japan's Asian empire, and road and rail links were built to the Korean coast closest to Japan and out into the Asian mainland.

Well-designed, well-plumbed cities housed Korea's burgeoning industrial workforce, some of whose children received schooling in the practical disciplines of maths, basic sciences and engineering. But of course the best schools were for the children of the Japanese plant owners, managers and the imperial administrators who also inhabited the best-built parts of town. Proportionally, three times as many Japanese as Korean children and youth went to school (and with no higher education for the latter). Korean students were taught a history that emphasised how Korea and Japan were historically joined at the hip. Anyway, all schooling was in Japanese, as was usually the press; colonial attitudes to Korean newspapers never quite reached tolerance.

In February 1936, those in the Tokyo government advocating a more moderate foreign policy were literally cut down and killed by fanatical army officers. By early 1937, it wasn't enough for Koreans to serve in Japan's war factories (although by 1945 two million Korean men were working in mainland Japan); they were to be needed for the front lines too. Korean women were rounded up and forced into work for the Japanese armed forces as 'comfort women', an outrageously effete euphemism for enslaved prostitution. The population was imbued with Japanese culture under the 'Transformation into Imperial Subjects' policy, from swearing the oath of loyalty to Japan's emperor to saluting the flag. Korean names were replaced with Japanese ones. Shinto shrines and ceremonies were brought to all Korean communities and families. Korea was the front-line state for Japan's imperial plans, not just a route into the Asian mainland but a supplier of food, workers, war materials and (subservient) spiritual brethren. The Koreans were welcome to celebrate and embrace this entirely usurious assimilation, or just suffer it anyway. But being Koreans, they could not seriously be expected to put up with that.

RESISTANCE AND WAR Indeed, soon after the Western powers' eviction from the region as the century had turned they found themselves diverted away from Korea's annexation by their upcoming (first) world war. Meanwhile, hundreds of thousands of Koreans took flight into Russia, America and China. But those that stayed hadn't trusted those fickle foreigners anyway, and the idea of a Korean nation, a concept in part realised realised through contact with the outside world, wasn't to be buried by any colonialists.

In the 1910s, the Japanese authorities so keenly sensed any whiff of rebellion that many Koreans were imprisoned, tortured and killed on suspicion of crimes they hadn't even considered. Incidents were just that, isolated expressions of malcontent while no coherent resistance formed, although Japan's land and administrative reforms dispossessed, displaced and ruined Koreans from every social strata.

All the Koreans needed was a rallying call, which came in early 1919. Intellectuals, Yangban, professionals and students joined together in signing a 'Declaration of Independence'. Hoping to catch the eye of the Western powers emerging from Europe's Great War and tap US president Woodrow Wilson's spirit of independence, they sent a delegation to Versailles. However, they were ignored (as was a young Ho Chi Minh, who was petitioning the Americans to end French colonial rule in Vietnam). Undeterred, the declaration of independence was proclaimed in Seoul on 1 March, two days before the funeral of former king Kojong. Japanese police arrested the leaders, but a crowd gathered, grew restless and shouted *Manse!* (which literally translates as '10,000 years' age' but is poetically meant to mean 'long live' or 'viva!'). They were fired upon by military police, the army and the navy, but Korean turnout reached the thousands. Two months of demonstrations followed and a million people joined the Samil or 'March 1 Movement' on the streets, demanding independence, wrecking colonial buildings and fighting the army hand to hand.

The international attention this gained focused less on Korea's independence movement and more on the savagery used in suppressing it, and the only concessions were a few Korean-language newspapers and limited opportunities in education.

Nevertheless, 1 March had demonstrated the huge, latent sense of Korean nationalism, smouldering away. The anti-Japanese guerrillas, beaten into the Manchurian hinterland, were invigorated in their struggle. In Shanghai, a self-declared provisional government of Korea was set up by Syngman Rhee, a Korean imprisoned by the Japanese before escaping to study in the US. Shanghai was also home to a Korean Communist Party, set up in opposition to the provisional government-in-exile, but it was not the only political party to take that name. Socialist societies were founded in Seoul and Tokyo, and in 1925 the Korean Communist Party was secretly founded in Korea. As former emperor Sunjong died in 1926, the communists sought to use the anniversary of his passing to attempt another 'March 1'-style movement, a valiant if futile effort that illustrates both how full of vigour, but also how confused, Korean political resistance was. Factions across the political spectrum reached for any symbol of Korean nationalism. The Japanese were, in contrast, eerily singular in their purpose of suppressing insurrection. However, despite mass arrests, imprisonment (with some leaders emerging from prison only in 1945), torture and executions, resistance movements regrouped, reformed and reorganised. In the 1920s, farm and factory disputes and strikes racked up from dozens to hundreds and thousands. Wonsan and Seoul went on general strike in 1929 and 1930 respectively, and in 1930 some 54,000 Korean high-school students were involved in disturbances across Korea.

Resistance groups were already operating from Manchuria, and following Japan's annexing of the area in 1931, Chinese and Korean guerrillas co-operated in carrying out merciless attacks on Japanese troops. By the mid-'30s, three anti-Japanese armies were operating in the Manchurian area, called the North Eastern Anti-Japanese United Army (NEAJUA) and which had Chinese and Soviet support. Russia had built its own fully-fledged communist empire, the Soviet Union, into which many Korean partisans fled, and where they were armed, trained and filled with political thought. Japanese forces were harried, pinned down and cut up in Manchuria's cold, harsh terrain. It was in this hell that the future leader, Kim Il Sung, spent his formative years, enduring daily a bitter life-or-death existence of sub-zero temperatures, starvation and traipsing through hinterlands festooned with roaming Japanese troops and treachery. The experience forged Kim's outlook forever after. In addition to the various northern China-based anti-Japanese groups that Kim joined, he became a member of the Communist Party of China in 1931. The Communist Party of Korea was still going but in the 1930s would later be thrown out of the Comintern for being too nationalist – a trait that runs through Kim's own political philosophy, Juche (see box, pages 26–7). Although later DPRK historians would shroud his early years in myth, what's not in doubt is that this charismatic young leader (born in 1912) wreaked enough havoc to warrant the Japanese assigning a crack unit to track him down.

Japan's imperial plans led to full-scale war with China in 1937 and the US in 1941. Imperial overstretch required Koreans to take the higher jobs they'd always been denied, and enter the Japanese army, for which they would later be branded collaborators. By late 1945, Japan was on the brink of defeat. As he had promised the Americans months earlier, Soviet premier Josef Stalin prepared to launch war against the collapsing Japanese forces in east Asia. To hasten its surrender and draw an awesome close to the east Asian war, US president Truman dropped two atom bombs on Japan, days before the Soviets were due to attack. The Soviets carried on, routing and taking prisoner Japanese forces in the east and landing their own forces in northern Korea.

The US proposed a joint occupation to 'share the burden' of rebuilding the country, dividing it into North and South by the latitude line of 38° across Korea's midriff. The Soviets agreed, and in early September US forces arrived at Incheon to take their zone of control. The Soviets wanted a friendly communist nation on their borders, and the Americans wanted anything but another communist nation slap next to their new Asian base, Japan. With the two worlds of communism and capitalism about to collide on a global scale in the Cold War, the Americans and Soviets set about looking for suitable leaders in their halves of Korea, and with French and British agreement, the Soviets and US agreed a five-year trusteeship of Korea in which time they would instigate elections for one national government.

Although they disagreed on many things, none of Korea's indigenous political groups took well to the trusteeship, but the trustees considered them too incoherent and politically immature to run the country, as in fact it had been run by the Japanese for the last 35 years. So neither the US nor the USSR paid much attention to the wishes of the Koreans. There was already a government-in-waiting in Korea, the Korean

People's Republic (KPR), formed by political leader and former political prisoner You Un Hyong and presided over by Syngman Rhee, president of the self-proclaimed Korean government-in-exile. But US forces' commander General Hodge regarded the KPR as crypto-communist, mainly for its popular policy of land reform, and, governing the South with remnants of the Japanese colonials' assistance, set about closing down all 'communist' activities, banning left-wing groups, labour unions and communist newspapers, and imprisoning advocates of land reform. Korean Communist Party leader Pak Hon Yong fled north. In the North, the Soviets had reluctantly cobbled together a coalition of communists, nationalists and Christians as well as considering the KPR, but their trusteeship would be pointless without installing a good communist in charge. In that they already had the youthful but very resourceful officer Colonel Kim Il Sung, freshly arrived in October 1945.

KIM IL SUNG AND THE KOREAN WORKERS' PARTY Only 33 years old, Kim had spent most of his life outside Korea, with years in Stalin's Soviet Union, leading his own reconnaissance brigade into Manchuria for the Red Army. Tough, straight-talking and respected by his Soviet supporters, he had a loyal core of fellow guerrilla-fighters. His military background and impressive record of nationalist resistance were key to his ability to organise and get the forming People's Army on side. He was placed to lead the provisional government of the Communist Party, set up in 1946.

In August 1946, the communists merged with their political opponents, the more social democrat New People's Party, a group led by Koreans formerly based with the Chinese communists in Yanan during the war years and which appealed to the educated middle class. The merged party was called the North Korea Workers' Party, thus a politically broad church with mass appeal. Cadres toured the country, appealing to the peasants to join the party and break their bonds with their suppressive landlords in the new Korea. A rural groundswell signed up for the party that swiftly dominated all politics, and they were rewarded with a revolutionary land reform that dispossessed landlords and distributed the land among the peasants, while the Japanese-owned industries were nationalised as a Soviet-style two-year economic plan for industry was put in train. To be sure, soon enough, the Christian and nationalist politicians would be made redundant, if not arrested. Meantime, the Yanan faction were more useful than obstructive to the functioning of government.

In the South, Syngman Rhee, now in Seoul, survived the KPR's demise and agreed to the trusteeship if the Americans helped crack down on any political protest against him, which, being usually from left wingers, the US command did so approvingly. With US provision of financial incentives for his supporters, and some local military arm-twisting for his detractors, Rhee became South Korea's dominant political leader. Not dissimilar tactics allowed the Soviets to establish Kim Il Sung as the key political leader and he set up a military-based administration in Pyongyang.

By 1947, both sides of the parallel had their own government, with Kim Il Sung's Soviet-backed regime in Pyongyang and Rhee's right-wing, US-supported regime in Seoul. These provisional governments were necessarily authoritarian to quell sporadic but violent unrest and factional fighting, and get their economies going again. But Korea's unification was a fading vision. Nationalist efforts to negotiate a unification treaty floundered because the two domestic governments' temporary set-up gave them questionable political and legal power. Their leaders were getting along as badly as their Soviet and American supporters, without whose backing no meaningful deal was possible.

Realising its increasingly heated relationship with the Soviets was obstructing unification, and that the Soviets were too stubborn to agree on anything, the US decided that a unitary government should be selected by the Koreans themselves. In late 1947, the US requested the United Nations to organise a general election for all Korea. The Soviets suspected foul play, justifiably as both powers had helped ban, incarcerate and assassinate (including Yo Un Hyong) the more radical opponents to their favoured leaders. Fearing their man Kim Il Sung wouldn't win, the Soviets refused elections for their half, but elections in the South were held in May 1948. This election established, under President Syngman Rhee, the Republic of Korea (ROK), recognised as Korea's legitimate government by the Western powers. The Soviets then organised their own northern election in August, delivering Kim Il Sung as president of the new Democratic People's Republic of Korea (DPRK) which the Soviet bloc recognised as Korea's legitimate government.

Korea had stable governance, if under two groups and not one. Resistance to Rhee's government continued but was pushed underground and into the hinterlands. The farms and factories were producing, although the idiocies of a divided economy were immediately manifest, with most of the factories and power in the North and the farms in the South. The North–South border was closed and there were regular, large skirmishes across it by opposing militia. But the situation was stable enough for US forces to withdraw in June 1949, leaving a few military advisers and promises of military aid. The Soviets departed the North, leaving weapons and arms factories for the North's 'defence'.

Independent at last, Rhee and Kim immediately began to whip up their halves about the urgent need for unification, and persuading their populace that only military force could achieve this. Barely five years after Japan's hated rule had collapsed, Korea was heading to war with itself. Pre-empting Rhee's plans for unification, Kim Il Sung and Pak Hon Yong visited Stalin in April 1950, assuring him that they had enough supporters in the South to ensure a swift, decisive victory. On 25 June 1950, some 70,000 North Korean troops smashed southwards across the 38th parallel. The Korean War had begun.

KOREAN WAR In the West it is firmly believed that the DPRK was the aggressor, with Northern forces invading the South in June 1950. Pyongyang's version is the south, at the behest of a belligerent US, attacked first, and the North simply responded in kind. If that was the case then the southern offensive into the north must be deemed as spectacular a failure as the success of the north's counter-attack.

The initial triumph of the DPRK assault suggests a long and hefty build-up, but the North was not totally devoid of provocation. The war was as good as inevitable following the division of Korea, the political gulf between the two states and border incursions by both sides, which had been going on for years. But both states then, as now, were and are committed to reuniting one country, a country split by outside forces with a map and a pen. It was always going to be a mess.

Northern forces hammered southwards with the lightly armed, poorly trained southern forces retreating in such panic they destroyed bridges that their own troops couldn't retreat across. Within a week, the North had taken Seoul, but as swiftly, the US and United Nations had voted to intervene on the South side. Fifteen countries' forces were combined into one UN command under US general Douglas MacArthur. The decisive move came in early September: as the DPRK army compressed the South around Pusan, a US Marine division landed at Incheon and cut the DPRK supply and reinforcement routes. The UN force heartily battered the DPRK army back over the 38th parallel, then pressed on to unite Korea under UN auspices. However, China's newly established communist government was very wary of losing its brothers in Pyongyang, and worse, a Korea united under American hegemony would only serve to harass China. China's premier and foreign minister Zhou Enlai threatened direct military intervention if US forces crossed the parallel and didn't leave the liberation to South Korean troops. Nonetheless, MacArthur was eager to finish the job, and by October's end, having taken Pyongyang by land and Wonsan by sea, and pounding every city from the air, UN forces had reached the Yalu. The Chinese, as they'd threatened, counter-attacked in late November with hundreds of thousands of troops, pushing the surprised UN forces 30 miles south of Seoul as the evil winter set in. But then the UN dug in, and the Chinese suffered their own staggering losses in April and May. Herein the war ground into stalemate as both sides went back and forth around the 38th parallel.

Armistice talks were proposed in June 1951, to which the UN commander General Ridgeway (who replaced the too-hawkish MacArthur) agreed. Two years of negotiations followed while scores died in futile battles every day. Along the way, US president Eisenhower, elected on a promise to end the war, threatened the DPRK with atomic attack.

On 27 July 1953, the US, China and the DPRK signed an armistice at the small village of Panmunjom, south of Kaesong, ending the fighting but not the war: peace has never been officially declared. The cost of the war has been estimated at around three million Korean civilians and 700,000 soldiers, a million Chinese troops, 54,000 American soldiers and 3,200 from the other allied countries. Many of the northern civilians were killed in air raids, in which a greater tonnage of bombs was dropped on Korea's cities by the US air force than either Nazi Germany or Imperial Japan ever received.

That was the injustice visited upon a Korean who dared to try to unite his divided country – and Kim Il Sung had gotten so close to unification. Now, however, Korea would be divided all the more so by the massive US and UN military presence in the South, to protect against his belligerence. In the eyes of the West he had gone from being just another communist leader to a warmonger with whom no peace could be made. Forever after Kim reciprocated this view by fortifying the North.

THE REIGN OF KIM IL SUNG TO TODAY'S DPRK

The DPRK domestic set-up The war hadn't achieved a unified Korea, nor dislodged or destabilised either government. So now we will look at the set-up of the DPRK government and its development. Notwithstanding minor constitutional changes, the balance of power (at least in theory) hangs between the main branches of government, namely the civilian state, the party (Korean Workers' Party, KWP) and the military (the Korean People's Army, KPA). All are made up of various agencies and committees with varying levels of interdependence and autonomy. Each branch of government also has its own supporting bureaucracy, and also ownership and control of different elements of the economy, including autonomous firms engaging in various businesses. All these departments and agencies compete for scarce resources and their own survival, as well as power.

From the DPRK's founding, the top state post was that of premier, a post that with a cabinet known as the Administration Council ran the country through numerous ministries. Kim Il Sung held that job until 1972 when the more senior post of president was created. The president and the council are elected by the Supreme People's Assembly, which consists of 674 representatives, voted in by popular election every five years. This body appoints the judiciary, passes laws and calculates the annual budget.

1

Juche (pronounced ju-chay), also known as Kimilsungism, is the sociopolitical philosophy developed by Kim Il Sung and expounded by Kim Jong Il, and which is infused into, and underpins, many if not all facets of the DPRK's governing philosophy, society and culture. Juche is a Korean word of two syllables, *ju* meaning 'master' and *che* meaning 'oneself', so literally translated it means 'Master of one's self'. Although the term first became widely used in 1955, most DPRK histories trace its origin back to June 1930 when the young Kim Il Sung outlined a new path for the Korean revolution at a meeting of revolutionaries in Kalun.

Kim Il Sung's father Kim Hyong Jik, when president of the Korean National Association, advocated the idea of Chiwon – 'Aim High' – to achieve Korean independence. This idea and the tenets of Marxism were important sources for Juche ideas, but to the standard Marxist emblem of the hammer and sickle Kim added the calligraphy brush, to include the intellectuals who he felt the Russians had sidelined at their peril. Not that other intellectuals would influence Juche, so much that Juche would influence them and all else. As stipulated in Article 3 of the 1998 DPRK Constitution, Juche is the state's governing philosophy, aimed at realising the ultimate communist state. Juche is celebrated by its followers for its 'scientific' answers to questions of man's destiny and, as the plaques at the base of Pyongyang's Juche Tower show, Juche has (small) followings worldwide. For all its international appeal, however, Juche is heavily Korea-centric.

Briefly, Juche states that man is the master of everything, and decides everything. Man is distinguished from the other countless physical and organic entities surrounding him by possessing the three attributes of creativity, consciousness and *Chajusong*, the last meaning 'independence', or man's innate will to live, to develop independently, and master his own destiny and world.

Chajusong involves man subordinating nature to his own ends, adapting the environment to suit him, as opposed to adapting to the environment as plants and animals do.

And while animals may mould the environment for themselves, their endeavours are purely instinctive, whereas man has developed and learnt (eg: building shelters that have developed from mud huts to tower blocks) and is improved by his creativity. Man's consciousness allows him to observe and understand the properties of his environment and manipulate it thus.

Chajusong and creativity are related as mastering the world involves recreating it, and consciousness realises that Chajusong requires creativity to achieve mastery, recognising Chajusong's needs and directing man's energies into moulding his surroundings accordingly. Therefore, all subjugation is to be resisted, and Juche strongly denounces dogmatism and flunkeyism. Man's social and political life are critical because man can only move beyond his instincts and fully realise his consciousness, creativity and Chajusong through education and thought development. Man needs the strong governance and guidance of a socialist state to fully realise those attributes needed to live in individual autonomy in the communist utopia, ie: to live in a world without states, one needs to be prepared by the state. Juche argues for that but in a Korea-specific way: man's Chajusong, creativity and consciousness are what will enable him to live in the autonomous nirvana, but to bring those attributes out needs the strong DPRK state under the helm of the Kims.

Juche affords no value to anything beyond its potential use or harm to man. Capitalism understands value and worth through monetary form, and greed prevents serious scientific advancements from benefiting society (consumer durables are in fact designed to break). This value system is also subjective and therefore unscientific and irrational and no way to run a society. Juche insists it must be in the interests of the individual to be engaged, but engagement comes through exciting and channelling his energies towards society's ends. Machines and materials can never be valued over man, for they are useless without men and exist only to serve him and society.

Marxism espouses that socio-historical progress comes from developments in the production of material wealth. Transformations in social history have come about through changes in the productive forces, production relations and production of material wealth.

Juche argues that history is the process of the masses enhancing their position and role to realise Chajusong. The masses struggle for Chajusong; when society's structure denies or constrains Chajusong, then society is changed. In international diplomacy, Juche demands each nation stand its own ground and defend its collective Chajusong against outside meddling. Hence the DPRK's steadfast independence and neutrality during the Sino–Soviet split, its refusal to join COMECON (the Soviet bloc economic union) and its resistance to pressure from the US. Further, a nation's true Chajusong can only be achieved through economic self-sufficiency, for any reliance on others shifts power into their hands. And to prevent the wrong class from controlling and abusing the power of the state, the masses must seize control of the state and its economic means of production. Society's structure is underpinned by its forms of economic production, so seizing them is the first means to change society into more advanced states as the masses need. History is a series of struggles, from primitive society through feudalism to industrialisation, involving the struggle to subdue nature, wherein the creative processes are fostered, practised and developed.

To realise Chajusong the masses must be brought up to be the masters of society, and be free of all exploitation and oppression. But old ideas die hard and imperialists continue to infiltrate and spread reactionary ideas, so even the liberated need ideological remoulding to wipe out old ideas and retool them with progressive ideas. People need to be remoulded like nature.

In 1975 the line of the Three Revolutions was put forward – the ideological revolution, technical revolution and cultural revolution. Basically the ideological revolution was to be complemented by the technical revolution to free people from the shackles of outdated technology and liberate people from back-breaking work. The cultural revolution would bring everyone up to the standard of an intellectual. Progressive ideas mean a high level of scientific and technical knowledge, with a strong physique. Thought determines men's worth and quality. Knowledge doesn't mean respectability, because much knowledge and bad ideology is disastrous. Only sound ideology, via good ideological remoulding, can direct knowledge to society's benefit.

Juche serves the masses, so the masses must learn Juche and accept the organisation required to imbue them with the philosophy of revolutionary struggle, the struggle to defend their Chajusong, their life and soul. For revolutionary tasks to succeed, political work must educate and rouse people into action, and the fostering of their zeal must be prioritised over all other work. The political persuasion and education of people must be tailored to their backgrounds, trades, etc. One persuader per ten workers is a good ratio for instilling revolutionary fervour.

Above all, harnessing this zeal requires good leadership from the Party and its leader. The leader is the brain to the body of the masses and is the supreme representative and embodiment of their interests; his acts represent their will. He leads them to victory and so devotion to the leader is the highest expression of revolutionary zeal.

With many thanks to Dermot Boyd-Hudson for his help here. The above is sourced from The Immortal Juche Idea *by Kim Chang Ha, Pyongyang Foreign Languages Publishing House, Pyongyang Korea, 1984. For further information look up the Juche Idea Study Group of England, or the Association for the Study of Songun Politics UK (www.uk-songun.com/index.php) or the International Institute of the Juche Idea (http://juche.v.wol.ne.jp/en.htm).*

The KWP is not the only political party. There also exists the Tonghak-derived Chondoist Chongu Party and the Korean Social Democratic Party, concerned with peace, reunification and the imposition of a social democracy for one Korea. In practice, the assembly is dominated by KWP representatives and the assembly ratifies policies already decided by the KWP leadership. The top KWP leadership post is the general secretary, who works with a small advisory group known as the Politburo, and both consult with the Central Committee, a several-hundred-member group that discusses state and ideological policy. The general secretary, Politburo and Central Committee run the Party between party congresses that at the outset happened approximately every four years, although as the years passed the gaps between sessions grew ever longer. Congress involves a few hundred party officials from across the country debating policies put to it by the leadership. Congress elects the Central Committee and Politburo. A Central People's Committee was created in 1972 that would supersede the Politburo, but isn't considered much more than symbolic, although the Politburo isn't up to much either. The most important body within the Party is the Central Committee's Organisation and Guidance Department (OGD), which deals with affairs of the KWP's headquarters, the broader party, the army and administration. The DPRK's top leaders are all members of the OGD, and the OGD has traditionally been under the control of the Kim family – whether it still is is questionable, with the public and violent removal of Kim Jong Un's uncle Jang Song Thaek from it.

The final branch of power is the military, the Korean People's Army (KPA), whose top posts are Supreme Commander and the Chairman of the National Defence Commission, ultimately commanding millions in service and industry.

As stated above, each branch has its own sector of the economy under its governance. What these sectors produce, the people they employ in what conditions, income generated and to what end the goods and income are put, all have a bearing on the relative balance of power of the three power branches. Nor is any one branch totally independent of the other. If the KWP dominate the agencies of the state, then the KWP is de facto the state, then the general secretary of the KWP wields great power. The army, however, has a firm monopoly on employing the nation's fit young men who themselves have a firm interest in joining up and working in the army's own economy sectors and networks. Commanding the army is critical, and when the Korean People's Army (KPA) was founded in early 1948, its leader Choe Yng Gn and its tens of thousands of troops were the hardy stock of guerrilla-fighters in Manchuria; Kim Il Sung's kind of people, and he was their kind of leader.

The different branches of government indeed have their own newspapers. While the subject matter may obviously differ, the unquestioning support and veneration of the Kims does not. Dissenters are noted and their opinions discounted; if they persist, they're publicly named, denounced and demoted (they used to disappear). This is largely the result of the extremely personalised rule of the country that Kim Il Sung inculcated from the immediate post-Korean War period, for the top posts mentioned would soon all be staffed by one man: Kim Il Sung.

Elections do happen. Michael Harrold, in *Comrades and Strangers* (see page 277), describes the visit he made for the election of the People's Assembly, explaining that he could see that the official turnout figures of 100%, of which practically all were voting for the Korean Workers' Party, were not inconceivable considering how much 'fun' voting is. Taken by his friends, wearing their 'Sunday best', he says:

> At the polling station – for the Ansan Guest House it was a nearby secondary school – there were crowds gathered and music being played. The people were organised into large circles, dancing.
>
> Taking the lead were, as usual on such jolly occasions, the old women, and they were pirouetting madly yet gracefully, coloured scarves held aloft, to the sound of some pretty uninspiring music being scratched out by a gramophone. I knew it was going to happen and so I tried as best I could to fade into the background. But it is hard for the proverbial sore thumb to become invisible, and it was with a shout of glee that one old lady spotted the foreigner in their midst. 'Have you come to vote?' she cried, to laughter from those around her. 'Vote for the glorious Workers' Party!' shouted another.

Kim takes charge Before the Korean War was over, Kim Il Sung took action to consolidate his position as leader. Across every echelon of the DPRK government were Koreans with a variety of backgrounds in terms of class, education, and their roots in the country with lifelong ties of friends and family. Aside from these loyalties, their individual political opinions, and the factions thus created, were influenced by where they had served their political apprenticeships during the anti-Japanese war, in the Soviet Union, China, in Korean guerrilla activities or outside Asia altogether. Kim was not one to wait for any disagreements with his policies to snowball into opposition and challenge to his leadership. Purges of the KWP began in 1952 when he indicated that some cadres were infected with sloth and other vices. He upped the ante in his expurgation of potential opponents and, by the end of 1955, a dozen senior figures had been imprisoned or executed on charges of spying for the US, including the former Korean Communist Party leader, Pak Hon Yong.

Thus emboldened, Kim set out his own vision for Korea, to set up the country's political economy along the same lines as Stalin had done in the Soviet Union from the 1930s and '40s where Kim Il Sung had been trained and based for years. Kim Il Sung committed the DPRK's economic growth to heavy industry, a very centralised form of governmental control and unquestioned, highly personalised leadership, which has drawn many parallels with Stalinism. But simply transposing the 1930s Soviet model onto Korea wouldn't take into account Korea's unique circumstances and history, certainly not for Kim. His Juche philosophy, Marxism infused with Korean nationalism, was soon to become the governing philosophy of the DPRK.

Everywhere, everywhere, everywhere in the DPRK there are images of the 'Great Leader' Kim Il Sung and his son the 'Dear Leader' Kim Jong Il. The leaders' portraits hang side by side from high on the walls of the largest public halls to the commonest private rooms, in primary school classrooms and the carriages of Pyongyang's metro, with the frames cleaned with dustcloths assigned only to that task. Their faces peer out from the paintings and mosaics emblazoning buildings, walls, junctions and the badges on people's lapels. In paintings, they loom larger than other people. In print, their names are in larger type. Bronze statues of the Great and Dear Leaders dominate town squares and city hilltops across the country, and front public buildings and farms. The leaders' philosophical treatises, teachings and signatures are carved into great stone tablets that flank public squares, factories and highways, and are chiselled into the rock faces of Korea's holiest mountains and boulders.

During his leadership, Kim Il Sung managed to visit nearly every city, town, village and farm, factory, military base, construction site, port, nursery and hospital, dispensing 'on-the-spot guidance', every occasion being marked on maps set up in Revolutionary Museums across the country. His every word was noted and filmed by accompanying officials and journalists, to be looped in print and film. His birthplace at Mangyongdae is a shrine, visited daily by throngs of pilgrims. All that he touched or commented on has become hallowed ground: the seat he took on the metro; a tree he remarked upon in Wonsan, the chopsticks he used, the railway carriage he travelled in, rooms he visited in rural schools have plaques detailing the comment, the time and day it was made. The same detailed recording would happen for Kim Jong Il, also for Kim Jong Suk, and these days at least in terms of unbridled adulation in the state media, for Kim Jong Un, although the Respected Marshal has yet to appear in statue form or on a lapel pin as he's very 'humble'.

Buildings are named by the date that the leaders visited them, or have meaning built into their grouting. The number of stone slabs on Pyongyang's Juche Tower, built for Kim Il Sung's 70th birthday, equals the days that he had been alive. The log cabin where Kim Jong Il was reportedly born in 1942 is exactly 216m from a mountain behind it, a distance that miraculously mirrors Kim Jong Il's birthdate of 2/16, a day marked by a double rainbow and a bright star in the sky, and the news spread fast (the Son was born in a lowly hut in midwinter as a bright star shone in the sky, the news spread far and wide, the Son would grow to become the only one able to interpret and spread the Juche word of the Father – which all sounds a little familiar!).

Every subject taught from nursery to university is infused with the wisdom of the Kims and their guiding philosophy of Juche. Primary schools have dedicated rooms housing large models of Kim Il Sung's childhood village, around which the children sit and hear stories. Entire departments at Kim Il Sung University are devoted to studying their writings about everything from economics to art and opera. Films and plays exist to propagate the greatness of DPRK socialism, more so Juche, its ultimate victory over imperialism, and the Kims' role in this.

Kim Il Sung has affected time itself. His birthday is a national holiday and the DPRK's calendar is based on Juche Time, counted since 1912, the year of Kim Il Sung's birth, eg: Gregorian 2013 is Juche 101. And he's still in charge. In 1998, four years after his death, Kim Il Sung was made 'Eternal President' of the DPRK by the Supreme People's Assembly.

As Kim Il Sung's rule became sharply more personalised and authoritarian from the 1950s, so his deification commenced. His leadership was based on an expanding personality cult that was partly inspired by Stalinism, with himself commanding a single-party state and centralised, command economy. From 1967, Kim Il Sung's ideology became the party's sole ideology. Success bore out the ideology's supremacy – failure meant someone wasn't applying it properly. The KWP Congress sessions became increasingly infrequent, and ever more solely to accolade Kim Il Sung as a military hero, a philosopher, the father of the nation, a genius whose comments were canonised and whose critics disappeared. A high turnover of senior KWP members was sustained, shaking out those who didn't adhere to the 'monolithic ideology'. The 1980 KWP congress was the only one convened in the last 24 years of Kim Il Sung's life, and that was to affirm Kim Jong Il's rise to power. The son Kim Jong Il himself had already laid down the 'Three Revolutions Teams' of economic management as the means to embed total ideological conformity – and Party control – at every level of the economy. In 1982, as the country's economy and international standing began to wobble and unification seemed ever more elusive, Kim Jong Il's solution was to affirm the 'monolithic ideological system of the Party', ie: more of the same, and he began to push the idea that the DPRK's destiny was one great arduous struggle to achieve global revolution, whatever the cost. Meanwhile, the old man increasingly only conferred with his comrades from their Manchurian guerrilla days, a coterie of an ageing old guard, all mutually enforcing one another's views and providing an ever more redacted outlook and detached hold on reality.

That reality was increasingly manifest architecturally in gigantism. From the late 1960s, ever larger prestige buildings, monuments and mosaics were built, dwarfing all those standing before them, and matching the monumentalism of his character over all others. The DPRK's history became ever more simply his story, with all the embellishments and singling out of his own achievements that inevitably come from the same source retelling the same stories over and over. But he still had his earthy side, his connection with the people. He'd still sit on the farmyard floor to talk corn with the farmers or pose for a photo with a teenager who'd won a trophy. He spent more time touring the country than in the capital in the 50 years that he dominated the country's public life, and many if not most people would have seen him in the flesh at some time in their lives. He led them through the holocaust of the Korean War and out of the ashes, rebuilding the country with some spectacular successes. When he died in July 1994, the almost wild outpouring of grief that beset the land was genuine. Many felt they'd lost a parent, and many Koreans today become visibly upset when remembering his passing.

For years Kim Jong Il had been promoted in government and print as the only man able to succeed his father; finally in July 1997 he added the post of general secretary to his battery of senior government and military titles, after three years of official mourning for Kim Il Sung had elapsed. In 1998, Kim Jong Il became Chairman of the National Defence Commission, while his late father became the 'Eternal President'.

The dynastical transfer of power from Kim Il Sung to Kim Jong Il, and now to Kim Jong Un, may conflict with the accepted norms of socialist governance, but concurs perfectly with Korea's history of Confucian, dynastical rule, which Kim Il Sung didn't invent, but merely reprised and modernised after it was suspended during the Japanese colonial rule. Confucian societies have rigid social hierarchies, overseen by a strong state and headed by a king venerated almost like a god, in life and in death, and unquestioning deference from subordinates to superiors (still seen in South Korea). In addition, the Korean distrust of outsiders, entire families being punished for the crimes of individuals, the existence of an 'untouchable' class whose loyalty and prospects are beyond the pale, were all in place from pre-Japanese days and were simply reprised when they left. The Soviets not only schooled Kim, they supported his war against the Japanese, put him in power and supported the DPRK until the USSR no longer existed. To all that, Kim Il Sung added many socialist aspects to the government – a command economy, state provision of housing and education, the abolition of private property, etc. Kim's governance was 'Red Confucianism'.

There was also the personality cult, which purists of Sino-Soviet socialism could accept as following the examples of Stalin and Mao, but the Kims were heading for outright deification, and Marxist-Leninists have no time for religion, rendering hell on earth to the holy. Of all the religions in the DPRK, Christianity fared worst, not just because of communist ideology, but also from a historical distrust between Korea's leaders and the Church. Regal Korea thought Christianity to be the most pernicious and malevolent foreign influence, as missionaries – usually American – converted the masses away from worshipping the Chosun and instead to worship Christ. The one-time Christian Kim moved swiftly upon taking power to eradicate the threat from the Church – there is an idea that the Korean War was really a war of Christianity versus the communists. However, Kim also appropriated some of Christianity's facets for his own cult.

The codification of the cult came in 1974 with the 'Ten Principles for the Establishment of the One-Ideology System', to whit a North Korean Ten Commandments. Indeed principle two of the Ten Principles – 'We must honor the Great Leader comrade Kim Il Sung with all our loyalty' – is akin to the Bible's first commandment: 'Thou shalt have no other gods before me'. The second commandment – 'Thou shalt not make unto thee any graven image', – has been inverted wherein images of the Kims are everywhere, but damage, deface or destroy them at your absolute peril. The equivalent of the third Commandment – 'Thou shalt not take the name of the Lord thy God in vain' – is to dare any citizen to speak ill of the omniscient Great Leaders, something they wouldn't even confess to in the weekly self-criticism sessions. Even if Lenin and Marx were turning in their graves, nobody would take notice. The picture of Marx hung on the Ministry of Foreign Trade in Kim Il Sung Square is gone, and work has been under way for a while to expunge any mentions of Marx, Lenin and communism from publications, as the Korea-centricity of Kim Il Sungism is made absolute. Kim Il Sung's heart wasn't really with the communist bloc, he fell in and out with the Soviets and Chinese, while he preferred the Non-Aligned Movement. But he got on famously well with Billy Graham and the Reverend Moon.

Kim consolidates However, the Soviet Union's premier Nikita Khruschev denounced all things Stalin in 1956, and a few Soviet-Koreans in the KWP criticised the leadership for the direction in which it was taking the country. Beating his detractors with the stick of nationalism, by late 1956 most of the Soviet-Koreans and the Yanan Koreans from the former New People's Party had been purged from the KWP for their 'foreign influences'. Up through the ranks of the party and the state bodies, Kim promoted his anti-Japanese guerrillas, rough, tough, hardy folk, of common stock and educated as such, promoted more for their ties to Kim than for their technical or political talents. Meanwhile, party membership was growing into millions across the country, taking in a groundswell of farmers and peasants, the people whose origins paralleled those of Kim's senior appointees in the party and agencies of government. By the end of 1958, through purges and promotions, Kim's grip on the KWP was iron-tight. Over the next decade he consolidated his personalised rule through fewer party congresses, more purges and a developing personality cult with a heavy military flavour (see box, *The Cult of the Kims*, pages 30–2).

Foreign policy It's something of a misnomer to write of the two Korean regimes' relations to each other as 'foreign relations'. The DPRK and ROK have always been the two halves of the Korean whole, yet undeniably their want and efforts for reunification have dominated their political environments. However, as both regimes recognise only themselves as Korea's legitimate government, reunification would pretty much require one regime to remove the other, and with no peace ever declared since 1953, the peninsula has been on a war footing ever since. Tensions between the three sides (for the US has long had a permanent, well-armed, military force in the ROK) oscillate to this day, and the last half-century of relations has been a cycle of negotiations, brinksmanship, spasms of violence and rapprochement.

For the DPRK, the creator and perpetuator of Korea's division has always been the US and its puppet government in Seoul. To the West, the DPRK has been a warmongering pariah, either as a Soviet puppet or on its own initiative, and reunification is impossible with the uncompromising regime in Pyongyang. If the DPRK regime were determined to be free of all outside pressures or coercion, as Juche aspired, then the country would be assisted into isolationism by throttling US economic sanctions. The continuity of the situation partly stems from the longevity of Washington's anti-communist policy and Pyongyang's military regime, topped by the Kims. The DPRK and ROK have always argued about the same things, just at times with much more violence than others, although relations have improved since the ROK became a democracy in 1989, and the DPRK's backers in Moscow died away in 1991.

The DPRK and ROK did try to reconcile immediately after the armistice. At the 1954 Geneva Conference, Kim Il Sung proposed an all-Korean commission to discuss reunification under a confederation of two Koreas, empowered to oversee their own foreign and defence policies. But the idea died. Pyongyang's offers of rapprochement in 1960 following Rhee's removal from office were rebuffed by the new junta in Seoul.

But no matter for Kim, as socialism was working. By 1960, the DPRK GNP was at US$140 per capita, hammering the ROK's US$100. The DPRK's impressive recovery was partly explicable by Soviet and Chinese aid, between which powers the DPRK jostled, playing one off against the other and being the pawn of neither. Nonetheless, Kim saw Khruschev's favouring of coexistence with the capitalist West as tantamount to defeat. Deteriorating Sino–Soviet relations in the 1960s led the

DPRK to back China at the cost of its Soviet aid, but Kim was worried that if the two really fell out, their shared beliefs would suffer. He castigated China's apparent failure to publicly lambaste America's engagement in Vietnam. However, China's Communist Party was lurching into extremes, soon to culminate in the Cultural Revolution, and returned fire that Kim was too pro-Soviet. As Sino–DPRK relations soured into the late 1960s, a spate of violent incidents marked US, ROK and DPRK relations, and feeling ever more isolated, Kim directed the DPRK to become ever more militarised (see pages 52–3). Paranoia bubbled over into proactive assaults. In January 1968, most of a team of DPRK commandos were killed in a raid on the ROK president's house (see box below). Two days later, an American spy-ship, the USS *Pueblo*, was captured by the DPRK navy and the crew held captive for a year. All 31 crew members of an American EC-121 spy-plane were killed when it was shot down by a DPRK MiG fighter in April 1969, and in August a US helicopter was downed as it strayed across the DMZ into the DPRK.

In the early 1970s, thawing Sino–US relations and reduced US forces in the ROK goaded more inter-Korean talks. High-level talks alternated between the two capitals and a crucial joint communiqué was issued in July 1972, which was a milestone for ROK–DPRK relations (another milestone that year was the creation of the post of president of the DPRK, to which Prime Minister Kim Il Sung was elevated). Work towards reunifying the country would be without foreign interference, without force, and fewer vitriolic slanging matches in the media. A Pyongyang–Seoul hotline was set up, as was a South–North Coordinating Committee (SNCC) for further negotiations and implementing the agreement. But it was a false dawn. The SNCC met only three times. The DPRK stressed that reducing inter-Korean armed confrontation was a prerequisite to all else, demanding in particular that US aid to the ROK must stop. Seoul preferred both Koreas' political systems be recognised, with mutual non-interference and economic co-operation preceding arms reductions.

Pyongyang proposed replacing the armistice with a peace agreement. The ROK side was worried by a reduced US presence and the communist victory in Vietnam.

BLUE HOUSE RAID

On 21 January 1968, a DPRK special forces unit of 31 men set off with a mission to assassinate ROK president Park Chung Hee in the Blue House in Seoul. Issued with ROK uniforms, the men crossed through the DMZ undetected, but a lone woodcutter stumbled across the group. They let him live, only for him to alert the ROK security forces. ROK troops stopped the unit not far from the Blue House, and in the ensuing gunfight, 28 of the raiders were killed. Only one raider was caught and under interrogation confessed that they were to also attack the US Embassy. The other two commandos were never caught.

The ROK sought to respond entirely in kind, creating an assassination hit squad called Unit 684 comprising 31 criminal desperadoes, targeting Kim Il Sung. Seven died in training on their base camp of Silmido Island, and the attempt was called off. Then 20 of the remaining fighters were killed in a violent mutiny at the base, and the four remaining were executed at a tribunal. It's speculated that when the plan was cancelled, the unit was to be liquidated to keep the story quiet, which the ROK government denies, but admits the unit existed and never denied its purpose.

A call from the DPRK for South Koreans to overthrow President Park's government wasn't conducive to successful negotiations. Tensions escalated along the DMZ and the Pyongyang–Seoul hotline was cut. In 1978, the US and ROK began what would become an annual event, the Team Spirit wargames that would aggravate the North and help justify a build-up in troops. At the beginning of the decade, the Korean People's Army had some 400,000 frontline troops; by the end, this figure had topped a million. Evidently the two sides weren't getting along so well and arming themselves to the teeth was one way to deal with relations.

Casting further What with the jostling for favour between China and the Soviets, and the apparent unending aggravation with the ROK and US, the net for friends and funds was cast further in the early 1970s. From 1972 to 1974, the DPRK government procured large loans of foreign capital, machinery and funds from countries like Sweden, France and Japan, to create new export industries that would repay the lenders. To further its nuclear power programme, it joined the International Atomic Energy Association (IAEA) in 1974, and the DPRK was accepted into the Non-Aligned Movement (NAM) in 1975.

Kim presupposed that this neutral group of developing nations, not really involved in the machinations of the Cold War, would be a good place to promote his anti-imperialism and be a supporting crowd for the DPRK, especially in United Nations negotiations. While NAM held Kim in high regard, it wasn't quite the coherent and cohesive freelance political force he had envisaged. Nor were the capital loans from elsewhere being paid off by DPRK exports, and the Ministry of Finance defaulted on the country's foreign debts, which would cost it dearly later (see *Economy*, pages 50–62).

By the end of the 1970s, the DPRK leadership was somewhat galled by China's warming relations with America and Japan, but this spurred some further discourse between the two Koreas in 1980 and a plethora of meetings ensued. They led nowhere, however, as General Chun Doo Hwan established his military rule in the ROK and was not interested in negotiating. He rejected Kim Il Sung's idea for a Democratic Confederal Republic of Koryo, with both sides equally coexisting in lesser forms under an overarching national assembly and a confederal committee with charge over national defence, foreign affairs and economic co-ordination. Kim responded to Chun's snub by ordering the assassination of Chun's cabinet in Rangoon in October 1983. It nearly worked (see box, page 36, for more details).

Somehow North–South relations improved and DPRK assistance and relief to the flood-stricken South in 1984 led to discussions on humanitarian and economic co-operation. In 1985, performing arts groups and sports teams were exchanged and separated families briefly reunited for the first time. In the KWP's higher circles, ideas of minor economic reforms similar to those being undertaken in China were bandied about, as the DPRK economy slowed and the last seven-year plan hadn't delivered. Capitalist enterprise zones were considered and a joint-venture law enacted, but there that train of thought halted. A visit by Kim Il Sung to the Soviet Union in May 1984 led to a new rapprochement and new economic, military and diplomatic links, lifting the DPRK's fortunes – except that the DPRK's fortunes now rested very heavily on the Soviets.

Talks with the ROK petered out and were given up in early 1986, with Pyongyang blaming Team Spirit exercises. Usually though the DPRK resumed talks when the games stopped, but not this time. Kim saw little to gain and had thrown his country's lot in with the USSR and NAM; what the rest of the world was doing didn't really seem to matter.

On 9 October 1983, the ROK's leader President Chun Doo Hwan, while on a state visit to Burma, went to lay a wreath at Rangoon's martyrs memorial. Due to traffic problems, Chun's car was delayed in arriving, and just as he did arrive a bomb exploded at the memorial, killing 21 people and wounding 46. As well as four Burmese dignitaries, 17 ROK government officials, advisers and journalists were killed, including the ROK foreign minister and deputy prime minister.

Burmese police managed to arrest their first suspect two days later, despite the man trying to blow himself up with a hand grenade. Two more suspects alerted to the police by villagers also tried to commit suicide with grenades, but only one succeeded. The two surviving agents were interrogated into revealing their DPRK origins.

Beijing scolded the DPRK leadership and froze them out for some months. Rangoon's leaders expelled the DPRK's diplomats. Burma–DPRK relations remained frozen until the 2000s, when the military dictators running a now isolated Burma found the DPRK to be a useful friend in supplying military tech and know-how, a relationship that goes on today.

But it would matter The international situation was changing. By the late 1980s, the ROK economy was soaring, approaching output levels ten times those of the DPRK, and the former's growing success and power tempted the USSR and China towards similarly capitalist economic reforms. China and the ROK started humanitarian and sports exchanges. Indeed, the ROK had been wooing communist nations since 1984, and in 1988 the ROK's newly elected president Roh Tae Woo's outreaches to the North cemented ROK relations with the Soviets and China. The world was presented with the ROK's new glories at the glittering 1988 Seoul Olympics, attended for the first time in 12 years by virtually all communist and capitalist invitees, with the ROK star ascendant. The DPRK's offer to co-host the games having long gone by the wayside, they accepted ROK financial aid in return for a promise not to disrupt the games.

The DPRK leadership seethed as its rich brother befriended all its old allies. So, unseen, DPRK diplomats in Beijing made contact with their American counterparts just after the Olympics finished, a prescient move as a year later the DPRK's greatest allies in eastern Europe evaporated with the Soviet bloc. Soviet trade declined in 1989, and in late 1990, the Soviets announced no more aid and no more barter – if the DPRK wanted something, they paid in dollars. The DPRK's world of friends disappeared practically overnight. Suddenly, for this stumbling industrial power, things looked extremely bleak.

Japan One route out could be Japanese investment, but that would need better relations. For many Koreans, Northern and Southern, Japan is still the great unforgiven for its colonial rule of Korea, for Korea being divided when Japan was the aggressor, and Japan's economic revival stemming from massive US investment to make it an operational base from which to fight the Korean War. Kim Il Sung was brought up mind and soul in fighting the Japanese, and resistance to them was infused into Juche and every history book in the country. Japan meanwhile would prove utterly indifferent to the malevolence of its imperial past and even be insanely litigious about it. It was not until 1965 that the 'treaties' of 1905, 1907 and 1910, which formally annexed Korea to Japan, were finally annulled and no longer could any diehard imperialist in the House of Yamato brandish those papers. But there was genuine Japanese ire at DPRK agents having kidnapped several Japanese citizens back to the DPRK, and Pyongyang's blithe defaulting on earlier loans.

Still, while the Japanese government recognised only Seoul as Korea's legitimate governing body, there were DPRK–Japan relations through informal channels, including trade links via the association of Koreans in Japan, Chochongnyon, that gained several hundred million dollars of investment over the decades. By the 1980s Japan was a major trading partner with the DPRK. In 1990, Pyongyang suggested to a Japanese delegation there – trying to release a fishing-boat crew from spying charges – that relations be normalised. Haggling would continue for the next decade, but it was a start.

Still, destitution loomed. China's economic reforms were glanced at and a free trade zone was set up in 1991, but substantial economic reforms were an anathema to Kim and everything five decades of socialism had cost. While capitalism increasingly infected the Soviet bloc during the late 1980s to '90s, Pyongyang's Politburo and Council were staffed more by ageing anti-Japanese guerrillas as Kim buttressed his beliefs with the backing of his oldest cronies. What could they do about the ROK's economic success threatening the DPRK's military superiority? he asked. They answered: build a nuclear bomb. And it was over nukes that Kim's regime would show its old mettle in brilliant lustre.

Nukes in Korea By the 1990s, concerns over the DPRK's nuclear ambitions had been brewing for a while. The DPRK Foreign Ministry was vague but cited the threat from the US's tactical nuclear weapons on the peninsula. IAEA inspections of the DPRK's nuclear facilities were repeatedly refused. Tensions rose and some US senators advocated bombing DPRK facilities at the Yongbyon nuclear facility, north of Pyongyang.

The DPRK had hankered to enter the exclusive club of atomic powers practically since the country's founding, and in 1974 had joined the IAEA, the international agency that gives out nuclear know-how – for strictly peaceful means, mind. So were the DPRK's apparent intentions in signing the Non-Proliferation Treaty of Nuclear Weapons in 1985. Only by 1990 was it obvious that DPRK's nuclear electricity reactors weren't really big enough for serious electricity production but could deliver lots of plutonium and enriched uranium: bomb material. But a

KOREAN AIR BOMBING

On 29 November 1987, Korean Air flight 858 between Baghdad and Seoul blew up over the Andaman Sea, and all 104 passengers and 11 crew on board the Boeing 707 were killed. The bombing was carried out by two DPRK agents, who had come via Moscow, Budapest, Vienna, Belgrade, Baghdad and then Abu Dhabi, where they'd put the bomb aboard the flight as it stopped over. Their getaway unravelled in Bahrain when their forged Japanese passports were exposed. One succeeded in suicide by cyanide cigarette, but Kim Hyon Hui failed to die, and under interrogation she revealed the incredible plot. Just as incredibly, ROK president Roh Tae Woo later pardoned her as a victim of brainwashing, and she wrote a book *The Tears of My Soul* that told of her training in the Korean People's Army and how she'd been personally briefed on the bombing mission by Kim Jong Il himself. She now lives in the ROK under guard.

slew of landmark agreements arose. However, Pyongyang did agree to talks at the prime-ministerial level with the ROK and, following rounds of bi-capital talks, in September 1991 the five permanent members of the UN Security Council approved both Koreas' membership of the UN.

The following month, US president George H W Bush announced the withdrawal of US tactical nuclear weapons from the peninsula, heralding a breakthrough in inter-Korean relations. In December, both Koreas signed the Agreement on Reconciliation, Non-aggression, Exchanges and Cooperation between the South and the North. The DPRK officially recognised the ROK's existence for the first time, and vice versa, and they agreed to negotiate a formal end to the Korean War, with joint sub-committees on developing economic ties and communications, cultural exchanges, united sports teams, familial reunifications, and measures to deflate military tensions. They also agreed the joint Declaration on the Denuclearisation of the Korean Peninsula, to set an effective bilateral nuclear inspection regime. But peace proved elusive.

ARE THE NORTH AND SOUTH IRRECONCILABLE?

Dr James Hoare, Chargé d'Affaires of the British Embassy to Pyongyang 2001–02

The division of Korea in 1945 had little to do with any historic or cultural differences on the peninsula. For about 1,000 years, Korea had been a unified political entity, with a remarkable homogeneous population. There were linguistic and other differences among those people, but the 38th parallel, the line chosen in 1945, bore little relation to them. Rather it was selected by the United States since it seemed the very least that the Soviet Union would accept. Just as important, in those opening days of the Cold War, it gave control of Seoul, the country's capital since 1392, to the Americans. But the Korean people never accepted the division.

However, the failure of either side to win an outright victory in the 1950–53 Korean War meant that the division has been perpetuated to this day. The war ended the 38th parallel's formal role. The line of actual military control, which became the Military Demarcation Line (the De-Militiarised Zone runs on both sides of this) with the signing of the Armistice on 27 July 1953, though it ran close to the 38th parallel, did not follow it exactly. Instead, the South Koreans held territory above the parallel to the east of the truce village of Panmunjom that had been in the North before the war. The North, for its part, held Kaesong, capital of the country in the last but one dynasty, and the Ongjin peninsula, both south of the parallel and both in South Korea before June 1950.

After the signing of the Armistice, while both Koreas claimed to work for the reunification of the peninsula, each set about the creation of a separate state. They did not deny the essential historic unity of the peninsula, but each side drew on cultural and historical material that could be used to stress its legitimacy, and in the process downplayed the claims of the other side.

In the South, this meant stressing the role of Seoul, the capital of a united Korea from 1392. The speech of Seoul was presented as the 'national language'. At the same time, South Korean propaganda emphasised the tradition of the Silla kingdom. Silla, one of the traditional 'Three Kingdoms' of Korea, with its capital at Kyongju in the southwest, had unified much of the peninsula under its rule from AD668. Silla's role assumed particular importance after Park Chung Hee came to power in 1961, since he came from that part of the country. The tradition of

In 1992 IAEA inspectors noted discrepancies between the amounts of plutonium produced and how much they found, and complained of restricted access to plants. Tensions roller coastered, with the US Congress demanding sanctions if not bombing, while the DPRK shook its stick at them. With the economy stalling through diminishing harvests and a lack of energy supplies, the DPRK threatened to cancel its treaties unless dialogue and aid began. US president Clinton ordered sanctions in mid-1994 and the DPRK withdrew from the IAEA. In desperate diplomacy, former US president Jimmy Carter visited Kim Il Sung in July and brought some defusion of tensions with a possible 'aid for atoms' agreement. The octogenarian Kim Il Sung, his back to the wall, was still demanding no surrender, not without a good price anyway. But then on 8 July 1994 he died suddenly of a heart attack. He was 82. His passing was profoundly traumatic for the DPRK people. He had led them out of the bitter ruins of the Korean War, and placed himself at the helm of the country's reconstruction and development into a fiercely sovereign state that provided all of one's needs in life – to the loyal. Dazed with

concentrating on Silla continued under his successors, since they too came from the southwest.

Although for North Korea, Seoul was to remain officially the capital until 1972, with Pyongyang listed only as the 'temporary capital', much stress was laid on Pyongyang's much longer history compared with that of Seoul. Indeed, Pyongyang was proclaimed to be the site of the capital of Tangun, the legendary ancestor of the Korean people. The speech of Pyongyang was promoted as the 'standard language' in the North. Historically, North Korea looked to another of the 'Three Kingdoms', Koguryo. Koguryo had been the largest of the kingdoms. At their greatest extent, Koguryo's territories stretched north far into what are now China's northeastern provinces, and south to the Han River valley around Seoul. The kingdom's warriors also acquired a reputation for fierceness in battle.

North Korea has placed much emphasis on these themes. There has never been any claim that these are the only strands in Korean history but the stress is on the importance of the Pyongyang region and the superiority of Koguryo over Silla. The role of Pyongyang as an older capital than Seoul has been boosted by the claim that this was the capital city on earth of Korea's mythical founder, Tangun. Even more conclusive evidence, in North Korean eyes, for the sacred nature of Pyongyang and its claim to centrality in Korean history was the alleged confirmation in the early 1990s that a tomb just outside the city was that of Tangun and his family. Refurbishment of the tomb of King Tongmyong, the supposed founder of the Koguryo dynasty, also just outside the city, reinforced the claimed importance of Pyongyang in the (unified) nation's history. No doubt an additional factor was that Kim Il Sung, ruler of North Korea from late 1945 until his death in 1994, came from the small village of Mangyongdae, just outside Pyongyang.

In addition to these factors, the continued North–South division has enhanced a sense of separateness. In vocabulary, customs, politics and general behaviour, North and South have grown apart. They no longer sing the same words to traditional songs, for example, even though the tunes remain the same. Increasingly, it is unlikely that they would even use the same instruments. None of this is irreversible, but the emphasis on separateness means that eventual reunification will be that bit harder.

grief, the DPRK still signed the Agreed Framework with the US, freezing its nuclear programme, staying in the NPT and allowing inspections in return for 500,000 tonnes of fuel oil annually (replacing the lost imports from Russia) and the US leading a consortium to build two light-water reactors by 2003 (nuclear reactors but less potent) through the Korean Peninsula Energy Development Organisation (KEDO). The DPRK received some guarantee of energy supplies and a nuclear-free peninsula finally looked possible. But this was a time of national mourning, with a new leader at the helm, and dreadful years to come.

The succession From the early 1970s, the man feted and groomed as the DPRK's next leader, the rightful heir of Kim Il Sung's power and authority, was none other than Kim Jong Il, Kim Il Sung's first son. From 1980, Kim Jong Il was announced as the heir designate to his father's throne, and his already considerable portfolio of senior positions in the government and party were further bolstered. His own thoughts on Juche were published shortly after. Little was known about the man, however. He was rarely seen in public in the way that Kim Il Sung toured the lands, and was rumoured to be a recluse, who spent too much time watching the Western films in his incredible collection, films that if anyone else had been caught with them would have led to a one-way trip to the mines.

What kind of man would Kim Jong Il prove to be? Technocrat? Ideologue? Pragmatist? Could he successfully succeed his father atop a system of governance built so solidly around one man's personality? Questions arose over who was really in power. The posts of general secretary of the KWP and president of the DPRK remained empty while the country stayed officially in mourning for three years.

During this time the country, through floods, droughts, the loss of energy supplies and its economic partners and backers, all compounded by overall malgovernance (see *Economy*, pages 50–62), entered into its first great famine. The trickle of defectors crossing into China was turning into a stream of refugees fleeing over the Yalu. In 1995, United Nations relief organisations received unprecedented requests to see the situation. Food and medical aid were forthcoming over the next months and years, from, among others, the US, Japan and ROK, but the politicking going on in the country's leadership was impenetrable at best. An indication of business as normal north of the DMZ came in December 1996 when a DPRK submarine ran aground off the ROK coast. Twenty-six commandos swam ashore and so began a violent manhunt that led to the deaths of all the commandos and 13 ROK soldiers and civilians.

The most serious indication of internal dissent was the defection to the ROK of the ageing International Affairs Secretary, Hwang Jang Yop, in February 1997.

A THRILLER YOU COULDN'T MAKE UP

Kim Jong Il had a distinct fondness for film femmes. While there are many scurrilous stories about the Dear Leader with very little truth underpinning them, the following story is true and says much about the lengths to which Kim would go. In 1978 South Korean actress Choi Eun Hee was kidnapped in Hong Kong and taken to Pyongyang. Her ex-husband, the acclaimed director Shin Sang Ok, suffered the same fate when he went to investigate her disappearance, and the pair would spend the next eight years in the DPRK where they were 'encouraged' to 'help' invigorate the DPRK's film industry by starring in and making dozens of films. They eventually escaped at a film festival in Vienna in 1986 by seeking sanctuary at the US Embassy.

Hwang was a senior Party member and committee chair, an interpreter of Juche philosophy and a man of very high standing with bountiful perks of state, had he wished to indulge. But he was an aesthete and a man of principle who told his southern hosts the regime was collapsing from within and couldn't have long to live. The rest of the world looked on, awaiting implosion.

But Pyongyang was opaque as the country was still officially in mourning for Kim Il Sung. Only in October 1997 did Kim Jong Il take power, with the post of general secretary of the KWP, and later as commander-in-chief of the Korean People's Army, taking charge of both halves of the power duopoly that runs the country. His first few months of official rule brooked little change. To the poker table of the diplomats' casino, the DPRK brought its sophisticated multi-stage missiles, firing a Taepondong 1 projectile over Japan in August 1998 to tell the world that despite all the rumours, the regime was alive and well. Seriously unimpressed, the Japanese government promptly withheld US$1bn earmarked for the already delayed reactors. The US Congress would also suspend some oil shipments over DPRK missile sales to America's enemies.

But all that was something of a very noisy backdrop that was otherwise very much at odds with positive developments on many fronts. Further US–DPRK talks in late 1999 led the Clinton administration to lift some sanctions and offer food aid in exchange for the DPRK freezing its missile programme. Indeed, DPRK–US relations had all the while been improving through the late 1990s, and Bill Clinton was poised to be the first US president to visit the country (notwithstanding the fact they were still technically at war), though US secretary of state Madeleine Albright instead visited in October 2000.

A campaign of outreach had delivered full diplomatic ties, or a measure of working friendliness, with over a dozen European Union states (including the UK, France, Italy, Spain and Germany), Canada, Australia, and the Philippines (completing the ASEAN nations, except Burma). By 2002 even full diplomatic ties with Japan looked possible, notwithstanding the DPRK's demands for hard currency compensation for Japan's colonial crimes (including 'comfort women' in Japan) and Japan's demands for its kidnapped citizens to be returned. While Japan had contributed to aid and foodstuffs going to the DPRK, it also supported sanctions against the DPRK out of fear of Pyongyang's bombs and rockets. Japan admitted it had 'caused tremendous damage and suffering' to Korea under colonial rule and sought to help normalise relations with grants and low-interest loans.

Peace between the DPRK and the US wasn't declared, but the potential for war to break out was enormously reduced as those countries' respective media employed far less colourful language about the other. Not least, the US sat back and let ROK president Kim Dae Jung carry out his Sunshine Policy towards the DPRK, which marked the greatest diplomatic advances seen between the two Koreas.

A former political prisoner and activist, Kim Dae Jung's policy was a more pragmatic acceptance of the North, encouraging permanent economic and diplomatic assistance and cultural exchange, which the DPRK reciprocated, starting with the exchange of basketball teams in 1999 (possibly inspiring US former basketball star Dennis Rodman years later) and leading to the historic summit in Pyongyang between the two sides' heads of state in June 2000. Stepping out of the plane at Pyongyang, Kim Dae Jung was surprised to see Kim Jong Il awaiting him at the foot of the stairs, a warm and cordial moment that set the tone for the summit.

Family reunions followed in August, and in September the ROK and DPRK teams marched together at the Sydney Olympics. No ROK team games were shown on DPRK TV from the ROK-hosted World Cup of 2002, but after the tournament the two sides had their own friendly, with one flag and a traditional folk song replacing their respective anthems. It was a fitting 0–0 draw. The ROK promised to finance the rehabilitation of the DPRK's infrastructure, building road and rail links across the DMZ to reach the massive South Korean investments in industry and tourism in Kaesong and Kumgangsan.

In January 2001, three central DPRK newspapers published a joint editorial proposing development of the economy in a profitability-oriented manner, the state's way of announcing a major step towards market liberalisation. In January 2002, the official 'Arduous March' phase of the country's development (or contraction) was declared over and the 'Construction of the Powerful State' began.

Bombs and rockets But nothing moves without energy. KEDO (the Korean Peninsula Energy Development Organisation) was dragging along, and as the

NORTH KOREA: A CINEMATIC EPIC IN THREE PARTS

An extremely effective introduction to the modern DPRK and its people would be to watch three documentaries that Nick Bonner co-produced with director Dan Gordon from the Sheffield, UK-based company VeryMuchSo productions.* The films are truly ground-breaking in terms of access and insight into the ordinary lives of North Koreans (although the films' subjects would rightfully be considered to be extraordinary people in any scenario) and have been highly acclaimed in both the Western media and the DPRK itself.

The first was the barnstorming *The Game of Their Lives*, catching up with the thousand-to-one-against DPRK football team in the 1966 World Cup, who, incredibly, beat the much-fancied Italians 1–0 and made football history by becoming the first Asian team to make the tournament's quarter-finals. There the North Koreans astoundingly were leading Portugal 3–0, before the latter came back to win 5–3. Nothing was heard of the players after 1966, and rumours abounded that they had come home in dishonour and were sent to labour camps.

None of it was true. Seven of the original team were still alive when the film was first suggested, and after four years of negotiations, the film-makers won unprecedented access into the lives and homes of the surviving players, who in 2002 were brought back to a heroes' welcome of 33,000 in the football stadium at Middlesbrough, UK, the city where the team had originally played and stayed. It is the first film to have official access to ordinary North Korean citizens and unfettered, uncensored interviews with them as they talk openly about their memories of 1966, the post-Korean War aftermath and their lives today. *The Game* also shows never-before-seen archival footage, filmed by the North Koreans in England in 1966.

'Even for an American, it was enough (no lie) to bring tears to your eyes,' reported CNN *Sports Illustrated*, and among its four awards *The Game* won the Royal Television Society award for Best Sports Documentary. Kim Jong Il saw and lauded the film.

VeryMuchSo then won permission to make a second documentary, *A State of Mind*, about two young gymnasts, 13-year-old Pak Hyon Sun and 11-year-old Kim Song Yun, and their families, in the lead-up to the 2003 Mass Games. Over subsequent visits, the characters warmed and relaxed in front of camera, and access century turned it was clear the light-water reactors would not be finished by 2003. George W Bush's neo-conservative outfit promptly agreed to an indigenous ROK missile programme, and responded to the DPRK's expression of frustration at the very tardy implementation of the Agreed Framework – such that Pyongyang was considering deeming it defunct – by calling the DPRK the 'road-kill of history' and later putting it on the infamous 'Axis of Evil' list, substantially alarming Pyongyang and irritating Seoul.

US aid in food and monetary terms declined sharply. Oddly, as it would turn out, in April 2002, the White House posted that the DPRK was in full compliance with the Agreed Framework and that funds for the very late reactors would be released, for which a ground-breaking ceremony was held in August. But just two months later, in talks between the US and DPRK in Beijing, US special envoy James Kelly reportedly presented evidence to the North Korean foreign ministry officials that the latter's country was engaged in enriching uranium, in violation of the Agreed

to home life, days out and an intimate portrayal were attained – a remarkable insight into a part of North Korean society never seen before in the West.

The most contentious film followed, the 2004 production *Crossing the Line*, concerning the fate of US soldiers who defected to the DPRK during the 1960s – when the Cold War was at its height and a second Korean war was not just possible but probable. Four US soldiers, sent to the DMZ to keep the peace and protect the 'free world', instead stepped across the demarcation line and defected to the DPRK. Not until 1996 did the US admit that had happened.

The film concentrates mainly on James Dresnok, or 'Comrade Joe', who defected in 1962 and with whom the West had no contact until two years of negotiations gained Gordon's team access to him in 2002, by which time he had had three sons from two wives and spoke Korean as his daily language. Another defector, Robert Jenkins, had married a Japanese national, Hitomi Soga, one of 13 Japanese that the DPRK had kidnapped over the years to teach language and customs to Korean spies. One allegation was that the DPRK kidnapped foreign women to marry the Americans so they would have Western-looking children who could be sent to the West as spies – ie: a deliberate spy-breeding programme. Nonetheless, Dresnok's boys are fully integrated into North Korean society, with one working in the diplomat service and another serving in the Korean People's Army, patrolling the DMZ from the northern side.

Dresnok and the three others gave their signatures to propaganda leaflets dropped on the ROK about the virtuous wonder and wealth of their new-found home, and voiced propaganda tannoyed over the DMZ to the US and ROK soldiers. They acted in DPRK films vilifying the US, with Dresnok typecast as an evil American, while he befriended several North Korean film stars who also appear in *Crossing the Line* and discuss the importance of film to the DPRK's propaganda machine. But the unreal existence of the four and their families would come to a rude, bitter end. As filming is underway, the departure of Soga from the DPRK forces Jenkins to follow her and ultimately surrender to US forces, to whom he denounces Dresnok, who responds on camera in what is an extraordinary documentary.

VeryMuchSo Productions, in association with Passion Pictures, the BBC, E Pictures, Koryo Tours, IFG2, Cinequanon and Dongsoong Art Center.

Framework. The North Koreans apparently denied this, and then supposedly later confessed to the breach.

In November President Bush unilaterally suspended oil shipments, presenting ROK, Japanese and EU delegates sent to discuss the matter with a fait accompli. Winter set in and a third famine loomed for the DPRK as food donations plummeted through overstretch and political malice. In December the plutonium-producing reactors at Yongbyon were re-activated as the war of words stoked up again. If the US is ready to strike at us for our nuclear programmes, we had better make a load of nukes to ward them off, Pyongyang reasoned.

Rising tensions

> The imperialists ... make aggression and war their means of existence. Aggression and war are constant companions of imperialism ... The situation has become aggravated to the extreme in Korea today and has engendered the danger that war may break again at any moment not because we committed any act of violating the territory of the United States of America or menacing the sovereignty and security but because the US imperialists have come to our country, thousands of miles away from theirs and stepped up policies of aggression against the Korean people.
>
> Kim Il Sung

Throughout 2003, the situation deteriorated. In January the IAEA urged the DPRK to 'co-operate fully and urgently' with the agency or be deemed non-compliant, so the DPRK booted out its inspectors and withdrew from the Non-Proliferation Treaty, then let off some missiles, timing one for the inauguration of the new South Korean president, Roh Moo Hyun (what a day to start work!), who with some courage vowed to carry on the the Sunshine Policy.

There didn't seem to be much sense in the US claims about the DPRK making a bomb. The White House had already said the DPRK was in compliance with the Agreed Framework and the reactors were about to begin being built – albeit a decade late. Bush's Axis of Evil speech may have scuppered years of thawing relations between Pyongyang and Washington, but at last they seemed ready to deliver on the deal – more than the Clinton administration, which admitted it had agreed the deal with Pyongyang back in 1994 thinking the DPRK would not be around to take delivery years later.

But the DPRK's enrichment of uranium made sense in so far as the promised light-water reactors would still need enriched uranium to operate, and intermittent deliveries of fuel oil from the US suggested reactor fuel deliveries might be as irregular, if not more so. And the Agreed Framework didn't prohibit enriched uranium, it covered plutonium. But the West's agreed narrative had no time for questions: the DPRK was a natural aggressor, it had its million-man army, and the US attack on Iraq was about to begin. Washington refused bilateral talks on an equal footing with the DPRK, or any security guarantees with the DPRK (they're technically not at peace), and opted for six-party talks involving Russia, Japan, the ROK and China.

The DPRK was convinced the US was only being consistently hostile, and air-raid drills in Pyongyang were being taken very seriously. The Six-Party Talks started and stalled all through 2003 and 2004, only interspersed by the DPRK stating it had reprocessed some 8,000 nuclear fuel rods, enough to make six bombs, then the ROK helpfully admitted its nuclear scientists had secretly experimented with uranium enrichment in 2000. In 2005 Pyongyang claimed it had made a bomb. Then a breakthrough came in the summer when the DPRK agreed to abandon its nuclear programme in exchange for economic aid and security guarantees. In September a joint statement was announced.

Something broke down somewhere. In July 2006, the DPRK fired a fist of missiles into the Korean East Sea. This was condemned by the UN Security Council, which then urged the DPRK to return immediately to the Six-Party Talks and embargoed trade in missile-related materials, but with fertiliser and food aid also cut off – again.

The DPRK responded thus: 'The field of scientific research in the DPRK successfully conducted an underground nuclear test under secure conditions on October 9, Juche 95 at a stirring time when all the people of the country are making a great leap forward in the building of a great, prosperous, powerful socialist nation,' KCNA announced. The DPRK had become the world's ninth nuclear power.

Western intelligence agencies estimated the blast at a few kilotons, with the US government, having done so much to talk up the hypothetical threat, now downplaying the reality. Indeed, CIA director Michael Hayden later called the blast a 'failure' and said that 'the United States does not recognise North Korea as a nuclear weapons state,' right as the US sat down to talks with the DPRK.

Still, it was 'provocative' and the UN Security Council imposed sanctions against the DPRK, demanding that Pyongyang cease its pursuit of 'weapons of mass destruction' (WMD). China stated its 'resolute opposition' to the 'brazen' act, the PRC's delicate way of saying 'we are apocalyptically unimpressed', and the DPRK swiftly agreed to rejoin talks that resumed in December. Low farce was still on the menu when the following month the US banned cognac, jet-skis and iPods from export to the DPRK to punish its 'elite'.

Progress came in February 2007 when the DPRK said it would shut down and seal Yongbyon and invite the IAEA back for verification, in return for a million tonnes of fuel oil and the promise of talks about a light-water reactor – in essence, reprising the terms of the 1994 Agreement, with more scope for a 'peace' of sorts to be settled between the DPRK and US.

It was a good year. Over the summer the row over ABM (Anti-Ballistic Missile) was resolved and the DPRK shut down and sealed Yongbyon. In October, Pyongyang committed to disabling its nuclear facilities and declare all its nuclear programmes by the year's end, and the presidents of both Koreas agreed to start talks to end the war; the following February the New York Philharmonic performed in Pyongyang (playing the 'Star Spangled Banner' first). But too much progress is never a good thing on the peninsula. In 2008 the ROK's new conservative administration under Lee Myung Bak said further aid to the DPRK depended on nuclear disarmament and progress on human rights, to which Pyongyang responded by closing the Kaesong industrial zone and letting off some missiles. Then in July came the fatal shooting of a South Korean tourist in Kumgangsan. This was doubly a shame, as the US and DPRK foreign ministers had met, the US removed the DPRK from its list of terrorism-sponsoring countries and Pyongyang agreed to access to its nuclear sites. But then suspension of US energy aid was met by Pyongyang threatening to slow the dismantling of its nuclear programme and cut off all overland travel with the ROK. In January 2009 Pyongyang accused Seoul of hostile intent, declared all military and political deals with the South to be dead, then launched what it called a communications satellite, but everyone said was a long-range missile. Rebuke from the UN Security Council led the North Koreans to flounce out of the Six-Party Talks, say the 1953 armistice was invalid and cap it by all by letting off a nuclear bomb, earning them more sanctions.

So would follow a carousel of fortunes that were entirely predictable in their erraticism. Pyongyang sent a delegation to the funeral of Kim Dae Jung, agreed

Since the Sunshine Policy of the 1990s, inter-Korean relations have, loosely put, improved, albeit with some sporadic outbreaks of violence. Curiously, for all the talk of Pyongyang's unpredictability, it's the North's governors who are most consistent, with variables affecting peninsula relations depending on the political hue of who's in Seoul or Washington, DC.

Annual US–ROK wargames always upset Pyongyang, while the North's missile launches and nukes worry the whole region, as does the torpedoing of ships and shelling of islands. But then positive steps are taken amid the greatest showdowns.

In 2004 while the nuclear crisis raged, the two Koreas' top military chiefs met in what was called a 'breakthrough of monumental proportions', setting up a hotline, sharing radio frequencies and stopping propaganda broadcasts across the DMZ – and cutting the phone lines and the recommencement of insults are very obvious clues to displeasure.

Tourist numbers to Kumgangsan climbed all through the tense noughties until the 2008 shooting of the South Korean visitor in Kumgangsan, where the DPRK has since confiscated the hotels. ROK firms still invest in the Kaesong industrial zone, although that too has closed in crises, notably during much of 2013. The effect of fluctuating intra-Korean relations impacts most bitterly on divided families, with people separated for decades finding their fleeting reunion cancelled at the drop of a diplomatic hat.

Hostilities are acted out online. The DPRK's military, KWP and cabinet all employ thousands of agents engaged in denial-of-service attacks against the ROK's state and financial institutions' IT systems, causing hundreds of millions of won in damage, and psy-ops including posting mass slanders against South Korean politicians and candidates. Little is known of any ROK counter-attacks, but the DPRK's lack of IT-based infrastructure suggests there'd be not much damage anyway. But ROK's intelligence agencies do very well in spreading scurrilous rumours about the leaders in Pyongyang, stories that the world's media lap up, despite very little of these tales being verified in any way.

But at the time of writing, the process was under way for the return from the DPRK of the remains of dead US soldiers and the normalising of relations is at last being discussed on both sides.

When the US, DPRK and ROK will ever formally end the war is not known. Questions hang over whether the Koreans can ever unite, not least because their economic successes and political systems are so divergent, and new generations come to accept the status quo as permanent reality. Korea's division in part stems from how factional they are and the violence that comes with that – see how often fistfights break out in Seoul's parliament. The Korean War, for which Pyongyang blames the US, was in fact a Korean civil war arising out of a division only five years in the making. Both sides want reunification on their own terms, and both sides engage in violence in various forms and depending on their governments – there is a theory that Pyongyang's outbursts are cyclically inspired by their own five-year election cycle, for what that's worth. Violence seen in the Sinchon Museum for example may well have been perpetrated by the Koreans themselves. When one considers how fierce the battles between different factions of monks became centuries ago (see page 14), one might consider how bad factionalism can get in Korea.

to resume family reunions, made positive noises about resuming Six-Party Talks and called for an end to hostile relations with the US. Then in March 2010 the DPRK torpedoed the ROK ship *Chenoan* with the loss of 46 crew, and in November revealed a new secretly-built uranium enrichment facility at Yongbyon.

All of which were collectively interpreted be the final flails of a dying man. On 17 December 2011 the Dear Leader succumbed to cancer, to a national outpouring of grief at which the rest of the world gawped in awe. His son Kim Jong Un had already been anointed as successor, but what would the reign of the very young man bring?

The chances of the region collapsing into a firestorm and the sky truly falling are really quite remote.

For the DPRK, any attack on the South, where there are better armed and better fuelled ROK and US forces, would basically be total suicide. Any ensuing apocalypse would lead to millions of refugees flooding into South Korea, China and Russia while millions more would die within from the catastrophic breakdown of infrastructural flows. The impacts would lead, not ironically, to US forces being ejected from the peninsula – an imploded DPRK would no longer require an external presence.

A US strike on the North's nuclear reactors risks sending radioactive fallout across the DPRK, the ROK, China, Russia and Japan. That, and a 1961 defence treaty between the DPRK and China, makes the latter very unlikely to look favourably on any attacks on Pyongyang – China entered the Korean War principally to counter advancing US forces from its border and subsequent attacks on Chinese territory.

The West's view that the DPRK is an aggressive little dictatorship that seeks to use nukes as a bargaining chip for aid sidesteps the fact that the DPRK is not at peace with a global megapower armed to the teeth with nukes. And the nature of the allegations about Pyongyang's uranium enrichment were non-existent: they were based on 'hearsay' of an apparent confession made in a corridor. However, in 2007 David Albright, president of the Institute for Science and International Security, compared the Bush administration's intelligence on Pyongyang's uranium enrichment programme to its claims on Iraq's WMD programme, writing that a large enrichment plant 'likely does not exist; perhaps it never did' and the 'vast majority' of the DPRK's plutonium was made after December 2002. The Senate Armed Services Committee also queried the State and Defense departments' intelligence on the DPRK programme. The West's default is everything Pyongyang says is a lie, but anything said about Pyongyang by its foes is true.

Anyone would know that making the allegations public would only force Pyongyang to dig its heels in, and feeling under threat, go ahead and make a bomb. So why did the conservative US government stoke the situation? Was the White House seeking a confrontation to exaggerate the power of the 'threats' facing the US and its regional allies, to justify its continued military presence there and drum up more orders for weapons from Asian allies for anti-ballistic missile systems?

Another theory was that the DPRK, Iran and Iraq were all listed on the Axis of Evil as they all sought to dump the US dollar as their hard currency and use the euro instead. For Iran and Iraq, mega oil-producing nations, this would smash international demand for the US dollar and the US's ability to import oil – apocalyptic and galling, when fellow net-energy importer the DPRK would profit from rising-value reserves of euros and encourage other Asian states to follow suit. DPRK funds in the Macau-based Banco Delta Asia (and also later the Gold Star bank in Vienna) were meanwhile subject to allegations of money laundering and currency counterfeiting, with tough financial sanctions being imposed despite Ernst & Young finding the allegations against BDA to be unfounded. The smear was an effort to curtail the DPRK's growing sales of its indigenously produced gold bullion, with gold prices rising, and at the time beyond the scope of sanctions (although some of the key chemicals for gold mining and processing have been sanctioned for purchase by the DPRK due to their dual use in WMD). With limited access to international capital markets, the laundering claims further eroded the DPRK's ability to earn hard currency and buy oil, fertiliser and food surpluses, already restricted by cuts in trade and aid, and leaving the DPRK all the more dependent on trade with China, selling its commodities there at knockdown prices. Anything but Juche, and some say the DPRK would rather be an ally with the US in competing with China – a buffer state between the two.

Raising the stakes on the peninsula enables the DPRK military to reassert itself within the state and put the brakes on any reforms and efforts to engage with the world. Everything takes a back seat to the military's needs and its outlook. Inter-Korean relations have been shaken if not stirred with the DPRK's self-confidence bolstered – the US lost most face in the nuclear showdown. Regional belief in US power faltered as the lesson was learned: 'to defy the US, you need a nuke as soon as possible'. Such crises also allow right-wingers in Japan to reassert themselves and fuel their call for Japan to change its pacifist constitution and allow the country to intercede abroad.

Not least, threatening the DPRK just doesn't work. It fought through an appalling war and built itself out of the ashes. It's both prospered and starved over 60 years in the face of a military holocaust, threats, blanket economic sanctions, energy starvation and mass famine, yet it's survived. It is not a suicidalist state and reports of its imminent death are always exaggerated – sanctions hurt the weak and the poor first and worst. Always the DPRK is talked of as that odd little starving land of bombs and rockets, run by an elite seeking only to terrify the world, and populated by brainwashed automatons. But the people are not mindless droids. They're people like you and me. Nor is the regime going anywhere anytime soon, not least as its youthful leader has so many years ahead of him.

Kim Jong Un Readily stepping into his dead father's shoes was Kim Jong Un, who on 30 December 2011, barely a fortnight after his father passed away, was appointed Supreme Commander of the KPA. 'Kim Jong Un, who came from the blood of the revolutionary family of Mount Paektu, has all qualifications and traits befitting a statesman and military strategist of modern times,' as KCNA put it. More outgoing than his father, he bears a strong resemblance to his grandfather, something that some think is played up by the DPRK media, but he has had no statues or lapel pins made of him so far, as 'he's humble'.

He's also very young and confirmed facts about him are few. Born in January 1983, he boarded at a preparatory school in Switzerland, then studied at Kim Il Sung Military University. He inherited the mantle of leader-to-be after his two elder brothers proved themselves unfit for high office. In 2009, when Kim Jong Il's health was first known to be failing, Kim Jong Un began appearing in official photographs. He came of titular age in 2010 when he was promoted to general in the KPA, was elected as a member of the KWP Central Committee and a vice chairman of the Party Central Military Commission. And then at the end of 2011 he inherited the crown.

Will Kim Jong Un's reign brook an epic shift in ideas? Or do children educated at elite prep schools in secretive banking states really learn how to bring liberal democracy to militarist autarkies? Can he do anything about the retrenched interests in Pyongyang, would he want to if he could? It's very early days, but it's been as dramatic as one might hope with the recent arrival of a new youth upsetting what had long been a soap opera dominated by fogies. There has been as much reform as retrenchment, as many bold acts of confidence as desperate feats of a young man proving something. In April 2012, as KWP delegates loudly shouted 'Hurrah!' for Kim's election as first secretary and his energetic Songun leadership, his grandfather's 100th birthday was celebrated by a (failed) satellite launch. The UN glowered that it was really a long-range missile test that had been banned along with nuclear tests in return for US food aid. The DPRK said the agreement was void. When floods led the DPRK to demand food aid shortly after, no aid was forthcoming, and a new US–ROK missile deal led the DPRK to retort with another missile launch in December and a nuke blast two months later.

Fresh rage and UN sanctions flowed, but then the annual US–ROK wargames got under way, and were far beefier than usual. Pyongyang restarted Yongbyon, closed the Kaesong industrial zone and launched more missiles. The rhetoric from both sides rapidly became much more shrill than it had been for years, with Seoul at one point warning the North would 'evaporate from the face of the earth' if they used a nuke. Sager minds observed that the world's press was giving this war of words a lot of unnecessary volume, and by September it had all died down again, but it was still the young one's first big game of brinksmanship.

The toing and froing, highs and lows at the Six-Party Talks continue. In October 2013 Kim snubbed a visit from one of Pyongyang's few friends, Mongolia's president Tsakhiagiin Elbegdorj, with Kim preferring to watch an artillery display. On the other hand, there is the continuum of keeping in well with the Chinese and the Russians, and Kim has hosted several visits from Dennis Rodman.

But Kim's had a few clear outs of the regime's top guns, most being associated with Kim Jong Il. In July 2012, several of the DPRK's senior military leaders, including army chief Ri Yong Ho, were purged from the KWP, and Kim Jong Un was anointed as 'Respected Marshal', as if wresting control from the missile men. In 2013 he purged many of the civilian big bosses, most spectacularly in December with his uncle Jang Song Thaek arrested in front of his comrades and TV cameras at the Supreme People's Assembly. Tried and executed within days, Jang went from being a major power broker and mentor to Kim Jong Un to becoming 'despicable human scum' and a 'traitor for all ages', who'd plotted to destroy the economy and then launch a military coup. Or so claimed the one remaining article on the Korean Central News Agency's website (*www.kcna.kp*) that mentioned Jang, after tens of thousands of articles from before October 2013 were deleted in an epic Ministry of Truth wipeout.

Previous purges were all in private, but Jang's fall was a very violent, very public statement – but of what? Was Jang simply suffering the fatal fate of all mentors as their princely charges assert themselves when coming of age? Had Jang gotten too big for his boots, and done deals that fatally excluded other important players? Was Kim keeping the peace among the court's factions? Was Jang's purging a sign of strength or weakness? Would it ensure absolute loyalty, or simply stifle voices of innovation and encourage defections?

Had the shadowy Organisation and Guidance Department been behind the purge, agreeing as much while Kim was outside Pyongyang, and presenting him with a fait accompli? Some Pyongyangologists, citing among other things how television reports dedicated to Kim are edited and the tiny nuances of where subordinates stand and their body language, observe that Jang was publicly accused of 'factionalism' and adultery as most significant, because just stating factionalism is an assertion of disloyalty to Kim's absolute authority, while adultery charges against Jang are a slur on his wife, Kim's aunt. Remember, the Kim family are national deities – but they're suddenly being publicly framed within a tawdry Greek tragedy. What this means for the House of Kim is entirely open-ended, although in March

2014 the young Kim won a decisive 100% victory in the national elections. Much of the global media's reporting of the affairs of the DPRK are ill-informed. There is an ever-growing list of outlets for detailed analysis of the country's affairs, of which a few can be found in *Appendix 2*, pages 274–83.

ECONOMY

The DPRK economy has historically been a command economy, built along a similar system of centralised control as the Soviet Union's economy in the 1930s. In both cases, the ultimate communist state was to be achieved through mass industrialisation based on huge increases in agricultural output, with the state providing cradle-to-grave jobs, housing, food, medical care, education, goods and clothing.

In command economies, output is not dictated by the laws of price, supply and demand, but according to targets set by the government. Successive multi-year plans (in the DPRK starting with a One-Year Plan in 1946 and getting longer ever since) demand certain economic sectors to produce quantitive targets (usually increasing) by a certain date. For example, the DPRK's 1978 Seven-Year Plan demanded that coal output in 1984 would rise from 80 million tonnes to 120 million and fertiliser from five to seven million tonnes. The plans include the inputs and incentives needed to increase production.

There is very little private ownership, the state 'owns' and runs industries, banks, transportation, financial institutions, etc as monopolistic enterprises. Workers are assigned to task-oriented work units that compete to (over-) achieve the targets, with rewards or cuts depending on their collective results. Mobilisation and propaganda campaigns exhort the workers onwards and upwards, and the workers can be rewarded from the total of their productivity increases.

Centralised governmental control and direction of each economic sector comes through ministries, committees and agencies at the national level down through committees and agencies at the provincial, county and city levels. The lower levels provide the statistics and information on developments, bottlenecks and issues their superiors need to plan, decide and overcome problems. Party control, as a distinct influence from solely state directives, comes through Party cadres occupying key managerial and committee posts in these sectors.

Planning has become more complicated as the DPRK economy has developed from being predominantly agricultural to an advanced industrial economy, with increasingly complex sectoral interactions and input needs. Ministries and agencies have varied and developed over time in response to planned (and unplanned) situations, the most dramatic being the collapse of the Soviet Union in the early 1990s, but we shall come to this after the following history. Also the various departments and ministries are in fierce competition for increasingly scant resources.

Korea's division in 1945 left the North with the industry and power, but the greater agricultural resources were in the South. The infrastructure of industry, road and rail installed by the Japanese colonialists had been run by Japanese, not Koreans, as the Japanese kept Koreans excluded from the higher echelons of education and government of their own country. Hence, most of the North's population were agricultural and were educated only to that level.

Between 1945 and 1950, the Party prioritised the 'Revolutionising' of the country's agriculture to produce abundance, not famine, and allow its workers to migrate to the cities' industries. A minority of landlords owned most of the land, with the overwhelming majority of peasants living as tenant farmers paying rent in kind (from

50% of crops upwards). Reform came as communist agitators had promised: all land, livestock and buildings held by Japanese, traitors, absentee landlords, religious organisations and Koreans with over five chongbo (2.45 acres) were confiscated and re-distributed among the peasants; theirs but not to sell, rent or mortgage.

Landlords were harassed by police and Party cadres, shunned by the peasants and investigated for anti-communist activities. Large and absentee holdings were confiscated first in a seemingly random fashion to avoid inciting any organised backlash by the landlords; lesser landlords either hoped to be spared, or collaborated. At best they received smaller plots, or were run from the province, southwards; otherwise it was hard labour. The peasants were encouraged into the Party, more land was appropriated, cultivated and funds released for fertilisation and irrigation. Farmers paid tax in kind and sold the rest, although 'patriotic rice' was occasionally appropriated for patriotic ventures, like large building projects.

Then the Korean War of 1950–53 wiped out the North's cities, industries and millions of workers, and agriculture as the mass call-up for the army and factories left crops unattended, while raging battles destroyed those that grew. The smoking husk of post-war Korea meant that nothing short of complete reconstruction was necessary. Rapid industrialisation was sought, but that needed a strong agricultural base, and that needed greater agricultural output.

During and after the war, and into the late 1950s, the farms were collectivised into co-operatives, ie: individual farms were combined into larger social, work and administrative units called *ri*, eliminating the final vestige of capitalist ownership in the countryside. Collectivisation was a practical necessity as the land and labour were pooled to make up for the missing men, but it was also a move of emancipation for women, who both achieved collectivisation and ran the farms, as is still the case today. By late 1958, all farms were collectivised into 3,800 co-operatives of around 300 households each, introducing new planting techniques, chemical fertilisers, industrialised and mechanised agriculture, and electrification through generators and hydro-electric power.

Farming joined the other economic sectors of industry, trade, culture, etc, that were all under state control by the end of the 1950s, and the productivity rises allowed for increased rural–urban migration to the city factories, based on cheap food at fixed prices for the urbanised workers. Government investment (there being no private) from the 1954–56 Three-Year Plan poured into agriculture, housing and education, but half of that investment was in heavy industry, in mining, coal, steel, copper, chemicals, and manufacturing of machine tools.

These developments were built upon in the 1958 'Chollima Undong' (Flying Horse) movement, the first great mass-mobilisation campaign (and it's never really stopped) where increased output was to be attained through the implementation of the Chongsanri Method and the Taean Work System. In the Chongsanri Method, Party officials were given much greater input in the production process of the farms and factories. Party cadres were placed as hands-on managers empowered to solve any of the problems and use the ideas that workers confronted them with, in a micro-version of Kim Il Sung's own highly interventionist style – basically, get down on to the shop floor and find out what's going on. Output was also to be increased by whatever means worked, usually increased shares in the output or other material rewards to the group. Group rewards besides, the workers were exhorted to produce ever more with ever fewer means and less time, and were bombarded with slogans like: 'Let us produce more with existing labour and facilities'. This kind of management developed into the Taean system, with more committees between the numerous work levels in a factory from shop floor to CEO, that remains largely in

1

use today. As with Kim Jong Il's 'Three Revolutions Movement' from 1975, the point was to have party hacks present and operating at all levels of economic production, ensuring everything was ideologically correct and serving the right ends, whoever's they may have been. So the party's economic and political control infiltrated every level of production, and industrial and agricultural management were of concern to the Party as well as the factory managers, but it was a top-down affair, and very effectively removed any means to innovate from the bottom up.

The fire of the 1950s economic growth was stoked in the 1960s. At this point the economy of the DPRK was racing ahead in income per capita over that of the ROK, and Kim Il Sung confidently predicted that if the ROK got anywhere under capitalism, it would collapse soon enough anyway. Nonetheless, the DPRK economy saw high rates of growth in all sectors, and critically for its 'defence' and socialist cause, its economic growth and per capita income outstripped the South's throughout the decade. As Juche prescribed, the DPRK had to propagate revolution by force and defend itself from attack from US and Japanese imperialists. In 1962 Kim Il Sung laid for the 'Byungjin' or 'Tandem' line, where the military would be developed on a par with the broader economy. However, the needs of the military were prioritised pretty much over all else. A huge proportion of manufacturing capacity went towards arms (defence industries were estimated to be up to 30% of GNP in the late 1960s and 1970s, and as high as 26.7% of GNP in 1995 as the

SONGUN

An integral part of the DPRK's governance, socially, economically, politically, is the idea of *songun*, or 'military first'. To reconstruct the country, to throw off oppressors, to project the revolution, in good times and bad, the military must be in the vanguard of everything: 'The pivotal, leading role of soldiers in arms is the major guarantee for effecting a radical turn in the thinking, mentality and fighting spirit of all members of society for the latter to bring about miracles and innovations in all fields of socialist construction including the economy and culture,' according to the 2012 publication *Questions and Answers on the Songun Idea*.

The idea that a nation's independence, sovereignty and prosperity is dependent on being organised and well armed was laid out by Kim Il Sung during the 1930s when battling Japanese colonialism, but the kernel for the idea came from Kim Il Sung's father, Kim Hyong Jik, who in 1926 gave his son two pistols to fight the Japanese – which has become a common motif in the DPRK. Arms delivering independence was borne out by the Korean People's Revolutionary Army's role in the liberation of August 1945, the Korean War and defending the realm thereafter. Of course, all countries need standing armies, but most socialist states assign the role of defending and projecting the revolution to the workers and proletariat, whereas in the DPRK it's the military that's entrusted with that task, employing its 'revolutionary soldier spirit'. And the spirit of songun would come to permeate all before it, infusing into the Juche philosophy of independence for Koreans.

The country's division and war left the North with a third of the Korean population, and a heavily armed South with a permanent US army presence. Unsurprisingly, the North's pursuit of economic reconstruction and reunifying the country became inseparable from means of arms. In 1962, with the communist world shaking from the Cuban missile crisis, and the Sino–Soviet split, Kim Il Sung announced his plan to ensure how the DPRK would survive and flourish. Along with modernising the armed forces, conscription was far expanded into 'songun' or 'military first' principle took over). Although Juche advocated the economy develop independently, ie: with minimal trade and capital flows from beyond its borders, the DPRK's Soviet, Chinese and eastern European socialist brethren supplied material aid and trade throughout the mid-1980s.

Nor was the DPRK averse to foreign investment from capitalist countries, only that inflows of capital to diversify the economy's output in the 1970s didn't fit the bureaucratic, insular economy and the DPRK defaulted on its foreign debts, excluding it from Western capital markets. Similarly to the other command economies of the socialist bloc, the DPRK's multi-year plans' overemphasis on heavy industry and commodity export suffered in the commodity market crashes of the late 1970s, while heavy bureaucratic control stifled technical and productive innovation. Capitalist investment from abroad was encouraged. Joint ventures were allowed from 1984, tourism was promoted in Kumgangsan and special economic zones were set up in Rajin-Sonbong on the Russian border, around Sinuiju and Kaesong. Foreign interest has fluctuated but steady Chinese and ROK investment has been inflowing since the late 1990s. Aid slowed as the other socialist economies spluttered, while minimal foreign trade meant the DPRK hadn't the foreign currency to buy what it couldn't produce itself. Because a quarter of the country's output and technical investment was monopolised by arms industries producing for domestic use, what the economy couldn't produce was a lot. The idea of diverting

the civilian population to establish 'a military basis for the daily life of the entire population with weapons training, military drill and instruction from kindergarten to retirement age' (Buzo, *The Guerrilla Dynasty*, 68–9). This manifested in economic policy under the 'Byungjin line', emphasising both economic and military developments in tandem, but which in effect prioritised the military's needs over all other economic considerations. The country was being turned into a fortress, and state investment in the military quintupled to 30% of GDP by 1967, from which level it's never far retreated.

Kim Jong Il's interest in military matters started in his teens, touring Korean People's Army units in the 1960s. In 1969 he nominally brought the KPA under the leadership of the Korean Workers' Party – great, while the country was still growing economically and internationally. But in the early 1990s, after the socialist world collapsed, the wolves of imperialism started circling the camp and the outlook for the DPRK was at its bleakest, the power relationship irrevocably changed in the army's favour.

On 1 January 1995, the army was made the supreme authority in preparation for the dark days of hunger ahead – the second 'Arduous March', named after Kim Il Sung's desperate days against the Japanese (see box, pages 248–9). The KPA would save the state it had in effect taken over, but how far would the military's needs wade in on those extremely finite resources, and who'd be left out? KPA units and individuals did suffer and carried out valiant works for the benefit of all, but many observers charge that their rule simply served them first and foremost.

Upon Kim Jong Un's arrival, he was hailed by Korean Central News Agency for his Juche-based army thinking and 'energetic Songun leadership', and missile tests and bomb blasts ensued, graphically illustrating what the DPRK's cabinet chief would later confirm in December 2013, that the country would 'stay the course' on Byungjin.

resources into a nuclear power-cum-weapons programme and development of intercontinental rockets was to use them to bargain, but would bombs and rockets earn more in bargaining than they could lose in sanctions and diplomatic reproach? Well, at least the rockets can always be sold for hard currency.

The DPRK's trade deficit with the USSR became unaffordable. Barter-trading with the USSR was curtailed by the latter for hard currency in 1991, as the Soviet economy staggered towards free-market economics. China followed suit. Soviet trade fell from 55% of the DPRK's 1990 total to 14% in 1991, worsening as the Soviet economy crashed. Soviet fuel imports, principally oil, collapsed by 85%, throttling the DPRK's transport and industries' ability to operate. The ensuing energy crises, compounded by failing hydro-electric power output, affected industrial output of goods and food (see page 59) with which to trade and earn foreign currency, as flagship state industries' output fell to 20% of the norm.

Simultaneously, aid and trade with the DPRK's eastern European allies died with their socialism, and the DPRK hadn't any significant manufacturing capacity for quality consumer goods to sell elsewhere. The DPRK's trade with 'imperialist' free-market economies (mainly Japan) existed but the links were minimal, its credit record poor, debts accumulating and US sanctions kept the DPRK from markets that the pro-independence spirit of Juche might yet have allowed. The DPRK's industries were worn and decades of insulation meant they were comparatively outdated. In late 1993, it was announced that the Third Seven-Year Plan had failed, a staggering admission in itself. The worsening energy crisis then began to break down the country's agricultural basis that had made the DPRK's industrialisation possible. Rations given to the bulk of the population from the centrally run Public Distribution System, graded as per the social position, work and age of the recipient, had been successively reduced since the late 1980s, and the DPRK tipped towards famine.

FAMINE COMES TO THE DPRK Korea's agriculture has historically been prone to calamity, as the mountainous peninsula has little fertile land in a country prone to flooding and drought. A terrible drought of 1812–13 reportedly led to a million deaths, and during rice riots in 1833 rioters burnt and trashed many parts of Seoul.

The division of Korea left the South with most of the country's arable land, and with the quality, fertile land at that. Regardless of tremendous output increases achieved since the Korean War, food has been rationed for Koreans for many years, with rations based on occupation, age and region, supposedly averaging around 220kg per capita annually as a solid supply. Agricultural output increased due to mechanised farming in production and transportation (tractors and trucks replacing men and oxen), the vast expansion of land under pumped irrigation and the production and use of chemical fertilisers and pesticides. The DPRK was more than self-sufficient, or self-reliant, in food output. The DPRK's Juche was grown from the fields.

But by the early 1980s, food shortages were being reported as the economy stagnated, and by the 1990s, the situation became disastrous as rations for farmers were reduced, causing upset, and Chinese and Soviet subsidies ended. The DPRK's contracting economy reduced fertiliser and pesticide output, as well as production of new tractors and pumps, and spare parts for those already in use. Broken machines couldn't be fixed, and harvests couldn't be reaped or sown. But the critical issue was energy; oil imports from the Soviet Union died with it, and the DPRK literally ran out of fuel. Two-thirds of the DPRK's electricity comes from hydro-electric power, in irregular supply due to droughts and flood damage, and

Along with the evaporation of foreign trade, aid and fuel, in the mid 1990s the DPRK suffered an onslaught of floods and droughts that destroyed its agricultural base. In 1995, the DPRK Ministry of Foreign Affairs announced flood damage to be some US$15 billion. Both floods and droughts have continued to hammer the country every since.

The floods don't just destroy growing and stored crops. Soil, tended and fertilised over years, is washed away with irrigation systems, agricultural landscaping, equipment, farms and people's lives. Silt and debris give the floods more physical clout to damage other areas, blocking and demolishing channels, roads and structures, and the best land is left under a thick scum of sand and silt, which the petrol-less bulldozers cannot shift. Floodwaters also contaminate water supplies and spread more diseases among an already malnourished population and overwhelm a health service that is run-down and ill-supplied, unable to source medicines locally or from abroad.

People escaping direct death and injury have to deal with the loss of land, livelihood, food stores and clean water. Damaged and destroyed communications hinder the ability to deliver aid; conversely, people are unable simply to flee to unaffected areas.

Either it rains, or it doesn't. In 2001 the worst spring drought in 80 years followed the coldest winter in 50 years. Spring's wheat, barley and potatoes were affected, then the drought prolonged to scuttle autumn's rice and maize. Droughts reduce Korea's hydro-electric power plants, which make up about 70% of the country's baseload capacity, causing power cuts: refrigerators for vaccines and pumps for sanitary water turn off. It also cuts power to the train lines that then prevents food being distributed and coal supplies from mines to other power plants, compounding the knock-on effect on the overall power crisis and the country's ability to produce goods to sell for export to buy in foodstuffs.

Deforestation has worsened the impact of flooding. As the food situation developed from precarious to crisis, the hills were first deforested to grow more crops, while the energy crisis led people to burn anything made of wood. The famine drove them to eat anything left in the fields and hills, reducing harvests further but also leaving no blade of vegetation to stop rainwater, and unusually heavy rains at that, from cascading down the hillsides that have so much more surface area than the planes below, with the rainwaters washing away the crops, soil, farms and villages in the way. Efforts to reforest the country have been ongoing and clumps of new trees bedeck the fringes of farms and barren hillsides. One can see posters with slogans like 'let us plant more Acacia trees'.

As the British Red Cross reported in 2013, 'not much land in the DPRK is suitable for farming. In an attempt to cultivate more land for food production, the country has seen large scale deforestation over the last decade. But this scarcity of trees during the rainy season results in landslides and floods,' leading to severe floods in 2012, making over 241,000 people homeless and destroying some 1.2 million square kilometres of farmland, compounding the country's food deficit. That, and the increasingly unstable climate wrought by the ever eastwardly expanding Gobi Desert, make for a bleak outlook.

so irrigation systems didn't work when needed – aside from the mass destruction caused by drought and floods on the crops and farms (see box, page 55). Much of the land was exhausted from overuse or fertiliser saturation. Unfortunately, depleted foreign earnings meant they hadn't the money to import fertilisers, pesticides, parts and oil, or food. Workers, soldiers, women and children went from the factories to the fields to supplant the shortfalls in mechanical power, but output slipped then plumbed below minimum subsistence levels. In 1995 and again in 1997 international aid was requested as rumours ripped through the international community of a calamity in the making. The United Nations Food and Agriculture Organisation (FAO) and World Food Programme (WFP) found in late 1995 that the 220kg average was closer to 170kg, below that needed for minimum nutritional requirements. WFP estimates for 1995 showed that Korea needed some 4,740,000 tonnes to meet minimum calorific intake, but was deficient in 1,250,000 tonnes, a quarter of a billion dollars' worth in rice alone.

No words suffice to describe the scale of the human cost. Estimates of mortality from starvation from 1995 range from under a million to over three million, or nearly 15% of the total population. Either estimate is astounding, all the more, however, because there is a discrepancy of two million that leaves a great deal to the imagination about the perception of the omniscient state or what it's prepared to divulge to the world.

UNICEF states mortality rates in the 1990s for children under five rose from 27 to 48 per 1,000, while over 45% of under-fives are still suffering chronic malnourishment and/or stunted growth. Malnutrition compounds people's susceptibility to flood-borne gastro-intestinal diseases, like diarrhoea.

The WFP, among other international organisations, has worked to rehabilitate the country's agriculture through variations in crop and fertiliser use, but restricted access to information and parts of the country has been frustrating. The deficit in domestic food production fluctuated by up to 1.8 million tonnes in 2001, but international aid in oil and food was forthcoming, particularly from China. Nevertheless, aid from the ROK, Japan and the US has sometimes been delayed by wrangling over the North's nuclear programme on top of long-standing bad relations, and accusations that aid goes to the army first. Aid-funding targets have also frequently not been met on programmes for food relief, vital drugs, immunisation, nutrition, water and sanitation, and education.

The WFP and UNICEF have since gained more access to areas, but the floods and droughts continue and their restructuring projects perennially seek funding.

Noted historian and observer of the DPRK Andrei Lankov has theorised that the country has missed out on the single greatest reform of its agriculture, that of giving farmers direct ownership of the land and a direct reward and interest from selling the produce. He argues that the dissolution of China's state farms in the 1970s led to the country's bounteous rise in food output as farmers became directly incentivised to produce more, and had the DPRK reformed its agriculture by the 1990s as per the Chinese model, 'not one single North Korean would have died from starvation'.

Possibly, although that may seem to overlook the impact of natural disasters and the energy crisis. However, citizens setting up illicit markets to buy, sell, get incomes and buy food was what kept many alive. They had to, as the state's public distribution system that had always provided the overwhelming bulk of people's food totally collapsed in the face of the disaster, and some say came to serve its masters more than the masses. As one theory goes, the songun system (see box, pages 52–3) decrees not only where one stands in the pecking order, but where one does any pecking, if one is to peck at all. Those northern provinces furthest flung from Pyongyang that suffered worst in the famine were populated by the people and the descendants of people that Pyongyang had flung furthest – people doing the dirtiest jobs at the bottom of the pile, who got paid the least and fed the least by the state. And when the Public Distribution System was tightening belts, such people were not fed, but neither were they paid so they could buy food. Nor could they leave work to go to the countryside for food, nor forage beyond their home districts (see Barbara Demick's *Nothing To Envy*). The famine laid bare the black bones of such a system that doomed so many.

Then again, this was a country that had descended from a rapidly industrialising economy to famine in less than a decade – a profound shift. No-one had predicted the collapse of the USSR, but there it went. And under such a controlling structure of governance, who would have known what to do? Who would have been able to act, for want of initiative, information or resources? For so long the famine became embedded not least because there was no-one to offer any alternatives. They just didn't exist.

REHABILITATION The Kim Jong Il era saw some major moves to rehabilitate the economy. He personally led delegations to Russia and China to observe how they evolved from command to free-market economies.

With the end of the 1990s ended the economy's long contraction, and in 2000 GDP growth of 1.3% was recorded, followed by 3.1% in 2001.

Business follows the flag and the late 1990s and early 2000s saw hugely accelerated diplomatic initiatives with the European Union, Japan, the ROK and the US, which relaxed many trade sanctions in 1998. The Bush administration sought to reimpose those sanctions, and the World Bank could not loan to the DPRK as it was part of the 'Axis of Evil'.

The Pyongyang Chamber of Commerce was accredited by the International Chamber of Commerce in Paris in 2000, followed by the European Business Association being founded in Pyongyang five years later. More foreign companies moved into Pyongyang as the Six-Party Talks sputtered along. Joint ventures involved banking, shipping, pharmaceuticals, IT, mining production and consumer goods, and European companies seeking opportunities to combine low-cost and skilled labour working on labour-intensive production lines. DPRK-made pianos went to Austria, French television employed North Korean animators (a section of the Disney film *The Lion King* was produced in Pyongyang). North Koreans undertook investigative trips abroad while investors were invited in to set up shop.

Foreign investment was encouraged in all industries – from mining to steel and manufacturing.

In early 2004, the first billboard advertisements for goods were put up – for South Korean cars assembled in the DPRK, which was far-sighted indeed as very few DPRK citizens had the money to buy such a vehicle, let alone the petrol to run it or the permits to get on highways that wreck the things!

Investment and development in hi-tech industries, principally IT, were given high priority in a state with a highly skilled technical workforce but without the reliability of a modern, efficient infrastructure to put them to best use. Numerous Chinese and ROK IT firms came and set up joint ventures in software and hardware factories and fairs, while North Koreans went out for training, and western companies have outsourced file management and transcription to firms in the DPRK. Co-operative ventures were set up with the Pyongyang Informatics Centre, the South's Pohang University of Science and Technology (PUST), the Korea Advanced Institute of Science and Technology, and the DPRK's State Software Industry General Bureau, to name a few.

The biggest players were the South Korean companies, building on the Sunshine Policy of investing in the North's infrastructure and building the massive Kumgangsan tourist zone and the Kaesong industrial zone, ultimately providing remittances worth hundreds of millions of dollars a year to Pyongyang.

ROK investments and trade flows into the North have proved remarkably resilient. In 2004, during a nuclear stand-off, a convoy of trucks took sand from the North to the South across the DMZ in the first intra-Korean trade by road in decades.

For all the triumphs, the DPRK's lack of energy remained a fundamental issue. As the noughties went on, the completion of the Korea Peninsula Energy Development Organisation deal and the light-water reactors staggered out of sight. The state's history of an erratic relationship with business would also take time to overcome, as would its propensity to hoard information and deny firms the up-to-date data they need to to function. It takes time to build trust, and Pyongyang has a proven lack of trust in free markets.

Whatever the indices say, above all else it was the groundswell of private markets and private trading that kept millions alive, and the economy going, when the state's public distribution system collapsed in the 1990s along with the issuance of state rationed goods. The presence of markets as supplanting the state's monopoly on the supply of goods was pragmatically recognised in 2002. The government ended the state's provision and rationing of some goods to leave it to the markets that were anyway expanding from alleyway affairs selling foodstuffs to large warehouses selling material goods from China, Russia and Japan. Many basic foodstuffs would now be obtained by money, not coupons. Private initiatives in shops and trade appeared, the 'foreigners' won' was abolished in favour of hard currency trading. The local won was dramatically revalued from 2.12 won to the dollar to over 200 won to the dollar, establishing nationwide what had been going on in Rason for years. Supply and demand permeated into the workings of factories, power plants, restaurants and street kiosks.

There was also a rescinding of the state's ownership of land. Whereas all accommodation had been provided by the state, with residents paying nominal maintenance fees for apartments allotted to them for life, land reforms allowed some individuals and businesses to take ownership of apartments and lease land from collective farms. The Swiss Agency for Development and Cooperation set up micro-credit schemes in the more remote rural areas and for farmers to apply business strategies to their investments.

Yet the food situation remained unsettled. In 2005 Deputy Foreign Minister Choe Su-hon requested the UN cease food aid as the country had enough from a good harvest. He accused the US of using aid as a political weapon – despite six million of the country's most vulnerable still receiving it – and he asked all NGOs to leave. It was really an argument about foreign donors' monitoring requirements amid concerns about where aid was ending up, but it defied the reality of the situation, that as the WFP observed, the average seven year old was 20lb lighter and eight inches shorter than his seven-year-old peer in South Korea, and mothers were searching the hills for acorns and bark to feed their families, against a backdrop of rapidly rising food prices. The public distribution system for grains, especially rice, had to be reintroduced, albeit with limited success. The embracing of capitalism as the means to survive supplanted not only the state's monopoly of supply, but its ideology as well, and while the state's antipathy to markets grew, its experience of dealing with them didn't. The government pushed back with bizarre demands like demanding that only women could work in the private markets, but there were also concerns about hyperinflation and worse about growing inequalities between a new, rich merchant class and everyone else. Bills and rents were rising to levels akin in wage-rent ratios to capitalist economies.

To counter these trends, in November 2009, the state revalued the won by knocking two 0s off the notes and limiting the changeover period to one week, and capped at 150,000 won. But the richest traders used foreign hard currencies and emerged from the revaluation all the stronger, while the won's black market value against the US dollar fell from 30 to the dollar to over 8,000. The savings of millions were destroyed, and traders and buyers were hammered and the private markets, which had gone from keeping so many alive to becoming the undertow of the economy, were badly hit. The revaluation was later admitted to be a disaster in 2013, but was conveniently blamed on Jang Song Thaek (see page 49).

Jang was also a major advocate for Chinese-style reforms of the economy – moves to introduce a form of market-Stalinist economy where, simply put, the one-party state sits monolithically atop a broadly capitalist, entrepreneurial economy. This has worked very well for China, which some say the DPRK follows with a 20-year lag. But the DPRK's current system works very well for certain vested interests there, and there's a lot of debate about the extent to which it is willing or able to shift in that direction.

If Jang had been so inclined at all, did his death kill any such reforms? Months before his downfall, in April 2013 the Party Central Committee had announced a 'new' political and economic line to accomplish the revolutionary cause of Juche, namely the 'simultaneous development of nuclear weapons and the economy' – reaffirming Kim Il Sung's Byungjin line from 1962, when, as the communist world quivered, the Great Leader rigged the economy to the military. Whether Kim Jong Un's regime is feeling equally defensive, it surely also means no change to the military's prominence in the economy.

The Kaesong industrial zone, albeit closed for much of 2013 during another stand-off, continues to expand, with the ROK's Ministry of Unification hoping to attract about 2,000 manufacturers there and hundreds of ROK firms engage in intra-Korean trade.

There is still the energy crisis. Too much of the DPRK's electricity comes from hydro-electric power that's subject to disruption by droughts and floods that smash up the turbines. KEDO might be dead and there's still the oil shortage, but China does supply oil and electricity. The Russians want to pipe in gas. In Pyongyang at least there are many more lights and nearly no blackouts, creating an illusion of rising prosperity. There is something of a consumer class, many people have mobile phones and indigenous iPad clones like the Samjiyon, a locally produced tablet that's come out of the big investments in IT and manufacturing from years before.

More and more DPRK businesses have email addresses. There is a burgeoning IT market in DPRK, for brand-new Chinese-made computers with Microsoft Windows software, cheap secondhand ones and the order at least for compulsory computer classes in schools.

While Westerners are still shown bizarre excuses for functioning shops, they're not allowed to see the flourishing markets that exist as large warehouses in the cities, or long covered open spaces or alleyways lined with rush mats and wares stacked on them in the towns and villages. These can be glimpsed but not visited.

Pyongyang has far more new cars built in the DPRK. Whether that's really progress in terms of all the dirt, noise, pollution, traffic deaths and road rage that come with them is debatable, but there are also far more bicycles than before as well. People are out and about, they look better off, more relaxed, while many new multi-storey buildings are going up in the city, much of those buildings and other larger infrastructure projects come from Chinese investment, such as the US$300 million suspension bridge between Dandong and Sinuiju.

Other massive infrastructure projects include the rebuilding of Pyongyang airport to the east coast highway to serve a proposed tourist zone around Wonsan – projects being built with the free manpower provided by the military. Tourism is being promoted, and apart from the infamous Masik ski resort, new hotels are being built, old ones are being renovated, towns like Pyongsong are appearing on itineraries, and cities like Wonsan, Hamhung and Chongjin are becoming regularly visited by train. The country is now open all winter, and Kumgangsan has reopened – albeit by the North confiscating the South's hotels there, which isn't the way to attract investors.

Nonetheless, Chinese investors are expanding Rason's factory base and its ports' cargo handling capacity, a game that Russia wants in on by having rebuilt the 54km of railway from Khasan to Rajin. The ports in the Rason Special Economic Zone are being expanded, but the whole SEZ enterprise has been revived and expanded to over a dozen cities and areas. Annual foreign investment into North Korea is

INVESTING IN THE DPRK   *Roger Barrett*

There are many good business opportunities in the DPRK, with a wealth of mining, manufacturing and trading groups acting as autonomous companies and seeking foreign partners according to their needs, and the rewards from successfully partnering into some of the pioneering opportunities can be great. Like anywhere, there are also risks, including not choosing the right partner, challenges due to poor infrastructure, the effects of sanctions and fluctuating tensions on the peninsula. But risk and reward are often related.

Possibly the biggest barrier to investment in the DPRK are very wrong perceptions held about the place, not least that you can't do business there and that the DPRK spurns foreign trade and investment. These incorrect perceptions arise partly because of poor international media coverage that gives a narrow and negative view of the land and its people.

It also overlooks the huge opportunities in manufacturing, mining, minerals and metals, areas in which the country is especially rich, with reserves estimated in the trillions of dollars. The country's energy supplies have been systematically improved through the development of hydro-power, and renewable energy sources are being developed in many areas.

The country's other rich seam is its people. Levels of education are high, and science, technology and foreign languages are taught in the country's schools and universities (of which many are vocational and allied to specific industries). That high level of education translates into excellent IT skills, and Pyongyang is a growing centre of software development in many languages. Egyptian conglomerate Orascom invested in the mobile-phone network in 2007, and in 2012 it was the world's fastest growing mobile network. Other examples of 'Equity Joint-Venture (EJV)' are well-scripted, and so too are some of the 'Contractual JVs (CJVs)' of which DHL and Kumsan JV gold mine are successful examples.

The DPRK has businesses that are diverse and well-structured, but have suffered from a lack of investment in recent years. Since the USSR broke up, the country's main trading partner has been China, but the Koreans do not want dependence on any single trading partner – and therefore partners from other countries, especially Australia, Britain, Canada, the EU, Hong Kong, Malaysia, Singapore and reaching US$2 billion. Australian mining firm SRE Minerals has started a joint venture to mine rare earth deposits at Jongju.

Sanctions are also still in place and being added to, and they're broad, ranging from an embargo on arms and related materiel and efforts to prevent WMD, missiles or related technologies coming in or out (a drawback as so much North Korean industry is devoted to making arms), all the way down long lists of goods, technologies and services, with some companies and specific funds also targeted. The much-hyped ban on luxury goods is just an add-on, and China, Pyongyang's greatest ally, has also supported UN sanctions against the North's nuclear antics. No North Korean finished product can be exported to the US, including Samjiyons sold by eBay (see the broad outline of US sanctions against the DPRK at www.treasury. gov/resource-center/sanctions/Programs/pages/nkorea.aspx and UN sanctions at www.sanctionswiki.org/North_Korea).

How open is the government to accepting change, and would it be wholesale change or just incremental bits and pieces? There are many vested interests that will not initiate reforms that threaten their own position. Possibly the most radical

South Africa, are warmly welcomed. The Ministry of Foreign Affairs and Ministry of Foreign Trade, including the Korea Chamber of Commerce, are staffed by many hard working and diligent officials, working to build bridges with foreign organisations and companies.

The power of the introduction is a centuries-old cultural tradition on the Korean peninsula and it is key to starting successful businesses there, furthering another old Korean adage: 'Well begun is half done'. Business fact-finding missions are available to gain an overview or achieve more specific goals and objectives, and while there your host company or organisation is responsible for all aspects of your well-being, including achieving the stated objectives of the visit. If you stick to business, you won't go far wrong.

The country has attracted its fair share of untrustworthy foreigners over the years and continues to do so – best to check with people who have a proven track-record in and with the country before investing in or through any foreign investor facilitator. Do also check that their claims, or the claims of their local partner, are bona fide.

The country does generally suffer from poor infrastructure in energy, roads and manufacturing basics, but it is resourceful in making 'a little go a long way'. However, the DPRK is in need of investment – and good and well-structured investment can provide great benefit to investors and local parties alike.

It is true that most Koreans don't have much contact with, or understanding of, the West, and most foreigners have little understanding of the country or its business needs or opportunities. But never underestimate their knowledge about the outside world; they know much more about it than foreigners do about them and will have researched your company. Check it out for yourselves, and enjoy the visit, and then you can be sure they will enjoy having you there, and maybe even do business together.

Roger Barrett is an investment consultant and chair of Korea Business Consultants www.kbc-global.com. See also ad, second colour section.

change accepted at the top were the grass-roots private markets, but even then the state's acceptance has been ambivalent, with markets bedevilled by petty regulation, shutdowns, crackdowns or 'currency revaluation'. But the markets are proving resilient. People's incomes are now very much buttressed by, if not mostly derived from, private enterprises and the black market, and the state no longer has total hegemony over paying, feeding and clothing them.

The current set up serves some elements of the state extremely well, but is it sustainable? Many observers say it can't be. Others might believe that, under the aegis of a near-perfect surveillance state, that endured and was emboldened by the death of millions of its own civilians, what can't they survive? A new, young leadership may augur a new influx of the young into the institution of power – but there the embedded interests break down these young idealists, and make them realise rocking the boat doesn't so much disbar promotion as guarantee being purged.

One way or another, the country still has a food crisis. The WFP continues to demand hundreds of millions of dollars to carry out food, health and water sanitation projects on an enormous scale. The year 2013 saw the second year of one WFP programme seeking to counter acute malnutrition in some 2.4 million mothers and children, and in March that year the UN said over a quarter of all children under five still suffered chronic malnutrition. In November 2013 the FAO and WFP reported that staple food production in the DPRK had increased year-on-year for the third year running, with total output 5% up on 2012, at 5.03 million tonnes. The promotion of sustainable farming practices, better price and market incentives for farmers and improved farm mechanisation were working. But 84% of households still had 'borderline or poor food consumption'. Child malnutrition had declined, but rates of malnutrition-related stunting continued. Heavy rains had wrecked plans to counter protein deficiency by increased soybean production. Overall, the public distribution system was facing 'immense logistical challenges' and the importance of markets and barter for families to access food was rising all the more. Whatever the state decides to do, people are digging deep into their Chajusong as the means to stay alive, and the hardy vines of change will continue to grow.

However the economy is reformed on paper, the fundamental obstacles remain – the need to secure peace with the ROK, the US and Japan, and from that reduce the prominence of the military and be rid of sanctions on trade and banking. The DPRK also needs to reform its dubious regard for law in business, the sovereignty of private assets and defaulting on debts, and redress the free flows of finance and information. Overall, to live or die requires fuel and food.

PEOPLE

Koreans are an ethnically and culturally homogeneous people, as seen in terms of their racial heritage, facial features, language and history. No wars or feuds are as long-standing and bitter as those between two brothers, which describes Korea's division perfectly. The people of both states want unification, but cannot yet agree as to how this will come about. The most obvious difference is that the ROK exists with a significant Western influence, visibly present in capitalist pop culture, that has flowed in through the development of the ROK economy and the presence of American forces there. In the ROK are also some minorities of other Asian nationalities and expats.

The number of minorities in the DPRK is restricted to Chinese and some Japanese, and a minute expat community, whose presence will never undo the country's decades of hermetic existence.

Children in the DPRK attend state nurseries or crèches so that their parents can work normally, and from age four receive a universal, compulsory 11 years of education, beginning with a year in kindergarten. Hence the DPRK has a very high literacy rate. School uniform is universally blue shorts/trousers/skirts, white shirts and a red neckerchief. Pupils may have on their arms small badges with horizontal stripes and little asterisks, the number of both patterns indicating a position of responsibility (asterisks determine job) in the school, class or class group (shown by the stripes).

Education has three strong themes of practical knowledge (maths, sciences) and political knowledge (Juche); the third involves 'social education', which Juche prescribes in detail. Children join the Pioneer Corps and the Socialist Working Youth League where they learn the workings of collective life, and they can engage in many extra-curricular skills and activities at the children's palaces around the country. Older children are drafted in at the right times of year to help with harvests and other labour tasks that introduce them to the workers and their world. Pupils progress to high school, then the forces, college or into specialist work units.

MEETING THE PEOPLE Beyond your guides, when in North Korea you may not meet that many Koreans, and Koreans themselves might seem cold or indifferent if they acknowledge you at all.

This is not a country where a whole village will pile out to see a foreigner. Historically, foreigners have often not been of great service to Korea and the government puts this point to the people in extremely colourful terms.

Consider also the strains afflicting this country. No family can have escaped unaffected by Korea's division, the war and the recent famines. The DPRK's reconstruction has taken decades of back-breaking work with scant resources, against reciprocated aggression from other countries and based on insecure flows of trade and aid. As the country's allies were lost in the 1990s, so all the health and nutritional gains evaporated as the economy ground to a halt, and millions died in a time referred to with some understatement as the 'Arduous March'. Within sight of many of the cities beyond Pyongyang are hillsides covered with graves from that catastrophe of which the locals are forever reminded. These people have had a time of it.

So it's not surprising that here more than anywhere, friendships take time to build, and a lot of trust. That said, those friends made are friends for life and are notably generous and warm. Most Koreans, like anyone else, like a drink and a dance and a picnic in the woods, because all Koreans are people like anyone else. Those much-espoused notions in Western media that the folks in DPRK are lifeless automatons should be ignored. A walk in the park on a weekend is a great way to meet the locals, particularly if it's a national holiday when dancing and drinking start early in the afternoon, and if you're passing and invited to join in, do so! Otherwise, be sure to wave and smile while travelling through the country, and more and more they smile and wave back.

SOCIAL SET-UP The old Confucian-based order of royal Korea demanded respect for age, learning, filial piety and authority, the last justifying a society based on hierarchy and class. Providing for the individual was secondary to serving the

Background Information PEOPLE

1

collective. Confucianism is no longer officially practised in the DPRK (and scarcely in the ROK), and the DPRK order has been overturned by a half-century of communist revolutionary rule, but the underlying influence of Confucianism is discernible. Age is still revered (see who gets served first at a table), and so is education. A great success for the DPRK has been the implementation of universal, compulsory education for all. Education is one route to escaping the poverty of one's origins and theoretically makes the basis for a classless society, as communism suggests.

Familial devotion and filial piety are Confucian social currents that the Party puts great emphasis on. Still, the revolution's social impact has been the erosion of old ties of family and broader networks based on kin in the countryside. These ties took a great shock from Korea's division (affecting one in seven Koreans) and the losses of the Korean War. In the DPRK, small villages were merged into large co-operative farms, family and kin moved to the cities as the country industrialised (60% of the DPRK's population is urban) and travel restrictions were introduced, all further eroding the links. However, the family is officially the most venerated, virtuous social unit (if not the kin network) and the above strains have for many people accentuated the importance of their own families.

In the past, one's position in society was inherited as much as earned, and due respect and reward for one's social position underpinned social stability. Today, whether in the Party, the army or just a normal civilian, like anywhere else, people of different livelihoods in the DPRK earn different amounts of money a month. However, two distinctions with the West are that it's the state and not the market that decides levels of pay, because the state owns everything, and second, pay is (or has been until very recently) of secondary importance to the other lifestyle elements provided by the state, namely accommodation, food and some clothing. Apartment size and food rationing have been graded by job and affiliations, and location. The distinction between town and country isn't just a matter of city limits and checkpoints; the material supply and support for the cities is notably better than for rural areas, and Pyongyang outstrips all cities.

Aside from the distinction of military and Party members, people are categorised according to their general field (workers, farmers, officials, co-operative units) then graded by specific job, and paid according to scale. There are three main classes, subdivided into 51 sub-grades, into which you are born and from which you can rise and fall.

Regarding social stratification, your starting point in life, your job and location depend on your songbun, your gauge or 'karma' of political reliability and commitment to the Great Leaders and the Party. Your songbun weighs heavily on your career prospects (and the wage that comes with it), where you will live (town, country, apartment), who you might marry or befriend, and access to necessary supplies.

Songbun isn't determined solely by your achievements, but sources from familial backgrounds as well, for songbun is recorded by the security services and updated continuously. People's loyalties are constantly monitored and social order maintained through a very comprehensive system of social surveillance that stretches right down to the neighbourhood level. The proportion of the population dedicated to keeping an eye on others, be such practices a result of one's profession or simply from the state making it in some people's 'interests' to keep their eyes peeled, is beyond the scale of that seen in East Germany. Families suffer the sins of the individual, be the latter alive or long dead, and your ancestors' victories and crimes provide the social context of your birth and your future. As Kim Il Sung explained in his tomes on Juche, control of the state and its economy was seized from the controlling class and given over to the masses in a remarkably comprehensive overturning of society. Korea's pre-1950 rulers are now ruled by those who are (descendants) of good 'revolutionary' stock, and songbun sustains that changeover. If your forebears were anti-Japanese fighters, then you probably rule today. Top songbun gets good military posts, college, careers, apartments and families, and the privileges start young. Children of the elite attend the Mangyongdae Revolutionary Institute near Kim Il Sung's birthplace.

If you are descended from factory workers or peasants, your songbun has a good grounding. Middling songbun means hard work (revolutionary fervour as Juche demands), can get a job or military posting proximate to Party cadres who might look kindly on you, and higher education is not impossible. If your forebears were Yangban or some form of middle-class professional, well, the odds are stacked. Kim Il Sung stated that 'after liberation we did not reject the old intellectuals because they came from rich families', and intellectuals as an educated class were essential for Korea's rebuilding. But that didn't mean they, or their descendants, were innately trustworthy. Good jobs of choice are attainable through Party membership, not possible for someone with bad songbun, as is higher education and the military; they go where the farms, factories and mines need them, and the only way up is to demonstrate exemplary 'right-thinking' through your work and life. Juche, as every person learns, emphasises self-sacrifice and hard work; dedication and revolutionary spirit can achieve everything, including good songbun. As the Koreans put it, the best are considered 'tomatoes', red all the way through; 'apples' for the superficially committed; and 'grapes' are nearly irredeemable.

These indicators have deep roots. The use of familial records and professions in songbun takes precedence over the aged genealogies and land registers used through much of Korea's history to determine people's social class and their entitlements. Today, uniforms are one obvious distinction between the services and the civilians, but the more subtle distinctions in people's apparel – ie: suits and the lapel pins with different styling and colours – could be said to have origins right back in the Sillan bone-clan system that required visual indications of one's social position.

So the system wasn't set up by Kim Il Sung as such. The highly rigid, stratified social structure of castes and profession and an underclass of 'untouchables' originated with the Koryo, who also demanded officials prove themselves eight generations clear of any 'untouchable' family. The practice of punishing the family for the crime of the one was continued right up until its abolition by the Japanese (who punished everybody for the crime of being Korean). Punishing the family was reprised by Kim Il Sung.

Joining the Korean Workers' Party (KWP) is a good idea, and it has over three million members today, mostly industrial workers, bureaucrats and intellectuals. Weekly meetings on political thought and individual 'behavioural' issues are compulsory, which some might liken to confession. The most diligent members, exemplary in their knowledge and understanding of Juche, economics and sociology (so very likely well educated), and selflessness in Party work, may become Party cadres. Cadres are posted into every element of life here, and the extra hours of study a week are outweighed by enhanced career prospects and raised social status. In addition to the KWP, there are other mass organisations for people to join, although it seems most are variations on a theme of collective work in the name of the country and the leaders.

WOMEN In olden Korea, women were lesser beings, for as Confucius said, wives are subservient to husbands, as the yin-yang symbolises. Women were not allowed to be seen in the streets, effectively under social arrest in their walled homes during daylight, where they tended to their duties as homemakers and mothers. Women had to be veiled to leave the house. The traditional game of see-sawing (jumping up

WHO'S WHO: HOW TO TELL

As a description of the people in uniforms, the list below is not comprehensive, but some colours have been identified approximately as follows:

- khaki-green, thick cloth, boots: Korean People's Army, although the detail's in the hatbands – red for army, blue for intelligence
- khaki-green, lighter cloth and red stars on the beret: Workers and Peasants Red Guard Paramilitaries (or Union)
- dark blue: air force
- blue and white, bell-bottoms: navy
- black: civilian police; black with florescent epaulette piping: metro
- azure blue: traffic police and railway police (so, are you in the road or at the station?)
- light grey; construction brigade

'Shock brigades' have their own uniforms for the tasks to which they are detailed.

Civilian clothing provides clues about people's positions or contacts. Until relatively recently, North Koreans were clad in a pretty uniform set of clothes, issued by the state, with men wearing classically timeless suits in heavy cloth and women in drably coloured blouses and skirts. For these civilian outfits, the darker the cloth, the greater the seniority of its wearer. Japanese suits, presumably lighter in cloth and colours, used to denote those with the money and connections to get such things; however, this is beginning to change as foreign imports and consumer spending power is making for greater diversity of clothing fashions and status indications less discernible.

Virtually everyone in civilian clothing wears a lapel pin of the Great and/ or Dear Leaders. This indicates first that you are indeed a citizen of the DPRK;

and down on either end of a see-saw) was devised so women could glimpse village life over the garden wall. Things have changed quite a lot since then.

Women in modern Korea are emancipated and educated, and in the DPRK their equal status and social rights are enshrined in the constitution. At work, the gender balance is just about 50–50, while professional women have made their careers in the Democratic Korean Women's League Party and the judiciary, and many co-op farms are still run by women in an overhang from the depleted male reserves around the time of the Korean War. Nevertheless, not even the DPRK's social engineering could eradicate traditional male chauvinism that still half expects little more of women than to smile and file.

LANGUAGE

The origins of Korean language go back to the earliest invasions of the peninsula by ancient Asian tribes, and Korean is considered to be part of the Altaic family of languages. Modern Korean is derived from the language of the Silla, with some influence from China's Mandarin language. Another similarity is with Japanese, in that both languages have different grammar and vocabulary according to the level of politeness with which a person of a particular age, gender and social status addresses another. Many Chinese and Japanese words have been borrowed over the centuries, their meanings and pronunciation changing with time.

it's also thought that the size, metal and colouring of the pin indicates a wearer's union affiliations, department and possible seniority. But the quality and style of the pins also vary according to income and age, suggesting the societal hierarchal positionings denoted are more generational than deliberate. Wearers of Kim Il Sung lapel pins used to heavily outnumber those wearing Kim Jong Il lapel pins, but these days a very common design is a flag with both leaders depicted. Children of the higher classes in Pyongyang are reputedly notable not just for their snazzier, foreign clothes, but also in that they might wear their badges on the tips of lapels in a somewhat louche expression of youthful insouciance – they've also been seen in platform shoes. Schoolchildren are usually clad in the classic blue trousers or skirts, white shirts and red neckerchiefs seen in schools across China and Vietnam – outside school, though, they are increasingly seen wearing fashionable clothes. The most racily attired youth are likely of Chinese Korean origin, being the most moneyed and Westernised.

Vehicles also say a lot about who is driving them, where they're from, possible connections, etc. Vehicle registration plates indicate their origins and sometimes purpose. The most common plate colour is white, for 'public', vehicles from particular government or local departments. On 'public' plates, first is written the vehicle's home city or province, then the vehicle's department number (eg: 88 is tourism, 30 is Ministry of Foreign Affairs, 50 for taxi), then the vehicle's number in that department fleet. Black plates are army, yellow are privately owned (probably donated from Japan), dark blue is diplomat, white with a red star is VIP. There's also red, thought to be for high-ranking Party officials. You might witness the spectacle of a VIP visit; the roads are closed as a fleet of black limousines flash and wail past, all flags waving.

Historically, imported Chinese texts for Buddhism and Confucianism meant that Korean scholars had to read Chinese, and so used Chinese characters for writing, as can be seen on ancient (and recreated) sites around Korea. Various attempts were made to create an indigenous script over the centuries, until King Sejong's initiative led to a brilliantly simple phonetic script being developed by the mid-1440s. Called Hangul, the new written language had 17 consonants and 11 vowel sounds represented in very simple characters, from which all the syllables could be constructed (since then the number of characters has dropped to 24).

Korea's educated elite damned Hangul as an idiot's or commoner's means to communicate. The simplicity of Hangul meant it spread with relative ease among the non-elite. The literati argued that this proved their point, while the dual use of Chinese characters and Hangul would be a written indication of education and class. Conversely, the literati's opposition solidified Hangul's suitability for Kim Il Sung, as a language for commoners was more revolutionary.

The attempts by Japanese colonialists to expunge the Korean language didn't succeed. From 1948 in the DPRK, all foreign influences, from borrowed words (especially Japanese- and English-derived ones) to Chinese characters, were expurgated. All DPRK texts are completely in Hangul. The DPRK 'dialect' uses Pyongyang as its standard, and northerners think the Seoul accent is nasal. Northern dialect also differs from the South in the former's complete absence of any modern American or Japanese slang. 'Polite' language has also been reduced in the North, from five noted levels down to three. In the ROK, the original number of polite levels and the use of some Chinese characters in writing continue. For words and phrases, see *Appendix 1* on pages 271–3.

RELIGION

The most important religions (ie: with long traditional bases or regional impact) that have succeeded historically across Korea and that still have a presence today are Shamanism, Buddhism, replaced by Confucianism, and following that, Christianity. None 'thrive' in today's DPRK, and there is much documentation on how that is manifest, which cannot be summarised in this book, but from the other perspective there are deep-seated themes for the state's historic opposition to religions in general and the situation is changing, glacially, incrementally, for the better.

Official DPRK figures estimate there to be just 10,000 Protestants, 10,000 Buddhists and 4,000 Catholics in the state today (although ROK church groups cite higher figures), and some 40,000 practitioners in the government-supported Chondogyo Young Friends Party, an adjunct of the Chondoist Chongu Party, which possibly has most official 'favour' for its revolutionary history in the Tonghak movement. These are small numbers compared with pre-1945 Korea and the present-day ROK (it is estimated that in 1945 up to a sixth of Pyongyang's 300,000 residents were Christians). The government exercises extremely close scrutiny and control over religious groups, activities and practitioners – the constitutional provision for 'freedom of religious belief' is not a right many in the North exercise.

In Korea particularly, much of the religious sites, staff and followers were ill treated by the Japanese. Many of those pastors and practitioners then headed south in 1945 and those that survived the Korean War and remained in the North ceased their worship for their own good.

In China and the DPRK, Christianity has, with some historical basis, been perceived as the vanguard for less benevolent channels of outside influence and control. Some contend that the vehemence of the opposition to the DPRK, particularly in the US, comes from the loss of the worshippers' base, and the proselytising and anti-DPRK stance comes from the same American religious right that most sharply castigated the 'loss of China' to communism in 1949. Communism is inimically antithetical to religion, and the cold pragmatism of its adherents would argue prayers, cathedrals and priests don't grow rice, stop floods or guard against invasion, particularly in a state like North Korea.

The philosophy of Juche also celebrates the power of man and the state and people's independence of thought, and is widely manifested in forms to capitalise on the fervour of worshippers, endowing supernatural phenomena and powers to the lives of its leaders (and there are the curious parallels between the Son of God, the nativity and miraculous powers – see box, *The Cult of the Kims*, pages 30–2).

The 1972 constitution said 'citizens have religious liberty and the freedom to oppose religion'. Twenty years later article 68 of the 1992 constitution dropped the 'anti-religious' clause and allowed for 'the construction of religious buildings and the holding of religious ceremonies,' but a pithy insert summarised the state's view of religion: 'No one may use religion as a pretext for drawing in foreign forces or for harming the State and social order.'

In the 1980s, there was a relaxation of sorts when the state allowed for greater freedom of religion, albeit under the auspices of official bodies like the Korean Buddhists Federation and the Christian Federation. In 1988 Pyongyang's Pongsu and Changchong churches were built. In 1989 a religious studies programme was set up at Kim Il Sung University. Also the DPRK began to use foreign religious organisations as channels for dialogue, 'neutral' diplomacy, humanitarian works and business, at a time when the old Soviet networks were winding down.

In particular these have proved fruitful conduits of dialogue with the ROK – and by extension the US, as the churches mainly founded by American missionaries proliferate in the South compared with their absence in the North – and on the question of national reunification through Buddhist groups as well.

Since 2005, delegates to the DPRK have included the Venerable Beop Jang, head of the largest ROK Buddhist group and chair of the ROK's national council on religious leaders, and the Catholic archdiocese of Seoul led by the director of the National Reconciliation Committee. Members of the DPRK Christian Federation also attended an international solidarity meeting in Germany.

Religious aid groups like the Buddhist Join Together Society and the Catholics of the Seoul archdiocese have been running food production centres for almost a decade, and the Lighthouse Foundation is preparing to open the Potong River Sheltered Workshop in 2007. The Catholic charity Caritas is the conduit for Catholic aid into the DPRK.

Since 2000 there has been a Protestant seminary in Pyongyang, reopened with assistance from foreign missionary groups, and in 2003 the Pyongyang Theological Academy for training pastors and evangelists was completed. The ROK's Unification Church, led by the Reverend Moon (who was born very near Jongu in what is now the DPRK), built an inter-faith religious facility in Pyongyang, the Peace Embassy. The Church was also a major investor in the Kumgangsan resort, Pyeonghwa Motors plant in Nampo and the Potanggang Hotel.

The Korean Presbyterian Church is working with the North Korean Christian League to build a third Protestant church in Pyongyang, along with the existing Pongsu and Chilgok – although foreign attendees to services have talked of more being done in the spirit of appearance than actual genuine worship. Pyongyang's first Russian Orthodox church was consecrated in 2006, with Russian and Korean staff trained in Vladivostok, which officially arose from Kim Jong Il's visit to an

1

Orthodox cathedral in Russia in 2002. A memorial service for Pope John Paul II was held at Pyongyang's Changchun Catholic church.

Buddhism is the religion given the greatest latitude, there being an estimated 300 Buddhist temples with religious activities and resident monks in some. They possibly serve to preserve the historical and aesthetic qualities of 'the Korean nation's cultural heritage' more than anything else, as the spotlessness of the sites suggests the monks are the only practitioners.

The ROK government and foreign tourists sponsored the reconstruction of the Shingye Temple, destroyed during the Korean War. Kaesong's Ryongthong Temple was renovated in 2005, with a growing residency of monks. Others are undergoing rebuilding, restoration and rescue from neglect, and many of the temples are popular tourist sites.

RELIGIONS

SHAMANISM The oldest religion in the peninsula that took root particularly in the North, shamanism is devoted to the worship of numerous spirits and gods believed to inhabit the elements and, in particular, animals. The spirit believed to inhabit Mount Paektu is one long-surviving example of shamanism. In the North it came to be supplanted by Buddhism.

BUDDHISM Buddhism arrived from India in the 6th century BC. An Indian noble eschewed his wealthy upbringing and through meditation achieved 'enlightenment'. Enlightenment here means to escape the cycle of birth, ageing, sickness and death through the renouncing of worldly desires and living in moderation. The soul enters nirvana, a paradise without want. It was Korea's state religion from the 6th to the 14th century AD, and through government patronage, beseeching the Buddha to protect their Korea, grew into a powerful sub-state over the years. This was partly why the religion was swiftly replaced by Confucianism as the state religion from the late 14th century onwards.

CONFUCIANISM Similarly to Buddhism, Confucianism was originally more a code of morals and conduct but attained quasi-religious elements over the course of its 2,500-year history. Although scarcely practised in the ROK, let alone the DPRK, Confucianism is still evident in Korean thinking, shown through reverence for age, learning and desire for social harmony. Confucius was a Chinese scholar from the 6th century BC, who believed study was the way to the truth and the virtues of benevolence, righteousness, decorum and wisdom. These attributes ensured social harmony and stability. He formulated a detailed behavioural code to govern the relationships of the family, community and state, on the premise that stability would arise from everyone knowing their place in society. He espoused that authority and hierarchy continued from the family to the emperor and that there were five relationships to adhere to: sons showing respect, obedience and filial piety to their fathers; subjects' loyalty to their rulers; the young revering the old; wives subservient to their husbands; friendships governed by mutual trust. Confucianism increasingly underpinned the structures of government and administration in Korea.

Chinese philosopher Zhu Xi in the 12th century expounded upon Confucianism to form Neo-Confucianism, with more religious undertones and involving ancestral worship, and it was this form that replaced Buddhism as the state religion in the 14th century.

CULTURE

CINEMA 'Like the leading article of the party paper, the cinema should have great appeal and inform the audience of reality. It should play a mobilising role in each stage of the revolutionary struggle,' wrote Kim Il Sung.

Should you get to settle in a cinema seat with a bucket of popcorn, be aware of the educational value of what you're about to see. Categories for DPRK films include historical and literary classics like *The Flower Girl* or *The Sea of Blood*, with healthy infusions of revolutionary thought; socialist-realism films, promoting the success and development of socialism, like *Girl Chairman of the Cooperative Farm* or *The Flourishing Village*; themes of revolutionary tradition, with the Party and its ideals at the centre; and war films, fighting Japanese imperialism (since forever) or

CHRISTIANITY Christianity was first brought into Korea by freelance missionaries moving on from China, and then seeped in via traders and explorers. Christian teachings of paradise in the afterlife and an early release from poverty appealed to the poor and thousands converted, but their teachings were an anathema to the ruling classes, for Christianity dismissed ancestral worship (and therefore the legitimacy of the state rulers!) and encouraged individualism. Several purges killed thousands of converts in the 1800s, but by the 1880s, Protestant missionaries were pouring into the country, and like teachers and doctors were tolerated for their poverty relief, but only up to a point. Nonetheless in 1907 came the 'Pyongyang Revival' or 'Pyongyang Great Revival', where from out of a city of 'sin abounding' exploded a spiritual awakening that somehow augured a massive surge in Koreans worshipping Christ. Some 50,000 converts came that year, and Pyongyang would be called 'The Jerusalem of the East'. While ill-treating Korean Christians (although their religion was secondary to their offence of existing at all), the Japanese did not seem so pressed to check the spread of more missionaries coming to spread the word, but in 1945 many Christians took the chance to head south, particularly as the northern government made its position on the Church terrifyingly explicit. The ROK is today home to 25,000 churches, while Pyongyang has one Catholic, two Protestant and a Russian Orthodox church. That said, Kim Il Sung's parents were Presbyterians, and there are micro-detectable influences in Juche philosophy and the cult which surrounds the Kims.

TONGHAK This confluence of Buddhism, Taoism and Christianity was known as 'Eastern Learning' to the Koreans and was propagated by a squire's son, Choe Chun. It preached salvation from destitution and placed all men (and women) on an equal footing with heaven, so envisaging a world without any class constraints or barriers. It appealed greatly to the majority of poor farmers, while causing panic in the upper classes. Peasants and disaffected Yangban rallied to the cause in their thousands in the early 1860s and throughout the decades to 1894, when the Tonghak mass-peasant uprising came close to destroying the House of Chosun (the Japanese 'rescued' them). The movement morphed into a less spiritual political philosophy that actually survives in some form in today's DPRK as the Chondoist Chongu Party. The proto-Marxist tenets of Tonghak must have saved the movement from the chop of the KWP.

American forms (since the late 19th century). Overarching themes are the oneness of the Korean nation, the realisation of Juche's teachings being the only way to live, and a strong spirit of selflessness and sacrifice being essential to achieving any collective goals, from reaching output targets to achieving national reunification.

In historical outings, common motifs include injustices and atrocities being piled upon lowly villages and families. Fathers get killed early on, providing the rage and reason for the remaining unlikely heroes to 'find themselves' and engage in amazing acts of self-sacrifice. Mothers not performing their own selfless feats, like storming a Japanese-held fort in *The Sea of Blood*, give their children to the revolutionary tasks (ultimately to Kim Il Sung's guidance, who fills the spiritual void of the deceased fathers and becomes the 'father of the nation'). The *Story of a Nurse* celebrates the bravery and vision of a young nurse who follows the army over 1,000 ri behind enemy lines. Just after her efforts are rewarded with Party membership, her unit is bombed. 'Breathing her last,' says a throaty voice, 'she asks that her Party card and her Party fees be forwarded to the Party Central Committee, and dies a heroic death.'

Everyone must watch out for those of aristocratic heritage, inherently unstable people who might try counter-revolutionary activities. In *The First Party Commissioner* a former anti-Japanese revolutionary fighter is sent to the country to form a party organisation in an iron smelter. There, workers of former aristocratic stock conspire to kill him, but he crushes their reactionary subversion and establishes the smelter's first Party cell.

In *Three Revolutionary Red Flags* and *The 100 Days Battle*, the workers are taught how Juche can make them self-reliant to meet the targets of the country's Chollima speed campaigns, which means films also cover issues of the day. From the 1970s, with Kim Jong Il's promotion as Kim Il Sung's successor, a sub-theme became the son taking over the revolutionary charge, and later revolutionary films touch on the class conflicts of the country's new technocrats.

Films were Kim Jong Il's passion; aside from his own reputed private collection of 15,000 movies, including many foreign ones, he had a hand in many of the DPRK's cinematic products, and secured the success of many silver-screen starlets. Such was his love of cinema that he wrote extensively about it, including a book, and had he not been destined to run the DPRK, he would have been a film director instead. In fact, in a plot straight out of a creaky thriller, in 1978 South Korean film director Shin Sang Ok and his actress wife found themselves accepting an invitation to Pyongyang that couldn't be refused, and during the following nine years in the North as the guest of Kim Jong Il, Shin made a dozen films that went down very well (see box, page 40). However, there was little technical advancement in how films were put together, and pictures right into the noughties seemed to have the print-film image quality, scene editing and melodramatic characterisation of 1970s Hong Kong martial arts movies, ie: there was a set trope in how a film should be.

That is beginning to change. Imports of films and television shows, as well as music, are officially restricted to those from China and Russia, albeit with the forces of modernity and racier ideas filtering in, for the increasingly large number of North Koreans who own CD, VCD and DVD players. But that is not the only way to see foreign films. Every two years, since the late 1980s, an international film festival is held in Pyongyang, usually in September, at the Pyongyang International Cinema on Yanggak Island (see page 152). *The Game of Their Lives* won the Special Award in 2002 and *A State of Mind* was shown at the 2004 event (see box, pages 42–3). Small numbers of locals are able to visit with tickets distributed through neighbourhood offices, and high-level political figures from the Supreme People's Assembly and the cabinet, including the Minister of Culture, also attend. Tour operators can arrange this to be the central fixture of a visit.

For many years the only films shown were from the Korea International Film Production Agency, together with international films from allied communist and non-aligned movement countries such as Iran, Lebanon, Vietnam, China and the USSR (a lot of which would be compelling stuff and not seen at the 'free' festivals in the West). But the range has increased of late to include films from Japan and hits like *Fahrenheit 9/11*, *Cry, The Beloved Country* and *Bend It Like Beckham*, which would be the first foreign film shown on DPRK TV. Such was the success and popularity of *Bend It* that Brit Nick Bonner was inspired, along with Belgian film-maker Anja Daelemans, North Korean director Kim Gwang Hun and producer Ryom Mi Hwa, to make the rom-com *Comrade Kim Goes Flying*. There is also the beautifully shot Chinese film from 2012, *Meet In Pyongyang*, to seek out.

The DPRK has also featured as a villain for Hollywood, starting with *The Manchurian Candidate*, the Bond outing *Die Another Day*, the satire of *Team America: World Police* and *Red Dawn* in 2012. Look up the rather droll weblog http://northkoreanfilms.com or the writings of Johannes Schönherr for more info about DPRK cinema.

MUSIC There is not much by way of a contemporary 'pop' music scene of the hysterical teen type visible in Russia, China and the ROK. Pyongyang has no equivalent of Justin Bieber. Those of you who are appalled by the degenerative influence of beatniks with mop-top hairstyles might fit in with the DPRK's take on popular beat combos. Here groups and bands normally involve formally attired men and women in front of suitably suited bands stashed behind panelled music stands, knocking out crushingly sentimental (and quite sexless) numbers about long-distance relationships of friends and family, home towns, reunification and landscapes, like 'Doves Fly High', 'My Home, Sweet Home', 'The Peak of Mount Gumsoo' and 'Yearning For My Beloved Mother'.

The Moranbong Music Band, a quintet of young ladies who debuted in 2013, marked a modicum of a departure from that, sashaying across the stage in their evening gowns right up to the seated audience of KPA and KWP bigwigs who are having a riot as lots of pyrotechnics go off, but the television playing a loop of the group's concerts contrasted with their rumoured fate.

Otherwise it's down to the minstrels in the Korean People's Army Choir to provide the top tunes, including 'Soldiers Hear Rice-ears Rustle', 'The Leader Has Come to Our Outpost' and 'Warm Feelings Creep Over the Ridge', with a heavy accent on Russian military music.

The state actively promotes and supports the teaching and production of dance and music in many forms, as long as the output is healthily infused with politically correct ideals as reflected in Kim Jong Il's views on opera: 'The creators of music must complete revolutionary opera songs as in The Song of Kumgangsan Mountains: For fifteen long years through snowstorms, He fought for the rebirth of this beautiful country, The towering peaks and crystal-clear streams, Praise Marshal Kim Il Sung's kindness in Song.' *Tell the Story, Forest, A True Daughter of the Party* and *The Fate of a Self-Defence Corps Man* are all hit operas from the 1970s.

Apart from the mass spectacles of Arirang and the Mass Gymnastics, and the medley presented at the Mangyongdae Schoolchildren's Palace, opera, dance and music recitals can be enjoyed in Pyongyang, mainly at the Mansudae Arts and Moranbang theatres. North Korean children have more opportunity than in many other countries to have state-funded tuition in musical instruments and many are markedly proficient in playing them. Korean men enjoy beers very similar to those drunk in England and they like a good singalong around a piano, although karaoke is also becoming as widespread as it is elsewhere, replacing the communal singing.

A selection of top tunes can be heard through Andy Kershaw's excellent BBC Radio 3 documentary on the country (*www.bbc.co.uk/programmes/p005y2n0*), which also shows how Koreans are prepared to spontaneously belt out a number, including Sinatra's 'My Way', and the brilliance of youthful musical expertise.

Specialist tours focusing on the meeting of musicians at places like the Isan Yun Conservatory are possible.; just ask your tour operator for more details.

PAINTING For depictions of 'ordinary life', the socialist-realism view of the communist world, committed to canvas mostly from the 1930s to the 1960s, is still being exhibited here and produced, albeit on a reduced scale.

The rosy-cheeked, flag-flying workers and farmers are depicted gaily hailing each other amid bumper crops, gleaming tractors and glowing blast-furnaces in the rural and urban idyll of the DPRK, while stoic-faced soldiers, chins up and eyes fixed amid blizzard-blinded battle against big-nosed foreigners, are shown defeating imperialism and advancing socialism. A great many paintings are celebrations of the life and achievements of the Kims, who dominate the pictures

TOURISM, ENGAGEMENT AND NORTH KOREA

Dr James Hoare, Charge d'Affaires in Pyongyang, 2001–2

Among those who attempt to understand the DPRK, there are periodic debates about engagement with the country and the nature of that engagement. To me, engagement is a fairly neutral term. Like diplomacy, it covers a wide range of ways in which countries interact with each other at both official and private levels. But in the North Korean case, as previously with Myanmar, for some of those debating it clearly carries a far more charged meaning. From the way some arguments are presented, engagement seems to mean support. By this logic, a tourist visiting North Korea is automatically backing the country's nuclear and human rights programmes not only morally but also financially through the money that comes from tourism.

A moment's thought might have cast doubt on this proposition. North Korea is not the first country to run labour camps or to develop a nuclear weapon capability. Yet there are few voices calling for boycotts of countries such as China and India, which remain popular tourist destinations. Many countries do things of which I do not approve but nobody has ever rebuked me for visiting the United States or Japan, which execute people, or Spain, which allows bullfighting. There are many aspects of my own country's policies (in the UK) that I do not like, such as the demonising of immigrants. Should I therefore stay quietly at home? To state the case is to indicate the absurdity of it. I suspect that if I did protest at any of the above, I would be seen as grandstanding rather than making any real contribution to the debate on such issues, and the governments concerned would reject my criticism.

The DPRK is no different in this respect. Its response to public criticism is also to reject it and to counter-accuse the accusers. Suggestions that it might change its ways are vehemently rejected; if you have perfection, why change? Engagement, however, is different. It involves mutual acceptance of the other side and careful consideration of its concerns. There are benefits for both. It is a slow process but it can also be one that leads to more understanding.

by the positioning, size and colouring of their figures. Another favoured medium is coloured woodcut prints.

There's little in common between such official art and the traditional painting styles that depict natural scenes of mountainsides, flora and fauna and ancient Korea. These images are shown from a few, deceptively simple brushstrokes of black ink to the wall-sized paintings and murals in large public buildings. The first great examples of Korean painting are found in the earliest tombs and mausoleums, of scenes from court and portraits of the gods of the day. The Songhwa Art Studio in the Pyongyang International House of Culture is where current trends in DPRK fine art are found, and the Art Gallery on Kim Il Sung Square has an excellent chronological review of Korean art.

POTTERY The earliest Korean pottery found regularly is earthenware with combed surfaces, but this took plain surfacing during the Bronze Age. During the 2nd and 3rd centuries BC, a greyish-blue glaze grew prevalent, followed by the short-lived lead glaze. From China in the 9th century came the green-blue tinge of celadon. Celadon had been imported for centuries from China, where its production was universal, and the techniques and styles were built upon by the Koreans over the next 500 years of Koryo rule, eventually surpassing the wares of China itself and were

In the case of the DPRK, engagement has taken a number of forms. Since the famine of the 1990s, the most prominent of these has been the various types of humanitarian aid, which have ranged from full-scale government involvement to small non-governmental organisations. But well before that, the United Nations Development Program ran courses to provide training in modern economics and trading methods. There have been links with American and other Western universities and scholarly bodies. Some have worked well, others less so. But both sides came to know each other better and the Koreans, in particular, learnt that there were more ways than one of doing things. That was and is important, and, I believe, if such contacts are pursued, they would have a wide effect.

Tourism is a form of engagement that seems welcome to the DPRK. Some North Koreans clearly see it as dangerous and the visitor is likely to be far more tightly controlled than is now usual in most countries. Not so long ago, the DPRK approach was fairly common among socialist states. Those who visited the Soviet Union before glasnost or China before the mid-1980s will find the current DPRK treatment of tourists familiar. There is also no doubt that tourism generates funds. But, compared with other countries' earnings from this source, the DPRK is not a major beneficiary of tourist money. Cutting off this legitimate trade will neither stop the nuclear programme nor help to improve the people's lot. Encouraging it, on the other hand, is a two-way channel. For the visitor, it means learning about a very different society, albeit in difficult circumstances, and perhaps beginning to understand why North Korea is as it is. But it is not a one-way process. For the guides, drivers and hotel staff, it means coping with enquiring and demanding people and doing things in different ways. They may not react immediately and your particular group may not see any direct benefits. But they are learning and that learning process is important.

So my advice to the intending traveller is go to North Korea and keep your eyes and ears open – you may even enjoy it!

even exported to Japan. The most sophisticated designs and decoration of Korean ceramics is considered to have occurred in this period, charged by the demand for pottery resulting from the growth of Buddhism in Korea and its prescribed uses of tea and incense. Cranes, willow trees and peony blossom were common motifs, as were the Buddhist-related lotus flowers, carved onto the surfaces and filled with coloured glaze, carved right through the clay or moulded into sophisticated forms.

Meanwhile, the production of white porcelain was being perfected in China and these techniques were mastered in Korea by the late 14th century. Porcelain, being tougher than celadon, gradually supplanted it in common usage. Left plain white or lightly adorned with cobalt-blue designs, the simplified porcelain designs reflected the more frugal, less ostentatious Confucianism that was replacing Buddhism. Such were the skills of Korea's pottery makers that many were kidnapped to Japan by Hideyoshi's forces in 1592 and 1598. Light brown décor on porcelain's white surfaces had by the 18th century taken its place alongside the blue designs, but the most common form of pottery found across the peninsula is still the huge earthenware pickling jars for *kimchi* (a traditional Korean side dish of fermented vegetables with seasonings).

LITERATURE   A staggering amount of literature produced is dedicated to the works of Kim Il Sung and Kim Jong Il. Juche, revolution and the need for the struggle of anti-imperialism underpin all modern philosophical and historical works, which strive to prove the superiority of socialism over all other lesser societal creeds.

Similarly to facets of culture, writers in the DPRK are state-supported and state-subordinate. From poetry to popular novels, literature must serve to 'depict man and life and serve the popular masses truly', wrote Kim Jong Il. 'We need a humanistic literature, which gives prominence to the principle of independence, the development of independent individuals, and which creates the image of the truly typical man of the new era, thereby contributing to the transformation of the whole of society in accordance with the concept of Juche', clarifying how man prizes, glorifies and will die for independence.

2

Practical Information

WHEN TO VISIT

The rainy season, mainly July and August, is very humid, cloudy and sticky, and not brilliant for radiant photography as the rain soups up poorer roads and rail lines and curtails access. The best times to go are April to June and September to October, when it is cool, dry and colourful, from spring's heaving tides of white blossoms to autumn's cascades of gold and red. If there are Mass Games on (over the summer; see box, pages 138–9 for more details) they are an absolute must-see.

HIGHLIGHTS

IN PYONGYANG
Grand Monument on Mansu Hill You will appreciate its grand austerity and holiness.

May Day Stadium The best time to visit is when one of the Mass Games events is on. What a show, what a venue!

Moran Hill This park on the Taedong's east bank overlooks the May Day Stadium and is dotted with relics and pavilions dating across the past thousand years, as well as giving grand views of the city itself. The hill is a sea of cherry blossom in spring, a blizzard of snow in winter, and a cool haven of shade in Pyongyang's baking summers.

Juche Tower On the Taedong's east bank, from the top of this tower one gets the best panoramic view of the city and can see pretty much all there is to see, including the areas you'd otherwise have no chance to glimpse.

IN THE COUNTRY
Myohyangsan Another firm fixture of any itinerary, the mountains of Myohyang are on one hand a beautiful ridge of gulleys bedecked by waterfalls and steeped in Korea's Buddhist history, and on the other the location for the Great and Dear Leaders' showrooms displaying their hoards of astonishingly gauche gifts from international dignitaries over the years.

Mount Paektu A spectacular geological phenomenon in its own right, this volcanic mountain lake is the spiritual birthplace of all Korea and is celebrated as such across the peninsula: high, cold, remote and deafeningly peaceful.

Lake Sijung On the road south of Wonsan to Kumgangsan, this tranquil place is where the better-off Koreans, Russians and other old friends go to relax in mudbaths, with petrol-cooked clam parties and fabulously clean beaches beyond the electric fence.

Inner Kumgang It is unusual for visitors to gain access to the inner sanctum of this site, which is one of Korea's most sacred, both historically and ecologically. If a trip can be arranged, you should jump at the chance, particularly to visit the Podok Temple, high up on the hillside.

TRAVEL IN THE DPRK

For tourists, visits to the DPRK take at least two weeks to arrange, for visa applications to be checked out and for the trip's itineraries to be arranged and agreed upon by both sides. Tourists visit the DPRK only on guided tours, with private transport arranged by the Koreans. Even a solo traveller will have two guides, a driver and a car to zoom about the country, and a guide is with you virtually all the time. The guides have the permits that all Koreans need to travel from city to city, examined at checkpoints surrounding the cities, and which tourists cannot obtain themselves. Access to many parts of the country is completely prohibited, such that even workers for esteemed NGOs like the World Food Programme can't enter large areas. Foreigners' free movement around the country is as proscribed as that of locals, who need good reason to get permits. The severe shortages of fuel combined with an intermittent electricity supply means there is very little by way of a regular, practical public transport system in the country.

For tourists, the range of places open to visit is limited to the capital, Pyongyang, and a handful of other cities near to national parks that protect mountains deemed significant for their history or wildlife. Diplomats do not have guides and have some freedom to tour Pyongyang, but tourists have guides and they must stick with them. Long-term residents, businesspeople and NGOs may get hold of the DPRK's local won, needed to purchase things from all shops, local markets or utilise the metro or buses, for example, but not tourists who are expected to use hard currencies – CNY, euros or US dollars (see *Money*, pages 93–4). The point is partly that the autonomy of having cash is that it's only as good as where it can be spent, hence having a limit on who can use local won, and a limit on where officially accepts hard currency, theoretically restricts where foreigners can go, and thereby their movements are controlled, or at least curtailed. In effect this keeps them in the best parts of the cities and countryside, the well-tended, well-fed areas, where the needs of the locals are being met, so exposure for the average visitor to real deprivation doesn't happen much. Against the great diplomatic strides achieved in recent years, a very deep, historical distrust of foreigners is continually worked up by the state-owned DPRK media. That said, the locals are not outright hostile, but wary. They would never attack or insult, only keep their distance. To that end they are becoming increasingly friendly, and when the barriers are finally broken down they are a very warm and hospitable people. As long as visitors behave themselves within the parameters laid out, the risks to them are very, very few.

Kaesong to Panmunjom The ancient city of Kaesong is pretty and is worth a two-day trip with a couple of outlying ancient tomb sites thrown in, their serenity contrasting with the silent intensity of a trip into Panmunjom in the DMZ.

SUGGESTED ITINERARIES

Every tour involves Pyongyang at some point. A very common itinerary (broadly speaking) would last four to five nights and take in Pyongyang, Kaesong, the DMZ, and possibly Myohyangsan and/or Nampo. It's also possible to concentrate on the northern regions and take in Paektusan, Chilbosan, Rason, Chongjin and Yanji over a week. One could see pretty much everything there is to see in the country over 16 days or so, albeit in what would be a very intense fortnight and then some. But if you can afford it, it's well worth it.

TOUR OPERATORS

IN THE DPRK The Korean International Travel Company (KITC) runs numerous specialist tours, such as mud treatment, spa treatment, golf, riding steam locomotives (in Kaesong and a new one in Nampo) or trolley buses in Pyongyang, mountaineering in Kumgangsan, Chilbosan and Paektusan, tae kwon do (Korean martial arts), Korean language learning, Juche learning, plant tours for medicinal herbs and specialist wildlife expeditions. There have also been a great many exchange tours held in recent years, with foreign teams coming to play football, basketball, cricket and even ultimate Frisbee, while high-profile events have included the New York Philharmonic Orchestra performing in Pyongyang (starting their set, naturally, with the 'Star Spangled Banner'). The KITC has offices in China and Thailand too; see below and page 80. There is also the Korean International Sports Travel Company (KISTC) and Korean International Youth Travel Company (KIYTC).

Korean International Travel Company 8901/381 8574 or +850 2 18111 (ext) 8283;
(KITC) Central District, Pyongyang; ☏ +850 2 381   f +850 2 381 7607/4407; e kitc_1@silibank.com

OUTSIDE THE DPRK There are many other tour companies, national and international, offering tours into the DPRK. **The Korean Friendship Association** is a pro-Pyongyang group seeking to build international ties with the DPRK. Its travel unit is on their website (*www.korea-dpr.com/kfa_travel.html*), while its numerous agents abroad can be emailed via this page: www.korea-dpr.com/organization.html. KTG offers trips for tourists and business people but is only contactable through their website (*www.north-korea-travel.com*) or by email (e *info@north-korea-travel.com*; see ad, second colour section). Below is a selection of tour companies listed alphabetically by country.

Canada
Bestway Tours & Safaris Suite #206, 8678 Greenall Av, Burnaby, British Columbia V5J 3M6; ☏ +1 604 264 7378, toll free +1 800 663 0844 (Canada & US residents only); f +1 604 264 7774; www.bestway.com

China
Korean International Travel Company (KITC) Yanxiang Hotel, 3rd Flr, Qianghuating A2, Jangtai Rd, Chaoyang District, Beijing; ☏ +86 10 6437 6666/3133; f +86 10 6436 9089; also at Xian Qian Rd, Yuan Bao District, Dandong; ☏ +86 415 281 2542/281 0457; f +86 415 281 8438 & in Yanji; ☏f +86 433 2529689.

Koryo Tours +86 10 6416 7544; f +86 10 6415 2653; e info@koryogroup.com, tours@koryogroup.com. This Beijing-based, British-run firm has done much to pioneer DPRK travel & is involved in cultural & philanthropic projects. See ad, 2nd colour section.

Young Pioneer Tours Room 2003, Unit 3-3, Saigao Block, Fengcheng Wu Lu, Weiyang District, Xi'an, Shaanxi; Office: +86 29 8621 2359, Gareth: +86 186 2902 7684, Shan: +86 186 8719 0181, Sophie: +86 132 7959 0968; e tours@youngpioneertours.com; www.youngpioneertours.com. Caters mainly for travellers on a budget.

Dandong Chosun Travel Service Jiangcheng Dajie 15, Dandong, Liaoning, 118000; +86 415 2300 133/2300 136; m +86 1347 000 2189; f +86 415 216 0867; e ddcts@163.com; www.ddcts.com. Offers tours to the DPRK.

Explore North Korea Dandong; +86 1594 154 5676; Skype: travelnorthKorea; e explorenorthkorea@gmail.com; www.explorenorthkorea.com

Czech Republic

Korea Discovery CK Svetlana Mikusova, Troja 147 E, 171 00 Prague; +420 720 409272; f +49 174 777 4975; e info@korea-discovery.com; www.korea-discovery.com

Netherlands

VNC Travel Postbus 676 6800 AR Arnhem; +31 26 303 0160; f +31 26 352 9391; e info@vnc.nl; www.vnc.nl

Republic of Korea (tours of the DMZ)

How To Go To North Korea www.howtogotonorthkorea.com. This company is contacted directly through their website.

Korea Travel Bureau Anguk BD 4F, 33, Yulgok-ro, Jongno-gu, Seoul 110-734; +82 2 778 0150; f +82 2 756 8428; e ktbmaster@ktbtour.co.kr; www.go2korea.co.kr, www.ktbtour.co.kr

Panmunjom Travel Centre Lotte Hotel, 2nd Flr (Main Bldg), Chung-Gu, Sogong-dong, Seoul City; +82 2 771 55935; f +82 2 771 5596; e jsa33@korea.com; www.koreadmztour.com

Spain

Viatges Pujol Corcega 214, 08036 Barcelona; +34 93 321 9303; f +34 93 419 0334; www.coreanorte.com

Sweden

Korea Konsult Rödklövervägen 79 165 73 Hässelby; +46 73 981 0372; f +46 70 116 5525; e postmaster@koreakonsult.com; http://koreakonsult.com

Thailand

Korean International Travel Company (KITC) 867139 Moodansilintheb Patanakan Rd, Soi 46 Soun Luang, Bangkok 10250; +66 2 321 5797/653 4083; f +66 2 322 1109

UK

Explore Worldwide Ltd e ops@exploreworldwide.com; www.exploreworldwide.com (central website). Subsites for the UK, Canada, Australia, Europe & NZ.

Lupine Travel 12 Warnford Street, Wigan Lancs WN1 2EQ; 1942 704525; e info@lupinetravel.co.uk; www.lupinetravel.co.uk. Specialises in unique destinations at budget prices. See also ad on the inside back cover.

Regent Holidays 6th Flr, Colston Tower, Colston St, Bristol BS1 4XE; (Asia) 020 3588 2971; e regent@regent-holidays.co.uk; www.regent-holidays.co.uk Se ad, second colour section.

Undiscovered Destinations PO Box 746, North Tyneside, NE29 1EG; 0191 296 2674; www.undiscovered-destinations.com

Voyages Jules Verne 21 Dorset Sq, London NW1 6QE; Sales: 0845 166 7003/020 7616 1000/01306 744795; e sales@vjv.co.uk; Visas: 0845 166 7040/020 7616 1050; e visa@vjv.co.uk; www.vjv.com

Juche Travel Services 35 Farington Acres, Vale Road, Weybridge, Surrey, KT13 9NH; 07841 408462; e info@juchetravelservices.com; www.juchetravelservices.com

US

Asia Pacific Travel PO Box 350, Kenilworth, IL 60043-0350; +1 847 251 6400, toll free: +1 800 262 6420; f +1 847 256 5601; www.northkorea1on1.com. DPRK trips have their own division – see their website for details.

New Korea Tours 1733 Aspen Glen Dr, Hamden, CT 06518; +1 203 613 5283; f +1 530 325 3462; +1 201 588 3874 (Skype); e info@newkoreatours.com; www.newkoreatours.com

Uri Tours PO Box 62, Cliffside Pk, NJ 07010; e info@uritours.com; www.uritours.com

TOUR COSTS On a tour, the cost is determined by numerous factors – hotels, meals, tickets to shows and where in the country is to be visited, etc.

As tours are usually presented as cost per entire trip, a comprehensive breakdown of individual elements is difficult to obtain and of no great use anyway, particularly as tours are long-standing arrangements brokered between the agencies inside and outside the country. As said in the *Accommodation* section below, the DPRK side prefers visitors to stay in the higher-band, higher-price hotels (and you'll appreciate the quality, with relatively regular power and hot-water supplies), and foreign-operator packages can be at least 20% cheaper than what going with KITC direct might cost. In addition, there are now many more tour companies – European, British, American, Chinese – than there used to be. Prices for tours range from as low as €400 for a three-day off-peak tour, up to £3,000 for a 19-day summer bonanza. Prices reflect overheads and expertise.

Most packages include hotel accommodation and all meals, guides, transportation in-country and the price of return flights and trains in and out of the DPRK – although a very common entry–exit set-up these days is in by plane and out by train (or vice versa). Some packages also include the cost of the DPRK visa and a night's stay in Beijing with transfers to and from Beijing's airport or rail stations. Not included are pocket money for gifts and extras beyond mealtime, tips for the driver and guides (which are now considered something of a norm, albeit still discreetly given) or flights and visas to and from China or Russia (a double-entry visa for China cost £99 in 2013). The main variables affecting cost per person are the season, the length of the tour, group size and destination in the DPRK. Larger groups reduce the overall costs – the daily cost per person of a group of ten of more (group sizes being a usual maximum of 16) can be 40% less than a package for three to five. Those travelling as a 'single', within groups, incur a supplement of

TOURIST INFORMATION

There is no longer such a dearth of up-to-date information about travel in the DPRK. More and more blogs are appearing all the time and most Western companies taking tours there have a blog on their websites. Travel discussion forums about the DPRK include www.tripadvisor.com – which has done so much to demolish the traditional paperback travel-guidebook industry. Bear in mind that the writers on such websites may not be who they purport to be and may have other agendas behind their comments.

Overall, though, one no longer has to rely on vague and out-of-date information provided in print by the indigenous tour operators, although do not discount the gloriously glossy publications *Korea Today* and *Democratic People's Republic of Korea* that are available on the Air Koryo flights into the country, and in most hotel shops. Visitors often assume that their guides are the local equivalent of Google, they know everything in a land infamous for the paucity of reliable information about it, especially in-country. To that end, quite often different guides will provide different answers to the most anodyne questions, and do not assume they're lying or engaged in some conspiracy to deceive; the fact is they simply don't know and are in all good faith giving a best guess, or they might not feel empowered to tell you. The DPRK is a black hole of information, and the situations about food, transport and power all change rapidly, just like itineraries. Which all adds to the fun. For further tourist information see *Appendix 2*, page 283.

€25–40 a night. A trip can be arranged with two weeks' notice but this is very, very rare – four to six weeks are what operators normally demand at the minimum and really the longer the better.

A 'short break' tour to Pyongyang is often at least three nights, possibly being solely based in Pyongyang to see the Mass Games (assuming they're on) and possibly oriented around another major public holiday. 'Standard' tours, taking in Pyongyang, Myohyangsan and another site or two range from five or six days up to 11 days; fully comprehensive excursions go up to 16 days (some offer 19 days) – taking in practically everything there is to see. These would be very, very intense, involving a lot of bussing and possibly even charter flights, but are nonetheless great fun. More focused specialist tours, such as to Mount Paektu, can be arranged.

RED TAPE

The UK government's foreign travel advice (*www.gov.uk/foreign-travel-advice*) says passports need only be valid for the proposed duration of the stay in the DPRK. However, visitors will most likely be going via China or Russia, and China needs a passport valid for six months from the date of issue of the visa, whereas Russia needs validity for at least six months following the visa's expiry. Going in from China and back into China also requires a double-entry visa to China. At the time of writing, visitors spending less than 72 hours in China could get 72-hour transit visas on arrival in China, but as this may change this must be checked with the tour operator and visa-issuing embassy.

For DPRK, visas – which are usually single entry – are given for set arrival and departure dates and are designated for exit/entry specifically for where the visitor is going in or out, say Pyongyang and Sinuiju. Visas must be obtained before going, and require letters of invitation, whether the visit is for business or pleasure, and your passport should be valid for a year after the travel dates. Because tourists must go on tours, they will either let their travel operator deal with the Korean International Travel Company (KITC) or do that themselves but applications take at least ten days because of how much needs arranging. Along with the application forms of the respective tour company and two (or more) passport photos, travellers must submit a CV and a letter from their current employer verifying the applicant's details. The CV and letter details have to be updated to the day they are checked: a wrong number or date can scupper the keenest tourist. Journalists need special visas, they are not allowed in on tourist visas, and any caught sneaking in are thrown out at their own expense. More importantly, they endanger everyone associated with them, the other tourists, the external tour firm and particularly the Korean guides. It is tantamount to spying. Sneaking into any country without a visa is a bad idea, and the authorities are not amenable. In 2009 American journalists Laura Ling and Euna Lee waded across the Yalu into the DPRK, got caught, and ended up having to be rescued by former president Clinton. In short, don't do it. Most people need visas to visit another country; North Koreans need visas to leave theirs.

If you're staying in the DPRK for more than 24 hours you must register with the Foreign Ministry, something the hotel should do for you, but they will need your passport for an hour.

Until 2008, South Korean tourists could visit on tourist visas, albeit only to the Mount Kumgang complex via the Hyundai ferry or buses across the DMZ and on other occasional tours that are very limited in comparison with the norm. That said, they can and do go by the thousand to the Chinese side of Mount Paektu and to the Yanbian Autonomous Region in China, also known as the 'Third Korea' (see page 268). US tourists constitute a surprisingly high proportion of visitors to the DPRK. They were banned in 1995, then a few dribbles were allowed back in 2002 for the Arirang Mass Games. These days US tourists can almost visit everywhere that other nationalities can, albeit with some restrictions, such as they're still unable to leave by train from Pyongyang to Beijing. These allowances (or restrictions) can fluctuate, so it is necessary to check with tour operators.

By far the biggest numbers of tourists into DPRK are Chinese. You'll likely see many jolly bands of middle-aged, prosperous Chinese men wandering around and you'll share the audience with them for the set shows and other events or venues to which KITC directs its tourists. Many Chinese come in homage to battle sites where their forebears fell during the Korean War. Others come for what feels like a nostalgia tour, as it is often observed that DPRK is very similar in looks, organisation and feel to China 20-odd years ago. Sometimes the locals think the Chinese seem to lord it up a bit. Whether the perceived gap between China and the DPRK is growing or narrowing is a question of perception.

Remember: you'll need double-entry visas certainly for China or Russia if you're coming through them, which is likely.

CUSTOMS Don't bring in any texts critical or derisory of the regime. There is no restriction on the amount of money you can bring in, but you have to declare the amounts you're bringing on a customs form given upon arrival, on which you must also list cameras, mobile phones, laptops, iPads, etc. It's prohibited to take local won currency out of the DPRK. The usual restrictions also apply for what you can't bring in regarding narcotics, firearms, live organisms, biochem and hazardous products. Pornographic literature is banned.

EMBASSIES AND CONSULATES

Since 1998, the DPRK has more than doubled its cache of fully established diplomatic relations with other countries, with the number of Western countries growing. Still, many don't have an actual embassy in Pyongyang but cover the DPRK from their Beijing embassies. Pyongyang's embassy district is Munsudong, on the east side.

🅔 Bulgaria Munsudong District, Daedonggang, Pyongyang; ☎ 02 381 7343; f 02 381 7342; e embassy.pyongyang@mfa.bg

🅔 Cambodia Munsudong District, Daedonggang, Pyongyang; ☎ 02 381 7283; f 02 381 7625; e camemb.prk@mfa.gov.kh

🅔 China B Kin Mal Dong, Mao Lang Bong District, Pyongyang; ☎ 02 381 3133/3116; f 02 381 3425. This stands out as the biggest embassy & the most efficient. Very good for getting visas back to China – you can get a business visa in a day, starting around US$100, but try not to rely on these things.

🅔 Cuba Munsudong, Taedonggang District, PO Box 5; ☎ 02 381 7703; f 02 381 7703; e embacuba@rpdc.embacuba.cn

🅔 Czech Republic Taedonggang Guyok 38, Taehakgori, Puksudong ,Pyongyang; ☎ 02 381 7021; f 02 381 7022; e pyongyang@embassy.mzv.cz

🅔 Germany Munsudong District, Pyongyang; ☎ 02 381 7385; f 02 381 7397; e info@pjoengjang.diplo.de

🅔 India 6 Munsudong District, Daedonggang, Pyongyang; ☎ 02 381 7277/7274/7215; f 02 381 7619; e amb.pyongyang@mea.gov.in, hoc.pyongyang@mea.gov.in

🅔 Mongolia Munsudong, Pyongyang; ☎ 02 381 7322; f 02 381 7616

🅔 Poland Munsudong District, Daedonggang, Pyongyang; ☎ 02 381 7333; f 02 381 7637; e pjongjang.amb.sekretariat@msz.gov.pl

🅔 Romania Munhengong District, Pyongyang; ☎ 02 381 7336

🅔 Russia Choson Minjujuii Inmin, Chuji Soryong Tesagwan, Conghwaguck, Pyongyang; ☎ 02 381 1301; f 02 381 1302

🇪 Sweden Daehak St, Munsudong District, Daedonggang, Pyongyang; ✆02 381 7904; f 02 381 7485. US & EU countries without their own diplomatic presence are represented & given consular assistance by the Swedish Embassy.

🇪 Switzerland 3 Yubo St, Munsudong District, Daedonggang, Pyongyang; ✆02 381 7645/7646; f 02 381 7643

🇪 UK Munsudong District; ✆02 381 7980/4, international dialling: ✆02 382 7980/2, local dialling: ✆02 381 2228; f 02 381 7985, international dialling: f 02 382 7983, local dialling: f 02 381 4482, out of hours; ⊕ 00.00–08.30 Mon–Fri

DPRK MISSIONS

🇪 Australia 57 Culgoa Circuit, O'Malley, Canberra, ACT 2606; ✆+61 2 6286 4770; f +61 2 6286 4795; ⊕ 09.00–12.00 & 14.00–17.00 Mon–Fri

🇪 Austria Beckmanngasse 10–12, A-1140 Vienna; ✆+43 1 894 2311; f +43 1 894 3174

🇪 Bulgaria Mladost-I, Andrei Sakharov 4, 1784 Sophia; ✆+359 2 975 3340/974 6100; f +359 2 974 5567 / 6111

🇪 China Ritan Bei Lu, Jianguomenwai, Beijing, 100600; ✆+86 10 6532 1186/6532 1154 (protocol); f +86 10 6532 4862. The biggest DPRK embassy & one of Beijing's biggest.

🇪 Cuba Calle 17 No 752 esq a Paseo, Vedado, Havana; ✆+53 7 662313 f +53 7 333073

🇪 Czech Republic Na Zaacutetorce 6/89, 160, 00 Prague 6; ✆+420 2 2432 0783; f +420 2 2431 8817; ⊕ 08.00–12.00 & 13.00–17.00

🇪 France 47 rue Chaveau, 92200 Neuilly-sur-Seine; ✆+33 1 47 47 53 85; f +33 1 47 47 61 41

🇪 Germany Glinkastrasse 7, D-10117, Berlin; ✆+49 30 2062 5990; f +49 3022 6519 29; e info@dprkorea-emb.de

🇪 Hong Kong DPRK Consulate Room 4007, 40/F China Resources Building, 26 Harbour Rd; ✆+852 28034447; f +852 2577 3644

🇪 Hungary Beckmanngasse 10–12, 1140 Vienna; ✆+43 1 894 2313; f +43 1 894 3174; e d.v.r.korea.botschaft@chello.at

🇪 India D 14, Maharani Bagh 110065 New Delhi; ✆+91 11 26829644; f +91 11 26829645

🇪 Indonesia Jl. Teluk Betung No. 2, Jakarta 12050; ✆+62 21 3190 8425/8437; f +62 21 3190 8445/8419; e dprkorea@rad.net.id

🇪 Italy Via Ludovico Di Savoia 23, 00185 Rome; ✆+39 6 7720 9094; f +39 6 7720 9111; e permerepun@hotmail.com

🇪 Lebanon Mousaitbeh, PO Box 9636; ✆+961 (1) 311490/868722

🇪 Malaysia No 4, Persiaran Madge, off Jalan U Thant, 55000, Kuala Lumpur; ✆ +60 3 4256 9913/4251 6713; f +60 3 4256 9933/4251 6719

🇪 Mongolia Huvisgalchdiin St, Chingeltei duureg, PO Box 1015, Ulaanbaatar 15160; ✆+976 11 326153; f +976 11 325663

🇪 Netherlands Only the Dutch Embassy in Seoul: Koybo Bldg, 14th Flr, Chongro 1-ga, Chongro-gu, Seoul 110-714; ✆+82 2 737 9514/6; f +82 2 735132

🇪 Poland ul. Bobrowiecka 1 A, 00-728 Warsaw; ✆local: +48 022 840 5813; f +48 022 840 5710; e korembpl@yahoo.com

🇪 Romania Sos Nordului nr 6, sector 1, Bucharest; ✆/f +40 (21) 232 9665; ⊕ 08.00–17.00 Mon–Fri

🇪 Russia (& Ukraine) 72 Mosfilmovskaya St, Moscow, 119590; ✆+7 499 143 6231; f +7 499 143 6312; ⊕ 09.00–12.00 & 14.00–18.00

🇪 Singapore 7500A Beach Rd, 09 320, The Plaza, 199591; ✆+65 6440 3498; f +65 6348 2026

🇪 South Africa 958 Waterpoort St, PO Box 1238, Faerie Glen Pretoria; ✆+27 12 991 8661; f +27 12 991 8662; e dprkembassy@lantic.net

🇪 Sweden (also for Latvia, Denmark, Lithuania, Finland) Norra Kungsvaegan 39, 181 31 Lindingoe; ✆+46 8 767 3836; f +46 8 767 3835

🇪 Switzerland Pourtalesstrasse 43, 3074 Muri bei Bern; ✆+41 31 951 66 21; f +41 31 951 5704; e dprk.embassy@bluewin.ch

🇪 Thailand 14 Muban Suanlaemthong 2 (soi 28), Phattanakan Rd, Suan Luang, Bangkok 10250; ✆+66 2 319 2686; f +66 2 318 6333

🇪 UK 73 Gunnersbury Av, London W5 4LP; ✆+44 20 8992 4965; f +44 20 8992 2053

🇪 US 820 Second Av, 13th Flr, New York, NY 10017; ✆+1 212 972 3105/3106; f +1 212 972 3154. The DPRK Mission in the US is really the Permanent Mission to the United Nations. DPRK officials are restricted to within a 25-mile perimeter of the building.

GETTING THERE AND AWAY

BY AIR The DPRK's national carrier is **Air Koryo** (*http://www.airkoryo.com. kp/en*). While that airline technically no longer has the monopoly on flights to the country (Air China now does a regular thrice-weekly Beijing–Pyongyang hop), Air Koryo acts as if it still does and its customer service is in want of renovation.

On the plus side, Air Koryo has upgraded its international fleet to new Tupolev 204-100s and 204-300s. The airline website says of these planes that 'Tupolev 204-100 is expected favourable comments as in case of Tupolev 204-300.' Unfortunately, however, that has materialised in the form of the EU repealing its 2004 ban of the airline from its air space, but then again Air Koryo hadn't flown its good-old-socialist-days routes to Berlin and Sofia via Moscow for years before that. Its Tupolevs may be known for cross-dressing as military planes on occasion, but its ex-forces pilots are known for their skill and have been noted for not taking risks that other pilots under greater commercial pressures might dare take. And its website, derided on debut for being defunct, now works. That said, you can't book a ticket without a visa and visas come via whoever's inviting the visitor.

Air Koryo operates regular international flights to Beijing, Shenyang and Vladivostok. The airline has also semi-regular flights to Khabarovsk, Bangkok and Macau, and there have been occasional/one-off charters to Seoul, Kuwait, Singapore and Kuala Lumpur. The airline's domestic schedule reputedly flies Pyongyang to Chongjin, Hamhung, Kaesong, Kilju, Kanggye, Sinuiju and Wonsan, but times, prices and availability for foreigners are not in the public domain. Specialist charter flights to Chongjin for visits to Mount Paektu are arrangeable (see page 245).

Baggage allowances are 20kg for economy class, 30kg for business. Don't get upset if you see these that restrictions do not seem to apply for locals. Chinese airports used to charge a 'construction tax' for those leaving on international flights, but this is now included in ticket prices. Air Koryo's prices to Russia have gone down of late, and to China they've gone up. Prices, times and schedule numbers for the international routes are listed here for late 2013 from the website, exclusive of tax and subject to exchange, so they're nominal and more illustrative than fixed. The same is true for the flight schedules.

Off-peak season is 1 January–31 March and 16 October–31 December. Peak season is 1 April–15 October. All flight listings below are run by Air Koryo unless otherwise noted.

From/to China
Flights between Pyongyang (FNJ) and Beijing (PEK) One-way:
economy US$287, business US$404; return: economy US$507, business US$725.

Tue & Sat JS151 leaves Pyongyang 09.00, arrives Beijing 09.55
Tue & Sat JS152 leaves Beijing 12.55, arrives Pyongyang 16.00
Mon & Fri JS151 leaves Pyongyang 09.00, arrives Beijing 10.00

Mon & Fri JS152 leaves Beijing 12.00, arrives Pyongyang 15.00
Thu JS251 leaves Pyongyang 09.00/10.30, arrives Beijing 10.00/11.30
Thu JS252 leaves Beijing 12.00/14.05, arrives Pyongyang 15.00/17.00

Air China's schedule is as follows:
Mon, Wed, Thu & Fri CA121 leaves Beijing 13.40, arrives Pyongyang 16.20
Mon, Wed, Thu & Fri CA122 leaves Pyongyang 17.20, arrives Beijing 18.05

85

Flights between Pyongyang (FNJ) and Shenyang (SHE)
One-way: economy US$224, business US$262; return: economy US$432, business US$465.

Tue, Wed & Sat JS155 leaves Pyongyang 12.00, arrives Shenyang 12.10
Tue, Wed & Sat JS156 leaves Shenyang 14.10, arrives Pyongyang 16.20

Flights between Pyongyang (FNJ) and Yanji (YNJ)
During the year's more clement months there is a charter flight to Yanji in China's Yanbian province, admittedly a route that's hogged by Yanbian travel agents, going at US$650 for a round-trip.

Thu JS541 leaves Pyongyang 09.00, arrives Yanji 09.30
Thu JS542 leaves Yanji 10.30, arrives Pyongyang 13.00.

From/to Russia
Flights between Pyongyang (FNJ) and Vladivostok (VVO)
(There is no departure tax for Russia's airports at present.) One-way: economy US$206, business US$273; return: economy US$372, business US$517.

Mon & Fri JS271 leaves Pyongyang 08.20, arrives Vladivostok 12.00
Mon & Fri JS272 leaves Vladivostok 14.20, arrives Pyongyang 14.00
Wed JS271 leaves Pyongyang 08.00, arrives Vladivostok 11.50
Wed JS272 leaves Vladivostok 13.50, arrives Pyongyang 13.40

Flights between Pyongyang (FNJ) and Khabarovsk (KHV)
This route used to fly on Mondays & Fridays at the following times. Any resumption in service might see prices very approximately around US$300 one-way, US$600 return.

Mon & Fri JS253 leaves Pyongyang 09.50, arrives Khabarovsk 14.00
Mon & Fri JS254 leaves Khabarovsk 16.00, arrives Pyongyang 16.10

From/to Shanghai, Bangkok and Macau
The following information about Air Koryo charter flights to Shanghai, Bangkok & Macau is solely illustrative, for possible destinations, flight numbers & duration.

Flights between Pyongyang (FNJ) and Shanghai (PVG)
Pyongyang–Shanghai (PVG) flight went twice a week: JS 551 Pyongyang–Shanghai 17.00; JS 552 Shanghai–Pyongyang, taking over 3hrs.

Flights between Pyongyang (FNJ) and Bangkok (BKK)
These used to go once a week: JS153 Pyongyang–Bangkok & JS154 Bangkok–Pyongyang, taking 5hrs.

Flights between Pyongyang (FNJ) and Macau (MFM)
These went twice a week: JS187 Pyongyang–Macau and JS188 Macau–Pyongyang taking 4hrs. Charter flights to Harbin & Xian have also been available in the past.

Air Koryo offices abroad
China Swissotel, Hong Kong-Macau Center, Dong Si Shi, Tiao Li Jiao Qiao, Beijing 100027; +86 10 6501 1557/1559, (airport) +86 10 6459 1253; f +86 10 6501 2591; e airkoryo_bjs@hotmail.com. Also at Qibaoshan Hotel (Chilbosan Hotel), No 81, Shiywei Rd, Heping District, Shenyang; +86 24 2325 1922/1937; f +86 24 2325 1936; e gacasy@silibank.com
Germany 65 D-10117, Berlin; +49 306 765003; f +49 306 0540496; e ber-airkoryo@hotmail.com
Kuwait Office 10, 2nd floor, Mghateer complex 31, Block 40, Al Farwaniyah; +965 2392 0460; f +965 2392 0461; e airkoryo-kw@live.com
Macau Rua da Praia Grade 55, 20 Andar-C, Centro Commercial 'Hoi Vong'; (town) +853 353 6634/353 6635, (airport) +853 861329/861111 (ext) 3878; f (town) +853 356631, (airport) +853 861329
Thailand Room 942/135.4, 4th Flr, Charn Issara Tower, Rama 4 Rd, Bangrak, Bangkok 10500; +66 2 234 2805/6, 535 3974, (airport) 535 5974; f +66 2 267 5009
Russia 101000 Mosfilmovskaya 72, Moscow; +7 95 143 6307; f +7 95 1476300; e moscow-minhang@stream.ru; Also at 41 Portovaya St, Artyom Primorski Krai, Vladivostok airport; 692800; f +7 4332 307684; e airkoryoinvvo@mail.ru

Other airlines have come and gone over the years. **MIAT Mongolian Airlines** has been known to charter, and in 2004 **China Southern Beifang** airlines commenced 45-minute flights from Shenyang to Pyongyang, Mondays and Fridays, departing Shenyang at 07.30 and making the return leg from Pyongyang at 10.00, but these dried up. So did **China Northern** flights between Beijing–Shenyang–Pyongyang. **China Southern** (*www.cs-air.com/en*) had at times a thrice-weekly route from Beijing to Pyongyang, CZ6021 going there and CZ6022 coming back, and also from Shenyang to Pyongyang, but no more. In good times with the ROK, Korean Air and Asiana Air have flown to Pyongyang on charters. Direct flights from Seoul to Pyongyang remain the preserve of high-level diplomacy. Aeroflot flew to Pyongyang until 2000 – check www.aeroflot.ru. What may happen with upgrades to the DPRK's airports is anyone's guess.

As of 2013, the distinctive old-style concrete and glass terminal at Pyongyang's Sunan airport, with a picture of Kim Il Sung and 평양 PYONGYANG in massive red neon, has been knocked down. While a new airport is being built, the temporary arrangement is for all arrivals and departures to go through a large, open-plan hanger-like building, with not much by way of duty free and a café at the entrance selling espresso at US$5 a go. One can see on touchdown, however, much of Air Koryo's Soviet-era fleet, which aviation enthusiasts can check out on specially arranged tours.

BY RAIL
From/to Beijing There is a very regular international rail service from Beijing to Pyongyang. The T27 leaves Beijing railway station (just inside the second ring road, south of Jianguomenwai Street) at 17.29 on Mondays, Wednesdays, Thursdays and Saturdays, arriving in Pyongyang the next day at 18.00. The Pyongyang service T28 to Beijing leaves at 10.40 on the same days. The Saturday train used to have a carriage ultimately bound for Moscow and getting the train directly from Moscow to Pyongyang was becoming increasingly popular in the noughties, but is not running as of 2014. Fares are substantially higher now (mainly due to increases in the price of crossing the border, a Chinese hike).

At Dandong and Sinuiju, the two cities straddling the Yalu River border between China and DPRK, the international carriages (Chinese, Korean and Russian) get detached from the long local trains and pushed across the bridge, from the arms of one side's customs officers into the clutches of the other. Both groups take two hours to sift through your papers and possibly bags. Snack pedlars trawl the train corridors and platforms on the Chinese side, selling noodles to be cooked from each carriage's scalding hot-water urn. If possible, bring lots of savoury picnic foods with a mind to share them with your Korean co-passengers, who'll likely share theirs with you. The charmingly shabby Korean restaurant car has many dishes for around €3–5 and loads of *soju* (see page 97). The restaurant car on the Chinese side can do a spread for 80CNY each, but be prepared to grab a table early and then wait, as they don't cook until the train starts to leave. And even if you're there before everyone, any delegation of government officials will get served first.

As many tours involve a plane going in and a train going out (or vice versa), the cost of the train is included in the tour price. Add to that that return tickets aren't available as such, instead one would buy two one-way tickets, and booking fees and your nationality are all variables to the final price. But as an idea, in 2014, they were quoted as 1,692CNY for a soft-sleeper and 1,164CNY for a hard-sleeper.

Boarding points *en route* are Tianjin, Shenyang and Dandong. In China, either buy the tickets from the station or go to the informative, English-speaking BTG 69

Ticketing Co Ltd (*Tourism Tower, 28 Jianguomenwai, Beijing 100022, China;* \+86 10 6515 0093/24, 6515 8844/2111; f +86 10 6515 8564/5292).

From/to Vladivostok There is also the rail route direct from Pyongyang via Rajin-Sonbong into Russia to Vladivostok (a route that was used by Kim Jong Il who preferred going by train to flying). For foreigners it's an irregularly plied route to say the least and not available at the time of writing. But it's worth asking about: every question becomes a suggestion.

Rail developments Pre-division Korea was traversed by railways, with the main lines being the Kyongi that went down the west coast and the Donghae along the eastern side via Wonsan. The country's division saw the tracks taken up and blown up in the war, but the rail lines were re-established across the DMZ in 2007. The Kyongi line is in use taking freight from Hyundai's Kaesong industrial zone into the ROK, but the Donghae line is not in use, as the ROK considers its Kumgangsan resort to be closed. Nonetheless, there is work under way to have all Korea linked again by rail and have the Trans-Siberian and Trans-Manchurian railways ultimately connect all the way through to the bottom of the ROK and transport Korean freight into Asia and to Europe far faster than by ship. One day...

BY SEA There's no direct sea connection from the ROK to the DPRK. Ferries run from Inchon port in the ROK to Dandong, China, and back three times a week (for details, see page 262), and from Dandong they can cross into Sinuiju, DPRK (see page 252). Tourists can also sail from the ROK port of Sokcho to Zarubino port in Russia, then go overland via Russia and China to the Chinese side of Paektusan (what the Chinese call Changbaishan) – but they can't cross into the DPRK there. Visas for China and Russia are required (see pages 82–3).

Hyundai Asan used to run ferries from its terminal at Sokcho port in the ROK to Kumgangsan in the DPRK, but that route closed in 2008. Also not running at the time of writing is the thrice-a-month ferry service from Wonsan port, DPRK to Niigata, Japan and back that served as a vital cultural and economic link for hundreds of thousands of Korean residents in Japan loyal to the North. A lack of diplomatic ties between the North and Japan always precluded non-Korean Japanese from taking this one-day voyage in any case. The situation for each of these services may change so ask tour operators.

BY ROAD Road access into the DPRK is bitty. There are a handful of road links into the DPRK from China – at Sinuiju, Namyang (to go to Hoeryong which has a bridge for Chinese visitors), and the Rason Zone and Tumangang, which also has a crossing point into Russia. Very short tours from Dandong into Sinuiju go by bus.

There are two road links from the ROK that cross the DMZ into the DPRK. Tourist buses used to run to Kumgangsan on the east coast, organised through www.hyundai-asan.com and www.mtkumgang.com, but that route closed in 2008 and those websites are moribund for now. Of greater use may be the south's official tourist office, via http://english.visitkorea.or.kr.

There is however a freight road from the Kaesong industrial zone that's still (usually) open, and in 2013 a motorcycle tour took that route to drive from the DPRK into the ROK. It was a one-off trip, however, that took a lot of preparation. Previously there had been motorcycle tours that came by ferry from the south into the DPRK, costing US$1,000 and run by the Federation Internationale de Motocyclisme (*www.fim-live.com/en*), the Korea Motorcycle Federation and the

Asian Motorcycle Touring Association, but that was years ago and overall it's an extremely infrequent mode of tourist travel.

HEALTH   *with Dr Felicity Nicholson*

VACCINATIONS The only requirement for vaccination is for a yellow fever vaccine for travellers over one year of age entering North Korea from a yellow fever endemic area. There is no actual risk of disease in North Korea. With regard to other vaccinations it is wise to be up to date with diphtheria, tetanus and polio (ten-yearly), hepatitis A and typhoid.

Hepatitis A vaccine (Havrix Monodose or Avaxim) comprises two injections given about a year apart. The course costs about £100, but may be available on the NHS; it protects for 25 years and can be administered even close to the time of departure. The disease risk in North Korea is considered to be moderate to high.

The newer injectable typhoid vaccines (eg: Typhim Vi) last for three years and are about 85% effective. Oral capsules (Vivotif) are a viable alternative for those aged six or above who are not immunosuppressed who prefer not to have injections. Three capsules taken on alternate days provide protection for three years. They should be encouraged unless the traveller is leaving within a few days for a trip of a week or less, when the vaccine would not be effective in time. For longer trips or trips to more rural areas, especially in the heaviest rain months of July and August, **Japanese encephalitis** vaccine will be recommended. The course comprises two injections over a minimum of 24 days.

Hepatitis B vaccine would be recommended for health care workers and those working with children. It is also likely to be recommended for longer trips or where there is a likelihood of risky behaviour. If Engerix B vaccine is used, the course comprises three doses given at zero, seven and 21. This rapid course is licensed only for those 18 or over, but can be used off license for those aged 16–18. For younger travellers the shortest course is over eight weeks, which means it is wise to organise vaccinations well in advance of your trip.

Vaccinations for **rabies** are ideally advised for all travellers as it is unlikely that North Korea will have all the treatment needed to protect against developing rabies. This is even more important for those visiting more remote areas as it will take even longer to reach help (see *Rabies*, page 91).

Tuberculosis (TB) is spread through close respiratory contact and occasionally through infected milk or milk products. It is very common in North Korea with an incidence of more than 409 cases per 100,000 population (WHO 2012). BCG should be considered if you have not had this before and are likely to be mixing with the local population for stays of three months or more. Experts differ over whether a BCG vaccination against tuberculosis (TB) is useful in adults: discuss this with your travel clinic.

There are no reciprocal health care agreements with Britain, so ensure that you have comprehensive medical insurance and that you carry adequate supplies of any prescribed medication that you usually take.

TRAVEL CLINICS AND HEALTH INFORMATION A full list of current travel clinic websites worldwide is available on www.istm.org. For other journey preparation information, consult www.nathnac.org/ds/map_world.aspx (UK) or wwwnc.cdc.gov/travel/ (US). Information about various medications may be found on www.netdoctor.co.uk/travel. All advice found online should be used in conjunction with expert advice received prior to or during travel.

Personal first-aid kit A minimal kit contains:

- A good drying antiseptic, eg: iodine or potassium permanganate (don't take antiseptic cream)
- A few small dressings (Band-Aids)
- Suncream
- Insect repellent; impregnated bed-net or permethrin spray
- Aspirin or paracetamol
- Antifungal cream (eg: Canesten)
- Ciprofloxacin or norfloxacin, for severe diarrhoea
- Tinidazole for giardia or amoebic dysentery (see below for regime)
- Antibiotic eye drops, for sore, 'gritty', stuck-together eyes (conjunctivitis)
- A pair of fine-pointed tweezers (to remove caterpillar hairs, thorns, splinters, coral, etc)
- Alcohol-based hand rub or bar of soap in plastic box
- Condoms or femidoms

IN NORTH KOREA Medical facilities in North Korea as a whole are basic, particularly in the rural areas. Hospitals and clinics in the latter are usually able to offer only the very minimum medical care. Clinical hygiene is poor, anaesthetics

LONG-HAUL FLIGHTS, CLOTS AND DVT   *Dr Felicity Nicholson*

Any prolonged immobility, including travel by land or air, can result in deep-vein thrombosis (DVT) with the risk of embolus to the lungs. Certain factors can increase the risk and these include:

- Previous clot or a close relative with a history
- Being over 40, with increased risk over 80 years old
- Recent major operation or varicose-veins surgery
- Cancer
- Stroke
- Heart disease
- Obesity
- Pregnancy
- Hormone therapy
- Heavy smoking
- Severe varicose veins
- Being very tall (over 6ft/1.8m) or short (under 5ft/1.5m)

A deep-vein thrombosis causes painful swelling and redness of the calf or sometimes the thigh. It is only dangerous if a clot travels to the lungs (pulmonary embolus). Symptoms of a pulmonary embolus (PE) – which commonly start three to ten days after a long flight – include chest pain, shortness of breath, and sometimes coughing up small amounts of blood. Anyone who thinks that they might have a DVT needs to see a doctor immediately.

To **prevent DVT**, try the following: keep mobile before and during the flight; move around every couple of hours; drink plenty of fluids during the flight; avoid taking sleeping pills and excessive tea, coffee and alcohol; and consider wearing flight socks or support stockings (see *www.legshealth.com*). If you think you are at increased risk of a clot, ask your doctor if it is safe to travel.

are frequently unavailable, and the electricity supply to the hospitals (even in the capital) can be intermittent. You should try to avoid serious surgery if you can. Take with you any medication you think you are likely to require because supplies are limited and very difficult to buy. Tourist sites may offer medical facilities.

Use bottled water for drinking and brushing teeth. Avoid dairy products, which are likely to have been made with unpasteurised milk, and boil milk (or use powdered or tinned milk, using pure water in the reconstitution process). Ensure meat and fish are well cooked, and served hot. Be wary of pork, salad and mayonnaise, and always cook vegetables and peel fruit. If in doubt:

PEEL IT, BOIL IT, COOK IT OR FORGET IT

Malaria There is a risk of malaria due to the benign *Plasmodium vivax* all year round. The risk is limited and is confined to some southern areas. At the time of writing, prophylaxis in the form of tablets is usually not advised though this advice may change for those considered more at risk, e.g. the pregnant or immunocompromised traveller. Prevention against mosquito bites is paramount so it is advised to use insect repellents containing 50–55% DEET from dusk until dawn (the mosquitoes that carry the disease emerge at this time). It is also wise to wear clothing to cover arms and legs and to make your sleeping accommodation as mosquito proof as possible.

Rabies Rabies is carried by all mammals but the most likely culprits are dogs and related species and bats. It is passed on to man through a bite, scratch or a lick of an open wound. You must always assume any animal is rabid as they can appear quite healthy, and seek medical help as soon as possible. Meanwhile scrub the wound with soap under a running tap or while pouring water from a jug. Find a reasonably clear-looking source of water (but at this stage the quality of the water is not important), then pour on a strong iodine or alcohol solution of gin, whisky or rum. This helps stop the rabies virus entering the body and will guard against wound infections, including tetanus.

Pre-exposure vaccinations for rabies is ideally advised for everyone, but is particularly important if you intend to have contact with animals and/or are likely to be more than 24 hours away from medical help. Three doses of vaccine should be taken over a minimum of 21 days to change the treatment needed. Contrary to popular belief these vaccinations are relatively painless.

If you are bitten, scratched or licked over an open wound by a sick animal, then post-exposure prophylaxis should be given as soon as possible, though it is never too late to seek help, as the incubation period for rabies can be very long. Those who have not been immunised will need a full course of injections and will also need a blood product called Rabies Immunoglobulin (RIG) injected around the wound. RIG is very hard to come by as there is a worldwide shortage. It is extremely unlikely that it will be available in North Korea so it will involve evacuating to a country that has supplies, eg: Hong Kong. If you have had all three doses of rabies vaccine before the exposure then you will no longer need the RIG and would only need to get two further doses of rabies vaccine, ideally given three days apart but can be up to seven days apart. Although the vaccine is moderately expensive the course of rabies vaccine provides long-term cover (unless you are a vet working abroad when regular boosts or blood tests are recommended). And remember that, if you do contract rabies, mortality is 100% and death from rabies is probably one of the worst ways to go.

Ticks and related diseases There is a possibility of tick-borne diseases in North Korea, including tick-borne encephalitis (Far East strain) and Lyme disease. Ticks are more prevalent during the summer months so travellers walking in forested areas would be advised to wear cover-up clothing including long trousers tucked into boots, socks, long-sleeved tops and a hat. At the end of the day always check for ticks. Pay particular attention to the hair line and behind the ears as ticks can easily be missed.

Ticks should ideally be removed as soon as possible as leaving them on the body increases the chance of infection. They should be removed with special tick tweezers that can be bought in good travel shops. Failing that you can use your finger nails: grasp the tick as close to your body as possible and pull steadily and firmly away at right angles to your skin. The tick will then come away complete, as long as you do not jerk or twist. If possible douse the wound with alcohol (any spirit will do) or iodine. Irritants (eg: Olbas oil) or lit cigarettes are to be discouraged since they can cause the ticks to regurgitate and therefore increase the risk of disease. It is best to get a travelling companion to check you for ticks; if you are travelling with small children, remember to check their heads, and particularly behind the ears.

Spreading redness around the bite and/or fever and/or aching joints after a tick bite imply that you have an infection that may require antibiotic treatment, so seek advice.

HIV/AIDS While North Korea still publicly declares itself as HIV-free, there are risks of this infection and other sexually transmitted disease, whether you sleep with fellow travellers or locals. The majority of HIV infections in British heterosexuals

TREATING TRAVELLERS' DIARRHOEA *Dr Jane Wilson-Howarth*

It is dehydration that makes you feel awful during a bout of diarrhoea and the most important part of treatment is drinking lots of clear fluids. Sachets of oral rehydration salts give the perfect biochemical mix to replace all that is pouring out of your bottom but other recipes taste nicer. Any dilute mixture of sugar and salt in water will do you good: try Coke or orange squash with a three-finger pinch of salt added to each glass (if you are salt-depleted you won't taste the salt). Otherwise make a solution of a four-finger scoop of sugar with a three-finger pinch of salt in a 500ml glass. Or add eight level teaspoons of sugar (18g) and one level teaspoon of salt (3g) to one litre (five cups) of safe water. A squeeze of lemon or orange juice improves the taste and adds potassium, which is also lost in diarrhoea. Drink two large glasses after every bowel action, and more if you are thirsty. These solutions are still absorbed well if you are vomiting, but you will need to take sips at a time. If you are not eating you need to drink three litres a day plus whatever is pouring into the toilet. If you feel like eating, take a bland, high carbohydrate diet. Heavy greasy foods will probably give you cramps.

If the diarrhoea is bad, or you are passing blood or slime, or you have a fever, you will probably need antibiotics in addition to fluid replacement. A dose of norfloxacin or ciprofloxacin repeated twice a day until better may be appropriate (if you are planning to take an antibiotic with you, note that both norfloxacin and ciprofloxacin are available only on prescription in the UK). If the diarrhoea is greasy and bulky and is accompanied by sulphurous (eggy) burps, one likely cause is giardia. This is best treated with tinidazole (four x 500mg in one dose, repeated seven days later if symptoms persist).

are acquired abroad. If you must indulge, use condoms or femidoms, which help reduce the risk of transmission. If you notice any genital ulcers or discharge, get treatment promptly since other infections increase the risk of acquiring HIV. If you do have unprotected sex, visit a clinic as soon as possible; this should be within 24 hours, though may be considered up to two weeks, for post-exposure prophylaxis.

SAFETY

Petty theft has happened from hotels and other accommodation, so be sure to keep your valuables and passport in safe keeping at all times. Incidents of other crimes against foreigners are very infrequently heard of. Take out full insurance coverage for health, belongings and flights, and cash to cover the trip because the ability to get hold of emergency funds is negligible. Bring all medication that you need and don't expect to get hold of any with any ease in the country. Some form of ID is needed at all times. Visit www.fco.gov.uk for up-to-date advice.

Children and babies on tours have been very well looked after, but under no circumstances should anyone, especially children and babies, drink the tap water.

Disabled travellers have also been well tended to.

WHAT TO TAKE

The DPRK's once rapid development stalled from the late 1980s, and the country's economic malaise and sanctions means there is a lot of very basic essentials you'll have to bring in. In the DPRK, do not expect to find batteries, chargers, memory sticks, camera memory cards, discs, etc.

The electricity system is 220v/60Hz, flat- or round-pin plugs but, outside Pyongyang's top hotels, power cuts are frequent, even regular and long. Use the time in Pyongyang to charge up your electricals, bring both flat- and round-pin plug convertors and don't be surprised if the plug socket disintegrates in your hand. Also take the following:

- Copies of all your documents. There are no facilities for you to photocopy anything in the DPRK.
- Insect repellent
- A small first-aid kit, with headache pills, contact lens solutions and enough of your own medication (do not rely on getting it in the DPRK; for a suggested contents list, see box, page 90).
- A powerful torch (and batteries) for the lack of street-lighting and evening power-cuts, preferably one that doubles as a lamp for night reading to supplement the low-watt lighting (when it's on)
- Cigarettes, including quality American brands, are appreciated as gifts for the male guides, while female guides go for chocolate
- Instant coffee and any snacks you can't live without
- Good reading matter, including this book (!) and any worthy tomes you can donate to the Taedonggang Diplomatic Club (see page 126) to please the fledgling expat community (for whom tonic water is worth its weight in gold!)

MONEY

The average visitor should forget credit cards, debit cards and cheques. It's a cash economy in which the hard-currency shops and bars take Chinese Yuan Renminbi

(CNY), euros and US dollars. The foreign hard currency that can be most easily used, but with the worst exchange rate, is CNY.

The DPRK's local currency is won, and it's obtainable for long-term residents, NGO workers and businesspeople at a conversion rate of roughly 130 won to the US dollar (obviously this is something to check; see www.xe.com for up-to-date rates), but short-term visitors will have next to no opportunities to get hold of any won – *except* in the Rason zone in the far northeast of the country (see page 232). It's as good as impossible to obtain DPRK won outside the country, and it is illegal to take it out of the DPRK.

Don't be misled by prices you see that are given in local won and then do some mental maths. Local won prices are as good as meaningless for what foreigners will pay. Low denomination notes and coins are best. The Koreans don't short change, but they may simply not have change, and you could get a mix of CNY and euros or be given another bottle or water, or maybe even a small cake or tea bag, which is really rather charming in a Paddington Bear kind of way. This can be an opportunity to ask for local won in small change.

If you've come unprepared and are loaded with notes from home, convertible currencies at the very few exchange facilities in Pyongyang are Japanese yen (JPY), British pounds sterling (GBP), Hong Kong dollars (HKD), Canadian dollars (CAD), Australian dollars (AUD) and New Zealand dollars (NZD). Foreign exchange is available at the Trade Bank or its agents, and at hotels and some restaurants. The Trade Bank opens from 09.00 to 12.00 and from 14.00 to 17.00 except Sundays, but don't bank on it, especially if you're on a tour. It's still an effort to spend money in the country. The tour company you use will specify the currency in which they need payment. Travellers' cheques issued in euros are usable in the bank but not in hotels or shops.

There is a local debit card system called *narae* ('wing') in use at major shops and restaurants, with which you may see your guides paying for a meal, but it's for locals and foreigners with long-term interests in the country.

The local currency was revalued in 2009 and notes from before that time may be bought as souvenirs, but they have no intrinsic value as useable currency. Incidentally, foreign tourists used to get 'foreigner won', a special tourist currency with suspiciously low serial numbers, a limit on the number of shops accepting it and a surprising inability to be converted back into hard currency. Luckily this near-as-useless Monopoly money was phased out in 2002.

For further information on budgeting and tour costs, see pages 81–2.

GETTING AROUND

DPRK transportation is limited, because to travel from town to town and province to province everyone needs a permit, locals and foreign visitors alike (you see the checkpoints around the cities). Locals need good reason to get one from the authorities, which also means the demand, and the need, for inter-conurbation transport isn't there. Foreign visitors' hosts arrange permits in accord with the visitors' itineraries. Tourists can only take **buses** and **trams** in Pyongyang as part of a tour. Local bus routes going beyond Pyongyang are for all practical purposes non-existent.

Cross-country travel by **train** is now becoming a regular possibility, with trains going to Myohyangsan, and over to Wonsan, Hamhung and Chongjin. Hitherto, rail travel was restricted to the Pyongyang–Dandong–Beijing train or very niche tours, and services were very intermittent in any case. But connecting the capital to the northeast of the country, an area once only accessible by plane, is a very interesting development, mainly as visitors will see the up-close pristine mountains and coastal areas that they previously flew over. They'll also take in views and towns that the road journeys miss, putting within range towns like Kimchaek or Sinpho, and on a far smoother mode of transport amid a moving time warp of 1970s carriages behind stylish Korean-built locomotives. Americans are also allowed on these trains (although they're still not allowed on the Pyongyang–Beijing train). Again, though, you don't just turn up and get on. Timetables are not readily available and tickets must be bought through agents before the day of departure – actions undertaken by tour operators.

For domestic **air travel**, foreigners can charter flights to Mount Paektu and Chongjin. As everywhere, reconfirm international flight tickets some days before travel, although this is likely to be done by the visitors' receiving party. **Bicycles** are scarce, are not available for hire and nor are **cars** except **taxis**. International driving permits are not valid but foreign nationals resident in DPRK can obtain local driving licences after taking a driving test. Locals walk short distances or **hitchhike** long distances in army trucks. It's unlikely you'll need to hold aloft your magic cigarettes. You and your group will be ferried about right from the airport in an **official bus or car**, which is clean and comfortable – and traffic jams are mostly unheard of, such that if you get involved in one in Pyongyang, it still counts as an 'event'. Beyond the cities, the roads stretch away as straight as runways, empty of cars, road markings, cat's eyes and lights but with beautifully tended verges and central reservations.

ACCOMMODATION

Hotels come in deluxe, first, second and third class, and there are also guesthouses. The local press often report that the top hotels are 'full' with foreign guests and delegates. It's preferred that you stay in the deluxe hotels, and you'll be informed that it's not because they need hard currency more but that this is the regulation, or the other hotels are too inferior for honoured guests; maybe their electricity and hot-water supplies are too unreliable (and yet they're all always full). In short, it is not impossible to go cheaper, and there are more hotels becoming available as new builds and renovated hotels are reclassified in higher grades. But tours are package deals, based on long-standing arrangements with the hotels already stated on the itineraries long before travel, and for the sake of hassle and considering just how good a top-flight DPRK hotel is, quibbling over a few notes ... well, most people don't. The prices and ranges listed are essentially a gauge for those non-tourist visitors or specialist tourists. The most common default position is tourists share rooms, and perfect strangers become 'roomies'. Any visitor should say before travel if they want a single room, for which they'll be charged an extra supplement.

There are still local hotels in which no foreigner can stay, but the grading of foreigners – the practice in which some nationalities stayed at some places while others stayed elsewhere – is becoming less marked. Nonetheless, Westerners tend to end up at the higher-grade places, for which the greater costs are justified by way of them having (more) secure hot water and power supplies; more restaurants with longer menus; more entertainment, from billiards to massage and sauna; and greater communications facilities.

It happens, though, particularly during busy times of year, that tour groups do not stay at their designated hotel but end up billeted somewhere else, possibly even in a different town, which is all part of the craic. If the new hotel is of the same class, that's that, but if it's of a lower class, there could be a fractional refund.

Hotels in the DPRK are banded as Deluxe (Top End), First Class (Upper Range), Second Class (Mid Range) or Third Class (loosely bracketed as Budget, and mostly only available to Westerners in the remotest parts).

Now it is said, in some parts, that the hotels and bars in the DPRK are so equipped that some folks don't have to actually be in the room to see and hear what's going on. No-one has satisfactorily proved that this is the case. However: 'We were in the lift of the Yanggakdo Hotel, going down from the 46th floor to the 44th. I pressed the floor 44 button and we started to descend, but the lift shot past the 44th, and I asked, "What's going on, we've missed the floor", whereupon the lift abruptly slowed, stopped somewhere around the 42nd floor, then rose slowly back to the 44th. We alighted without a further word!' (Anon)

EATING AND DRINKING

You will always be well fed in the DPRK. Apart from the handful of foreign restaurants in Pyongyang, North Korean fare is pretty basic stuff with many simple soups of eggs and bread for Westerners. The ubiquitous foods are pickled cabbage (*kimchi*), bread (*bang*) that comes as white-slice doorsteps, and white rice (*bab*) with vegetables and meat, and may contain remnants of husk; watch your teeth. Other regular dishes are potato (*gamja*) and egg (*dalgya*)-based soups (*gug*), stews (*jjigae*), casseroles (*jeon-gul*) and salads (*saengchae*). Chicken (*dakgogi*) and fish (*saengson*) are the most frequent meats (mullet fish and fish-head soups!). Neither pork nor beef is very commonly found, the latter because it's always been a 'controlled substance', rationed by the state, but it appears in Korean barbecues (beef is *pulgogi*, pork is *kalgi*) where a tray of coals are put centre-table and you fry away – great fun. Usually, set dinners are multi-coursed by separate, simple dishes that keep coming. A set of numerous small dishes for one is called *pansanggi*, and there's a version with spicier dishes of octopus (*nakji*), crab and salted fish like anchovies (*jeotgal*). For a feast on the coast, order steamed crab (*tang*) and a heaving great crab, intact and dead (hopefully) will be hurled onto the table. *Sinsollo* is a Korean version of hotpot, with sliced meats, vegetables and egg stewed and broiled together in a doughnut-shaped 'chaffing' pot. Pyongyang cold buckwheat noodles (*naeng myun*) are another speciality actually found all over the country: very chewy pre-cooked noodles garnished in ice-cubed water. Very tasty and very heavy, a bowl of cold noodles is a meal in itself.

Don't drink the tap water! Bottled mineral water is widely available with two or three bottles going for a euro (sometimes water's given as change), but wherever possible stock up for the day ahead. Soft drinks are still mostly local, with lightly fizzy, sweet lemon juice (*remonadu*), lovely pear juice (*baeju*) and an apple juice (*saguaju*, which they call cider but is non-alcoholic) in bottles, along with a bitter cranberry-type juice.

RESTAURANT PRICE CODES

These prices are based on the average price of main course:

Expensive	$$$$$	€15+
Above average	$$$$	€10–15
Mid range	$$$	€6–10
Cheap and cheerful	$$	€3–6
Rock bottom	$	€1–3

There's also canned peach juice, but in the DPRK a man drinking peach juice is equivalent to prawn sandwiches at a football match. Coke and Pepsi appear and part like ghosts.

There are a few common beers (*maegju*), namely the light blue and gold-label RyongSong, a pleasantly light, lagery brew, the dark blue and gold-label Bonghak, and the green-labelled brews from the Taedonggang Brewery No 3, which produces a nice heavy ale, but also a rice-based one that's pretty foul. As its name suggests, the Taedonggang Brewery No 3 is based in Pyongyang, and is kitted out with the brewery equipment bought lock, stock and barrel from Ushers of Trowbridge, Wiltshire, imported into the DPRK in 2002 and very briefly advertised on Pyongyang television.

There are various local brewed draught beers at many of the hotels and bars around the country, with a nice tan-coloured draught beer available at the Yanggakdo, among other hoppy ales, or a dark, malty flagon-filler. Imports of Bavarian, Erdinger, Tiger and Heineken are becoming more available, and a few lagers in cans that suspiciously resemble Heineken.

Soju is the local rice wine, about 25% ABV, which is not only very cheap and available, but goes down very cleanly indeed. There's very little grape wine (*podoju*), but there are the other rice wines flavoured with apple, blueberry and wotnot (*cheongju, makgeoli*) but they're best avoided; even if you're instructed to buy some by a guide they're only doing it for a laugh. Otherwise there are often imported spirits like the ubiquitous Johnnie Walker and Remy cognac, as well as other brands of spirits no-one's heard of, like Finest Coventry Gin and Loch Inverness Scotch.

What there is very little of is real coffee. Some is served at great cost at the Viennese café on Kim Il Sung Square, and a lot of what coffee exists is poor-quality instant. The Yanggakdo serves weedy cups of instant, while coffee is available on order for €1 a go from the third-floor breakfast buffet at the Koryo Hotel, and even then it's still only instant!

NIGHTLIFE

Nightlife is restricted to a handful (but increasing number) of joints in Pyongyang, with most of the hotels having karaoke and late-opening if not all-night bars, or the Diplomat Club, but the real charm of the cities after dark comes with their quietness, which is notable by day but deafening at night. In 2002 I wrote that 'Pyongyang is mostly as dark and quiet as Korea's other cities and towns… and if you get the chance, try a night walk in the city. It is spectacularly beautiful and, I found, romantic to behold such a black, eerie calm in a capital city.' While that's very much true for many of the major cities outside Pyongyang, it's no longer the case for the capital, which now has way more traffic. More to the point however, many of Pyongyang's grander buildings are lit up long into the evening, a relatively new sight for visitors as the city

Practical Information NIGHTLIFE

2

97

The country used to shut down for winter but now it's possible to have Christmas in Pyongyang.

1 January	New Year's Day
16 February	Kim Jong Il's birthday
15 April	Kim Il Sung's birthday
25 April	Army Day
1 May	May Day
27 July	Victory Day
15 August	Independence from Japan Day
9 September	Republic Foundation Day
10 October	Korean Workers' Party Foundation Day
27 December	Constitution Day

suffered total blackouts for many years. And there is nothing more empty and silent than Kim Il Sung Square at 22.00, and the leaders' statues at Mansudae are all the more impressive when floodlit while other grand buildings are laced in neon. Night tours per se do not really happen, and so it's a grey area what could or could not be visited – for example, the Mansudae statues are definitely off-limits after dark, for now. But if cruising back to the Yanggakdo from the May Day stadium or the Kaeson funfair, a scenic route can be requested and the guide might ask the driver if he can s-l-o-w-l-y pass the major sites, if not outright stop.

Travellers have written before how they've sneaked out of their hotels at night to tour the city on foot – but don't do it. It's not worth the trouble for you or your guides (for more details on cultural etiquette, see pages 103–5).

SHOPPING

The Mayor had, at my request, notified to all the shopkeepers that I was anxious to buy any curios in porcelain or bronze, but nothing of any kind was brought to me, and the shops and stalls seemed quite bare of anything of the kind. Even silk and cotton goods were hidden away in shops of a very humble appearance, and such things as were exposed for sale were of the very commonest description. Sandals, tobaccos, pipes, and basket hats, were the most prominent articles for sale. There was besides a considerable sprinkling of Japanese goods … [and those] from Manchuria – Everything in fact here, as at Soul, testified to the extreme simplicity of the life of the people, and to the absence of anything but a retail trade.

W R Calres, HM Vice-Consul Shanghai (and formerly Corea), 1887

Korean shop titles are simply by function, 'Electrical Parts', 'Groceries', 'Children's Clothes', etc, not by the brands carried or the proprietor's name. Many offer services, like barber's shops, watch or electrical repairs. They serve the surrounding blocks, an administrative unit having about 5,000 inhabitants and called a *dong*. Each dong has a public bathhouse, post office and other services which the locals are ascribed to use there and nowhere else.

For the most part, your chances for shopping are limited to the hotel shops and a few department stores in the large cities, if you can get the shop assistants there to serve you. Unless they accept hard currency directly over the counter, buying stuff in shops involves the three-way system of going to the first till or counter where an assistant writes down what you're buying and its cost; you then take this chit to the cash till where you pay a second assistant who rips or stamps the chit or gives some other receipt, plus change (which may be a small cake or tea bag if they haven't got small enough notes or coins), that you then take back to the first assistant to get your goods. This is quite a quaint system that's amusing enough if you've got time to kill, but a total faff when large groups of visitors descend on a place, sometimes surprising the staff who start shouting down corridors for colleagues to come quick and man the tills, and the time-consuming queues quickly wreck tight tour schedules. A suggestion for saving time with large groups is for four or five people to put all their goods together and have one person pay for the lot.

The same system is in use in the shops used by locals, who pay with local won (which tourists aren't supposed to get, except in Rason), hence foreigners cannot shop in most stores and they often get shooed out as soon as they walk into a local grocery or whatnot. Rationed goods need ration coupons, which locals have, and foreigners don't.

Rumours of credit cards being accepted in a very few places are rumours. You can haggle up to a point in some shops, eg: if you're buying paintings, but they're not yet big on bartering so be discreet, and expect that North Korean haggling often goes along the lines of: they state the price, you make a lower bid, to which they say 'no', you raise your bid, they say 'no', you raise your bid again, they say 'no' and so on until you've bid back up to the original price.

But there are new trends. Farmers' markets have been in operation in the DPRK for some time, and these markets have now expanded to include all manner of other articles being bought and sold by middlemen trading items ranging from televisions to bicycles, or so it is reported. There are also growing numbers of small shops, variously backed by private retailers, by consortia of works units or as commercially run enterprises managed by the local resident units.

Where these markets are located however can be a sensitive question, and foreigners' access to them is still prohibited, but in southern Pyongyang there now exists the big blue Tongil market, full of stalls of foodstuffs and goods much like those found in Beijing, and this is surely the shape of things to come. There are still the large department stores, eg: Pyongyang's Department Store No 1, that have held a special place in the hearts of shoppers seeking to ferry coupons and chits from counter to counter just to buy a pair of socks. Even Pyongyang's Paradise supermarket with its dinky trollies sticks to this chit–cashier–receipt ballyhoo.

Western correspondents have traditionally loved to cite the big shops as the greatest proof of Potemkin pretensions, being filled to the ceilings with goods no-one is supposed to buy, but the days of such scoffing may be numbered. Markets are morphing into malls. There are as yet no chains of the likes of WalMart, Tesco or Carrefour, and plans by China's Zhongxu group to take over Pyongyang's Department Store No. 1 fizzled out. The DPRK has not yet got a retail market anything like on a proportional scale compared to China's, but the economy is growing, along with a consumer class and goods to serve them. In any case what one sees on streets everywhere are little private-owned gazebo-like kiosks of private sellers, and one can sometimes glimpse covered markets as the state's domination of supply and distribution of food and goods has been substantially reduced. When this nascent business grows into a roaring retail trade of chains and shops is anyone's guess.

Practically every hotel, and a few tourist sites, has some kind of shop selling souvenirs of books, CDs, badges and DVDs. Also available for purchase in the Foreign Language Bookshop, the Mansudae Art studio, the Koryo Hotel, and the

Koryo Museum in Kaesong, to name a few, are some beautiful paintings, prints, excellent embroideries and sometimes the spectacular hand-painted socialist-realist propaganda posters (although beware, the latter are not allowed to be taken out the country, which is enforced with varying strictness) along with Korea's own fruit-powered rice wines and herbal remedies (mainly ginseng). Fantastic stamps are also available from the stamp shop next to the Koryo Hotel and Kaesong's Koryo museum. It's even possible to have Kim Jong Il suits and other attire tailor-made on the third floor of the Yanggakdo for around €100. Whether the locals appreciate visitors dressing up in this way hasn't yet been fully gauged.

PHOTOGRAPHY

You can photograph fairly freely, but your guide might suggest (read: insist) you don't, so don't. All and everything military is off-limits, and if going through a military check point on the roads, it's best to lower your cameras completely. In the DPRK, as elsewhere, it is unacceptable to photograph local people without permission, and many people will refuse to pose or will ask for a donation. However, they're becoming more amenable to pictures being taken, and can like shots being taken with visitors. Asking permission may lose the spontaneity of a shot but it will avoid genuine ire, and if they say no, respect that.

Many indoor exhibitions forbid photography. Photographing poverty isn't appreciated, nor are shots of construction sites (because the building isn't finished and is therefore imperfect). Sometimes when on the bus guides will ask you not to photograph out of the windows (photography from the bus is difficult anyway as the roads are bad and you can end up simply denting your lens against the window), and restrictions are enforced with varying strictness around the country. Pyongyang is relatively relaxed but Chongjin for example is tight on restrictions, to the point that the local tour bus driver may be the one who reports the group, using the rear-view mirror to watch the tourists, and admonishments follow. Follow the guides' advice and permission, and if they say no, respect that: first because it's rude not to, but also they're actually often enough protecting you and aren't out just to spoil your fun. Going along with the guides' requests builds trust and it's when they trust you that things loosen up. They can demand to see, and delete, your pictures. It doesn't happen often – but it does happen. Do not sneak photos.

There is a photography shop on the second floor of Pyongyang's Koryo Hotel (see page 122) that can develop film and does passport photos, while 35mm camera film (usually 200) is becoming as unavailable as it is in the rest of the world, as digital's won that war. Assume, however, you will not find film, memory cards, batteries and other camera things in the DPRK so bring all that with you. Restrictions for bringing optical equipment into the country include camera lenses over 150mm or video cameras with higher than 24x optical zoom, and binoculars or telescopes over 10x power, although these limits have become loosely enforced to the point of being non-existent. Essentially, double check with your tour operator before going in.

MEDIA AND COMMUNICATIONS

The Korean Publications Exchange Association (*PO Box 222, Pyongyang, DPR of Korea;* ✆ *850 2 18111, ext 8842;* f *+850 2 381 4632/4416/4427*) is the definitive source for the DPRK's English-language publications.

The DPRK's indigenous newswire is the Korean Central News Agency (*www.kcna.kp*) with news in English and Spanish. The DPRK's most frequent English-language publications, namely the *Pyongyang Times, Korea, Korea Today* and *Foreign Trade*, are excellent for geting the look, feel and themes of the state's output and outlook, and are all accessible online through the 'naenara' website (*www. naenara.com.kp*). Other DPRK media outlets are www.rodong.rep.kp/en and www. uriminzokkiri.com.

The Society for Korean American Scholars is at www.skas.org, and a quite natty portal by Frank Hoffman has links to many other sources of Korea-related information at www.koreastudies.com. There is an absolute gamut of websites on pages 278–83.

TELEVISION AND RADIO There are three television stations: Korean Central Television, broadcasting daily, and Kaesong and Mansudae stations at the weekends. Their content follows two main themes, the greatness of the DPRK with focus on the Great Leaders' current and past deeds, and how appalling the southern puppet regime/Japanese/Americans are, all with a strong military accent. There are 11 radio stations on AM and FM. There are long-running drama series and soap operas aired which can be overwhelmingly sentimental. Examples of what's shown on DPRK television, and some of the equally single-minded propaganda put out by Western media about the state, can be seen on YouTube and Google Video.

POST AND TELECOMMUNICATIONS Post can be sent through the main post offices and those in the larger hotels. What you write on cards and in letters can and will be read by the authorities, so write lovely things to maximise the chances of delivery. Postcards cost €1 to send and take ten days. Any philatelists must visit the stamp shop next to the Koryo Hotel, although they might never leave. DHL has an office on Sungri Street, Jungsongdong Central District, Pyongyang (☏ *+850 2 381 8053;* ☉ *09.30–17.30 Mon–Fri*).

The landline telephone system is divided three ways (and so are the conversations): local calls, and the two lines prefixed 381 and 382 for companies and foreigners. First are local calls, for which you dial 18111/222/333… 999 for the central switchboard; then you need a four-digit extension number. Numbers beginning with 5 are all local and should be seven digits. Please note that the area code for Pyongyang is 02, which must be dialled from elsewhere in the country. Second are the domestic lines for foreign firms, organisations and embassies and a very few select Korean firms with the numbers 382xxxx; they don't need an operator. International lines used by these organisations are 381xxx or 382xxx. It's impossible to dial 381 numbers from a 382 line, and vice versa. Some hotels have IDD connections, which can also be used for in-country 381 calls and hotels can provide international calling services. It's not cheap, with rates at euros per minute. Telephone, fax and telex calls can be made at the International Communications Centre in Pyongyang in the Ryugyong-dong, Potonggang District, Pyongyang. For local calls from phone boxes, 10 chon coins are needed. Local calls can also be made from hotels and post offices.

Mobile phones are now firmly established in the DPRK, being on the road to ubiquitous among locals in the bigger cities (handsets costing around US$150) with subscribers running into millions – they're not solely for use by the elite. Mobile services were first available in 2002, with Nokia and Motorola mobile phones sold to serve a network built by a Thai telecoms company, but it was exorbitant in cost and intermittent in use, as officials suspected it of being used to enable illicit border trading and defecting, before being withdrawn in 2004. Since 2008, the Koryolink 3G network has been set up and spread to several hundred base stations covering the capital and scores of other cities and can be used by visitors to the DPRK.

Visitors no longer have to give up their mobiles on arrival at the airport (although they must declare they have a mobile) and can buy SIM cards from a Koryolink booth at the Sunan airport. Numbers begin 00850 (0) 192 xxxxx.

Like the landline system, there are distinct lines for different purposes and people.

There is a network for Koreans, and a network for non-Koreans, and they cannot call one another. Koreans cannot call the outside the DPRK nor can they access the internet. For non-Koreans, the situation is broadly as follows, with prices valid for 2013: short-term visitors including tourists get SIM cards, with pre-loaded balances that cost from €50 (including €30 preload), that are valid for 14 days, or longer if you pay more. Local calling and receiving rates, and texts, are €0.2/minute. At the time of writing, tourists cannot use their phone to access the internet.

Longer-term visitors/residents can get SIM cards for €50 and pay monthly fees of 800KPW (approximately €6/US$8), with 200 minutes/month and 20 free SMS to other local lines. The calling rate is 4.20KPW/minute (€0.03), receiving rate is 3.50KPW/minute (€0.02), and SMS is 2.80KPW (€0.01) and MMS is 7KPW (€0.05). Longer-term visitors/residents can access the internet for their phone and computers, but this is another add-on package of connection fees and monthly costs.

For both short- and long-term visitors, international-calling, per-minute rates are China and southeast Asia €1.43; Russia €0.68; France and Switzerland €0.38; UK and Germany €1.58; and the US €5.

You may pick up a Chinese or ROK network signal in border areas, of interest if not of any use. Overall, however, a lack of people shouting 'I'M ON THE TRAIN' in your ear is so rare it's quite nice to experience the silence. Upon landing back at Beijing airport one can be surprised by how unfamiliar the sound of mobiles has become, as the passenger cabin suddenly comes alive with the chirping of phones waking out of hibernation. So if you don't have to faff about getting a mobile, instead just savour the isolation!

INTERNET AND INTRANET As outlined above, longer-term foreign residents can subscribe to internet access, but at the time of writing, tourists could not access the internet on their mobiles. Tourists can access the somewhat pricey internet at the Kumgang Hotel in Kumgangsan or Masik ski resort, and this might meanwhile spread to all hotels, but it's a situation in flux. It could all as easily be turned off.

Since 2000 (the year Kim Jong Il met then US secretary of state Madeleine Albright and asked for her email address), there has been a domestic intranet called Kwangmyong ('bright'), with its own browser, search engine, email, chat rooms and even dating websites. One can see it in use in libraries and in schools and there are intranet cafés with children playing online games, but it is an intranet nonetheless. Access to the World Wide Web for ordinary citizens doesn't exist. The government has internet access: a very select few can access the web and search for materials of use to the state, and there is talk of enabling greater access to the internet but this will undoubtedly be under very proscribed conditions. The DPRK's designated domain suffix, .kp, is in use with a few state-sanctioned websites, with most of its international domains operating from Japan and China, but the list of DPRK-hosted websites is growing.

Email is available to most people involved in business and trade, and broadly throughout the education system of schools and universities, with the main limit being a shortage of computers, but that is changing. Foreign embassies and NGOs that might have web access through satellite connections will not readily lend them, except for the tidiest sums, and they have better things to do. Tourists are best off sticking to the traditional and much more reliable postcards and letters. Forget spending the evenings updating blogs in sweaty internet cafes.

Fax machines are still in use in the DPRK: in fact in late December 2013 the Military Defence Commission, upset by the burning of noteworthy effigies in Seoul and apparently continuing something of a Christmas tradition of kicking off, sent a fax to the ROK threatening a 'merciless' attack. The ROK's reply by fax was equally robust.

TIME ZONE

DPRK time is GMT plus nine hours, so midday in Pyongyang is 03.00 in London, 15.00 in Wellington and 21.00 in Vancouver the previous day. Years are given in the Gregorian calendar and the Juche calendar. The latter marks the years since Juche evolved, ie: 1912, the year Kim Il Sung was born. So, 2000 for example is Juche 88, as 1912 + 88 = 2000, and 2003 is Juche 91, etc.

CULTURAL ETIQUETTE

First and foremost, disrespecting the Great Leader, Dear Leader or Respected Marshal is the surest way to cause heinous offence to your hosts, be they guides, businessmen, or whoever. This will mar your relations with them in the immediate sense and for the rest of the trip. You'll be asked to 'pay respect' to statues and shrines of Kim Il Sung and Kim Jong Il, usually by standing quietly in front of them and giving a solitary nod of the head. Just do it. Sometimes flowers must be brought. Do not disfigure in any way any image of either leader in printed material and leave newspapers and magazines high and dry and not screwed up in the bin – newspapers are already specially folded to prevent the photos of the Leaders being creased. There have been anecdotal reports of foreigners falling foul of this, chucking newspapers in bins or defacing pictures accidentally or not, and incurring a public dressing down at the least.

However, your hosts will be knowledgeable on a great many worldly matters, and ranging debates about politics and economics may start up. On the other hand, they're civilians and human beings who don't know everything – if they don't give a 'satisfactory' answer to your question, it's because they don't know. Why should they know the intricacies of the state's missile programme or incarceration system? If you want to know about the details of the Leaders' love lives, look up the DPRK edition of *OMG!* – except nothing like that exists even in the imagination. Bombs, rockets, camps, tittle-tattle, hive off the *what to talk about* list. Guides may talk about the famine, but as up to one in ten Koreans died in that time, it's a sensitive subject. Just be aware, but not paranoid. One visitor read in an Australian paper that the guides were trained to be charming (well, um, yes, it'd be poor form for guides to go scowling around the place), which he was talking to a friend about in a DPRK hotel bar – and when he saw his guides next morning, they were quite cold to him. Had they heard what he'd said? Had the conversation been *bugged*? The short answer is no, the long answer is don't be ridiculous. There again, avoid glancing around if you think you've said something controversial.

Prevent causing offence unwittingly by avoiding overt criticism in favour of suggestions: how things can 'be improved' or 'made even better', if the need is felt to say such things. Koreans are fiercely proud people and there is always the overhanging cultural concept of 'loss of face'. In conversation no-one should be boxed into a corner and be forced to apologise, concede defeat or accept criticism (which no-one enjoys anyway). The Korean variant is *kibun*, similar to face, which values keeping personal relations harmonious. You just have to be diplomatic. Watch for the silences or titters. On another note, here's an extreme example of how to get it all wrong:

> At the Myohyang International Friendship Exhibition, one gift to Kim Il Sung that stuck out for me was a fanciful corrugated cardboard galleon from a Portuguese printers' union. Somehow, inexplicably, having padded for hours through the incredibly long showrooms in the exhibition's highly sombre atmosphere (the Exhibition is the holiest of holies, enshrining the world's gifts of tribute and homage to the Great Leaders), this little ship cracked me up. The exhibition guide stared at my mirthful writhing in chilled disbelief, while my interpreter haltingly asked, with quiet, incredulous menace, what was funny. I realised I had well and truly crossed the line and only another tourist's intervention with a more harmless explanation saved me.
>
> Anon

Your guides are your means to get around, and they need to trust you as you must trust in them. If you're prone to ignore basic manners, antagonising your guides will wreck any chances of more spontaneous endeavours and cloud the trip's atmosphere. Western journalists have made great hay of running away from their guides, and some tour companies have suggested in their literature that tourists can, for example, leave their hotels at night without their guides. Indeed this book ambitiously claimed in its first edition that 'Pyongyang is a city where you can wander freely without guides', but did stress, 'but do not run off and leave them', and that's the maxim – do not leave your guides, it's not allowed, you'll get nowhere fast without them, no-one will take you anywhere and there are very few places beyond a few bars or restaurants to go. Most importantly your guides will get in trouble. They're civilians who are responsible for you and the blowback for any problems arising will be borne by them. The consensus is that there is little to be achieved from abandoning the guides except trouble. Much, much more can be seen and done if you ensure your guides can trust you – they can open doors, you can't, and legging it will mark you out as a worry. That so many journalists write up so much about their exploits of running away from their guides might suggest that, as a result, they end up with little else to report.

The final point doesn't need writing but I'll put it anyway, so don't take offence. The tours can perhaps feel claustrophobic; you're always on the go from here to there and may tire; you're with your guides and fellow travellers for all the hours you're awake. Realistically, nearly nobody can get along with everybody all the time, so check your mood and step back. But you're going to the DPRK because you know it is a truly worthwhile, once-in-a-lifetime experience. So endeavour not to ruin a unique adventure and try to get along with your hosts and co-travellers, who'll be of all ages and backgrounds from around the world, and are joining you on this thrilling sojourn. And the locals are great. If they offer a drink and a dance, pile in.

IMPORTANT TITBITS Tipping is not expected but obviously appreciated. If you do tip then do so with great discretion.

Wave people towards you with the palm down and fingers batting back and forth. Don't point. Pour drinks by holding the bottle with both hands, serving elders first. Never sit with your soles pointing at anyone, so sit cross-legged with the feet tucked beneath your thighs, or side-saddle. Women and the young used to sit on their heels as a matter of course, and children would stand up when addressed, something still occasionally seen. Receive business cards with both hands and study appreciatively on receipt before placing in a breast pocket. Nearly every man in the DPRK smokes, and they smoke in bars and restaurants, and getting upset about that won't change anything.

Public petting isn't appreciated, and nor do Korean men take well to Korean women being pawed by anyone, especially foreign men, although it's the women who will incur greater repercussions. One traveller put it this way: 'It's certainly not on the *Sex and the City* scale, but they're not quite the Taliban either.' Korean women making advances to foreign men isn't known to happen. The sheer thrill of being in the DPRK, and the unceasing close proximity of the guides, can bring on all levels of infatuations for visitors who mistake professional charm and attention for amour. Failure to find the middle ground may be costly. For homosexuality, it's occasionally hoisted in the DPRK media as a vague, decadent imperialist plot, but it's not illegal. This is largely because at a social level, pretty much like Victorian Britain's view of lesbianism, it's just not a concept. It's not illegal because it doesn't exist. How that view conflicts with reality is a whole other story. A rule of thumb is: it's not about Koreans being bothered by foreigners' sexual orientation, it's that they don't want to be presented with sexuality at all.

Part Two

THE GUIDE

3

Pyongyang 평양

*39.1°N 125.45°E; Pyongyang City District,
capital of the Democratic People's Republic of Korea,
Korean peninsula*

Pyongyang, the DPRK capital, is a showcase city, the political, cultural and educational centre of the country, a city built to impress the world with the success, progress and fortitude of the DPRK and its people.

The tiled apartment blocks and concrete high-rises strut alongside the city's wide, tree-lined boulevards cutting from titanic state buildings to monuments striking for their powerful shapes and size. Roads stretch arrow straight into the distance, linking monuments and plazas set in alignment over the horizon, across the river, across the city. In sunlight, the streets and squares, without a fleck of dust, can literally dazzle. In rain, the harsh, grey geometries meld into the sky while vast, sweeping Korean-style eaves hurl the rainwater away. Into all this order and space some 200 parks and open spaces have been carefully slotted. Most fume-producing factories have been banished to the city's outskirts. Pyongyang reputedly has 58m² of green belt per citizen – four times the amount prescribed by the United Nations, and in spring its hills heave with green. It is, as Kim Il Sung meant it to be, a city without parallel in Korea, or Asia. 'The capital of our socialist homeland, Pyongyang is the political centre, the centre for culture and education and a wellspring of our revolution' – and a well-ordered wellspring at that.

In few parts of the city can be found the higgledy-piggledy mash of streets that comes from the organic growth of other cities, as individual people, firms and authorities fight over space and time; this form of Pyongyang's layout has been virtually obliterated. Every corner of every block has been approved according to one overall, unitary plan, and there is an extraordinary homogeneity in the buildings' design. For the parts and the whole, one design fits all as a handful of factories produce the designs of even fewer design institutes. The same singularity of purpose is visible in all the pictures, placards and slogans round the city, for which and only for which all neon gets used. It is still very much mostly the case that advertisements in Pyongyang and beyond do not promote material goods or recognisable brands, but are for promoting the ideals and leader(s) of North Korea's socialism. Pyongyang is a mindset, an ideal, an idea, the city as the manifestation of the state, the state as the manifestation of the man.

The city limits drawn on the plans are clearly visible on the ground. The grey cliffs of the perimeter high-rise provide a sharp, vertical barrier to the fields and lowlands lapping round the city. Pyongyang doesn't sprawl like other Asian cities, forever absorbing rural–urban migrants. The population is relatively stable at a little over three million because people do not live and work in Pyongyang without permits, which are as valued as the gold dust mined in the city's outskirts. Koreans cannot in fact leave or enter the city without permits, as the checkpoints on the perimeter roads verify, and as a result the lack of inter-urban public transport is deliberate: if no-one needs it, why have it?

The lack of traffic spares the city from pollution and the flying dust brought in and whipped up by vehicles. Incoming rural lorries and buses are hosed down just outside the city perimeters to make sure, and the regular trams and trolley buses are electric. Everyone mucks in to keep Pyongyang clean, as groups of families are responsible for keeping their immediate locale dirt-free, while brigades of older women tend to the public areas. Water trucks hose the streets. There are very few stalls or vendors and there's little litter because there is nothing to throw away: this is not a consumer society, and what's used gets converted. Watch out for small tools and appliances brilliantly fashioned from drinks cans and the like. On the other hand, you see very few deliveries for stores, post or parcels for business and other service personnel who make up so much of the melee of road and pavement traffic. That facet of activity is still to come, but there is much more bustle than there was say even in 2002 or 2003, when the whole country was staggering out of the famine. One sees more people and they look healthier, less worried – happier, even.

The relative lack of road traffic still means there isn't anything like the white noise of vehicles that outside cities have, but the streets are nowhere near as empty as they were and people are out commuting, milling and chilling. Still, visitors ask, 'where is everybody?' Well they're either at work, or at home, or out in the courtyards and spaces of their residences where most of their amenities are also stashed – just not necessarily hanging out on the major thoroughfares sporadically tracked by tourists.

GEOGRAPHY

'The beauty of its situation well deserves the praises that have been showered upon it by both Korean and European writers,' wrote Dr Philip Jaisohn (the Korean patriot, journalist, doctor and intellectual who was a staunch advocate for Korean independence). Situated in the southeast of the country, the city straddles the River Taedong, where this major waterway (450km long, 20,000km^2 catchment area) is joined by the rivers Potong, Japzang and Sunhwa. The flat plain on which Pyongyang sits is walled in on the northeastern sides by hills, in which coal and gold are mined, and open plains to the west and south. Pyongyang and its manufacturing industries produce mining and construction machinery and products, as well as locomotives, hi-tech electrical goods and IT, textiles and tools, with a burgeoning food processing industry.

HISTORY

Pyongyang has long been a city of importance, being the second or third city for those interludes in history when it wasn't the capital, and always a vital fortress city and trading centre. DPRK historians are adamant that they've nailed the 5,000 years of history myth on to King Tangun, who was in fact a real king and who did indeed establish the walled city of Pyongyang 5,000 years ago. It probably wasn't built exactly where Pyongyang is today, but 500 of an estimated 10,000 dolmen tombs have been excavated around today's city that date back some 5,000 years, along with 150 stone coffins, laden with jewellery and ceramics. There's also much from the Bronze Age, pre-dating the Tangun, with slaves' and slave-owners' graves identified.

A small town grew around 2,000 years ago south of Yanggak Island on the fertile Taedong plains, and under Koguyro a citadel was built on Mount Taesong in 247AD, with ancestral shrines, government offices and residences in the adjacent Anhak palace. The building of Pyongyang proper soon followed as it moved from Koguryo's second city to being the capital in 427, on order of King Changsu.

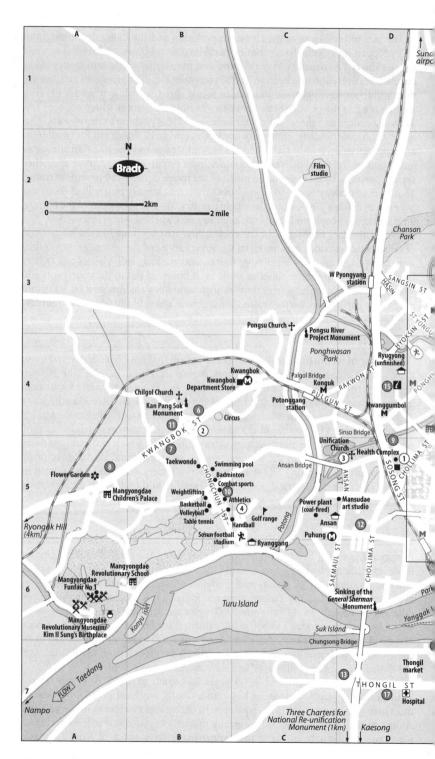

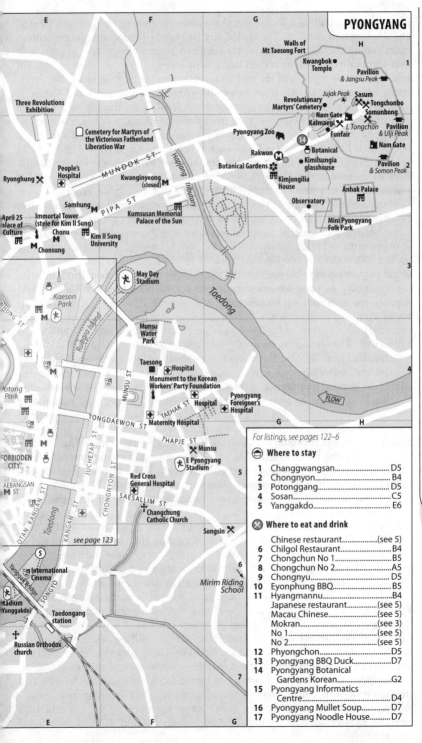

Walls of
Mt Taesong Fort

Kwangbok ●
Temple

Pavilion
& Jangsu Peak

Three Revolutions
Exhibition

Jujak Peak   Sasum

Revolutionary   Tongchonbo
Martyrs' Cemetery   ●   Somunbong

Nam Gate
Cemetery for Martyrs of
the Victorious Fatherland   Kalmaegi   *L Tongchon*   Pavilion
Liberation War   *& Ulji Peak*

Pyongyang Zoo   🐘   Funfair   Nam Gate

Rakwon Ⓜ   🔴 Botanical

People's   MUNDOK ST   Botanical Gardens   Pavilion
Hospital   ● Kimilsungia   *& Somon Peak*
Ryonghung ✕   glasshouse

HAJANG ST   Kwanginyeong   Kimjongilia
(closed) Ⓜ   House

PIPA ST   Anhak Palace

Samhung Ⓜ   Observatory

April 25   Immortal Tower   Kumsusan Memorial
alace of   (stele for Kim Il Sung)   Palace of the Sun   Mini Pyongyang
Culture   Chonu   Folk Park
Ⓜ Chonsung   Kim Il Sung
University

May Day
Stadium

Kaeson
Park

Munsu
Water
Park

Taesong   Hospital
Monument to the Korean
Workers' Party Foundation
Pyongyang
Hospital   Foreigner's
Hospital
TONGDAEWON ST   Maternity Hospital

THAPJE ST

Munsu
E Pyongyang
Stadium

Red Cross
General Hospital
SAESALLIM ST
Changchung
Catholic Church

Songsin ✕

see page 123

Ⓢ
International
Cinema   *Mirim Riding
School*

tadium   Taedongang
Yanggakdo)   station

✝
Russian Orthodox
church

Pyongyang HISTORY

3

Pyongyang was built as a walled city that eventually grew to cover today's Central and Phyongchon districts. The walled city consisted of four parts, inner, central, outer and northern, and its perimeter stretched 16km in length and in parts rose over 10m, with crenelated parapets lacing between up to 16 gates. These walls stood in some form or other until the mid 20th century, protecting the miserable streets inside with varying success from the invaders from the north, south and within.

In 598, a seaborne assault by Chinese forces heading for the city on a punitive venture (not enough tribute was paid from Korea to China) was luckily wiped out by a typhoon. Thirty thousand Tang soldiers marched into the peninsula in spring 661 as their half of the Tang/Silla alliance to defeat the Koguryo, and laid siege to the city. Although the Tang forces gave up the siege, Koguryo was weakened and, from its collapse in 668, Pyongyang was abandoned to become a 'city of weeds'. It was not until Wang Kon established Koryo in 918 that the city was reborn.

Wang Kon had Pyongyang reconstructed as a major garrison town to re-establish order in the north, and he contemplated moving the Koryo capital there. The city's administrative and material footprint was reset over the surrounding districts and Pyongyang thrived as second city to Kaesong, both becoming centres of learning from the late 900s with new libraries and academies filled with students from a burgeoning urban population of noble families. But the thriving peace was short-lived. In 1010, the Pyongyang garrison commander General Kang led his troops to Kaesong and deposed the youthful King Mokchong and his nefarious dowager queen mother to install a more suitable monarch. Unfortunately, into the melee from across the Yalu came the Liao, who trashed Pyongyang and burnt Kaesong. This led to the building of a great wall of fortified cities north of Pyongyang by 300,000 men from 1033.

A hundred years later, the threat was from within. In 1135, Pyongyang became the base for the bizarre Myochong rebellion, led by a prophetic Buddhist monk of that name who attained prominence in the Koryo court. Myochong had been persuading the then king, Injong, to move the court from Kaesong to Pyongyang, arguing that the Chinese Chin needed attacking and that Kaesong lacked 'geomancy', something Pyongyang apparently had in spades. Injong was taken in and a palace and several temples with deities were built in Pyongyang before making it the capital. Then another scholar, advocating peace with the Chin, sat Injong down and carefully explained that Myochong's theories weren't quite aligned with reality. Livid, Myochong set up with his followers a siege state in Pyongyang that took a year to crush.

In 1592, it was in Pyongyang that General Konishi of the Japanese army advancing from the south made fleeting contact with the fleeing Ri court, who over their shoulders exclaimed that they would return. After a final abortive night raid by the city's defenders, Konishi entered a Pyongyang empty of people but full of supplies. The Ri, however, did return that summer, with Chinese and Korean forces encircling Pyongyang, and in February 1593 an army of Buddhist monk soldiers led the city's retaking through the walls breached by heavy artillery.

In 1627 and 1637, the invaders came from the north as the Mongols ravaged Pyongyang on punitive raids, but these were the last significant military attacks for nearly 300 years. The intervening years saw invaders of a different, Christian kind. One 19th-century observer wrote: 'The Koreans of these northern provinces are, in the opinion of the missionaries, far more satisfactory than their southern compatriots. They are more honest and reliable, as well as more enterprising, diligent, and industrious, a view that is borne out by the foreign merchants who have had dealings with them.' And Pyongyang was 'an excellent centre for evangelistic works'.

The city's military significance didn't wane, however, for by the mid 19th century, Pyongyang had around 295,000 households and 175,000 men listed

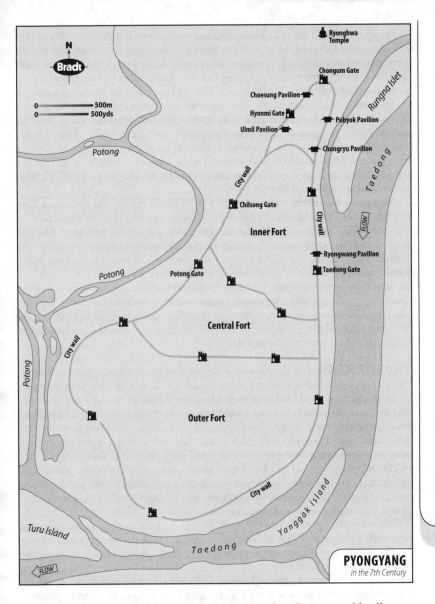

Map labels:
Ryonghwa Temple
Chongum Gate
Choesung Pavilion
Rungna Islet
Hyonmi Gate
Pubyok Pavilion
Ulmil Pavilion
Taedong
Potong
Chongryu Pavilion
City wall
Chilsong Gate
FLOW
Inner Fort
City wall
Ryongwang Pavilion
Potong
Taedong Gate
Potong Gate
Central Fort
City wall
Outer Fort
Potong
City wall
Yanggak Island
City wall
Turu Island
Taedong
FLOW
PYONGYANG
in the 7th Century

for military duty. It was reserves of such size that the Chinese would call upon decades later in the 1894 Sino–Japanese war, when Chinese armies in and around Pyongyang buttressed the city's forts and walls from Japanese attack. Still, three columns of Japanese troops converged on Pyongyang and routed the Chinese after days of heavy fighting, in which a third of the city was burnt. In *Fifteen Years among the Top-Knots*, Lillias Underwood reported scenes of carnage with one pile of dead troops and horses stretching 'a quarter of a mile long and several yards wide' that lay rotting for weeks, while bodies in the Taedong polluted the city's major water supply (for more details, see page 18). Cholera broke out the following year.

Pyongyang didn't seem to have benefited much from the decades of Japanese rule that soon followed. Most of the schools and hospitals were built and run by Protestant missionaries who provided desperately needed relief for the city's poor. In 1939, Jahisohn wrote that Pyongyang had only one notable thoroughfare that led along the riverbank from Taedong Gate. This was the business district, dominated by Japanese traders, particularly rice and bean merchants exporting to Japan and investment banks charging extortionate rates of interest. Jahisohn wrote that 'the remaining thoroughfares are extremely narrow and dirty. Most of the houses and shops are more or less dilapidated, while there are no buildings of striking importance.' Mud-plastered thatch-shacks were knotted together by dirt tracks flanked by stinking open sewers running into the river, itself jammed with Chinese junks trading legally and illegally.

Pyongyang was liberated in August 1945 by Soviet forces, and their man Kim Il Sung arrived in triumph the following month. The city became the capital of the 'temporary' state of North Korea, and some impressive buildings, like the Moranbang Theatre (just!), survive from the few peaceful years preceding the Korean War. During the Korean War, Pyongyang was wrested from both sides' hands, while hundreds of thousands of civilians here and elsewhere were killed in American bombing raids that had no palpable effect on the war's outcome: 'Bombing could inflict a catastrophe upon a nation without defeating it' (Max Hastings, *The Korean War*). The *Pyongyang Review* claims that the 428,000 bombs dropped equalled more than one bomb per citizen there. Except for a handful of buildings, the city was truly wiped flat.

RECONSTRUCTION The capital of the DRPK had to be rebuilt, quickly, simply. The city was planned around the River Taedong as a 'garden city' with over 200 green spaces, tree-lined roads and riverside walks. Buildings shot up using methods and materials stripped down and honed so that the absolute minimum in skills or resources was needed. Industry and manpower resources, recovering from the war, were faced with a colossal demand for materials and workers, and quantity took priority over quality. You don't have to stand very close to buildings to see that balconies, tiling, vertical and horizontal joints often depart from the plumb line. Interesting concave and convex patterns appear in prefabricated, hand-finished concrete walls. Windowpanes have bubbles, bands, fisheye and bottle-glass effects. Spaces exist under doors and their frames.

Still, the buildings of the late 1970s and 1980s are a great qualitative improvement over their predecessors that suffered poor wiring, low water pressure and uneven heating. Heating in many apartment blocks is of the traditional Korean type (called *ondol*), with stove-heated air piped under the floor and hot water provided from the city's thermal power plants. This does cool over a distance and there's no micro-control facility. Stoves are still the major source of heating in modern DPRK flats, such that you can see stovepipes protruding through 18th-storey windows. In the taller buildings, unevenly heightened floors and unaligned lift shafts prevent operational lifts. By day and night, the country suffers from power shortages (albeit in Pyongyang less so these days) and the low-energy bulbs and fluorescents flicker by day and emit zingy light at night.

But this is to run one's fingers along the mantelpiece of what is ultimately a stunning achievement, and the march of the high-rise stamps onwards. Pyongyang has many traditional single-storey brick and clay huts but they are screened from the main thoroughfares by the high-rises out to replace them, so be aware from highpoints and glance through alleys and archways. From the Juche Tower looking east there are many such houses on the fringes of the city, crammed between developments closer in, and the locals who visitors claim they don't see by day are either in those warrens or in the spacious courtyards of the larger blocks. Either way, everyone is expected to keep the place neat and trim. One can sometimes see the grass verges along pavements being tended by women with scissors, and children have been seen loading turf onto lorries for larger projects.

Pyongyang is the sister city to Kathmandu, and was the inspiration for Romania's communist dictator Nicolae Ceaușescu to demolish much of Bucharest and rebuild it as his own city-sized monument to his glories.

Design For the apartment blocks, the homogeneous designs give few architectural clues to indicate a building's age, purpose or occupiers' status, beyond the simple observation that if it's tall and grey it's probably residential, and the taller it is, the newer it is. There are three main types of grand, public buildings. The first is the classically derived grandeur, all pedestals, pillars and steps like the Moranbang Theatre, or the simplified classicism derived from Soviet-design shops, like Mansudae Assembly Hall and the Kumsusan Memorial Palace of the Sun. The second style literally was built atop the first. While the floor space of the classical structures was appreciated, the façades changed from the very late 1960s onwards with the plain Soviet austerity being at first augmented, then replaced, with the far more ostentatious traditional Korean-style fronts and sweeping roofs (examples include the Grand People's Study House, Pyongyang International House of Culture and Okryu restaurant). Some buildings combine the two styles such that the bottom half is Stalinist and the top is Korean. The neo-Korean architecture was made to reflect the emergence of the DPRK as a power and culture in its own right, cutting its own path in the world, as well as the styles being also technically and commercially affordable to use. Alongside this indigenous design philosophy came arguments advocating how spectacular concrete could be in imaginative hands (Pyongyang International Cinema, Chongryu restaurant, the Ice Rink, Chongchun Street, Ryugyong Hotel, East Pyongyang Grand Theatre, Monument to the Party Founding), and this would make up the admittedly broad umbrella term of the third style. Many of those projects were simply brutalist, which was taken up with the monumental residential developments of Tongil Street, south of Yanggak Islet, and Kwangbok Street in Mangyongdae district, which are overwhelming. The May Day Stadium stands alone as a brilliant project in flying steel.

'Let us build our city more beautifully at a faster rate,' the constructors were exhorted, and visitors will be regaled with statistics. The Pyongyang Maternity Hospital was knocked up in less than nine months before the sixth party congress in 1980. The Grand People's Study House, 600 rooms over 100,000m², was built in 21 months. Whole streets, like Chollima Street in the 1970s and Pipa and Ragwon streets in the 1980s, were built in months, under the so-called 'Pyongyang Speed'. This was also due to the strictures of the multi-year plans.

Interiors The most ostentatious features of any grand building's interior are their vast chandeliers that bear down through floors and stairwells like almighty drill-bits, and paintings of Korean landscapes that cover entire walls. Plastic 'wood' panelling, marble-print paper on pillars, painted metal slats nailed onto the walls, flock wallpaper – all are common features. There are evidently precious few factories producing the fixtures and furnishings. Try and spot the recurring wallpaper and curtain material from the DPRK's own IKEA. Tours focusing on architecture in the

DPRK have been run successfully for some time by Koryo Tours (see page 80 for details) in conjunction with the DPRK Architectural University.

GETTING THERE AND AWAY

By air, you arrive at Sunan airport [off map 110 D1], a 30-minute drive from the city, and by train at the Pyongyang railway station [123 A7], two minutes' walk from the Koryo Hotel. See also *Getting there and away*, page 85.

GETTING AROUND

METRO Pyongyang's underground railway, or metro (*www.pyongyang-metro.com*), has two lines running under the main streets on the west side of the Taedong: the Hyokshin Line going under Ragwon and Pipa streets, and the Chollima Line under Podunamu, Kaeson, Sungni and Yonggwang streets. This is important to know as the 17 stations are mostly not named by location but instead by good revolutionary terminology, like Hwanggumbol (Golden Fields), Pulgunbyol (Red Star) and Chonu (Comrade). Nor do any available maps show the precise location of the stations and streets, hence those maps available outside of the DPRK are compilations and close estimations. Without them, unless you're a local, there's no way of really knowing where you are.

Leaving that aside, apart from being a swift, smooth link across town, the stunning opulence of Pyongyang metro's architecture and the extraordinarily deep stations with their vertigo-inducing escalators are worth the visit. The Chollima line opened in September 1973, and the metro resembles Moscow's, though some say Pyongyang's is the more beautiful. The escalators take some leisurely minutes to plumb down 200-odd metres, arriving in marble-clad tunnels that bore away from blast doors to blast doors, for the subway doubles as an air-raid shelter for Pyongyang's citizens. The platforms are underground cathedrals to socialism, with their marble pillars, vaults and platform-length murals and mosaics of Korean countryside entitled 'Song of a bumper crop' and 'Builders at the construction of a blast furnace', while commuters may be seen reading copies of the day's news pasted up in metal stands. The chandeliers are themed by the name of the station, so at Yonggwang (Glory) station they look like fireworks, and at Hwanggumbol (Golden Fields) they're grapes of bumper harvests. Yonggwang and Hwanggumbol figure along with Kaeson, Konsol, Konguk and Ragwon as the worthier stations to visit. Some of the stations, like Hwanggumbyol, are absolute riots of neon at night, when the power's on.

Trains run every five to seven minutes, or every two minutes at peak time, reportedly carting some 300,000 commuters every day. None of this came without a price, however. The Korean National Intelligence Service disclosed in 1999 that during the metro's construction in 1971, over 100 lives were lost when part of an underwater tunnel at Ponghwa station collapsed.

That the stations most often shown to tourists (including Madeleine Albright) are normally Puhung and Yonggwang gave support in some quarters to the rumour that the metro system has only these two stations, or that these are the only stations 'in operation', with lots of well-dressed actors shuttling like commuters to impress the visitors. There are no depths that conspiracy theorists will not plumb. The rest of the network definitely exists and these days visitors are taken to a good half-dozen stations, and special tours are now able to see the entire network. One might have thought that the bulk purchase of hundreds of metro cars over the years from West and East Germany and China would make for an absurdly elaborate and expensive hoax, as well as a lot of redundant trains (the trains themselves also exemplify a bygone epoch of design. Yet, as www.pyongyang-metro.com outlines, there would seem to be far too much rolling stock for the timetables going along the two lines. What this may support therefore is the rumour of parallel metro lines that are run exclusively for the top military and government personnel, possibly connecting to a network of underground roads and even a 'square', with an underground line extending all the way out to Sunan airport. The building of underground complexes originated during the heavy bombing of the Korean War and it is highly understandable that the practice would continue, particularly with the US and ROK forces sitting just a rocket's throw away over the DMZ. But the extent and existence of such infrastructure will not be admitted to, let alone added to any tourist itinerary, beyond the metro, no matter how hard you ask.

Plans to link the western ends of the two lines and build a third line crossing the river remain just that. Tickets for all public transport on the metro cost 5KPW in local money, paid at ticket offices.

BUSES, TROLLEYBUSES AND TRAMS There are extensive trolleybus and tram connections across the city, plied by rusty, hard-working vehicles from regimes that time forgot, and which are usually packed out whether they're moving or are marooned, hunched down on their springs. Women and children have priority on public transport, with conductors in military-style uniform in control and not to be jostled with if they let you on. Tickets are 5KPW in local money that tourists don't have. All services are irregular due to power cuts. The trams and most of the trolleybuses are mostly Korean made, now with a few Chinese imports, dodging Russian, Czech and Hungarian petrol buses, and more modern Japanese buses and lorries. For lorries, the situation is a lot of Russian GAZ and KrAZ types, Korean and Chinese copies. On the sides of many vehicles are painted long lines of red stars. Each star shows 50,000km of safe driving, so it appears that some could have cruised safely to the moon and back more than once.

TROLLEYBUS ROUTES

1 Pyongyang station – Yonggwang – Sungri – Moranbong – Arch of Triumph – Ryonmotdong

2 Pyongyang station – Sosong – Chollima Street – Ryugyong Hotel – Moranbong Street – Sangsin – West Pyongyang station

3 Pyongyang Power station – Chollima Street – Ryugyong Hotel – Moranbong Street – Sangsin – West Pyongyang station

4 Ponghwa – Sosong – Haebangsan – Taedong Bridge – Saesarim – Songsin station

5 Pyongyang Department Store No 1 – Sungri – Okryu Bridge – East Pyongyang Theatre – Munsu

6 Pyongyang Department Store No 1 – Sungri – Okryu Bridge – Tongdaewon – Taehak – Sadong

7 Munsu – Youth Street – Rangrang Bridge

8 Friendship Tower – Arch of Triumph – Moranbong Street – Ponghwa – Ryugyong Hotel – Pulgun – Kwangbok

9 Ryonmotdong – Ryongsong (north)

10 Kwangbok (Palgol Bridge) Pulgun – Sosong – Yanggak Islet – Rangrang – Taedonggang station

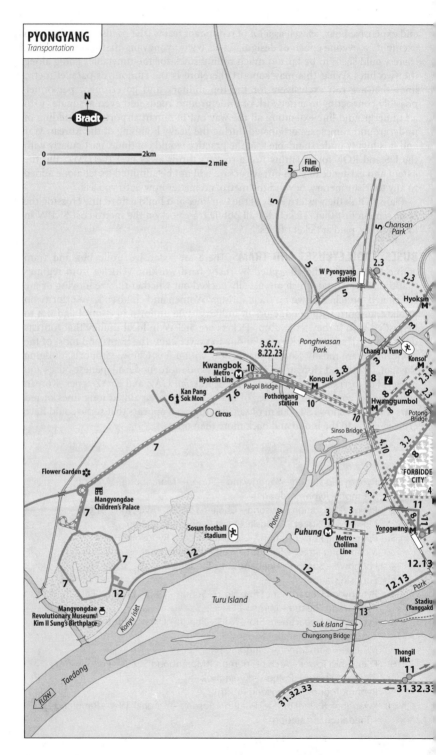

N

Bradt

0 ——————————————————— 2km
0 ——————————————————— 2 mile

5 Film studio

5 Chansan Park

5

W Pyongyang station

2.3

2.3

Hyoksin Ⓜ

3

3.6.7. 8.22.23

Ponghwasan Park

22

Kwangbok
Metro - Hyoksin Line Ⓜ 10

Chang Ju Yung

Konsol Ⓜ

Konguk Ⓜ 3.8

8

2.3 2.3

8

8

Kan Pang Sok Mon 6

7.6

Palgol Bridge

Pothongang station

Hwanggumbol Ⓜ

8

Potong Bridge

Circus

10

Sinso Bridge

10

FORBIDDE CITY

4.10

3.2

3

2

Flower Garden

Mangyongdae Children's Palace

7

7

Sosun football stadium

12

Potong

3

Puhung Ⓜ Metro - Chollima Line

3

11

11

11

4

8

11

Yonggwang Ⓜ

12.13

12.13

12

12

7

7

12

Konyu islet

Turu Island

13

Suk Island
Chungsong Bridge

Park

Stadiu (Yanggakd

Mangyongdae Revolutionary Museum/ Kim Il Sung's Birthplace

Taedong

FLOW

Thongil Mkt

11

31.32.33

31.32.33

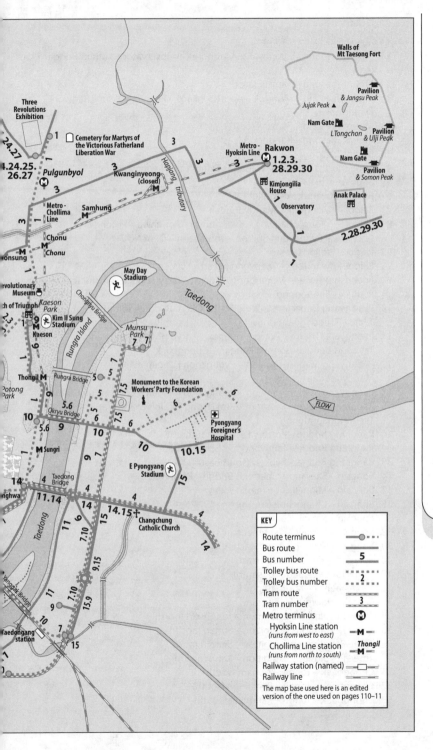

Three Revolutions Exhibition

Cemetery for Martyrs of the Victorious Fatherland Liberation War

Walls of Mt Taesong Fort

Pavilion *& Jangsu Peak*

Jujak Peak ▲

Nam Gate

L Tongchon

Pavilion *& Ulji Peak*

Nam Gate

Pavilion *& Somon Peak*

24.27

4.24.25. 26.27

Pulgunbyol

Kwanginyeong (closed)

Haplang tributary

Metro - Hyoksin Line

Rakwon 1.2.3. 28.29.30

Kimjongilia House

Observatory

Anak Palace

2.28.29.30

Metro - Chollima Line

Samhung

Chonu

Chonu

onsung

evolutionary Museum

May Day Stadium

Taedong

Chongryu Bridge

ch of Triumph

Kaeson Park

Kim Il Sung Stadium

Kaeson

Rungra Island

Munsu Park

Thongil

Rungra Bridge

Potong Park

Monument to the Korean Workers' Party Foundation

FLOW

Okryu Bridge

Pyongyang Foreigner's Hospital

Sungri

10.15

E Pyongyang Stadium

Taedong Bridge

Changchung Catholic Church

nghwa

Taedong

Yanggak Bridge

aedongang station

KEY

Route terminus	
Bus route	
Bus number	5
Trolley bus route	
Trolley bus number	2
Tram route	
Tram number	3
Metro terminus	Ⓜ
Hyoksin Line station *(runs from west to east)*	—M—
Chollima Line station *(runs from north to south)*	*Thongil* —M—
Railway station (named)	
Railway line	

The map base used here is an edited version of the one used on pages 110–11

1   Mount Taesong – Pyongyang Astronomical Observatory – Mirim Bridge (east)
2   Mount Taesong – Samsin (east)
3   Mount Taesong – Mundok – April 25 Palace – Pipa – Hyoksin – Ragwon – Kwangbok
28 Mount Taesong – Samsok (east)
29 Mount Taesong – Kangdong (east)
30 Mount Taesong – Pongwhari (east)
4   Sopo (north) – Three Revolutions Exhibition – Ryonmotdong
5   Sopo (north) – Film Studio
6   Palgol – Kwangbok – Chilgol
7   Palgol – Kwangbok – Mangyongdae
8   Palgol – Pulgun – Ragwon – Kyonghung – Ponghwa – Potong Gate – Chollima – Pyongyang Station – Yongwang – Dept No 2
22 Palgol – Wollori (west)
23 Palgol – Kwangbok – Taepyong (west)
9   Friendship Tower – Moranbong – Sungri – Okryu Bridge – Juche Tower – Pangjik – Sanopdong
10 Pyongyang Department Store No 1 – Okryu Bridge – Tongdaewon – Tapje – Taedonggangdong
11 Pyongyang Thermal Power Complex – Koryo Hotel – Yongwang – Taedong Bridge – Songyo Kangan – Chongbaek
12 Pyongyang Station – Yokjon – Pyongchon Kangan – Angol – Mangyongdae
13 Pyongyang Station – Yokjon – Pyongchon Kangan – Chongsung Bridge
15 Rangrang Bridge – Saesarim – Kim Hyong Jik University – Tapje – Taedonggangdong
16 Rangrang Bridge – Pottery Factory (southeast)
34 Rangrang Bridge – Taehyondong (southeast)
35 Rangrang Bridge – Ryokpo (southeast)
14 Songsin – Saesarim – Taedong Bridge – Dept No 2
17 Songsin – Mirim Bridge (east)
18 Songsin – Changchon (south)
37 Songsin – Ripsok (southeast)
38 Songsin – Sangwon (southeast)
39 Songsin – Tokdong (southeast)
40 Songsin – Rihyonri (southeast)
19 Tapje/Taehak – Sadong (south)
20 Tapje/Taehak – Mirim Bridge
21 Sangdangdong – Hyongsanri
24 Three Revolutions Exhibition – Tongbukri (north)
25 Three Revolutions Exhibition – Sunan (north)
26 Three Revolutions Exhibition – Sinmiri (north)
27 Three Revolutions Exhibition – Kanri (north)
31 Chongbaek – Tongil – Wonam (south)
32 Chongbaek – Tongil – Pyokjidori (south)
33 Chongbaek – Tongil – Kangnam (south)

It is possible on some tours to go on Pyongyang's trolleybuses and trams, tickets cost 5KPW paid to the conductor, but that is a planned option, not a spontaneous event, ie: a guide would never say 'O, let's just get the tram,' to get somewhere. If it's not on the itinerary it's not happening and tourists cannot go on them by themselves.

Opposite and on page 117 are lists of the trolleybus and bus routes for Pyongyang, with roads and landmarks indicated. This is really for the visitor's interest and *maybe* one day for their use, although previously including this information has notably traumatised one guide. Where the vehicles go into unmapped outskirts, their general direction is given (eg: north).

TAXIS Taxis were for many years mostly a decrepit fleet of 1970s Volvo and 1980s Mercedes saloons and some token Volkswagens with 'Taxi' on the roofs. That's still pretty much the case, but hundreds of Chinese-made BYD Autos taxis have permanently joined the fleet (all in Beijing taxi colours, so don't think they're just very lost taxis) and there are hundreds more on order. The fixed fee for the first 4km is 400 won, and 100 won each kilometre thereafter, which is very roughly US$4 or €5 upfront. They don't ply the streets for trade but loiter around the big hotels and Pyongyang railway station, and can be reluctant to take foreigners. Tourists will need their guides with them if they want to take a taxi – which happens next to never. Phone or get the hotel to call these taxi-centre numbers: ☎ 33428, ☎ 45615 or ☎ 42007. However, around here every Sunday is a 'walking day' – so spare some fuel and see more, and be seen, by walking as much as possible.

OTHER CARS There are supposed to be around 250,000 cars in the DPRK, and many of those have been kept on the road for extraordinary lengths of time, including early Russian Moskvichs and Volgas, very quaint Russian jeeps and secondhand, right-hand-drive vehicles imported from Japan. However, more and more newish and new Chinese brands, Volkswagens, Japanese saloons and 4x4s are appearing, imported from China. There are also increasing numbers of the locally assembled Pigeon brand of cars and vans, the only consumer product for which there is any advertising (one can see a handful of billboards around Pyongyang). Look out for the public announcement vehicles, minivans with four massive tannoys on the roof, reminding locals of the orders of the day. Until the 2010s, Pyongyang's wide boulevards remained blissfully clear, and as one businessman put it, 'Pyongyang is exceptional in that the journey times from one part of town to another are the same at any hour, now as ten years ago.' Now, in a sign of the times, people are experiencing traffic jams. While most cars are almost exclusively for 'public' use of some kind, there is increasing private ownership of vehicles, although there's also the tight supply of petrol to consider, causing drivers of all vehicles to flick into neutral gear as they coast downhill. Spare a thought for the ingenuity and effort needed to keep the older vehicles roadworthy, after millions of kilometres of driving. Parts supplies are irregular (if available at all, considering the age of some). If not rolling around on four mismatched tyres, many of the vehicles you'll see will be by the roadside, on jacks and/or with the bonnet up with legs protruding from beneath or oily hands reaching out. It's not known if these vehicles have ever served hitchhikers, but probably not as foreigners can't hitchhike here anyway.

BICYCLES There are now many more bicycles than there were (with round red registration plates), but no hotels as yet hire them out.

Most people just walk, and officially they do not jaywalk, which you will see them doing but must not emulate! Use the underpass or zebra crossings or the arm of the traffic police will befall you.

TOURIST INFORMATION

For detailed tourist information, see pages 81 and 274.

BEYOND THE CITY Public transport beyond the city's immediate limits is limited to very old buses, packed out, or being crammed into the back of an open lorry. You can maybe catch a foreigner's Land Cruiser, if you've the permits to get somewhere.

WHERE TO STAY

Most of the hotels in the DPRK date from the 1970s and have not been decorated since, so they have a now unique Soviet ostentatiousness, which is on the one hand charming and part of the trip, but on the other, particularly for hotels outside Pyongyang, they can be quite run-down, with ropey wiring, broken fittings, bath taps that snap off in your hand and toilets that don't flush (clue – if you find your bath is full of cold water and there's a pan floating in it, it's probably to flush the loo with). Longer trips involving numerous hostelries can become a veritable series of case studies for apprentice plumbers. That said, there is a process of renovations being undertaken for the country's hotel stock – albeit obliterating their faded charm – and a surprising number of new ones built with Chinese money are going up.

You don't have to stay in the top-class hotels, and indeed the DPRK media are always pointing out that the top hotels are already full with visitors, but you will be given the hard sell. Note that none of them, even the high-class ones, have heating in the public areas in winter, and even the top hotels have old-school bedside cupboards with built-in radios that don't work.

You can first dial (adding +850 2 if outside the country) 18111 which puts you through to the operator and you can then either give an extension number of the hotel or the name of hotel. But for international calls many of the hotels also have direct international numbers (or faxes) that run +850 2 381 xxxx. All listings are located on the map opposite, unless otherwise noted, and the map key below corresponds to the map on the opposite page.

DELUXE These hotels have guaranteed hot water & electricity. In theory, both the Yanggakdo & Koryo hotels, because they are so tall, add a little extra for rooms the higher up they are (a kind of 'view premium' tacked onto the price) but it's not in practice for tourists.

⌂ **Pyongyang Koryo Hotel** (500 rooms) Changgwang St; ☏ 02 381 4397; f 02 381 4422. Opened in 1985 & recently renovated. Near Pyongyang railway station & the Forbidden City. 45 floors in twin towers & many restaurants, with 2 that revolve. The hotel's twin towers are a Pyongyang landmark, with comfortable rooms, & there are a few bars, a mini-mart, a 15m swimming pool in the basement, billiards & a bookshop, among other features. **$$$$**

PYONGYANG *City Centre*
For listings, see pages 122–6

⌂ **Where to stay**
1	Haebangsan	B6
2	Moranbong	B2
3	Pyongyang	B6
4	Pyongyang Koryo	A6

⊗ **Where to eat and drink**
	Arirang	(see 3)
5	Gold Lane Bowling Alley	D4
6	Minjok Soktang	B6
7	Moran	C2
8	Okryu	C4
9	(Old) Taedonggang Diplomatic Club	C6
10	Pyongyang Boat Restaurant No 1	C5
11	Pyongyang Boat Restaurant No 2	C5
12	Rungwa Island Restaurant	D3
13	Songyo	C6
14	Taedongyang Brewery No 3	D5
15	The Pyolmuri	A6
16	Viennese café	C5

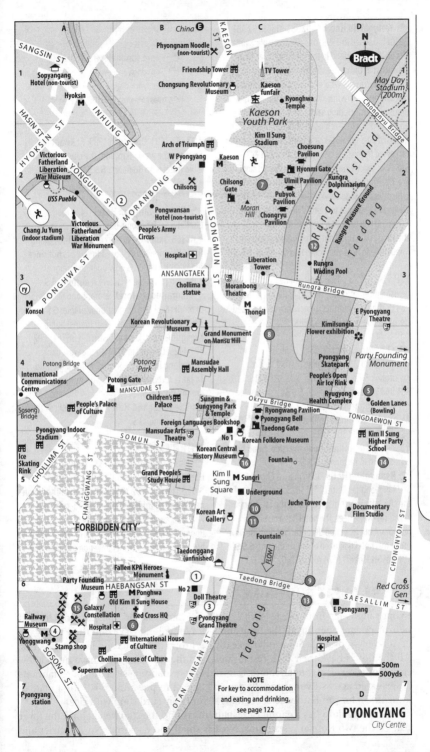

⌂ Yanggakdo Hotel ☎02 381 2134; f 02 381 2930/1. Opened in 1995, this 47-storey glass prism sits on Yanggak Island in the Taedong River, 4km southeast of the city centre. The hotel is 2nd only to the Koryo in the whole country, & has numerous restaurants, with a massive banquet hall wing, & amusements including sauna, bowling & karaoke, all stashed in a low-ceilinged underground warren accessed by a spiral staircase from the foyer, a casino (accessed from stairs next to restaurants 1 & 2), a 3rd-floor tailor who'll knock up Kim Jong Il suits, & a 'health centre' run by Chinese from Dandong who offer massage services for around € 15. The Yanggakdo also has foreign TV news in its rooms, assuming you can get reception. If bouncing from the Yanggakdo Hotel out of town & back it's not impossible to hold your room for €5 a night. **$$$$**

FIRST CLASS Five-digit phone numbers can be used internationally by first dialling (+850) 18111 then the number; hence they can be used from outside or inside the DPRK.

⌂ Chongnyon Hotel (520 rooms) Chukjondong, Mangyongdae District. Cnr of Kwangbok & Chongchun Sts; ☎02 381 6210; f 02 381 3681. Triangular design. **$$$**
⌂ Potonggang Hotel (162 rooms) Ansangdong, Pyongchon District; ☎48301; ☎02 381 2228/9; f 02 381 4428. About 4km west of Kim Il Sung Square, at the Potong riverside. Good hotel. CNN shown in its rooms. **$$$**
⌂ Ryanggang Hotel (330 rooms) Chongchun St, Mangyongdae District; ☎73825. In the west of the city, near sports district, where the Taedong & Potong rivers meet. The hotel has a revolving restaurant but its period décor cannot disguise how much this hotel is in need of refurbishment. **$$$**
⌂ Sosan Hotel (474 rooms) ☎02 381 6212;

f 02 381 3601. Opened in 1989. At Kwangbok Street in the west, 4km from the city centre, this is a big hotel with 30 floors. **$$$**

SECOND CLASS
⌂ Changgwangsan Hotel (420 rooms) Chollima St, Tongsong-dong, Central District; ☎48366. 3km west of the centre, at the Potong River. Was previously closed to tourists but since renovation in 2006 is now open to foreigners, although it is somewhat airy & austere. **$$**
⌂ Moranbong Hotel Moranbong St. Number of rooms & phone number unavailable. **$$**
⌂ Pyongyang Hotel (170 rooms) Sungi St, Kyongrim-dong, Central District; ☎38161; f 02 381 4426. Opened in 1961 on the west bank of Taedong River & opposite Pyongyang Grand Theatre, recently renovated with quite a glitzy ground floor. **$$**
⌂ Taedonggang Hotel Being rebuilt at the time of writing. **$$**

THIRD CLASS
⌂ Haebangsan Hotel (83 rooms) Sungni St, Haebangsandong, Central District; ☎37037; ☎02 381 6214; f 02 381 3569. South of the square, near Taedong Bridge, & the only 3rd-class hotel where foreigners can stay, mostly foreign students. Rooms are clean but not luxurious. Bathrooms with hot water. Weird sentinel tower on one corner. **$**

✖ WHERE TO EAT AND DRINK

Pyongyang is far from the level of London or Bangkok for eateries and bars, but new places are opening all the time and it is a long, long way from the Pyongyang of not-very-old-at-all. Some offer free dishes, group discounts and loyalty schemes. All the hotels have their own restaurants, and the top-class ones have quite a few each (some revolve!) but an interesting and ever-expanding selection of restaurants is sprinkled across Pyongyang. In general, expect to pay around € 3 for a plate of kimchi, € 8 for pre-barbecue beef and € 10 for bean-curd soup with rice.

The **Yanggakdo** has a gamut of restaurants round the stairwell behind the foyer bar. Of the two Korean restaurants, **No 1** is small and enclosed, **No 2** is airier and has a river view. Both serve a compromise of basic Western and Korean foods. Enclosed **Japanese** and **Chinese** restaurants sit opposite them across the stairs to the basement, where is the **Macau Chinese restaurant** (✆ *02 381 2134 ext 10808;* f *ext 10807;* ⏱ *08.30–03.30*), a very popular spot with expats – although Koreans are not allowed in – with long opening hours and a menu to match. The Yanggakdo's warm revolving venue serves its last meal at 22.00 but serves drinks until 23.00.

Changgwang Street has two dozen restaurants and bars that accept foreigners and their money. They all advertise as being open from 12.00 to 15.00 and 18.00 to 21.30, but may not be in practice and some open only for large bookings, for works' units on reward whom you may see queuing outside with their vouchers.

But several more accessible restaurants are there for wining and dining along, behind and around Changgwang and the Koryo. The stamp shop next to the Koryo has its own restaurant. Several are tucked into the block opposite the Koryo Hotel entrance. Across the Changgwang from the Koryo, heading for the side street on the right, and about 80m down on the left is a gated courtyard. On the immediate left is a white conservatory entrance to a multi-floored **Korean BBQ** ($$$$) and a **Japanese restaurant** ($$$). On the far side of the yard is another Korean venue with karaoke upstairs. Both are open until 23.00. Also look out for the two places below.

There is also reputedly a bar at the Jongbo centre at the base of the Ryugyong Hotel and a rarely used restaurant nearby, and word was once of a hamburger joint called Samtaesan. The TV tower has a restaurant that punters are welcome to tell us about. All listings are located on the map, page 123.

✗ **Minjok Soktang** (aka the National) Next to the Red Cross HQ & Pyongyang University of Medicine, over the road from the Koryo Hotel. Has a fun floor show most evenings & great ambience. $$$$

✗ **The Pyolmuri** (aka the Galaxy or Constellation) Changgwang St, 100m northwest of the entrance to the Koryo Hotel. A 1st in many respects, being the 1st place to offer pizza, pasta & hamburgers, & it has a good cocktail bar. The Dear Leader did not eat here. $$$–$$

WEST BANK The **Viennese café** on the northeast corner of Kim Il Sung Square offers real coffee, at some price & not so speedily when a large tour group suddenly rolls up & the three-way payment system can also slow things down – but it's all part of a pleasant experience. There's a shop selling interesting beers, cider & cakes.

✗ **Arirang** Part of the Pyongyang Hotel. There's an English menu with BBQ, beer & salad. $$$

✗ **Okryu** Sits in full Korean-style splendour on the Taedong's west bank. A massive restaurant built in 1960 that's just reappearing on tours. Best known for its cold noodles. $$$

✗ **Pyongyang Boat Restaurant No 1** Usually moors opposite the Juche Tower on the west bank.

Excellent BBQs. Can be hired out for events & cruises lazily along the river. $$$

✗ **Pyongyang Boat Restaurant No 2** Smaller than the No 1, this usually moors about 200m south of it, with pink net curtains & a welcoming smile. Serves black beer. $$$

AROUND THE CENTRE AND NORTH

✗ **Changgwang Health Complex** Next to the ice rink, has 2 restaurants, but the one on the terrace is only open in the summer. Both serve the higher end (& higher priced) of Korean fare. (The nearby ice rink has a restaurant & there is also reputedly a Japanese venue behind the rink.) $$$$

✗ **Eyonphung BBQ Restaurant** Just off a side road from Potong Bridge. €20 per head including beer & *soju* – does a good BBQ. $$$$

✗ **Mokran** (Magnolia) Japanese-based Western restaurant in the Potonggang Hotel, with excellent service & fine wine. In this hotel is a standard Korean restaurant that has recently had a makeover. $$$$

✗ **Pyongyang Informatics Centre** In the shadow of the uncompleted Ryugyong Hotel. Has a good, if expensive, Korean BBQ restaurant. Bars on the ground & first floors & a pool in the basement. $$$$

✕ **Moranbang Hotel** Has a Japanese–Korean terrace bar; lovely in the evenings. $$$
✕ **Phyongchon Restaurant** Just south of the bend in Chollima St, take the road running east; halfway along is this restaurant. $$$
✕ **Moran** In the middle of Moranbang Pk. Korean food. $$

EAST
✕ **(Old) Taedonggang Diplomatic Club**
🕐 for lunch & until 21.30; disco until 23.00 Fri/Sat. Through its corridors are a few restaurants, & it has been renovated & refitted of late to include karaoke rooms, bars & sports facilities. Simple servings of soups & salads, batting around €15 pp. $$$$–$$$
✕ **Gold Lanes Bowling Alley** 2 restaurants here & a bar here, serving draught beer. The stews here are well known. $$$
✕ **Songyo** Opposite the Taedonggang Diplomatic Club. A Korean restaurant. $$$
✕ **Taedonggang Brewery No 3** A few hundred metres northeast of the Juche Tower is an upstairs bar with 7 different beers from a microbrewery, great variations of barley to rice, €2 a glass. No 6 is a coffee-tasting stout. Also serves food. $$$
✕ **Taedongyogwan** Cross Okryu Bridge eastwards, follow Munsudong St straight through a 3-pronged fork, & on the right appears this drum-shaped Korean restaurant. $$

SOUTH
✕ **Dangogo Gukjib** Tongil St. Dog meat is the speciality here. $$$$
✕ **Pyongyang BBQ Duck** On the northwest corner of Tongil St & Chungsong Bridge junction; 🕐 until 21.30, serving duck cooked on BBQs at your table. Great fun & popular with the locals. $$$$–$$$
✕ **Chongnyu Restaurant** On the Potong riverbank before Sinso Bridge. This 4-storey building shaped like a ship serves the usual Korean fare, including *sinsollo*, with rooms dedicated to particular dishes. $$$
✕ **Pyongyang Mullet Soup Restaurant** On the Taedong's south bank between Chungsong & Yanggak bridges. Fiddly to get to. $$
✕ **Pyongyang Noodle House** Diagonally opposite from the Pyongyang BBQ Duck. Specialises in Pyongyang (ie: cold) noodles. $$

WEST
✕ **Chongryu Hotpot** Opposite the Romanian embassy, this upstairs restaurant is great fun, with individual furnaces to cook a hotpot. Downstairs sells drinks, ice-cream, snacks & tat. $$$$
✕ **Sherman Pizza** Changkwang St, near the Sherman monument. Has pizza worth waiting for – & you will wait as there's only 1 oven, so go in the evening as the last thing to do. The menu has pasta & Korean dishes & the Italian-trained staff provide karaoke & Italian-style fretting in the face of large groups. At least €12pp. $$$$
✕ **West Pyongyang** At the Taedonggang beer factory. Built with bricks from the west of England, this good restaurant now produces 7 types of draught beer & lager (inc black beer) that compete with the longer-set home brews of Pyongyang & Ryongsong beer. $$$$
✕ **Chilgol Restaurant** Opposite the circus on Kwangbok St. $$$
✕ **Chongchun Restaurant No 1** Kwangbok St, nr Tangsang flyover. A good place to mix it with the working classes. $$$
✕ **Pizza & Spaghetti Restaurant** Kwangbok St. Upstairs & serves its namesake food. $$$
✕ **Chongchun No 2** Kwangbok St, nr Tangsang flyover. $$
✕ **Hyangmannu** Kwangbok St, nr Tangsang flyover. $$

ENTERTAINMENT AND NIGHTLIFE

For nightlife, there's not that much to do. The city was once famed for the wits and other delights of its 'kisaeng girls', akin to the geishas of Japan, but these days they're rather thin on the ground. Most of the hotels now have some form of karaoke, which open until your larynx is frazzled. There's an interesting Egyptian-themed nightclub in the Yanggakdo Hotel basement that's open till the small hours, next to the DPRK's first casino (staffed only by Chinese; ⊕ *14.00–05.00*). Atop one of the Changgwangsan hotel's towers is Pyongyang's first disco, still going strong, for foreigners only. During the summer months, and/or when a large show or festival is on, numerous beer tents open around Pyongyang (particularly around the Koryo and to a lesser extent the Yanggakdo) selling drinks and sometimes heated snack foods until the small hours. These two hotels have white-boothed bars selling good, opaque, brown draught beer till midnight, and all the hotels at least have bars doing what bars do in the wee hours.

The Taedonggang Diplomatic Club has a disco until 23.00 on Fridays and Saturdays. The foreign residents by and large congregate at the Random Access Club, which tourists aren't allowed into. In true Pyongyang style, revealing its location requires an invitation.

But the quietness of Pyongyang at night is another unique attribute; no capital anywhere is as silent or dark. One guest at the island hotel of Yanggakdo leaned out of his top-floor window and heard a baby crying, which he realised was coming from an apartment across the river. If it's a special time of year, or a state visit is on, the main sites are illuminated.

If not, tiptoeing through the streets at night in the pitch black was one way to go round town without getting any kind of attention, with the presence of others only noted when you heard them talking as they passed. Pyongyang railway station at night was wonderfully romantic, full of waiting travellers, smoking, chatting, playing cards and sleeping, maybe one playing a flute for haunting tunes to waft through the streets.

Things change, however, and for all that, the streets are not as ill lit as they were. More to the point, sneaking out of your hotel without your guides is not an option.

SHOPPING

Beijing and some other Chinese cities have vast aircraft hangar-like covered markets, and Pyongyang now has one, Tongil market, just off Tongil Street. There are scores of stalls and cubicles selling everything from watches and radios to curtains and shirts while another hall has foodstuffs, including exotica like quail and turkey, squelching and spilling all over the shop. Otherwise your ability to buy things is limited to the large department stores, hotel shops and a few other outlets.

OTHER PRACTICALITIES

CHANGING MONEY You can change money in the big hotels, some restaurants & at the Trade Bank on Sungni Street, near Kim Il Sung Square. But better to bring enough in the first place.

HOSPITALS AND PHARMACIES
Foreigners needing to see a physician can contact, or get their guides to contact, Dr Melvin Padua in the WFP administration building (*21 Munsudong, Pyongyang*, m *0191 2500 624*, trunkline: *02 381 7220 ext 5115, or 02 381 7585*; e *Melvin.padua@ undp.org*; *€25 consultancy fee*).

POST OFFICE The main post office is in the centre, just southwest of Taedong Bridge [123 C6]. The International Post Office is in Haebangsan Street. The International Communications Centre is in Potonggang District, opposite the Pyongyang Indoor Stadium.

PUBLICATIONS *Korea* (monthly) & the *Pyongyang Times* (weekly) are multi-lingual publications available from the hotel shops. Much of the available literature in the DPRK concerns the lives & works of the Kims, or foreign affairs reviews like 'The US Imperialists started the war'. Otherwise there are glossy books on Korea's wildlife, & that's it. There is one foreign-language bookshop (⊕ *09.00–18.00, except Sun & Thu afternoon*), opposite the Pyongyang No 1 store on the same block as the Korean Culture Museum.

WHAT TO SEE AND DO

Guides and DPRK guidebooks give a lot of statistics: dates of construction, speed of construction, floor space, and the number of tiles, bricks or measurements that have symbolism for the cult of the Kims. The anodyne statistics are also proof of progress. Communist states in the heady decades of success from the 1950s to the 1980s were fiercely competitive among themselves in terms of output and progress, and the proof of a more advanced, more capable workforce was that they could knock up the biggest library in the world in the shortest time.

These statistics also make up for the dearth of other facts. It's quickly apparent that there are far fewer urban anecdotes than those you'd find in other cities, eg: 'This area used to be a red-light district, and that hotel used to be a brothel and Dickens was once caught there.' This is due to a combination of Year Zero and Ground Zero. The first comprised the DPRK's own cultural revolution, in which the communists expunged all the history of the corrupt and wicked past and outside influences, redacting the definition of interesting and worthy only to achievements and comments from the Kims (arguably, this cultural revolution has never ended). Ground Zero was what befell Pyongyang during the war. Nearly every building, including many of the 'ancient' ones, were built or reconstructed post-war, and the grander buildings are from the late 1960s and 1970s when the economy could afford more grandeur. In that sense, what you see is what you get. All those apartment blocks, tied together by weedy power lines strung from roof to roof, are and have always been apartment blocks. The purpose for which a government edifice was put up is the purpose for which that building is used today. You might disagree over what DPRK literature considers to be 'highlights', as the following from the *Pyongyang Review* suggests: 'The Three Revolution Exhibition is a centre for recreation for working people, and for scientific research. It is made up of pavilions, recreation, management, entrance, car park and lawn area, which constitute an ensemble.'

On the other hand, the list of highlights continues to grow. Where there's to be any change in the DPRK, it'll happen first and foremost in Pyongyang, and the list of sites, from old places opening to foreigners and new enterprises operating along more Western lines, can only really get longer.

KIM IL SUNG SQUARE [123 C5] At the centre of the city is this huge open plaza of 75,000m² of granite, set out in 1954, which is seen as Pyongyang's heart, through which the great military and torch parades and mass rallies pass during national holidays and anniversaries. Tourists have not usually been allowed to attend the more formal elements of these celebrations, such as the torch parades, but may catch parts of parades in other parts of town and may well see mass gatherings for rally practices around the city. One visitor to North Korea told me:

I was in the city one spring, walking back through town quite late, having had a few beers, and happened to see that, for once, the lights were on in Kim Il Sung Square, albeit very dimly. This was rare enough to warrant a look-see and, in a spy-like manner, I peered around the last wall to look out onto the square. What I saw was the entire square with what must have been thousands of people, in lines, in identical positions as they went through some kind of t'ai chi-like set of poses. The thing was the only noise was the completely in-sync swoosh and shuffle of moving arms and legs, and the breathing, thousands of people all breathing in and out in time. It was eerie, but incredible.

It is as good a place as any to start a tour and may well be the first place that you visit. Looking at the square's western half, the **Ministry of Foreign Affairs** is on the north side and the **Ministry of Foreign Trade** on the south, with both buildings dominated by the **Grand People's Study House** [123 B5]. The eastern half of the square has the simple classical grandeur of the **Korean Central History Museum** [123 C5] on the north side and, opposite that, the Korean Art Gallery. Huge placards of the national and KWP flags, slogans and neon add vibrant colour to an otherwise austere place.

The Study House truly rules the square. 'Its architectural ornaments are of light and quiet colours, which contribute to its magnificent yet refreshing appearance. In architecture, it demonstrates the elegance and majesty of the traditional Korean-style building,' according to local literature. The 34 hip-saddle roofs, capped with 750,000 green tiles, rise one above another like unfolded wings of cranes. Built for Kim Il Sung's 70th birthday in 1982 (as was the Juche Tower opposite), it is the facility that hosts the 'Study-While-Working' educational system for Party members and working people, and can accommodate 12,000 users a day. A huge white statue of the Great Leader sits in the marble-pillared entrance, flanked not by grand stairways but by two modern escalators. Enter the Kim Il Sung reading room with its half-computerised directory, half-carded index, and you'll see the music library with the foreign music section – where Koreans can listen to foreign popular music such as Vera Lynn's greatest hits right up to the most modern – The Beatles. Maybe you'll see a language class in action (Repeat after me!) and big reading rooms full of dull, flickering lights to strain the eyes of the library's visitors poring over its 30 million volumes, deliverable on a remote-controlled conveyor. Certainly the lifts are in tremendous demand on Saturdays, and seem to work in a way where 'catch a lift' is appropriate, as they zoom past floors where people are waiting to board. The upper balcony is also used to co-ordinate the march pasts and evening torch parades, and you can look out onto the mature metal roofs of the surrounding buildings. Also note that the Study House is symmetrically perfectly aligned with the **Juche Tower** [123 D5] (see page 145) across the river, and which is a totem to Kim Il Sung's own philosophy of Juche that underpins so much of politics and culture in the DPRK. The tower having been built at the same time as the study house, it is one of a few epic architectural vistas that Kim Il Sung visited upon Pyongyang and is fascinating for what it reveals of Kim Il Sung's beneficent ego. The Study House is itself a magnificent gift of philanthropy to benefit and educate the people – but as the thousands pour out of it, freshly laden with the learnings of the world housed in an entirely Korean edifice, the tower reminds them of the single body of learning bequeathed by the Great Leader that guides and inspires their lives, Juche.

On the square's northeast side is the **Korean Central History Museum** [123 C5] (⊕ *Tue–Sun*), providing a long, detailed tour of the peninsula's history, a lot of which is invasions, resistance and repulsions, feuds and wars between provinces, kingdoms and surrounding countries. It's a complicated tale that's difficult to tell coherently, and the museum could assist visitors' concentration by adjusting the lighting and ventilation. Look out for the world's first rocket batteries and the classic black ball and fuse of the world's first time bomb.

The **Korean Art Gallery** [123 C5] is well worth a visit. From its excellent reproductions of early Korean tomb paintings, it follows with large (roll mat) screen paintings illustrating court and common life in Korea across time. The guides provide an excellent interpretation of the paintings, from the decadence of feudal Korea up to the real meanings of seemingly innocuous paintings under Japanese rule. The big, bright, socialist-realism paintings on the upper floors are fascinating, especially the *Sailing Steel Works* that challenges Western notions of what constitutes beauty.

KIM IL SUNG SQUARE TO THE MANSUDAE GRAND MONUMENT Head north from the square along Sungri Street (that splits the square in two), and a block later on the crossroads with Somun Street is **Pyongyang Department Store No 1**. Reader Robin Tudge writes: 'None of the lights were on in the shop when I went there, so only daylight glinting off the polished floor permeated the shop's centre. This meant I could get quite close to the tills (for practically all goods are behind counters) before the shop assistants would see me and wander off.'

Opposite the No 1 is the **Foreign Languages Bookshop** (⏲ *09.00–18.00 Mon–Sat, closed Thu pm*). It's a good place to buy books, prints, pictures, embroideries and other souvenirs as well as maps and occasionally fantastic hand-painted posters. On the corner and riverwards along Somun Street is the **Korean Folklore Museum** [123 C5]. This is a much more manageable three-floor exhibition of the daily lives of Koreans, and the English-speaking guide gives a good account of what work and fun entailed for Korean men, women and children in times gone by.

On the No 1's west side, and accessible via a huge staircase leading down from the Grand Study House, are the hard-to-miss **Mansudae fountains** (firing up to 80m high), providing cooling mists in summer and pools for locals to play in. The fountains front the massive **Mansudae Arts Theatre** [123 B5], with its spectrum-coloured tower, and in which dance and music performances can be seen by arrangement. In good contrast with the theatre's monolithic simplicity are the more humanly scaled **Sungmin** and **Sungnyong** temples [123 B5], dating from 1325 and 1429 respectively. The latter was built as a shrine to Tangun and to the founder of Koguryo, Tongmyong. Continuing uphill and northwards to Mansu Hill, a good view of the city to the west becomes visible. Soon, on the left appears the monolithic DPRK building of the **Mansudae Assembly Hall** [123 B4], with a huge carved national emblem on its façade, surrounded by acres of empty car parks. The hall, built in the 1960s and revamped in the 1980s, is where the DPRK parliament assembles and votes, and visiting it is really worthwhile but is only possible by arrangement, ie: when it's not in use. Hallways hundreds of metres in length are lined with statues not of the great and the good as they would be in the West, but of workers and patriots, and wall-length paintings beam away from stairwells with chandeliers cascading down through the floors. The main assembly hall is cavernous, with an awesome glazed ceiling and an 18m statue of Kim Il Sung reminding any delegate who had (or has) forgotten quite who is still in charge. Observe the detail of the décor and count the number and location of microphones. Guides take you through the numerous private committee rooms and lounges, with boat-sized oval tables bedecked with towering flower arrangements, these structures sailing on lake-sized deep plush carpets, rooms which would normally be filled with the DPRK's own great and the good and all the smoke that goes with top-level decision-taking.

From the hall, the road tips down then up Mansu Hill towards the **Korean Revolutionary Museum** [123 B3] and what must be Pyongyang's most famous site, the **Mansudae Grand Monument** [123 B4]. Here are the towering 20m bronze figures of Kim Il Sung, arm out pointing the way forward, and Kim Jong Il, both standing in front of a 70m-wide mosaic of Korea's spiritual source, Mount Paektu. Local tourist literature says of the monument:

> The Korean People erected the monument from their unanimous desire and aspiration to have the immortal and revolutionary exploits of the great leader Comrade Kim Il Sung remembered for all time and to carry forward and consummate the revolutionary cause of Juche which he initiated.

Flanking the Great and Dear Leaders are the DPRK and KWP flags rendered in polished stone and lined with 228 bronze figures (5m high) symbolising the anti-Japanese struggle, socialist revolution and construction. The monument was first built in 1972 to commemorate Kim Il Sung's 60th birthday and a statue of Kim Il

THE GREAT LEADER'S GREAT WORKS OF ART

An increasingly frequently visited venue is the Mansudae Art Studio, where some 1,000 artists produce everything from massive oil paintings, prints, charcoals, and 'jewel' paintings laden with powdered stones to the massive statues and reliefs at the Mansudae Grand Monument, the huge winged-horse of the Chollima Statue and the Monument to the Founding of the Korean Workers' Party. Set up in 1959, the sheer scale of the studio, with 4,000 staff stashed across some 120,000m² (two-thirds being indoors), says a lot about the importance of the arts in the state's efforts to glorify the Kims and the regime. The entrance courtyard to the studio serves as an outdoor gallery of murals, paintings and statues, and a visit here should include seeing the artists in residence at work – producing work of such value they need picturesque guards with bayoneted-AK47s on the door. But just as the DPRK has exported its expertise in organising Mass Games, the Mansudae studio has an international wing, Mansudae Overseas Projects, doing good business building statues, monuments and even a palace in far-flung lands, projects ranging in scale from the Fairy Tale Fountain in Frankfurt to Africa's tallest statue, the 49m-high African Renaissance Monument in Senegal. This epic, macho structure, depicting a ripped man, a curvy woman and their child pointing to the sea, was unveiled in 2010 to an audience including the presidents of Zimbabwe, the DRC, Jesse Jackson and hip-hop singer Akon as well as various North Korean dignitaries. Africa has also proved a fertile ground for Mansudae's other projects, with monuments in Botswana, Zimbabwe and Namibia, where the artists built a patriotic 732-acre Heroes' Acre cemetery dedicated to the country's national heroes.

In case there is nothing in the studio's large shop that appeals (and remember you're only ever going to go there once), there are two major outlets in Beijing for North Korean art, one being the Mansudae Art Studio Gallery, which is Mansudae's 'official' outlet (*www.myinweb.com/mansudae/*), and the other being at the Koryo Tours office (*www.koryogroup.com*).

Sung stood alone until 2012 when it was joined by one of Kim Jong Il. However, the original Kim Il Sung statue that stood until 2012 did not have him smiling or wearing glasses as he does now, and the very first statue of Kim Jong Il had him wearing a coat very similar in cut to his father's – but now he wears a parka. The statues were made at **Mansudae Art Studio** (see box, page 131).

Slogans on the monuments' placards read 'Long live Kim Il Sung' and 'Let us drive out US imperialism and reunify the country'. A six-figure group on the left banner of the statue plot the overthrow of US imperialism, all imperialism, and the world revolution. The monument and the museum were built for Kim's 60th birthday, and the museum has over 4.5km of display halls of varying interest. Since his death in July 1994, it has become the focus for mourning. The statue in its dazzling glory stands atop a massive plaza, with music softly wafting from the nearby trees. It is an extraordinary, powerful place, and is one of the, if not *the*, most sacred sites in the DPRK. It is as good as an obligatory stopping point for any visitor, from whom the utmost decorum is requested and required (and advised to be followed without question). Some Koreans visiting the site, and it is a site that wherever North Koreans go in the country they will as likely come here at least once, are moved to tears. It's also however a site for newly weds to come and have their photograph taken.

It is obligatory to pay your respects and present flowers to the site which can be bought from the fountains just down the hill for around €5 a bouquet but will most likely be arranged by your guides in any case (careful of flowers wrapped in purple cellophane, the colour comes off on your clothes!). Photographs can be taken with discretion and the important proviso to observe is that no feature of the statue is cropped from any shot.

As part of another grand vista, the statues are symmetrically aligned not only with the Korean Revolutionary Museum behind, but to the Korean Workers' Party Foundation Monument 2km east across the river. One can also clearly see the Juche Tower, the May Day Stadium, the Chollima statue and other sites around town.

MANSUDAE GRAND MONUMENT TO THE ARCH OF TRIUMPH Northwards past the monument run little leafy paths down to Chilsongmun Street, which hugs the hilltop park of Chongnion on **Moran Hill** [123 C2]. First on Chilsongmun you pass the **Chollima** statue [123 B3]. Chollima is a fabled winged horse that could cover a thousand ri (400km) a day. The 46m-high statue was inaugurated in 1961 and 'symbolises the heroic mettle and indomitable spirit of our people who made ceaseless innovations for post war rehabilitation'. The rebuilding of Pyongyang after the Korean War was said to be carried out at Chollima speed.

The statue is composed of a worker, a member of our heroic class, spurring the Chollima on to a leap forward with the red letter of the Central Committee of the Workers' Party of Korea in his raised hand and a young peasant woman seated behind him with a sheaf of ripe rice in her arms.

Opposite Chollima is the classical portico of the **Moranbong Theatre** [123 C3], built in 1946 just after occupation and where the North–South joint conference, followed by the first Supreme People's Assembly (indicating who won that argument), was held in 1948. Rebuilt having been gutted during the war, it is now a great venue for performances of classical music and opera. It's nestled into Moran Hill, the slopes and trees of which provide shade and breeze as you descend to the Arch of Triumph. This road crosses over the road tunnel that bores under Chongnion and on to the Rungra Bridge. Kim Jong Suk nursery is on the left.

Eventually you reach the **Arch of Triumph** [123 B2]. Made of white granite, the 60m arch is dedicated to 'the home return of the Great Leader Comrade Kim Il

While there's been a marathon held in Pyongyang since 1981, the first Pyongyang Marathon with international competitors was in 2000, and was won by Kenya's Nelson Ndereva Njeru. The race's openness to foreign competitors has fluctuated over the years, but since 2009 at least it's been won by Chinese, Russians, Ukrainians and an Ethiopian, Ketema Bekele Nigusse in 2013, when 16 nations were represented (although the best time was posted by North Korean Kim Jung Wun in 1996). The women's race has consistently only ever been won by North Koreans, with Jong Yong Ok posting the fastest time in 2007.

The marathon is held in April, when temperatures are from 10° to 14°C. The flat and fast course starts and finishes at the 70,000-seat Kim Il Sung stadium, weaving through Pyongyang with a stretch along the Taedong, and 100,000s of Pyongyangians cheering the runners on. 'Several runners reported extremely tired arms as they decided to shake hands with the crowd over the last five kilometres,' said one organiser.

Marathon running is taken very seriously in Korea. The DPRK's top ten male runners consistently run about two hours ten–15 minutes and there are ten DPRK women who can run under two hours 30 minutes, including Jong Yong Ok. International participation in the Pyongyang Marathon – also known as the Mangyongdae Prize International Marathon Race – was restricted to top runners until 2014, when amateurs could at last apply. Their path was trailed possibly by participants in the capital's first 5km fun run in May 2013, when 50 tourists took to the streets to raise money for an orphanage in Nampo.

Sung who liberated Korea from Japanese colonialism' and has dozens of rooms in the interior as well as a lift going up to the viewing tiers atop the arch. It was built and erected in 1982 in one year on the 70th birthday of Kim Il Sung (symbolised by the 70 azaleas, Korea's national flower, that frame the arch). As written in the *Pyongyang Review*, 'Inscribed either side of the arch are the dates 1925–45 covering the period when Comrade Kim Il Sung set out on the 1,000 ri Journey for National Liberation to the time when he returned home in triumph after achieving his aim'. The *Review* continues: 'The three-tiered roof embodies the structural features of the traditional architecture – the pillars, beams, brackets and eaves are formed in a way congenial to modern aesthetic taste.'

Taller than the Parisian version we were told – interesting that the architectural styles are so similar! It's possible that you could arrive at the arch by way of nearby Kaeson ('triumph') metro station, where looming over the platform stands a golden statue of a very youthful Kim Il Sung, flanked by wall-length mosaics of ecstatic followers approaching, and again the theme relates to Kim's triumphant arrival in Pyongyang following Japan's collapse in 1945. Above ground and opposite the arch is where the Great Leader spoke to the masses at the 'Pyongyang Mass Meeting' where now stands **Kim Il Sung stadium** [123 C2]. Originally called Moranbong stadium, it was reconstructed with a capacity of 100,000 and renamed for KIS's 70th birthday. The Japanese had built it as a baseball stadium, but they were the last to use it for that purpose. These days it hosts football games and athletic events, and has been the venue for the Mass Games. The tree-shaded area nearer the metro entrance is also a site where many men hang out, playing draughts or chess or debating football, and there's a **shooting range**. Next to the stadium is a large stone with Kim Il Sung's autograph carved onto it, while to the left of the station entrance is a huge colourful mural depicting young Kim Il Sung addressing the crowds, and the large open area in front of the mural is a venue often used for mass dancing.

ARCH OF TRIUMPH TO THE REVOLUTIONARY MARTYRS' CEMETERY Beyond that, heading up the hill in the direction of the Pyongyang TV tower, is **Kaeson funfair** [123 C1], and it's well worth a visit if only to see hordes of locals, including entire brigades of Korean People's Army soldiers, relaxing and screaming like children. It's €1 to get in and then most of the big rides are up to €3. Foreigners with guides don't pay at each booth; instead they'll likely be taken straight onto the rides (don't look at the queues of glowering locals!). Then the punter must remember what

PLAZAS, DANCES AND PARADES

There are various large plazas around Pyongyang on which at the right times of year mass gatherings can occur. The spaces in front of cultural palaces and major landmarks like Kim Il Sung stadium, the KWP Foundation Monument and the People's Palace of Culture are venues for mass dances, joyful affairs where thousands of men in suits and women in red and pink dresses revolve, twirl and hokey-cokey, and to which sure-footed visitors are very welcome to join in (something the authorities encourage in order to depict on television foreigners having a good time engaging with local people).

Dances are most often held around the time of major national anniversaries or public holidays, as are the kinds of parade involving huge march pasts of soldiers, tanks, missiles and politically and patriotically emblazoned floats, which for outsiders all constitute probably the most readily identified motifs of the DPRK.

The chances of an ordinary visitor actually getting to see the huge march pasts in Kim Il Sung Square, or anywhere near there, are akin to being invited into St Paul's Cathedral during a royal wedding. But what can be attended are smaller parades – and 'smaller' means hundreds and hundreds of trucks full of soldiers taking hours to roll past throngs of cheering locals – and they're great fun, real street parties without the austerity of the main parades.

It's not guaranteed. In fact visitors expecting to be in Pyongyang the night before a parade might find themselves billeted miles out of town as hotel rooms are assigned to more important people. And on the day, while you can see the parades beginning on television, somehow your tour bus keeps being pointed the wrong way against the tides of locals tooled up with flags and flowers on their way to an amazing event. But more often than not, you will see something. Not so long ago ordinary visitors saw nothing, and instead would end up at some very empty site out of town where they could dwell on being excluded from an utterly epic event.

As there are several occasions for such parades, there are even more occasions to practise for them, so keep a look out for glimpses of rehearsals, with mass gatherings appearing in the plazas around the Juche Tower, Kim Il Sung Square, outside cultural halls and at points along the strip of parkland running along the Taedong's east bank, and see which way torrents of well-dressed locals are going. Nonetheless, getting to go up close and have a full-on gawp is unlikely.

rides he went on and pay their tour guide at the end. Particular favourites are the Drop of Death and the Pendulum of Death. Just west of the arch is the **Wolhyang department store**, which sells paintings and sometimes national football shirts, and the Pyongyang City People's Hospital No 1.

If you continue north on Kaeson Street, the 30m, somewhat chunky **Friendship Tower** [123 C1] arises on the right, celebrating the alliance of China and the DPRK. Built shortly after the Korean War, it is essentially a war memorial to Chinese forces lost in the conflict but a monument that has since been literally and figuratively enlarged upon into a more 'positive' commemoration of Chinese–DPRK friendship, also matching in height the monument built celebrating the Soviet–DPRK alliance.

The tower is bigger and more ostentatious than the more forlorn **Monument for the Fallen Heroes** [123 B6], which is still what it was, a memorial to the million or so Chinese 'volunteers' killed fighting on Korean soil. Neither site hence figures highly for Western tourists but both are points of poignant and proud homage to Chinese visitors, many of whom lay flowers in moving memoriam to long-lost forebears, if not loved ones. Opposite is the Chongsun restaurant and the **Chongsun Revolutionary Museum** [123 C1] and further along is the Phyongnam noodle restaurant. Kaeson Street crosses Pipa Street and there appears on the left the classically colonnaded **April 25 People's Army House of Culture** [111 E3] (west on Pipa Street), a 'centre of mass cultural education for soldiers of the Korean People's Army and the Working People'. Within the 50m-high, 176m-long building is a cinema and two theatres (one with 6,000 seats). While this is next-to-never visited, it's an important building as the Education and Agitation departments of the National Defence Council and the KPA have education sessions and military honours ceremonies here. The westward road opposite, guarded by a giant trident called the **Immortal Tower** [111 E3], a stele on which is an inscription in red to remind the populace that Kim Il Sung's spirit shall forever be with them. This is the master copy of 100s of stelae scattered across the country, built following the great man's death in 1994, and all of which were altered to add Kim Jong Il's name following his death in 2011. The tower stands over the road that ultimately goes to where the two Kims' bodies lie permanently in state, the Kumsusan Memorial Palace of the Sun.

Kumsusan Memorial Palace of the Sun [111 F3]

Kim Il Sung's final resting house is the Kumsusan Memorial Palace of the Sun, where lie in state both Kim Il Sung, and, since 2012, Kim Jong Il. Set in 100ha of trees, this was formerly where Kim Il Sung lived, worked and entertained and its interiors are lavish, so it is not a monolith built around a mausoleum but was a functioning residence refurbished to become a mausoleum. The cuboid mausoleum where Kim Il Sung lies in state is similar in design to that of Lenin, Mao and Ho Chi Minh, with a vast, dazzling plaza in front of it making it Pyongyang's other Kim Il Sung Square (much bigger in fact: the two halves of Kim Il Sung Square total 300m east to west, whereas the mausoleum's plaza is almost 500m at its longest). But it is not normally open just for people to turn up – Fridays and Sundays are 'open' days but notice must be given. Koreans like it if you do ask to be taken, although it is more likely for you to receive an invitation off the bat if you are part of a delegation, or resident.

If you do go, you are expected to dress smartly, ie: long trousers, shirt and tie, for men. No shorts for anyone. Visitors' shoes are scrubbed from beneath and the dust is blown off their clothes. Cameras are handed in and visitors must not have any mobile phones, memory sticks or electronic paraphernalia upon them. They go through a metal detector and then stand (do not walk!) on miles of moving walkways, past oncoming columns of solemn parties of army, Party and hoi polloi, the walkways and

3

corridors guarded by female sentinels in black velvet dresses who radiate austerity. Along a long corridor are photos of Kim Il Sung, genuinely in his element as he beams away in the company of farmers, teenagers and workers, and other photos of Kim Jong Il who seemed to prefer the company of his immediate entourage. Kim Il Sung was still mixing it with the people no matter how closed his ears and distant he became from the Supreme People's Assembly and the KWP, the provider, keeping it real to the end, while his reclusive son made a show of getting out and about but preferred making bombs and the escapism of cinema, the destroyer.

In lines of four, in a vast room visitors bow to statues of both Kims, before being taken to Kim Il Sung's encased body acentre a dim red lit room. Again in fours, visitors circle the body, bowing at the feet and sides but not at the head. They then go into a room bedecked with medals, honours and accolades from other dignitaries such as Nicolae Ceaușescu, Colonel Gaddafi and every nation in the Non Aligned Movement, followed by a room with maps of Kim Il Sung's travels to eastern Europe, North Africa and south Asia, and his railway carriage, and then his Mercedes.

Sometime between December 2011 and early 2012, the entire series of rooms was replicated identically for Kim Jong Il, differing most visibly only with the maps showing his travels were somewhat less far flung than his father's... there were fewer places to go by then, and he wasn't much of a traveller.

Three Revolutions exhibition and Cemetery for Martyrs

Pressing on north on Podunamu Street, you pass the Ryonmot restaurant on the left towards the **Three Revolutions Exhibition** [111 E2], about 6km from the city centre. It's a series of massive sheds in 100ha, and an almighty steel globe in which is housed an exhibition on the country's interstellar exploits. Other halls are themed as New Technical Innovations, Light Industry, Heavy Industry and Agriculture, with exhibits from the ideological, technological and cultural revolutions. The objectives of these revolutions, significant political milestones in DPRK policy, are 'to raise the ideological level of the people, equip the economy with modern techniques and to lift the people's technological and cultural level. They are considered essential for successful socialist construction.' The place is akin to a massive expo-centre for DPRK manufacturers, so you get to see loads of what's not in the shops, and if that doesn't appeal then see it as an exhibition of what's considered to be fascinating enough to show visitors.

Right opposite the Three-Revolutions exhibition, on the Sunan airport road side, is the **Cemetery for Martyrs of the Victorious Fatherland Liberation War** [111 E2] – marked by a massive flag-encloaked rifle and bayonet spearing out of the soil – where lie the remains of over 500 martyrs from the Korean War, and opened on 27 July 2013 on the 60th anniversary of the war's cessation of fighting. It's written

RIVER WALKS

The willowy Potong River Park is a balmy place to stroll, and you can find long lines of chaps casting lines into the water here.

Both banks of the River Taedong from Rungra Island down beyond the Yanggak have raised dykes topped by paths and shaded by trees, making for good walks of the city with grand panoramas and a chance to see the locals relaxing. On the west bank opposite Juche Tower, pedal boats operate in summer, and the river can freeze thick enough for skating in winter.

here: 'Heroic feats and undying exploits performed by the service personnel of the People's Army in the Fatherland Liberation War will always remain in the revolutionary history of our people in golden letters and they will be conveyed down through generations. Kim Il Sung.'

Back on Pipa Street, continue east straight to Mount Taesong. The street gets leafier and hillier along here as the land rolls up to Taesong's base, and where the city begins to peter out you pass **Kim Il Sung University** [111 E3], a severe-looking complex of buildings for 12,000 serious students (including not a few foreign ones) to do serious study – and by God they'll never have worked so hard in their lives, nor ever will again. It's Pyongyang's top multi-curricular university of the 30-odd universities in the city, which range from Pyongyang University of Foreign Studies to the University of Railways.

Staying at Moran Hill, the hill divides into two parks, Moranbong and Kaeson Youth Park, but the hill's contouring paths lasso the parks together seamlessly. In spring this park drowns in pink blossom and it's a favourite area for strolling lovers, and on weekends and national holidays groups of Koreans gather to drink and sing and dance – all day long. Tourists are welcome to join in the party and gulp the firewater.

One path leads to the highly prominent **Liberation Tower** [123 C3], built to commemorate the USSR's assistance in liberating Korea from the Japanese. The hill's southern slope overlooks the **Rungra Bridge** and **Rungra Island**, which is utterly dominated by the soaring steel arches of the fantastic **May Day Stadium** [111 F3]. This stadium, opened on 1 May 1989, has a seating capacity of 150,000, making it one of the world's largest, and is another venue for the truly awesome Mass Games (see box, pages 138–9). From above, the stadium's 16 arched roofs (peaking at 60m in height) circle to take the form of a magnolia.

Beyond the May Day Stadium on the island's north end is a series of sports facilities, but between Chongnu and Rungra bridges is the **Rungra Pleasure Ground** [123 D3], with its dolphin aquarium, wading pool (with some substantial water slides) and funfair rides, including 'mad mouse', 'nose diving tower', 'octopus merry-go-round', and 'temptation merry-go-round' (whatever that means), and is all open to visitors.

MORAN HILL TO THE WAR MUSEUM Staying on the west mainland and on Moran Hill, its paths connect a series of old pavilions, gates and sentinel towers that remain from old Pyongyang's fortress walls, which protected the city and formed the divisions of its inner districts. Pyongyang's walls were first built between 552 and 586 as the city was then the Koguryo capital and at the height of its prosperity had over 210,000 houses. The walled city went south from Moran Hill, filling the sac of land that rests between the Taedong and Potong rivers, natural defences for the city. All of the wall's gates and posts have been rebuilt at one time or another, with many rebuilt in the 1710s following a great fire. Under Moran Hill are tunnels and caves, where the government functioned during the Korean War.

On Moran Hill's Chilsongmun side is **Chilsong Gate** [123 C2], known as the 'gate of happiness' or 'gate of love' since the 6th century. On the hill's riverside is **Chongryu Pavilion** [123 C2], another gate to the walled city. **Pubyok Pavilion** [123 C2] (so named from the 12th century) on the Chongryu cliffs was an annex of the Yongmyong Temple built in 393. *Pubyok* means 'floating walls', as if it floats on the river. **Ulmil Pavilion** [123 C2] was originally 6th century, a northern command post, rebuilt in 1714 and named after General Ulmil who defended the place, and is famed for its picturesque location during spring. Just 100m downhill is **Hyonmi Gate** [123 C2], the northern gate of the walled city during Koguryo times, named after the black tortoise-serpent god Hyonmi that was fabled as this city district's spiritual defender. On Moran Hill's highest peak is the **Choesung Pavilion** [123 C2], originally 6th century and rebuilt in 1716. The height of the hill made it the natural choice as the city's central command point. **Chongum Gate** was the southern gate of the Koguryo's northern fort and was rebuilt in 1714. All were part of Pyongyang's Inner Fort, the walls of which traced down the riverbank a kilometre southwards past the Okryu Bridge to **Ryongwang Pavilion** [123 C4] and **Taedong Gate** [123 C4]. Ryongwang dates from the Koguryo period and the Taedong Gate

MASS GAMES

Almost every year, Pyongyang hosts what has been rightly called the most incredible show on earth, when around 100,000 artists, dancers, gymnasts, acrobats, martial arts experts, soldiers and children perform in the Mass Games. Combining scenes of ethnic dances, giddying acrobatics and folk songs, it's a 'compact' story of the DPRK, celebrating everything from the success of egg farms to the struggle against US imperialism, performed by thousands of participants in a stunning feat of choreography, not only in the precision of the dances but in how they all manage to evaporate off the stage in total darkness.

The DPRK's big games have been held since the 1950s, with thousands of participants in shows ranging in theme from Chongjin's nationalist 'Glorious Homeland' in 1962, to Nampo's provincial 'Flowering South Phyongan Province under the Benevolent Sun' in 1973, or the politically inspired 'The Ever Victorious Workers' Party' in Pyongyang in 2000. Since the 1970s all games have come under the aegis of a single production company, The Mass Gymnastics Production Company, which straplines itself as 'the Centre of Fantastic Creations', and has also worked on international shows in China, Angola, Namibia and Nigeria.

'The key to putting mass gymnastics on a mass basis is the school,' according to the FLPH book, *Mass Games*. Primary and middle school children are taught in drills and gymnastic movements in sometimes gruelling after-school and weekend sessions at schools and schoolchildren's palaces across the country over months. Individual school units are trained in particular scene segments, with units progressively combined and harmonised before final rehearsals. The huge backdrop of images comprises 20,000 coloured cards turned over by as many 13 to 15 year olds. In the pre-show warm-up, the columns of words turned over by the children display the names of the different districts from which they come.

Each 'pixel' is a child flicking over single-colour pages in large books, all directed by one man with flags and large illuminated numbers, just tucked out of sight. The larger the backdrop area (ie: the venue seating), the more 'pixels' can be used and the more sophisticated the image, and pixel books have grown from ten pages in 1955 to 170 in 2000 as more themes are covered in lengthier games and the venues have increased in size, while images now include movement, spotlights, lasers and fireworks. Hence, 'the slightest blunder will end up in making mess in the synchronisation in the rapid change of backdrops'.

Indeed the slightest mistake anywhere could ruin that scene, and avoiding that, or making the individual surrender to the discipline of the collective, is central to perfecting the show over months of preparations. The youth-oriented nature of the games comes from the Sokol movement of the Czech region in the 1860s, which sought to harness and direct youth by promoting physical and intellectual vigour through mass gymnastics. This spread across Slavic eastern Europe and was originally 6th century, as is the eastern gate of the inner fort. One plaque on the gate reads 'Uphoru', meaning a 'pavilion facing a clear stream', and one below it reads 'Taedong Gate'. Next to it is the 13.5-tonne **Pyongyang Bell**, cast in 1726 and used until the 1890s to tell the time and also to warn of danger. In the northern part of Moran Hill is **Ryonghwa Temple** [123 C1], a 20th-century construction where worship is allowed and is now graced by the 5m-tall, seven-storeyed pagoda, an 800-year-old Koryo-period pagoda that has, for all its granite weight, managed to move around quite a lot since its first location at the (disappeared) Hongbok

Russia and was ready-made for take-up by the socialist regimes that ultimately swept those regions, replacing the more nationalist themes with the kind of socialism and internationalism that led Sokol's ideas to reach the DPRK, and which is now supplanting socialism for Korean nationalism in a 'form of mass physical culture which is combined with physical skills and ideological and artistic value'.

Since 2002 the DPRK's main theme has been 'Arirang', a traditional Korean folk song with many variations, but the games' version is of young lovers split up by a wicked landlord's machinations, which very simply put is used as a metaphor for Korea's beauty, the sorrow of its division and hope for its reunification. The show story depicts Korea's bitter resistance against Japanese colonialism, the Korean War, division, prosperity and the joy and power of its prospective unification. The exact line-up changes annually, sometimes in a season, but the most important symbols range from the golden sun that symbolises Kim Il Sung; the flags of the country, Korea Workers' Party and Korea People's Army; the two pistols given to Kim Il Sung by his father to fight the Japanese; the Dear Leader depicted by the Kimjongilia flower; the Leaders' birthplaces at Mangyongdae and Mount Paektu, the latter being Korea's spiritual hearth; obvious military displays; and the flaming torch of Juche.

Tae kwon do exemplifies the ferocity of Korea's sovereignty. Political and economic achievements are shown by workers around a computer terminal or molten metal pouring forth from a mill, agricultural achievements have hundreds of chicken eggs running around or huge pigs suddenly giving birth to fleets of piglets. Children loom large. More transitory political themes may include the winged horse of the Chollima movement that has set alight the economy since the 1960s, while cars ascending a snowy mountain road at night depict the Arduous March of the 1990s. A rainbow extending from Pyongyang to the Forbidden City and then the Kremlin underscores old ties and new relations with China and Russia. Then there are more time-sensitive events, like 65 years since the founding of the DPRK, Kim Il Sung's 100th birthday, or the 2013 satellite launch.

With at least one in 100 Koreans involved in the show, from performing to making costumes, it's truly a national event. As such it's put on at great expense and some risk, hence it is not a rigidly annual event, although 2014 was the first year in a while to have no games. In 2006 and 2007 the games were disrupted and cancelled due to floods in parts of the country, and there are always rumours of this year's being the last. So seeing the games, while it incurs an extra cost, is very much worth it. Seats cost €50 third class, €100 second class, €150 first class or €300 VIP (first class are best). Go – and when you're there, it's arguably better to take in the spectacle than see it all through a viewfinder. Filming for longer than five minutes is prohibited and they'll ask you to stop. Finally, at the end, first-class sitters need to leave quickly as the rows of Koreans behind can't leave until you do.

3

Temple. The pagoda is covered in reliefs of Buddha and is topped by a carved lotus flower bud.

On the northern side of Moran Hill is speared the hard-to-miss, 150m-tall **Pyongyang television tower** [123 C1]. Built in 1967, it is in the same cocktail-cherry design as Moscow's lunatic Ostankino television tower, and, from where the DPRK started broadcasting in colour in the 1970s. Around its base have mushroomed an army of satellite dishes looking to the sky for answers. Daring the ascent in the shabby elevator will be rewarded with a rather good (yes, revolving!) restaurant. The tower site is accessible by a path on the north side.

Head back down south through the park and to Okryu Bridge, a modern, wide-arched concrete construction, with its east end now almost walled in by the soaring tower blocks on both sides of the west–east-running Mansudae Street. These 14 towers, up to 45 storeys and looking like illuminated steps when lit up at night, are a huge new presence on Pyongyang's skyline, succeeding some way towards 'changing the appearance of the capital beyond recognition'. They were part of a campaign to build 100,000 new residences by Kim Il Sung's 100th birthday in April 2012, and are the dominant feature of an extensive redevelopment of the area spreading north from these towers towards the Mansudae Grand Monuments. Ongoing since 2010, it features the large black-glass drum building (Mansudae People's Theatre) then a trio of black triptych shaped buildings (two of which are restaurants) dropped amid a maze of paths and gardens, and an underground shopping centre. It is as if 'a fire of new Pyongyang creation is blazing violently in the ongoing Mansudae area construction', according to *Rodung Sinmun* (see page 282).

Westwards Mansudae Street goes all the way to **Potong Gate** [123 A1]. This was the west gate of the walled city, first built mid 6th century under the Koguryo, and rebuilt several times since, most recently after the Korean War. It now marks the Potong Bridge crossing into Potonggang district, a heart-shaped area moated by two arteries of the Potong River. From here the Potonggang Pleasure Park curves northwest and is a beautiful venue for walking amid willow trees, confirming Pyongyang's moniker as 'city of willows'. Pyongyangians are seen relaxing and fishing all along the river. Compared with other Asian cities, Pyongyang is exceptionally quiet at most times of day, but the thin and lazy Potong is charmingly gentrified and serene. The park's paths can be followed as they curve northwest, past Mansu Bridge and the adjacent dome of the People's Army Circus, towards the **Monument to the Victorious Fatherland Liberation War 1950-1953** and the **Victorious Fatherland Liberation War Museum** on Yonggung Street [123 A2]. The monument was erected in 1993 'on the occasion of the 40th anniversary of war victory'. The setting consists of a 150,000m² white stone-flagged park with ten group sculptures in dark bronze depicting various battles on sea, land and air. It is dedicated to the 'Korean People's Army and Korean people who defeated the US imperialists and its allies in the Fatherland Liberation War'. On a sunny day, the contrast of the dazzling white floor and the nearly black sculptures is eerily impressive. The bronze *Victory* sculpture is the monument's focal point, representing a soldier shouting 'Hurry' at the top of his voice. Visitors are increasingly asked to pay respect here and give flowers on the way to the Victorious Fatherland Liberation War Museum.

The museum begins outside, with the monument's sculptures flanked by long open sheds of US and British tanks, artillery pieces and remains of aircraft from the war, as well as a collection of reconnaissance aircraft and helicopters brought down over the years. One such major trophy of captured spyware is the USS *Pueblo*, now apparently permanently moored on the Potong River and which takes up a good 30-minute part of the tour (see box, page 142).

As for the museum, the main building's entrance foyer is a palatial orgy of marble looked down upon by the figurine of a youthful Kim Il Sung. The museum was always large, but was extensively expanded in 2012 at considerable expense, with the new building being an intricate labyrinth of halls with life-size dioramas, battlefield reconstructions, baffling maps and compellingly arranged documents, as well as innumerable artefacts from the Korean War, its build-up and aftermath, all of which is impossible to digest in one visit.

The opening salvo in the depiction of the war may be a DVD detailing how the US sought and started the whole thing, then there is a series of halls charting the process of the war, heavily emphasising the North's early months of success, then the success of counter-attacks against the UN forces, then over two years of bitter fighting to a stalemate and China's intervention barely mentioned, until 'victory' over the US (defined as preventing them from winning). One life-size diorama has a surrendering US general with a waxwork corpse of a US soldier with its eyes eaten out. There are also gruellingly written confessions by captured US servicemen where the handwriting says a lot about what it took to make them 'confess'. It's impossible to see the whole museum in one visit but a staple is the extraordinary 360° revolving panorama of a battle with impressive special effects. Unlike in the West, the war is not forgotten here, not least because technically it's not over.

WEST AND SOUTH OF KIM IL SUNG SQUARE From every viewpoint in Pyongyang can be seen the great unfinished **Ryugyong Hotel** [110 D4], a vast 105-storey pyramid stabbing 330m high into the sky, topped of course by five revolving restaurants, and which many now think may have inspired the Shard in London. Started in 1987 to be complete for the World Youth Games in 1989, it would have been the tallest hotel in the world, with 3,000 rooms and facilities to warrant it being considered a district in its own right. However, it wasn't finished in time, and work petered out in the early 1990s as the economic crisis gripped the DPRK. For many years this building stood as a hideous concrete shell for people to point at as a monument to hubris, a hotel too far, calling it the 'hotel of Doom' (that had consumed a staggering 2% of the country's GDP), and ribbingly asking their guides when it would be finished, who could only roll their eyes in response. Then Egyptian telecom company Orascom bought it in 2008 as part of their deal to bring 3G to the DPRK, which would involve sticking phone masts on the building. One might guess that the Koreans demanded that Orascom at least shorn the edifice with glass, if not kit out the building completely, and not just treat it as a massive telegraph pole. Doubts remain whether the structure is actually useable or not, however work is ongoing inside to make something out of the space. Clad in glass though the building now may be, it's anyone's guess as to when exactly it will be finished – or indeed if it will serve as a hotel. Another site on the Potong River's western artery is the **Monument to the Potong River Improvement Project** [110 C3] and further west is **Pongsu Church** [110 C3], built in 1988 when Changchun Church was built. The official line is Pongsu has a head minister, a vicar and a bevy of elders, deacons and deaconesses and a congregation of 300 and is undergoing an expansion paid for by South Korean Presbyterian churches. It is known that foreign residents have attended services there. (Incidentally, there is a mosque in the grounds of the Iranian Embassy in the eastside diplomat quarter, but it's not thought to be for public use.) Heading south from Potong Gate along Chollima Street, it seems that the road broadens out and the buildings are given more personal space to flaunt themselves, lined up along the Potong and taking in the sun. You pass the huge neo-Korean-style **People's Palace of Culture** [123 A4], a labyrinth of rooms and halls

A highlight of the Victorious Fatherland Liberation War Museum is the Cold War trophy that is the USS *Pueblo*. In January 1968 the 850-tonne spy-boat, with Captain Lloyd M Bucher and 82 crew members, left Japan supposedly on an oceanographic research mission but really to conduct electronic surveillance off the DPRK coast. The North Koreans had recently expressed their heightened irritation over spy-ships loitering in their waters; indeed in January 1967 North Korean battery fire from their shores had sunk the American patrol-boat *PCE-56* near the DMZ, but their threats of an even more vigorous response weren't heeded. Surely, though North Korean planes and boats buzzed the *Pueblo*, its captain and crew considered themselves safe (the US insist that it was never closer than 15 miles from the DPRK, ie: in international waters – but the North Koreans claimed their sea border out to 50 miles from the coast). On 23 January one North Korean navy vessel aggressively approached the *Pueblo*. Bucher ordered his ship to weave away at speed, but it was not a speedy ship, and too soon its pursuers included torpedo boats and MiG 21 fighters. In the ensuing chase the *Pueblo* sustained cannon and machine-gun fire – the North Koreans were out for blood as the attempted assassination of the ROK's president Park in the Blue House Raid had failed only two days before (see box, page 34) – but the *Pueblo* did not return fire, its two 0.50 Browning machine guns remaining shawled under protective tarpaulins. A crew member was killed and several were injured, and realising the *Pueblo* was outpaced and outgunned, Bucher surrendered the ship. A haul of secret documents and equipment, neither destroyed nor dumped in time, fell into North Korean hands, later gleefully shared with the Soviets. More importantly, they had 82 captive Americans with whom they could torment President Johnson's administration for 11 months. The crew were initially not particularly ill-treated, but things changed permanently for the worse when the North Koreans rumbled that in photos released to the world, the crewmen weren't giving what they claimed was a 'Hawaiian good luck sign', but they were actually giving the finger. Only the signing of confessions alleviated any beatings.

Distracted by the increasingly heavy casualties being sustained in Vietnam – the *Pueblo*'s capture came only days before the North Vietnamese launched the Tet Offensive – the US had a very poor hand to demand the crew's return. The North Koreans doggedly refused anything less from the US than an admission of wrongdoing and an apology, upon the painful delivery of which the crew were ultimately handed back, with the remains of the one dead crew member, through Panmunjom on 23 December 1968, whereupon the US retracted its apology. However, the North Koreans kept the ship, mooring it in Wonsan until the late 1990s. Then, by somehow stealthily towing it around the ROK, they got it to Nampo before mooring it peripatetically along the Taedong, at first next to a monument celebrating the 1866 burning of the *General Sherman*, and now next to the War Museum, kept company by fisherman along the riverbanks. It also remains one of the oldest ships still in commission with the US navy, which wants it back. Visitors to the ship, with all its bullet holes gleefully circled in red, are briefed about the *Pueblo* incident by way of a short film that is a marvellous example of DPRK propaganda, with spinning newspapers and thrilling soundtrack, and even credits a 27-year-old General Kim Jong Il with a hand in winning the day for the DPRK. The film can be found on YouTube.

for the 'ideological and cultural education of the working people', in front of which grand public dances are held on national holidays. Next to it is the **Pyongyang Indoor Stadium**. Spacious roads break west to cross the Potong by the Susong Bridge (just over which is the silvery tower of the International Communications Centre) and Sinso Bridge. Just before Sinso is a knot of buildings [110 D5] including the **Changwang Health Complex**, **Ragwon department store** (also known as the Paradise supermarket), **Chongryu restaurant** and the 6,000-seat **ice rink**, dating from 1982, the 12 supports on its conical hat shape resembling skates.

A stopping-off point may be the **Paradise supermarket** on Chollima Street, a glitzy affair next door to the Air Koryo office, with goods ranging from doughnuts and frozen octopuses to beds, sports gear and random musical instruments. Tour around it with a tiny shopping trolly and pay for goods by the quaint time-consuming three-stage payment system, although the shop is one of the new kind in Pyongyang, where customers can take stuff off shelves themselves and not order everything across a counter. Similar things go on in the Pyongyang Hotel shop and the considerably larger Kwangbok Commercial Centre (a joint venture with Chinese Trade Company, opened in 2012 but not yet to tourists). Nearby is the Unification Church interfaith complex or World Peace Center, set up by the ROK's Reverend Moon in a rage of optimism that the building's somewhat moribund state no longer really imparts.

The **Pyongyang railway museum** [123 A6] is a brutalist grey edifice. Its entrance hall is taken up with a celebration of all of the railway developments and journeys undertaken by the Kims. There is a wonderfully brightly painted mural along the back wall of the Kims at Pyongyang station, in which they seem curiously taller than everyone else. The building is full of models of trains and some lovely dioramas, and a large room of real trains that also houses the very same carriage that Kim Il Sung's mother was transported in when laden with child. There's also a lot of incongruous displays about Kim Jong Il in essentially un-rail-related pose, with one painting depicting him looking quite saintly in the glowing forest of Paektu, and another where his fighter mother Kim Jong Suk stands in the snows, firing a pistol at the Japanese while holding the Dear Leader-to-be to her breast.

Continue south on Chollima Street until it intersects with Sosong Street and follow the rail tracks to **Pyongyang railway station** [123 A6], where you may have first arrived or perhaps will leave the country. The clock overlooking the square is said to be the time-standard for all the DPRK. The entrance door on the left is for foreigners; entering through the right door will lead to your swift exit back through it. The station, with its impressive arch, pillared colonnades and impressive octagonal lantern atop, was first built by the Japanese, but was obliterated in the war and rebuilt in the 1950s. The building was for many years fronted by a copse of trees, full of waiting travellers at all hours of the day, but this has been cleared to make the front plaza into a somewhat fraught drop-off/pick-up/parking area where unwary groups fragment and scatter. Pyongyang station department store is opposite. Yongwang Street goes towards the river, taking in the simple classical design of the **Chollima House of Culture** [123 A7], the bad-day-for-modernist-architecture creation of the **International House of Culture** [123 B7] and the sweeping fancy of the **Pyongyang Grand Theatre** [123 B6]. Like many of the grander edifices in the city, the theatre combines Soviet classical designs in its simplified pillars and plinths with neo-Korean-style pavilions and roofs. But it dates from 1960 (renovated in 2009) and is clearly part of the first surge of Korean styling beginning to manifest in grand civic building design, which the theatre does not achieve with much subtlety: two floors are built in Soviet style, then its is as if someone decided halfway through construction to just go

3

Korean and drop traditional pavilions and roofs on top. Although, that said, it could be seen as a metaphorical assertion of Korea's cultural sovereignty topping Soviet bloc conformity. Compare it with the classical portico of the **State Theatrical Company**, then go west along Haebangsan Street past two post offices to the **Party Founding Museum** [123 A6]. This schoolish edifice was a Japanese company headquarters before 1945, whereupon it became the headquarters for the party's Central Committee immediately following 1945, and has the hallowed rooms and residence where Kim Il Sung mapped and slept on the party's future. It also contains the pond in which Kim Jong Il's younger brother drowned when the Dear Leader was a child. You're walking in the grounds where the state germinated, just over the road from the 'Forbidden City' where the state lives today.

Spattered across Pyongyang are a handful of zones that are off-limits to most mere mortals, but the most significant exclusive area between Changgwang, Chollima and Jebangsan streets is what many foreigners refer to as Pyongyang's own **'Forbidden City'** [123 A5]. This compound is where many of the top echelons of the DPRK's society work and live, with roads heading into the complex blocked by security checkpoints of guards manning a chain barring the entry point, and surrounded by long strips of metal fencing. You'll quite often see saloon cars cruising in and out of this city-within-the-city and well-dressed types walking in and out, but your chances of getting in, like your average local's, don't exist. This is the best known of the large gated communities in Pyongyang and in other parts of the country, but none appear on any official DPRK maps or have any indications in name or symbol, and the surrounding roads and areas on maps can be (as in this case) somewhat moulded to underplay the size of the compounds. Some of the four- or five-storey white buildings in the leafy compound can be seen from the Juche Tower, but the best view is from Google Earth.

Return to Sungri Street dog-legging past the **Monument to Martyrs of the People's Army** [123 B6] and you're going back towards Kim Il Sung Square, or cross the Taedong Bridge to the city's eastern half.

EAST PYONGYANG This side of town is quieter and there's less to see, with most of the sites being situated along Juchetap Street, the major north–south drag right alongside the strip of neat parkland that runs the length of the river's east bank. The Taedonggang and Tongdaewon districts of East Pyongyang are home to the city's diplomatic quarter, a dozen universities and a few hospitals, including the top-flight 1,500-bed **Pyongyang Maternity Hospital** [111 F4]. Some have claimed this was built to dispel the myth that pregnant women were banished from the city but it would seem to be a somewhat dramatic response to a persistent rumour. Some tour itineraries now have visitors taking a wander through the hospital.

Just off Saeserim Street running from Taedong Bridge is the **Changchun Catholic Church** [111 F5], the first Christian house of worship to be built in the DPRK when completed in 1988. It was constructed in time for the 13th World Student and Youth Festival the following year, to show the world that religion was not banned in the DPRK, although the wall surrounding it does not impart that much freedom of association and there is no resident priest. The building's simple design, colours and layout are very similar to the Pongsu Protestant church that was commissioned at the same time.

Perhaps you can load up at the Songyu restaurant on Taedong Bridge's east end, or the **Taedonggang Diplomatic Club** [123 C6] opposite. As the clientele has expanded considerably over the years from Russians out for a vodka jag and a fight, the club has been substantially renovated to house numerous rooms and entertainments, from a disco and karaoke to massage to a bar with arcade games , and may make for a last night's revelry.

Going north along Juchetap Street takes one to the **Juche Tower** [123 D5], which dominates the eastern riverbank. This 150m stone-clad tower, with a 20m, 45-tonne metal flame flickering atop it, was built, as its name suggests, to celebrate the Juche philosophy of self-reliance (see box, pages 26–7) as expounded by Kim Il Sung and developed by Kim Jong Il. The two words Ju and Che appear in large form on the east and west sides. The sides' tiers add up to 70, Kim Il Sung's age in 1982, and for that birthday the tower was built, while each stone is for a day in his life.

At the east base is an open shrine of dedications to the Juche idea, containing over 500 tablets from around the world given in deference to the man and his idea, and to the left of these tablets is the entrance to the tower, a large stone door. Having paid €5 you then enter a large round room split by a lift shaft, with souvenirs one side and snacks the other. With a guide, the lift takes packets of visitors up and up, the ascent marked in stages by number lights (not related to floors in case you're wondering), before ultimately alighting beneath the base of the gold plinth of the flame, from where a very impressive all-round view of pretty much the entire city is available. Also note the tower lines up directly with Kim Il Sung Square and the Grand People's Study House (see page 115) across the river, as the Study House was built at the same time and you have the two edifices of learning mirroring one another across the river – global knowledge on the west side, and the Korea-centric Juche philosophy celebrated by the tower on the east. The statue fronting the tower on to the river has three people – intellectual, worker and farmer – holding their tools aloft into the KWP insignia. In contrast to the Stalinists in Russia who persecuted and alienated those who chose to think for themselves, Kim included intellectuals in the frame, or symbolically at least, their status rising the more they agreed with Kim's views. This statue is based on the Vera Bucking statue *Marching Women* exhibited in Paris in 1939, and the three of them look boldly out onto the 150m-high fountains blasting out of the Taedong. There are toilets in a tunnel at the southeast corner of the tower, with one room having a karaoke machine.

Across the road from the tower (the road being Juchetap Street) is the Korea Documentary Film studio where all things Juche are produced. Also across Juchetap Street are two tall white apartment blocks symmetrically either side of the tower and topped with large red neon Korean words – 'one heart' on the left and 'one unity' on the right. Further north along this road is a tall, plain building with a deep bronze tint that's noticeable only for the large KWP sign on its roof. This otherwise innocuous high-rise is the **Kim Il Sung Higher Party School** [123 D5], where Korea's brightest and best get trained in ruling the country.

Continue north along Juchetap Street, crossing over Taedongwan Street, which runs west onto Okryo Bridge, and on the right appears the brown **Golden Lanes Bowling** [123 D4] building where one can have a round for €2.50 per person, and makes for a fun if not humid hour. The computer scoring is erratic and larger-footed punters may have a job getting shoes to fit. Be careful to find a ball with smooth finger holes, as they can scratch. Non-bowlers can go to the bar, the two restaurants, play pool, try the one-armed bandits or peruse the upstairs food and clothes boutique. Opposite the bowling is the very modern black glass and wavy steel roofed **Ryugyong Health Complex** [123 D4], which offers saunas, an extensive gym, massages, jacuzzis, vibrating cocoons or just the chance to watch locals enjoying the same. Here is also the outdoor **People's Open Air Ice Rink** [123 D4] and next door is **Pyongyang Skatepark**, which is more about rollerblading than skateboarding. Rollerblading is quite popular these days in Pyongyang. All three venues were opened in 2012 by DPRK cabinet premier Choe Yong Rim.

Then further north along Juchetap come the peculiarly sculpted **Central Youth Hall**, with its anvil and armadillo roofs, and the slide machine of the **East Pyongyang Grand Theatre** [123 D3]. Around 3,500 people can pack in to see music or revolutionary opera here. Midway between these two buildings is a symmetrical street, and you realise it's in perfect alignment with the Mansu Grand Monument west across the river and the **Monument to the Korean Workers' Party Foundation** [111 F4] to your east just across Munsu Street. This staggering piece of work was erected in 1995 to celebrate the 50th anniversary of the Korean Workers' Party: a hammer, sickle and calligraphy brush grasped in the hands of a worker, farmer and intellectual. The sculpture's 50 granite-faced metres mark 1m for each of the party's 50 years.

The belt uniting the three tools has bronze reliefs lining its interior, emblazoned with the slogan, 'Long live the Workers Party of Korea, the Organiser and Guide of the Victory of the Korean People!' The inscription on the pedestal refers to the development of the Party from the roots of anti-imperialism, while the red granite disc at the centre of the monument's base signifies the Sun, who is Kim Il Sung. Speaking of which, this monument forms part of another grand vista, with a beeline view towards the Grand Monuments on Mansu Hill and the Ryugyong Hotel beyond. Behind the KWP monument are two symmetrical blocks of flats painted in rust red, their stairs-like structures designed to resemble billowing flags, while the slogans on their roofs read '100 battles' on the left and '100 victories' on the right. Between them is the muggy **Cultural Exhibition Hall**, a large upstairs space with photos, paintings and souvenirs for sale, as well as a downstairs tea room selling beer, tea and water.

A block north along Munsu Street from the monument is a new shopping mall, built with Chinese money solicited by Jang Song Thaek, and beyond that under a trio of pyramids is the large **Munsu Water Park** [111 F4], its indoor and outdoor aquatery covering 10.9ha according to local lore, with its 25m pool, high diving boards, pipes and slides open for €10 a visit. This has replaced the waterpark and funfair that were supposedly sited here.

Then some 11km east southeast of Pyongyang is the former KPA equestrian club now known as the Mirim Riding Club, which consists of some 60ha of land, and it

KIMILSUNGIA AND KIMJONGILIA: FANATIC FLOWERS

Deriving from the *Dendobrium* genus of the orchid family, kimilsungia is a tropical perennial with deep pink flowers, cultivated in Indonesia and named after Kim Il Sung in 1965 when he visited the country: 'The Indonesian president said that his respected excellency (Kim Il Sung) had rendered great services to mankind and deserved a high honour. The Indonesian president was so firmly resolved that Kim Il Sung could no longer decline his offer.'

Kim Jong Il received his own species of Kimjongilia, a blood-red bloom of tuberous begonia, in 1988 from a Japanese botanist, Kamo Mototeru, 'in the hope of achieving amity and friendship between Japan and Korea'. Both plants have inspired songs, won international competitions, and are cultivated countrywide for local shows and an annual festival for Kimjongilia flowers held in Pyongyang in February.

The flower shows are held at a special venue on the west bank, just south of the Rungra Bridge.

offers a half-day's riding for €30 a go with indoor and outdoor tracks, sauna, gym and so on. A good option for those interested.

FURTHER OUT OF TOWN

Korean Film Studio Far out into Hyongjesan district, about 10km due northwest of Kim Il Sung Square, is the other great factory of the DPRK's view on the world, the Korean Film Studio. With nothing to note on the way to this massive Korean Hollywood (except the Railways University) it's a must-see, churning out such thrillers as *Daughter of the Revolution*. You'll likely watch old melodramas being filmed and tour through reconstructed feudal villages which give a good insight into ancient Korean life, so it's partly a moving museum (although the crops grown in the village are for real). Note the German town, pre-revolution Chinatown and the totally decadent Seoul city, awash with US- and Japanese-run brothels, go-go bars, casinos and all so decadent that they don't eat dogs but pamper them. Despite having to pay to take photos (of the actors at least), the studios are well worth visiting to experience the dream world within the dream city. The number 5 tram ventures there from West Pyongyang railway station.

Mount Taesong [111 H1] Beyond the sprawl, about 10km northeast of the city centre, are Mount Taesong and its hills. The road with Kim Il Sung University and Kumsusan Memorial Palace of the Sun (see pages 135–6) continues to undulate eastwards, crossing the Hapjang River, which seems to be a border for town and country.

Physically, Mount Taesong is one peak, Jujak (192m), surrounded by a series of vegetation-covered summits capped with small pavilions, while many small lakes pock the valley that curves around Jujak and its surrounding peaks. A series of paths weaves the lakes and hills together and makes for a good afternoon's walking in balmy air, finding amid the scant ruined walls of **Fort Taesong** viewpoints over distant Pyongyang. The peaks were linked by a fort wall from the 3rd century, and the fort was bolstered for Pyongyang's defences after the Koguryo moved their capital to the city in AD427. Fort Taesong's walls reached 9.2km in length, and of its 20 gates, the most prominent 'survivor' is the **Nam Gate** [111 H2], rebuilt in 1978.

Looking from the bus terminus at Taesong's southwest foot, on the left is **Pyongyang Central Zoo** [111 G2]. It may have 600 species of all breathing things, many of which were gifts to Kim Il Sung, but it's a zoo in the very, very traditional sense. Attractions include Korean tigers in a seriously miserable cage, elephants penned in by spiked plates on the floor, and a collection of cats and dogs. Only the unconvincingly escape-proof baboon pen merits much more attention – that and a turkey, 2½ bears (well, one of them has only one arm) and the giant German rabbits – they were not all eaten as the press said they were, although people do eat rabbits.

Opposite the zoo are the **botanical gardens** [111 G2], of note for any of the 5,000 species there. The chance to see kimilsungia and Kimjongilia out of season is possibly the best reason to visit, and to investigate what's being bred in the 'experimental' section. The gardens also have some ancient tombs, possibly of Koryo origin. The gardens are next to the **Taesongsan Fun Fair**, with a charming Buddhist temple within its grounds (open on request) and beyond that, past a handful of restaurants, lies the main path for the pavilions of Jangsu and Sumon peaks around Jujak.

These are all light distractions compared with Jujak's crown, the **Revolutionary Martyrs' Cemetery** [111 H1]. Unless driven to the top, you pass through the large Korean-style gate and ascend a breathless flight of 300 granite steps up to a road (where the bus will otherwise stop), then the cemetery begins on a shallower slope up to Jujak Peak. Between a large medal and a huge crimson granite flag are interred hundreds of leading figures from Korea's resistance to Japanese colonial rule in what is an exceedingly austere, but nonetheless very moving, setting, as sombre music is piped around their bronze busts. While many of those interred here were scarcely adults when they fell fighting the Japanese, by no means did all of the cemetery's occupants die during that struggle; some were killed during the Korean War, many would die of old age years later, and there are still a few to come – but they are the ones Kim Il Sung had most dedication to. They were the ones who were with him during his formative years in the war against Japan, the bitter struggle where the likeliest outcome would be a violent death at the hands of an unshakeable colonial ruler. Whatever the hell of the Korean War or the successes of the country's rebuild that followed, it was those guerrillas from the Revolutionary War that Kim stayed loyal to in a way not really seen with Mao or Stalin. Even as Kim's rule became ever more personalised, as he came to ignore first the Supreme People's Assembly, then the Korean Workers' Party, he kept the guerrillas around him, and it was for them that he built the cemetery in the early 1970s high on a hill and rewarding them with a glorious view of the city. Still, Kim castigated himself for waiting so long in what he considered to be an oversight of respect, and this need to show gratitude nagged him – the busts were first made in stone but later replaced with bronze in the early 1980s as the cemetery was expanded.

The first to die are in the first line of graves, with age rising up the hill. It is expected that you pay respects at the medal and the flag, where stands a bust of Kim Il Sung's wife Kim Hyong Suk. There are grand views from up here of the capital. Otherwise, going left of the flag appears a road heading back to the bus terminus and another path heading up for the peaks. To the right of the flag is a viewing point from which can be seen the Taesongsan fun fair stretching along the valley, and then **Mini Pyongyang Folk Park** [111 H3]. This half-mile square park has large-scale models of the Korean peninsula's more famous landmarks, including pagodas, the Juche Tower, the Ryugyong Hotel and an old-world village sometimes used as a film set, and which all 'greatly helps the Korean people, including school youth and children, inherit and glorify the excellent tradition and brilliant culture of the nation'. Visitors pay €14 a go, and there's also a hospitality house with traditional music and *soju* served by young ladies in period dress. The park sits at Taesong's southern foot, between Pyongyang Astronomical Observatory on the park's west side and Koguryo's Anhak Palace on the east. The latter must have been a major sight to behold, for within its four walls (each measuring 622m and 6–12m high) the remains of 52 buildings, most linked by lengthy cloisters, have been found among gardens and waterways.

In the incredibly unlikely event that you're taking the bus from the Mount Taesong terminus, numbers 1, 2, 3, 28, 29 and 30 terminate there, but only the 3 is useful in running into central town along Hyoksin, Pipa and Mundok streets.

Far over on Taesong's west side is the **Kwangbok Temple** [111 H1], tucked up a small valley and with a handful of monks still seen to practise their religion. The site, if not the buildings, is one of Pyongyang's most ancient, for a temple has been here since AD392. However, the original burnt down in 1700 and its replacement was razed during the Korean War, hence the gleaming one you see today, built in 1990 following the 1989 World Festival of Youth and Students.

Mangyongdae district [110 A6]

This is the westernmost area of Pyongyang city, filling the banks of the River Potong's western artery. Two boulevards, **Kwangbok Street** and **Chongchun Street**, divide and rule this area in their roles as open galleries for the art of concrete architecture. Kwangbok Street, finished in 1989, is

By the 1860s, the Ri court was deeply alarmed that despite the prohibition and persecution of Christianity and its followers, Koreans were still converting by the thousand. The Tonghak rebellion of 1864 further shook the royal court, and drew the line in the sand – thereafter, anyone caught proselytising would get very short shrift.

So it was ill-timed that in August 1866, the armed steam-schooner the *General Sherman* should forge up the Taedong River, ostensibly to broach trade with Korea – but on board was the young Protestant missionary, Robert Jermaine Thomas. The *Sherman*, formerly a trading ship used by both sides in America's Civil War, was subsequently pressed into service in east Asia. Captain Page piloted the ship into Korea but it was evidently Thomas that called the shots. The *Sherman* was first greeted by an emissary for Governor Park Kyoo Soo of Pyung-an, who told Page, Thomas and the other Westerners aboard (including the ship's owner) that trade with Korea was illegal, but that provisions would be provided for the ship's departure from Korea.

Nonetheless, Thomas ignored the hint and piloted the *Sherman* upriver towards Pyongyang, where heavy rain and high tides made the river unusually deep and enabled the ship to reach Turu Islet, near Mangyongdae, from whence Thomas proselytised and his companions tried to trade with locals. Deputy Commander Lee Hyon Ik of the Pyongyang garrison was sent to the ship to convey the king's displeasure at the *Sherman*'s further intrusion and the Koreans now heavily suspected that this was less about trade than about Christian evangelism. A testy confrontation was imminent when, upon the call-out of the Pyongyang garrison, Lee found himself taken hostage as the ship turned to go. However, the wet weather had abated, the tide turned, and then fog sealed the futility of the ship's escape and it ran aground. Accounts differ as to whether the Pyongyang garrison or the *Sherman* fired first. Either way, the garrison attacked with fire-rockets and cannon, and the *Sherman* returned cannon fire on anything that moved, civilian and military alike. After four days of battle, on 2 September, Korean turtle-boats were tied together, set afire and pushed towards the *Sherman*. All the Westerners and the ship's Asian crew that had escaped gunfire or the fumes of the burning ship were caught, executed and mutilated. Thomas apparently followed his Bible riverward from the burning ship's deck, and was captured. Whether he died the brave martyr or was slain begging for his life is not clear.

The USS *Wachusett* was sent the following year to investigate the incident, but little was learnt except that the *Sherman* had indeed been destroyed. In spring 1868, the USS *Shenandoah* reached the Taedong River's mouth where Captain Febiger received an official acknowledgment that all the *General Sherman*'s crew were dead. The *Sherman*'s destruction was cited as but one 'depredation against Americans' that justified a punitive attack on numerous sites and forts by American forces in 1871: the incident and its repercussions also justified to the Ri that politeness was ultimately wasted on these foreign devils and their duplicitous ways, and stelae were put up nationwide that read 'Posterity should remember that unwillingness to fight the intrusion of the Westerners means reconciliation, and that insisting on negotiations for peace mean selling the country'.

described as a city in its own right, with 25,000 flats racked and stacked along this 6km-long, 100m-wide strip. Beginning at the Potong's Palgol Bridge, Kwangbok has the hexagonal spaceships of the **circus** on its west side. Here you'll see a fun mix of high-wire acrobatics and grotesque parodies of American troops and South Koreans. If you're on a tour, tickets to the circus are an extra € 10. Kwangbok ends in the embracing arms of the **Mangyongdae Children's Palace** [110 A5] and its bronze-coloured *Chariot of Happiness* amid sculptures from numerous tales told to children by the Great and Dear Leaders. Many of the various 690 rooms are for group classes where children learn the violin, accordion, dance, public speaking, tae kwon do, boxing, etc, and a tour should prelude an electrifying, technically razor-sharp 90-minute show of music and dance by the children trained at this DPRK version of *Fame*. Extended visits to the palace for observation only can be arranged.

Halfway along Kwangbok, Chongchun or 'Gymnasium' Street undercuts it. A series of nine sports halls, each dedicated to one sport, line this road down to the Angol flyover on the Taedong. Each hall's design apparently represents some facet of its nominated sport, but unless you're going to watch one, the buildings are bizarrely impressive enough, some being able to take up to 5,000 spectators, built as they were for the 1989 World Festival of Youth and Students (although originally planned to host the 1988 Olympics that in the event was awarded to Seoul). At the Taekwondo Hall tournaments can be attended or even courses arranged. Just off Chongchun is a professional shooting range where € 1 gets three bullets in .22 rifles or pistols, making for a great evening's entertainment of shooting targets. There was also once a golf driving range off this street.

Continuing northwest along Chongchun beyond the large junction where it crosses Kwangbok are two sites of interest. First, on the right, 350m from the junction, is a park and statue dedicated to Kim Il Sung's mother, Kang Pan Sok, a Presbyterian deaconess, and visitors to her small house here learn of her revolutionary exploits. On the same side of the road is the Chilgol Church, built in 1992 and dedicated to Mrs Kang, who was a devout churchgoer.

You may traverse Kwangbok and Chongchun going to or from the Mangyongdae Revolutionary Site, where the Great Leader was born and spent his first few years. Otherwise, you may hug the road on the Taedong's west bank down to Mangyongdae, spying the huge thermal power plant to the east, belching fumes profusely.

Just before Mangyongdae, you'll notice that the river has split around the rather large Turu Islet and its satellite islets. Here it's thought that the American missionary trader USS *General Sherman* was beached and destroyed in 1866. Official histories credit the burning of the ship to Kim Il Sung's great-grandfather Kim Ung U, but it's not clear whether that version of the story holds water, or has been left high by the receding tide of truth (see box, page 149).

Mangyongdae Shrine and its environs [110 A6] Follow the Taedong's west bank southwards and the landscape becomes rapidly green and rural. Some 12km south of the city centre, just before the River Sunhwa empties into the Taedong, is a site of nearly religious significance, the former village of Mangyongdae. Here Kim Il Sung was born and spent his childhood, and the handful of tiny thatched huts where his parents and grandparents tilled the land are now enshrined. They form the centre of some well-trimmed parkland to which throngs of Koreans are taken on Party, factory and school tours to pay homage. The huts sit beside the small lotus pond, and are surrounded by small sites of significance, including the graves of Kim Il Sung's forebears. The full, official history of Kim's forebears is within the **Mangyongdae Revolutionary Museum**, 100m from the huts. On

above   **Pohyon Temple,
Myohyangsan**
(GH/AWL)
page 191

right   **Rimyongsu Falls
pavilion in Paektusan**
(MT/S) page 247

below   **Court officials
and warriors are
represented around
the tomb of King
Kong Min, near
Kaesong** (AI/S)
page 164

left **A female employee at the Hungnam Fertiliser Complex in Hungnam** (EL) page 218

below left **A monk outside Pohyon Temple in Chilbosan** (RW) page 191

below right **A traffic warden in Pyongyang** (GH/AWL)

bottom **Soldiers in a military parade in Pyongyang, honouring the 100th birthday of the Great Leader Kim Il Sung** (A/S)

above Children performing at the Mangyongdae Children's Palace (GH/AWL) page 150

right Young pioneer girls wave flowers at a celebration in Pyongyang (EL)

below On 15 April, the late Kim Il Sung's birthday, many locals go into the parks to dance and drink together (EL) page 98

above   **Lake Chon, held within the volcanic caldera of Mount Paektu** (EL) pages 244–5

left   **Kuryong Waterfall in the Kumgang Mountains** (GH/AWL) page 214

below &   **Many tours may include a visit to**
inset   **a model farm** (both EL)
pages 202–3

above &
right
With a mountainous interior, rugged coastline and beautiful white-sand beaches, Chilbosan offers a great variety of scenery (both EL) pages 229–30

below
The new, controversial Masik Pass ski resort in Ryongjo-ri (BCT) page 197

KORYO
TOURS

The Experts in Travel to Rather **Unusual Destinations.**

We've taken more people to North Korea than anyone else. No one goes more than us. No one knows more than us.

koryotours.com

E.   info@koryotours.com

T.   + 86 10 6416 7544

27 Bei Sanlitun Nan
Chaoyang District.
Beijing. China

the lotus pond's opposite bank is a line of trees, each donated by visiting leaders from the communist bloc, a reminder of the world of comrades that has so recently disappeared. Mangyong Hill has a small pavilion atop it, and has two sites where Kim Il Sung studied and another where, according to legend, he wrestled with a larger foe and won. You're invited to drink from the well of youth.

Fighting through the throng of **Mangyongdae Fun Fair**'s [110 A6] reported 100,000 daily visitors, you'll find the grenade-throwing ground and machine-gun stalls as well as 50 other amusements visible from the gondola and monorail rides that link the two halves of the fair, and an impressive corkscrew rollercoaster. The fair was partly renovated and reopened in 2012, and is open on most holidays and some weekends. You might also get to see the DPRK's own little Eton, **Mangyongdae Revolutionary School**, just over the hill from the shrines. Here are trained the 'children of revolutionary martyrs to be political and military cadres. Kim Il Sung Higher Party school and Pyongyang Communist University (just east of the Koryo Hotel) train Party workers or give reorientation to them' (*Pyongyang Review*).

The refreshingly untouched **Ryongak Hill** sits about 4km north of Mangyongdae. On the edge of town, it's largely unvisited and appeals for being what it is, a hill set in greenery with a few forgotten sites around it. The Koguryo-dynasty Pobun Monastery and the Ryonggok Academy, dating from 1656, are to be found there. At 292m, Tae peak is the highest on Ryongak and gives splendid views of the city.

SOUTH PYONGYANG Chollima Street beams southwards to Chungsong Bridge, the westernmost bridge in central Pyongyang, which crosses the Taedong and attaches to Suk Islet on its easternmost point. Shortly after reaching the Taedong's south bank the road crosses the east–west-running Tongil Street, a breathtaking, massive, modern boulevard finished in 1993, lined with scores of brutalist apartment blocks. If the shock of the new does not appeal, Pyongyang's BBQ duck restaurant is to the northwest of the junction with Chongsung Bridge Street, and the Pyongyang Noodle restaurant to the southeast. Going east along Tongil on the north side is the entrance to the large Tongil market, which is open to foreigners seeking anything from foodstuffs to Chinese electricals. Beyond the market towards the riverfront is the Pyongyang Mullet Soup restaurant.

Continuing east along Tongil, again on the north side, set back a couple of hundred metres is placed the beautiful, brand-new Russian Orthodox church, also known as the Church of the Life-Giving Trinity, and is the first in the country. A stark white building complete with gold onion domes, it was consecrated in mid-2006 by numerous Russian political and religious dignitaries.

Tongil then bends northeastwards, becoming first Chungnyon, then Munsu Street that runs through the east side of the city.

Tomb of King Tangun The 5,000-year-old bones of the mythical King Tangun were identified in the early 1990s, an event so ground-shaking that 'Comrade Kim Il Sung was so please [*sic*] he asked dear Comrade Kim Jong Il if it was true'. At the base of Mount Taebak in Munhung-ri, Pyongyang, Tangun's tomb was reconstructed and opened in October 1994 (reflected in the number of stones used to rebuild the tomb), a nine-tiered granite pyramid without a point at the end of two colossal flights of steps. Inside, in polished wooden coffins are kept the remains of Tangun and his wife, guarded by a stone tiger, the 'biggest in the world' at 3.5m in height. The steps to the tomb are flanked by statues of Tangun's sons and ministers, while another monument celebrating the reconstruction stands between the two flights. Followers of Taejong, a Korea-centric religion built around the deity of Tangun, can now worship at the site, which also receives two pilgrimages on 2 October and 15 March every year, so the tomb has been awarded profound spiritual and political resonance.

YANGGAK ISLAND Apart from the triangular Yanggakdo hotel, Yanggak Island has a few things on it. A cruddy 9-hole golf course next to the hotel is being built upon by a Chinese funded health complex. Beyond that is the sprocket-shaped International Cinema Hall with six screens (one for 2,000 cinemagoers and then smaller ones down to two 50-seaters), which was built in the 1980s to host the showing of Korean films and those from allies in the Non Aligned Movement. Since then the biennial Pyongyang International Film Festival has broadened its remit to include films from countries with diplomatic ties with the DPRK, with over 100 shown per festival (*www.pyongyanginternationalfilmfestival.com*). And over the other side of the bridge, to the south-east of the island is Yanggak football stadium.

4

Pyongyang to Sariwon, Kaesong and Panmunjom

Pyongyang to Kaesong, 161 km, three hours by train and 90 minutes by road; Pyongyang to Sariwon 50km. Kaesong to Panmunjom 10km.

The road from Pyongyang to Kaesong 개성 – and it's not the smoothest of roads – starts at the capital end on Thongil Street, a monolithic housing development completed in 1993. The marker point for leaving the city is passing under the **Three Principles Monument** [off map, 110 D7], a 30m-high statue of two women from both Koreas leaning together over the highway, the symbolism of the location being that this is the primary road from Pyongyang to the ROK. Unveiled in 2001, the monument's longer title is the Monument to the Three Charters for National Reunification, and the two women representing the two Koreas, are holding aloft the symbol of the charter. The Army Film Studios are quite near this monument. Through the checkpoints, and 9km from Pyongyang, is the country's only turnpike, indicating Wonsan 191km and Kaesong 152km. As you cruise to Kaesong you observe the farms and the long slogan boards planted in the fields, then you can admire how well tended the verges are on the road itself.

Most of this highway, like much of the other highways in the country, is as straight as a runway, but the turns get sharper as the landscape gets hillier going south. And yes, the roads are always this quiet, although they didn't used to be: 'In this country, in which sumptuary laws prevent the humbler classes from travelling on horseback, and where wagons and steam roads are unknown, the roads are lively with numerous foot passengers,' wrote William Eliot Griffis in *The Hermit Nation* (1882), listing pupils, pilgrims, pompous functionaries on horseback, travelling players, picnickers, postal slaves on the pony express, packhorsed merchants, beggars, refugees of war and weather, and 'men dead of hunger in times of famine'. But the well-trodden roads did not support ye olde motel industry: 'The country is very deficient in houses for public accommodation. Inns are to be found only along the great highways, and but rarely along the smaller or sequestered roads. This want arises, perhaps, not so much from the poverty of the people, as from the fact that their numerous proverbial hospitality does away with the necessity of numerous inns.' Nonetheless, if a household hadn't the food to replenish a traveller, the travellers would be invited in anyway to cook their own.

SARIWON 사리원

38.3˚N, 125.4˚E; capital of North Hwanghae Province

A diversion off the road to Kaesong, 40 minutes' drive from Pyongyang, is the North Hwanghae Province seat of Sariwon. The city skyline is broken up by heavy

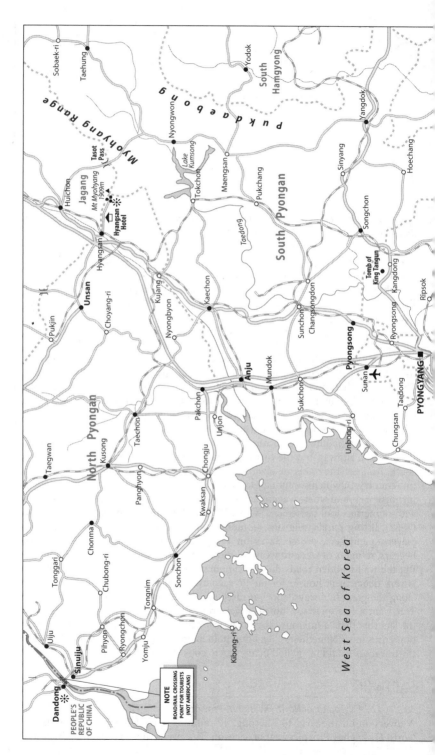

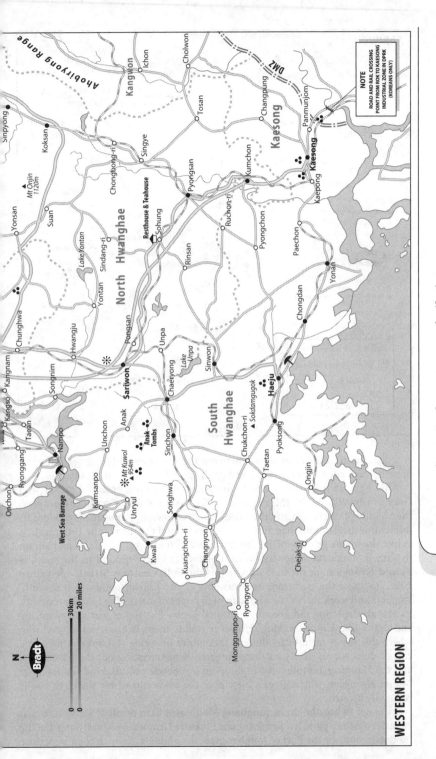

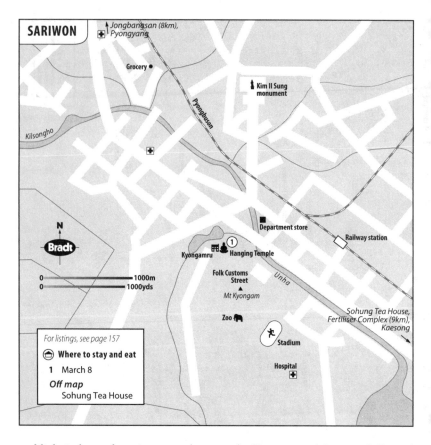

For listings, see page 157

and light industry factories strewn between the Kyongam and Sangmae hills, and there is also a bevy of universities serving the population of around 300,000.

Although you may be attracted to the **Sariwon Orchard**, noted for its 'Sariwon Grape', or be seduced by the allure of the **Sariwon Potassic Fertiliser Complex**, there's little of interest in an otherwise attractive town that mostly grew out of its interconnection of rail, road and river routes around the turn of the 19th century. While the town's gridlike plan runs northeast to southwest, the dazzling path up to Kim Il Sung's statue spears north. But the far bigger mound to the south is **Mount Kyongam**, at the base of which is the **Folk Customs Street**, open since 2007, 'to show the traditions and customs of the Korean nation to the youth, students and working people' and with high hopes of interesting tourists too, with its murals depicting old arts of traditional games like tug of war and wrestling and crafts like *kimchi*-making. However unless there is a festival or occasion where this site is in full use, there is little point in seeing it. Look out for some extraordinary trees, like great long-fingered hands, coming out the pavements, and the **Hanging Temple** hoist high up on a concrete pole. Behind is a track up Mount Kyongam, which gives a view over the town and where the city's zoo is reputedly located.

It's easier to breathe in the **Jongbang Mountains** 8km north of Sariwon, which were decreed as a park, the **Jongbangsan Pleasure Ground**, by Kim Il Sung. On the mountain slopes is the **Fort of Jongbangsan**, the grounds of which come very close to the Jongbang tunnel of the Pyongyang–Kaesong highway. It was a good enough site for the fort to be rebuilt in the mid-1600s and within its 12km of walls can be found the remains of its main armoury, garrisons and bits of 48 long-destroyed temples. The buildings of the Buddhist temple Songbul still stand, although they've been rebuilt many times since their foundation in 898.

Drive 30km due east from Sariwon via Chaeryong and you'll come to Sinchon, with the **Sinchon Massacre Museum** which, in customary micro detail, tells of an appalling atrocity committed by the US forces during the Korean War. The museum charts the massacre of over 35,300 civilians in and around Sinchon– men, women, children and babies. In a building much like a provincial boarding school are held the remains of 5,605 patriots, 400 mothers and 102 children killed in the massacre carried out between October and December 1950. Extremely graphic paintings depicting all manner of killings and torture hang alongside tortuous black and white photographs of the real aftermath. It is not for the faint-hearted.

Some 16km north-northeast of Sinchon is Anak, and it is between Anak and Sinchon that the three UNESCO-listed tombs of Anak lie, but arrangements need to be made to see these. Incidentally, Sariwon is twinned with Lahore in Pakistan, which is something to mull over back on the road to Kaesong.

WHERE TO STAY AND EAT You can stay at the **March 8 Hotel** (*29 rooms; $$–$*), a four-storey pink and white edifice that sits at the foot of Mount Kyongam. Notwithstanding restrictions on hot water and power, it has very comfortable rooms, some with the most attractive peach-melba coloured bathroom furniture. Otherwise, press on 30km further from Sariwon towards Kaesong until you reach the **Sohung Tea House** that bridges the road, where you can 'recover from fatigue and enjoy the nature' and have some tea, ginseng and beer, maybe some snake wine and dried squid as well as perusing books and embroideries, but sadly, they've long sold out of CD-ROMs about dogs. There used to be ostrich eggs on sale from an ostrich co-operative farm somewhere nearby that was once open for visits, but apparently that is no more. Further investigation has found that there was a rash of ostrich farms opened around the world in the 1990s, and the DPRK may have been the most exotic place that the ostrich farm salesman made a hit, but all went the way of the monorail. As you hang out here, be careful not to wander into the traffic!

Here on in, the road stops trying to avoid the hillsides and just bores straight through them. The tunnel entrances have precariously supported concrete obstacles, waiting to fall in the path of any invading tank or tourist bus, and that pertains to the point that the closer you get to Kaesong the more checkpoints you'll go through, and while you're not allowed to take photos of military things anyway, it's a very good idea at checkpoints simply to put any cameras out of sight. Otherwise keep an eye out for road signs to Seoul 서울.

Some 28km before Kaesong, just before Ryunggang tunnel, is evidence of a much older invasion. On the left at the bottom of a hill are a series of **dinosaur footprints**, 30 great plate marks from around 180 million years ago, found during the road's construction.

Eventually, you pass through the mist of the last seeping tunnel and a long flank of apartment blocks appears on the left; your vehicle curves right round under the highway and onto Thongil Street, matching the street you left Pyongyang by. Flanked by high-rises resembling the concrete stacks beside the highway, Thongil Street darts down and up a hill to a bronze statue of Kim Il Sung, who hails your arrival into Kaesong.

KAESONG 개성

37.55°N, 126.3°E; city and area under central authority

This former capital of Koryo is really a pleasant and interesting place to pass a couple of days. Most of the sites are within walking distance of each other and the city has the broad boulevards of Pyongyang, but none of the traffic (!), giving it a relaxed air that you wouldn't expect so close to the DMZ that lies only 8km away. Except for those lining the thoroughfares off Thongil Street, the buildings are low-storey and leave the surrounding hills to provide the shelter.

Kaesong means 'castle gate opening' and the city had long been a significant fortress city before King Wang Kon made it the capital of Koryo in 932, deeming it best located as a centre for the Koryo Kingdom. In the next 400 years, Kaesong grew and prospered not only as the kingdom's political centre but one of great commerce and learning, with schools, temples, and centres to study meteorology and astronomy. Buddhism was made the state's official religion and Kaesong its heart, as the aristocracy poured money into monasteries, temples and schools. It was also a fortified city, with three series of surrounding walls pulsing outwards over the centuries of Koryo's rule, like the rings of a tree, while all they built was laid out under the rules of geomancy.

HISTORY Although no longer the capital under the Ri dynasty, the city remained a significant commercial hub and military staging post, and became a centre for the cultivation and trading of the great medicinal cash crop, ginseng (*Koryo insam*), still a highly prized crop produced locally today. Until World War II, visitors noted a bustling business town, a great centre of the grain trade, with various mercantile guilds and roaring businesses in sesame oil, paper products, tobacco pouches, umbrellas and sheetings for walls and windows, and imports from Britain and Japan. Kaesong was fortunate to be set in a 'no bomb' zone that exempted it from the attention of US carpet-bombing, but it didn't escape the effects of the Korean ground war. The first armistice talks were held here in June 1951 before being moved to Panmunjom. In 1955, Kaesong was declared to be under direct central authority, and now constitutes one city and three counties.

Today, the city's main commodity is ginseng, with good trade in rice, barley and wheat until recently. The city's also known for its embroideries and porcelain, textiles and heavy industry, but there's more dust and rust here than in Pyongyang, and the real business goes on in the ROK-owned Kaesong Industrial Zone just outside town. Little remains of the city walls that once circled 15km around, its scores of temples and monasteries are largely vanished, and its population, at 335,000, is a sharp fall from its height of 800,000 under the Ri. Floods in recent years damaged the city's surrounding farmland, and once one could spot food-aid sacks with the stars and stripes on them. One would hope however that the Kaesong Industrial Zone (see box, pages 160–1) is improving things, and there's still much to behold from its past. In 2013 UNESCO gave 12 of the Koryo-era sites in the city World Heritage status, remarking that 'the geomantic layout of the former capital city of Kaesong, its palaces, institutions and tomb complex, defensive walls and gates embody the political, cultural, philosophical and spiritual values of a crucial era in the region's history'.

WHERE TO STAY AND EAT In addition to the places listed below, there is a charming **courtyard restaurant** right opposite the Folk Hotel serving not only cold noodles but also the traditional Korean multi-dish feast.

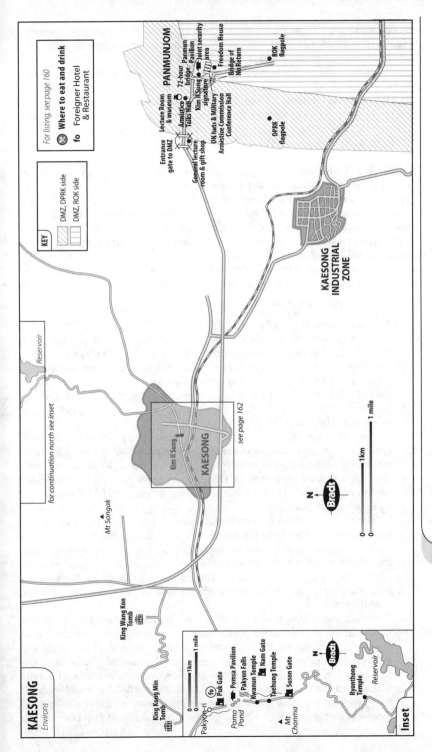

KAESONG
Environs

KEY
- DMZ, DPRK side
- DMZ, ROK side

For listing, see page 160
Where to eat and drink
- fo Foreigner Hotel & Restaurant

PANMUNJOM

72-hour bridge
Panmun Pavilion
Joint security area
Freedom House
Lecture Room & museum
Armistice Talks Hall
Kim Il Sung signature
Bridge of No Return
ROK flagpole
UN huts & Military Armistice Commission Conference Hall
Entrance gate to DMZ
General lecture room & gift shop
DPRK flagpole

KAESONG INDUSTRIAL ZONE

Reservoir

for continuation north see inset

Mt Songak

Kim Il Sung

KAESONG

see page 162

0 ─── 1km
0 ─── 1 mile

Inset

King Kong Min Tomb

King Wang Kon Tomb

Pakyon-ri
Puk Gate
Pomsa Pavilion
Pomo Pond
Pakyon Falls
Kwanun Temple
Nam Gate
Taehung Temple
Suson Gate
Mt Chonma
Ryonthong Temple
Reservoir

0 ─── 1km
0 ─── 1 mile

4

⌂ Janamsan Hotel (43 rooms) Next to Mount Janam up the road from Sonjuk Bridge. Quite old-school décor, with something of a flaky lift & power supply. The restaurant & bar are on the 1st floor. Also has billiards. **$$**

⌂ Kaesong Minsok Folk Hotel (50 rooms) Traditional 1-storey houses with courtyards built aside a stream during the Ri dynasty, & furnished as such. Absolutely charming place set in the city's old quarter; great fun. Also has restaurant where traditional Korean meals are served, & bar. **$$**

⌂ Foreigner Hotel and Restaurant At Puk Gate, by the Pakyon Falls. Prices unavailable.

✕ Thongil Restaurant At the foot of Mount Janam. Serves local cuisine like *pansnaggi, insam takgom*, Kaesong *posam kimchi*, Kaesong *yakbap*. Prices unavailable.

WHAT TO SEE AND DO Overlooking Kaesong is the pine tree-covered **Mount Songak**, with the smaller **Mount Janam** 'kneeling before it like a cute child to its father'. But it's around the latter hill that Kaesong centres, and Mount Janam is all the more dominant with its crown of bronze, in the form of Kim Il Sung, gesturing to the south. At night the statue is the lucky recipient of the city's only regular power supply, with the huge searchlights illuminating the statue and setting its shadow against low cloud.

By day, the 17ha of leafy slopes around it include a **revolutionary museum**, a **monument** and a marking point for 'on-the-spot guidance' from the Great Leader.

KAESONG INDUSTRIAL ZONE

Between Kaesong and the DMZ is the Kaesong Industrial Zone 개성공업지구, a theoretically ever-expanding enterprise built by the South Korean megalithic conglomerate Hyundai Asan, where South Korean firms are outsourcing production to the skilled but very low-cost northern workforce. This zone is not on the tourist itinerary and it has had negligible visible economic impact on Kaesong city itself, except some minor paint jobs (although the three planned golf courses may one day become a fixture), but is worth noting.

The plan as it panned out was to build an industrial city, as well as tourist and entertainment facilities and apartments, in three phases, with some 1,500 firms employing 350,000 workers from North Korea and managers bussed up from South Korea toiling to produce US$20 billion of goods each year. An expanded version was planned to add another 500 firms and take the total employment of locals to half a million.

With the zone linking the two Koreas by fibre-optic telephone cables, power lines running from South to North and road and rail links, this happier invasion of investment and ideas suggested much closer and more convivial ties between the DPRK and ROK. Indeed the DPRK so bought into the plan that the Dear Leader reportedly asked Hyundai Asan to draft special regulations for the Kaesong Industrial Estate, saying 'North Korean officials have made a futile attempt at this', according to NKchosun.com.

For positive influence, at the time, and maybe still, it seemed the DPRK was finally shifting from a mostly autarkic state-run communist economy towards an open-trade, capitalist basis, with the accompanying shift in mindset to accepting individualist inspiration and entrepreneurship – if they could avoid choking on the fact that it was all being provided by their gallingly successful brothers from the South. For the first phase, bids outnumbered allotments by 10 to 1, and although long preceded by Rason and Sinuiju as foreign investment zones, Kaesong has proven to be the most successful by far, but it's taking longer than planned. The

It's good for views of the city's **old quarter**. To the statue's left is the **Kwandok Pavilion**, built in 1780, where archery was practised in feudal times:

> The chief out-door manly sport in Corea is, by excellence, that of archery. It is encouraged by the government for the national safety in war, and nobles stimulate their retainers to excellence by rewards. At regular times contests are held, at which archers of reputation compete, the expense and prizes being paid for out of the public purse.
>
> William Eliot Griffis, *The Hermit Nation*, 1882

The pavilion is also a site for local parties to gather and play games on national holidays, for instance young girls racing around with bowls of water on their heads.

Cut into the eastern slope of Mount Janam is the charming **Sungyang Lecture Hall**. Confucianism was taught in this private hall, where lived the Confucian official Jong Mong Ju in the dying days of Koryo (he was assassinated on the Sonjuk Bridge). On a north–south axis, the school buildings were in the front and those annexes for sacrificial rites in the rear of the site, while to the east and west lie the dormitories.

Very visible from Mount Janam towards the southwest is Kaesong's old town, with its crooked, narrow-as-a-man alleys of single-storey, clay-brick houses, with gently

4

third phase was supposed to be complete by 2012, but by that time the zone had just over 120 South Korean firms employing some 53,000 North Koreans, mainly producing textiles, and also kitchenware and car parts. The rail line connecting the Koreas was revamped and reopened in 2007, but was in use only for a few months.

Pyongyang has sometimes seemingly randomly made unprecedented demands for tax and higher wages for workers (paid directly to Pyongyang). But then ROK firms can exploit too, paying North Korean workers a fraction of the wages earned in China, let alone the ROK. In 2012 a US$160/month wage for a textile worker was on a par with Vietnam, but just across the border from the ROK's markets, and without the faff and cost of long-range shipping and management.

Can North Korean-produced parts going into South Korean goods be exported to the US? It was hoped, not least by this writer, that the sight of investors piling billions of dollars into an industrial park right on the flashpoint of a future war suggested they were not banking on their investments being obliterated anytime soon, despite the war of words between the DPRK, the US and ROK, and with prosperity there'd also come peace. Incidents like a DPRK submarine sinking the ROK vessel the *Chenoan* in March 2010, with the loss of 46 crew, and the shelling of Yeonpyeong Island later that year (see page 47), notably didn't stop operations in Kaesong. But the showdown with the US in April 2013 sure did, with the DPRK throwing out the ROK's managers and closing the zone until September. Now maybe the DPRK had a point, their rowdy neighbours and their violent ally were wargaming just a few miles away, so it was hardly surprising Pyongyang didn't want their kids over to play.

And it was just a lockout, the factories weren't damaged. But interest on capitals loans was still being paid while nothing was being earned, and really, locking the owners and managers out of their own factories for months isn't really in the spirit of modern business.

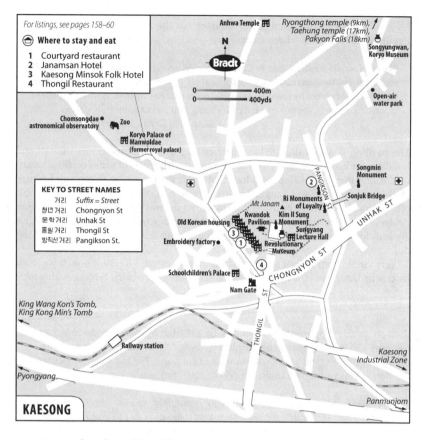

For listings, see pages 158–60

Where to stay and eat

1 Courtyard restaurant
2 Janamsan Hotel
3 Kaesong Minsok Folk Hotel
4 Thongil Restaurant

Anhwa Temple

Ryongthong temple (9km),
Taehung temple (17km),
Pakyon Falls (18km)

Songyungwan,
Koryo Museum

N

0 ——— 400m
0 ——— 400yds

Open-air
water park

Chomsongdae
astronomical observatory   Zoo
Koryo Palace of
Manwoldae
(former royal palace)

Songmin
Monument

KEY TO STREET NAMES

거리	*Suffix = Street*
청년 거리	Chongnyon St
운학 거리	Unhak St
통일 거리	Thongil St
방직선 거리	Pangikson St.

Ri Monuments
of Loyalty   Sonjuk Bridge

UNHAK ST

Mt Janam
Kwandok   Kim Il Sung
Pavilion   Monument
Old Korean housing
Sungyang
Lecture Hall
Revolutionary
Museum

Embroidery factory

CHONGNYON ST

Schoolchildren's Palace

Nam Gate

THONGIL ST

King Wang Kon's Tomb,
King Kong Min's Tomb

Railway station

Kaesong
Industrial Zone

Pyongyang

Panmunjom

KAESONG

sweeping roofs and an old-world appearance that both charms and appals. Though not all the roof tiles can be accounted for, it's fortunate that these densely packed houses are no longer thatched. This part of town's had some renovation in recent years, the most obvious aspect being some garish paintwork on their walls, and very recently it's become not impossible, with enough time and trust, that a walk can be done along the main road from Nam Gate (passed on the way in) to the Minsok Folk Hotel. Photos aren't allowed and gawping through windows will lead to curtains being tautly closed (quite right too). The Minsok Folk Hotel will very likely feature for the traditional Korean meal – lunch or dinner – that you may have there, with a dozen dishes in separate brass bowls. There's also a brothy dogmeat soup on offer (€5 in 2013) or a few could share a ginseng-stuffed chicken for €30. Back at Janam, there's an unmissable neo-Korean edifice, the **Kaesong Schoolchildren's Palace**, for 3,000 children to engage in after-school activities.

From Koryo times, Kaesong was a city bestowed with castles, with a royal palace stashed within an inner and outer castle. The southern gate to the inner castle, **Nam Gate**, has been reconstructed and dominates the crossroads just off from Thongil Street. Originally built in 1391, it stood as the southern gate of Kaesong's inner castle until it was destroyed during the Korean War.

The gate houses the **Yonbok Temple bell**, made in 1346 for Yonbok Temple and moved to the gate in 1563 when the temple burnt down. Weighing 14 tonnes, it's covered with figures of tortoises, crabs, dragon, phoenix, deer, and images of the

Buddha, and the two dragons on top of the bell indicate 'intrepid spirit'. The bell can be heard 4km away.

Bishop (see page 278) wrote that the road was lined with monuments to good governors, magistrates, faithful widows and pious sons. Very few such sites remain, but walking east along Chongnyon Street, possibly the same road that caused Bishop to call Kaesong a 'one-road town', you come to a bridge and a road going left. A hundred metres up here on the right is **Sonjuk Bridge**, a tiny stone crossing built in 1215 that now has a small fence round it and another crossing next to it. On this bridge in 1392, Ri Song Gye, in the process of establishing the Ri dynasty as rulers of all Korea (with himself as its first king), assassinated Jong Mong Ju, a civil servant and loyalist to the Koryo dynasty. Where Jong's blood fell, it stained the bridge (supposedly still visible today) or from the blood grew bamboo. To commemorate the incident, a descendant of Jong fenced off the bridge in 1780.

Jong's loyalty is also celebrated at the **Songmin Monument** just beyond the bridge, erected in 1641 along with two other monuments, one to the memory of the government official Gyong Jowho who was killed with Jong. Loyalty to the Ri dynasty inspired the monuments set across the road from the bridge, with two large stelae set on the backs of tortoises. The left dates from 1740 and King Yong Jo and the right from 1872 and King Ko Jong.

At the base of Mount Ogwan is the Koryo-era **Ryongthong Temple**, or rather the rebuild that was completed under the direction of the Koryo Art Studio in 2005, an effort partnered with UNESCO and South Korean Buddhist groups. A renowned Buddhist priest of the 11th century, Ui Chon, founded the sect of Buddhism in Korea and at one time resided at the temple which became a centre of Buddhist learning. It burnt down at the end of the 16th century and its pagoda was buried. That the temple dated from the Koryo era makes its current location near the DMZ all the more significant, with Koryo being the first unified Korean kingdom, and the temple being rebuilt with cross-Korean co-operation.

Songyungwan Situated past a children's large water park, this impressive but very picturesque complex of 20 education buildings was founded in AD992 as the Kukjagam, the highest educational institute for the civil service as Kaesong was directed towards being the intellectual heart of Koryo as well as its political capital. The children of Koryo and later the Ri aristocracy attended the school to learn the Confucian ways of administration and sacrifice. Renamed Songyungwan from 1308, it was expanded but burnt down during the Japanese invasion of 1592 and was rebuilt ten years later. The main buildings are on a typically Confucian north–south axis, with a pleasure ground for archery and swinging over the west side. Since 1987, the site has been home to the very picturesque **Koryo Museum**, where is stashed a good hoard of pottery, ironwork, prints and relics from the Koryo dynasty, with readable presentations of life in those times, and some thousand-year-old pagodas rescued from Hyonhwa, Hungguk and Pulil temples, a recreation of a royal tomb and a wall chart showing the relative pecuniary value of cattle, slaves and women in those times. This is all overlooked by 500-year-old gingko trees and a 900-year-old zelkova. One feat is for four people to link arms around the large tree just within the museum entrance. East of the museum are two mounds of a tomb that are worth investigating. Just outside the museum gates are two shops, with one having a very impressive selection of stamps and artwork while the opposite shop sells all things ginseng. The museum also has information about the following site that may or may not appear on a tour, namely the former **Koryo Palace of Manwoldae**. Manwoldae is located on the southern foot of Mount Songak, 2km north of Nam Gate, and dates from AD919 to 1361 when it was burnt down in a raid by Chinese rebels, the Red Turbans, as part of their campaign against the Yuan rulers. However the not inconsiderable stone foundations of the palace are still visible, and a joint North–South Korean archaeological dig in 2009 found quite a few artefacts. Part of **Kaesong outer castle** lies beyond, as do the remains of the **Chomsongdae astronomical observatory**, in most use between 1024 and the late 1300s.

A fleeting excursion could be made to **Anhwa Temple**, 4km from Nam Gate and built in AD930 on the mid-slope of Mount Songak. Here studied Wang Sin, a cousin of King Wang Kon. Obaek Hall's thousand Buddhas protected it from the ravages of war, and the seven-storey pagoda survived too.

OUT OF TOWN

King Kong Min's Tomb Fourteen kilometres southwest of central Kaesong and stacked up a steep hill is the charming tomb of King Kong Min, the 31st King of Koryo from 1352. Kong Min was a skilled painter and draughtsman, and when his wife died in 1365 he designed two tombs side by side (construction completed in 1372), the right one housing his wife and the left he entered upon his death in 1374. The statues are of military and civil officials. The 'older' military figure is on the outside, better able to defend the king from attack through his veteran experiences, and the older civil officials are nearer the tomb than the youthful assistants, as maturity guarantees better advice to the king. The tiger outside the tomb is representative of the Koryo ancestry and the sheep of his wife's Mongol descent. The location of Kong Min's body is not known however; the answer lies with the Japanese troops that looted the place.

Wang Kon's Tomb Just over 3km due west of Nam Gate in Haeson-ri, on the road to Pakyon Falls is the Tomb of King Wan Kon (AD877–943), the founder of Koryo. He was born into a wealthy farming family and his father held great influence as a local aristocrat and landowner. Wan Gon served as a civil servant from the age of 20 and achieved high rank. His coup d'état in June 918 overthrew the Thaebong state and founded the Koryo, inheriting Koguryo's remnants and bringing Silla and Paekche under the rule of Kaesong. He died in 943 and they built his tomb there, with lawns carpeting up to it. Statues of officials and animals, stone lamps for burning incense, an offertory table and images of 12 guardian gods all guard the tomb. But it is a bit new – possibly renovations were over-enthusiastically done.

Pakyon Falls Moving north from the tombs, the road gets grottier and tighter as you head up through the Jongmyongsa Pass and down into a valley of *insam*. You're *en route* to Pakyon Falls, a delightful waterfall 24km from Kaesong, tucked into a sharp valley fort on Mount Taehung.

As you turn right through the village of Pagyon-ri, there appears on the left a monument to the falls. Then there appears **Puk Gate**, a large edifice that fronts the Taehungsan Fort surrounding the falls. The fort, established before Koryo, was beefed up to defend the new capital Kaesong, and along its 10km of lacing walls still stand the Nam and Sosan gates. Puk is flanked by a **hotel** and **restaurant**.

Passing through the gate and past some large ponds, you come to the falls, dropping 37m down from Pakyon pond. To the right is the **Pomsa Pavilion**, dating from Koryo times, that gives a good view and a sit-down. A kilometre further up the valley from the pond is the beautiful **Kwanum Temple**, built when the fort was expanded. With its seven-storey pagoda, it's a fabulously tranquil location that could inspire the most agnostic to concede that, living in such settings and high architecture, the Buddhists were possibly on to something. Nearby is Kwanum Cave that was blessed with two marble Buddhas in AD970 by the temple's high priest.

Another 2km upwards is the private school where Wang Kon's son studied in AD921. The old temple of Taehung that was here burnt down. Later the school building was converted into the temple it is today. This is set dead in the centre of a reserve for the white-bellied black woodpecker, which could be spotted from the paths around Taehung Temple that lead to the fort's remaining gates.

PANMUNJOM 판문점 AND THE DMZ 한반도 비무장지대

Panmunjom 37.96°N 126.677°E, the DMZ 250km running from the Korean West Sea to the Korean East Sea.

Many moons ago there was a road linking Kaesong to Seoul. The road crossed the River Sachon, a tributary of the River Rimjin. People built a bridge with logs and boards and named it Panmun, but rains would wash the bridge away and prevent anyone from crossing, so an inn was built for delayed travellers, an inn called Panmunjom (board-framed shop) that lent its name to the village built here. The village itself was wiped from the map during the Korean War, but the name survived and it's now known as the venue for the Korean Armistice Talks. It's here that the 'US imperialists bent the knees down before the Korean people' when the US 'gave up' in 1953, and is the epicentre of the De-Militarised Zone (DMZ). The actual division line of Korea is the Military Demarcation Line (MDL) that snakes across Korea from the mouth of the River Rimjin in the west to the east-coast Walbisn-ri, and the DMZ is a 4km-thick buffer straddling the MDL. The DMZ is anything but demilitarised, and is one of the most heavily guarded, heavily mined frontiers in the world. This isn't surprising as a combined total of 1.5 million Korean and 28,000 American soldiers would clash along this frontier, and the DMZ bristles with artillery and troops ready to let rip at the drop of grenade. As you are driven in and out of the area, try and spot as many disguised sentry points, pillboxes, tank-traps, machine-gun and artillery posts as you can. Having said that, the atmosphere is overall surprisingly relaxed, especially compared with the Friendship Exhibition in Myohyangsan. While here more than anywhere permission for photos is needed, the officer guiding you will yay or nay with a friendly bat of his hand. Which you had better heed.

DMZ WILDLIFE AND THE PEACE PARK So little actual human activity for good or ill goes on in the DMZ (for obvious risks of being shot or blown up) that wildlife, particularly endangered species, have been seen to thrive in this fenced-in strip of land. It is unsurprisingly difficult for any '-ologists' to get in and check what hops amid the mines, but Manchurian crane, ringtail pheasant, spot-billed duck, black-tailed gull, white-naped and red-crowned cranes, and the black-faced spoonbill have been sighted, as have bears, wildcats, leopards, deer and Siberian tiger in the hillier parts, as well as freshwater turtles, terrapins and butterflies. The DMZ has become such a haven for species that are endangered elsewhere that plans are afoot to turn this buffer zone to keep the peace into a 'peace park', to protect a substantial slice of the peninsula's biodiversity. ROK president Roh Moo-hyun raised the idea with Kim Jong Il in 2007, and President Park Geun-hye also floated it again in 2013 and has set the Unification Ministry on the idea. Other backers to the scheme have ranged from Nelson Mandela to Ted Turner, and calls for the UN to endorse it have

4

come to fruition with Secretary-General Ban Ki-moon, a former foreign minister of South Korea, saying the UN was game – if Park Geun-hye could make headway with the DPRK on the matter. Symbolically, the park would convert the DMZ from a symbol of division into one of peace and unity. However, in an ironic twist, the haven is being threatened by those same forces of reconciliation; rail and road links across the DMZ will require the area to be de-mined, and this may lead to the destruction of these fragile habitats.

GETTING THERE AND AWAY
Visiting from the ROK On the DPRK side you'll be spied upon by UN troops with binoculars and may be dazzled by the flash photography of a tour group from the other side, mainly Americans, ROK citizens and Japanese who might otherwise never have a chance of stepping into the DPRK. Panmunjom is only a 90-minute drive from Seoul, and day-long bus tours running from the city can

THE ARMISTICE

On 23 June 1951, nearly a year after the Korean War had started, the Soviet Union's UN envoy Yakov Malik suggested that the opposing sides should try peace negotiations. The DPRK's forces had nearly succeeded in uniting the country, as had the United Nations Command (UNC) coming back the other way. A week later, UNC general Ridgeway got word that the communists might be favourable to armistice talks, which were arranged, unarranged and rearranged for Kaesong. The decision to move the talks from Kaesong to Panmunjom in September 1951 was the easiest decision reached by the communists (consisting of the Korean People's Army and the Chinese People's Volunteers) and the UNC, and it totally dominated discussions for two weeks. The agenda finally decided upon was to agree what a ceasefire meant, how it was to be implemented, where (which involved drawing a demarcation line while fighting continued) and what to do with prisoners of war (POWs). Two years of long, tedious and tortuous negotiations followed, while talking peace took second place to another day's fighting that could tip the balance in a side's favour. Both delegations, the communists led by Korean general Nam II, and the UNC by Lieutenant-General William K Harrison, engaged in time-wasting tactics and talks descended into vitriolic slanging matches, with the most colourful language coming from the communists. As soon as a point of conduct or principle of a ceasefire was agreed, one side accused the other of violating it and raised hell if they didn't storm out, resuming negotiations by letter days or weeks later.

The repatriation of POWs took the most debate. The UNC declared they held up to 132,500 POWs, and the communists held around 11,400 UNC and 7,150 ROK troops (a disputed figure), with fierce debate over how a POW would be defined. The lists lengthened as fighting went on and shortened as dribs and drabs of POWs were repatriated through Panmunjom. The communists demanded their POWs be repatriated whether they wanted to or not, which the UNC insisted was a matter of free choice. Thousands of POWs on both sides were slain after capture and others held in camps so foul that prisoners grew sick and died while their captors looked on. Nam II and Harrison signed an armistice on 27 July 1953. Accusations of violations of the armistice have flown from all sides every other week since.

PANMUNJOM AXE INCIDENT

On the lane to the Bridge of No Return, southwest of the huts, occurred a bizarre incident on 18 August 1976 that became known to the US side as the 'Panmunjom Axe Murders'. A group of ROK and US soldiers arrived near the bridge to prune a large poplar tree obscuring the view of two proximate UNC checkpoints. Captain Arthur Bonifas with First Lieutenant Mark Barrett and a Korean officer were overseeing the task when a group of Korean People's Army (KPA) soldiers arrived. The KPA officer demanded the pruning be stopped; when it didn't, the KPA soldiers attacked the group with axes, knives and clubs, killing Bonifas and Barrett and injuring ten more. The KPA claimed that the tree pruning was a cover for provocative attacks on KPA checkpoints. Over the next few days, tensions ran high as the KPA shot at patrolling US aircraft while both sides readied for further bloodshed. The US response was Operation Paul Bunyan early on 21 August. US and ROK infantry and artillery trained their guns on KPA positions as US air-force bombers scowled across the skies. A US 'task force' completed the pruning. The Americans now call the Joint Security Area (JSA) 'Camp Bonifas' (obviously the North Koreans don't), and the JSA was summarily divided, with the Bridge of No Return going into the southern half. The KPA built themselves a new bridge in three days, calling it '72-hour Bridge' and the axes from the incident are proudly displayed at the Armistice Talks Hall (see page 168).

include commentaries on the area's history and visits to the tunnels that the DPRK dug under the demarcation line into the South to sneak fully armoured attacks on Seoul. A series of monuments to the 15 countries' UN forces dot the route into the DMZ, and should you stray past a sky-blue obelisk saying DMZ, you know where you are. Tours do not run every weekday and not on holidays, so check with the operators listed below.

Tour operators

Korea Travel Bureau (KTB Tour) Anguk BD 4F, 33, Yulgok-ro, Jongno-gu, Seoul 110-734 ; ☏ +82 2 778 0150; f +82 2 756 8428; e ktbmaster@ktbtour.co.kr; www.go2korea.co.kr, www.ktbtour.co.kr. One-day Joint Security Area (JSA) tour is around US$75, while a JSA tour & tunnel is US$115. You must bring your passport on the day,

your hair must not be unkempt & your safety in the DMZ cannot be guaranteed.
Panmunjom Travel Centre Lotte Hotel, 2nd Flr (Main Bldg), Chung-Gu, Sogong-dong, Seoul City; ☏ +82 2 771 5593 5; f +82 2 771 5596; e jsa33@korea.com; www.panmunjomtour.com

WHERE TO STAY AND EAT There is nowhere to stay in the DMZ and tourists can only visit on day trips, but there is a large dining hall tucked away behind the hills with restaurants upstairs and down, and in summer there may be artwork for sale outside. It's fine as restaurants go, but the location is so quiet you forget where you are.

WHAT TO SEE AND DO The entrance to the DMZ is 8km south of Kaesong, and on the way down you can glimpse from the road Hyundai's Kaesong Industrial Zone and the smart silver-grey railway station built to serve the facility, with the first train crossing the DMZ in 2007.

Just before the entrance to the DMZ is a tight gate, these days often with a queue of buses backed out of it. Beyond is a courtyard of sorts, where disgorging tourists mill in and out of the building on the right, the **general lecture room and gift shop**, or take in the pungent toilet on the left, before being escorted into the DMZ. The more buses there are, the longer it'll take for you to be let in. You can photograph the pink-flowered united Korea mural, but do not take pictures of anything in the direction of the DMZ.

The shop sells masterpieces of propaganda about the Americans and their lackey puppets as well as much of the usual souvenir stuff, but most outstanding are the local hats and T-shirts almost of the 'I went to Panmunjom and all I got was ... ' sort. The tour begins when you're ushered into the general lecture room next door, where, against an impressive wall map of the area, an overview of the DMZ and its history is given by a Korean People's Army officer who'll be briefing you throughout the tour.

You're then taken outside, lined up and walked into the DMZ single file through the muscular entrance gate, past a row of precariously jacked tank-traps, and then led back aboard your bus along with a KPA officer (and any others needing a lift). These guys are quite chilled because they know no-one's going to misbehave. See how many block-obstacles, drop-down barriers, ditches and moats you can spot on the way to the **Armistice Talks Hall**, a pretty little hut with a small stele outside. This is 1km into the DMZ and is where the Korean War armistice talks were held. It took a year of fighting from 1950 for both sides' armies to grind to a halt pretty much back where they'd started, and talks began in June 1951 in Kaesong itself. Two more years passed in which hundreds of thousands of lives were squandered while talks continued in this hut, in what is now an eerily quiet part of the world.

Next to the Armistice Talks Hall is a large, light-coloured building with a dove on the roof, the hall where the armistice was **signed** on 27 July 1953, and the chairs, tables and flags are all preserved there in a museum with the usual impressive display of enlarged photos, documented 'proof' of US aggression and maps of the war. Incidents of several intruding ships and aircraft being shot down and captured are all divulged in detail on wall panels.

The Panmun Pavilions and the Joint Security Area

About 1km southward from the Armistice Hall, you cross the 72-hour Bridge over the Sachon River into the **Joint Security Area** (JSA). The JSA radiates 400m around a row of blue and white huts in which armistice talks continue to this day. From the DPRK side, you approach the huts from behind the elevated **Panmungak Hall**, an austere building flanked by a large stone panel on which is carved Kim Il Sung's signature, and the panel is filled with numerical meaning. The total height of the panel is 4.15m (April 15, Kim Il Sung's birth), the width of the top panel is 7.7m and the plinth is 9.4m – he died on 7 July 1994.

Opposite Panmungak on the ROK side was once only a small, raised pavilion but now there is also a remarkable building fusing hi-tech modern materials and traditional Korean building style that contrasts with the DPRK's Soviet-style hall. Between these two architectural emblems of Korea is a tidy row of huts straddling a thin concrete path indicating the military demarcation line between North and South, and the huts are seemingly all that staple the two states together. If you're allowed into the huts (the ability to access the huts does fluctuate – in 2014 Panmunjom was closed on the north side on Saturdays), the one you'll most likely enter is the **Military Armistice Commission Conference Hall**, which is still in use by the Military Armistice Commission and the Neutral Nations Supervisory Commission. In the middle of the hall is a table, across which are strung microphone leads, indicating the demarcation line in the hall, and it's at this table that representatives from the UNC, Korean People's Army and Chinese Volunteer Army sit and thrash out how each side is upholding the armistice, not always in the most cordial fashion. In the hall there's also a list of participatory countries in the Korean War against the DPRK side that the guides refer to apologetically as you may well come from one of them.

Tourists can orbit the table and thereby technically cross into the ROK, but this room is not a mock-up, so do not touch the microphone leads. As said, the huts are still used for negotiations, also for organisations like the Red Cross and Olympic committee, and such meetings are one reason the huts may not be accessed. Another touted reason is since DPRK–ROK relations soured after 2010, military phone lines between the two sides were cut, making visits to the huts problematical in case tour parties from both sides of the border clash. And under no circumstances should one try to cross the concrete demarcation line outside (for the record, one Soviet defector made it in 1983).

The JSA itself used to be pocked with equidistant United Nations Command and Korean People's Army checkpoints, for, until 1976, both sides had free run

DEFECTIONS, DECEPTIONS AND TUNNELS

The DMZ on land, and the DPRK–ROK borders at sea, have seen innumerable violent incidents over the years, not just shoot-outs and skirmishes inevitably arising from ongoing tensions, but attempted infiltrations and outright attacks. The worst era was the late 1960s and 1970s, and in 1968 alone there were 181 incidents, starting in January with the infamous Blue House Raid (see box, page 34), while a later seaborne incursion into Samchuk, ROK, in November led to 107 DPRK commandos being killed. While assaults from the sea continued into the 1980s, the DPRK was also busy underground. So far, the UNC has discovered four tunnels dug under the DMZ, three being unearthed during the 1970s and one in 1990, with investigating parties suffering fatalities and injuries from booby traps. Dug down to depths of 145m and extending over 1km into the ROK, some of the tunnels are big enough for tens of thousands of troops to come through each hour, and it's thought there is actually over a score of such tunnels, of which the DPRK denied any knowledge until the 1990 bust.

Spies have also been sent south across the lines, with many being killed on the way, and submarines and frogmen have been used in clandestine missions. In June 1998 a DPRK midget submarine caught up in fishing nets was spotted and seized off Sokcho, ROK. Rather than be taken prisoner, the nine crew aboard took their own lives.

Several acts of espionage have been caught coming north. A US Chinook helicopter was shot down over the DPRK in 1977, as was an OH-58a chopper that had got 10km into the DPRK's air space in 1994. The costliest incident happened 90 miles out over the Sea of Japan, however, when on 15 April 1969 (Kim Il Sung's birthday) KPA MiGs shot down a US EC-121 spy-plane, killing all 31 aboard.

The DMZ's also seen defections, including a Soviet tourist, a Chinese officer and a few DPRK soldiers going south, but a few have come the other way, some successfully, some not. In September 2013 a 47-year-old South Korean was shot dead by ROK troops near Paju in the south as he tried to swim across the river to the DPRK.

of the JSA and jointly maintained its security. This changed in September that year following the Panmunjom Axe Incident (see box, page 167), and the JSA was divided into North and South.

At various points along the road to the JSA, you can see two huge flag towers, one in the DPRK, the other in the ROK. The 160m DPRK flag mast, with its quarter-tonne flag, towers over the village of Kijongdong, with its brightly painted apartment blocks. Legend has it that the flag mast was built to outdo the ROK's 98m-tall mast that dwarfs the village of Taesong-dong, with which Kijongdong is not twinned. There are fields and fields of crops being grown around the main DMZ sites, part of the **Panmunjom-ri co-op farm**, so somebody's doing something, but the ROK calls Kijongdong 'propaganda village', claiming it's not a village but was built to serve as a honey trap for South Korean defectors, to house KPA soldiers, and as the place from where to broadcast high-volume abuse at Taesong-dong.

In fact both sides used massive loudspeakers to hurl abuse and propaganda at one another right up until 2004, probably when they both realised there wasn't really anybody close enough to hear it. ROK literature contrasts the villages with ROK photographs of Taesong-dong showing a beaming, happy population that are regularly helped in the fields by smiling soldiers, before darkness falls and the 23.00 curfew begins. So they're all at it, really.

Elsewhere along the DMZ you can see an 8m-high concrete wall, the **Wall of Division**, in the southern half, built from 1976 to 1979 by US forces along nearly all the DMZ. Due east of Kaesong's Nam Gate (27km) is a good viewing point of this coldly impressive wall, although very few tourists have actually been there in recent years. You can also see the **Bridge of No Return**, which is the southern bridge along the DMZ where POWs crossed from one side to the other.

5

Nampo, Mount Kuwol and Haeju

For a map of the region see pages 154–5.

From Mangyongdae in southwest Pyongyang goes the 'Youth Hero Motorway', so named for having been built by the young, a road that continues to point southwestwards as it tacks along the Taedong River, and 55km later reaches Nampo 남포 city. This route passes through one of the DPRK's most industrialised areas, including two plants of great repute and place in the DPRK's heavy industry sector, the **Chollima Steel Complex** and the **Taean Heavy Machine Complex**. Sited on the Taedong riverbank about 12km southwest of Pyongyang, the former complex at its peak was knocking out a million tonnes of steel a year. Here visitors unencumbered by hard hats can get right up close to the electric arc furnace that produces 'Juche Steel', and all three generations of the Kims have been here and done that. There's much by way of impressively colourful slogans and murals. It was originally built by the Japanese and became central to the DPRK's post-war strategies of reconstruction and advancing heavy industry. That is as true of another newly opened site a few kilometres further downstream, the heavy machine complex at Taean, where in vast hangers workers use lathes and machines to turn Juche steel into usable industrial products, turbine and generator blades.

North of the Youth Hero Motorway, about 27km west-southwest of Pyongyang, are the tombs of **Kangso** and **Tokhung-ri** (outside Taepyong) and then **Kangso** town where the 7,000m, 18-hole **Pyongyang Golf Course**, built and financed by Japanese-Koreans for Kim Il Sung's 75th birthday, awaits to give the golfing experience that no golfer could ever miss (a round for around US$100). Legend has it that the Dear Leader played a round here and scored 18 holes-in-one (quite a record and even more quite a drinks bill), but the legend, which has been in strong circulation in Western publications, is rumoured to actually be one of Western origin. Hmmm.

The area around Kangso is also noted for its numerous springs of mineral water which helps the 'function of secretion, absorption and motion in the alimentary canal, accelerates the formation of bile and excretion, increases the amount of urine and promotes the excretion of stones in the urinary canal,' according to the Korean Central News Agency (KNCA). When it is not being bottled and shipped to Pyongyang, it is the bedrock (as it were) of spa treatment centres in the area, the waters having somehow bucked contamination from industry, and facilities are open for visitors to bathe in mineral waters.

Around and south of Nampo is one of the DPRK's most important agricultural areas (notwithstanding the apparent maxim that if it's earth, grow something) and the region is best noted in Korean lore for its apples, although in recent years both the water and the fruits have been imperilled by increasingly intermittent rainfall.

NAMPO 남포

In that Inchon is Seoul's city on the sea for trade, so is Nampo for Pyongyang, being on the mouth of the Taedong River and only a short scoot or sail from the capital.

With a population of nearly three-quarters of a million, Nampo is to most intents the DPRK's second city, where cargoes for Pyongyang are unloaded, ships are built and repaired in the state's largest shipbuilding facilities, copper is smelted, electrodes, textiles and glass products are manufactured, and many a living eked out by fishing on the West Sea (or to non-Koreans, the Yellow Sea), and it's where the Moonies built their Pyonghwa car factory. South Korean companies are already operating textile factories, an electronics complex is under construction and an

TOMBS

Across Korea have been found thousands of tombs, forts, walls, gates, relics and settlements in varying states of repair, a great many of them dating from the Koguryo period (277BC–AD668). The most exceptional of these sites have intricate mural paintings depicting customs and other less salubrious goings on in the Koguryo court and country life. Koguryo also included parts of China, and UNESCO estimates that there are around 10,000 Koguryo tomb sites in China and across Korea, but only 90 or so have such wall murals.

Of those that have been long known, many have suffered the withers of time as well as ransacking and robbery over the centuries, most recently under the Japanese, plunder that can 'never be covered up … they will certainly be made to pay for their crimes despite the flow of time', KNCA commented half a century after the events.

But many of these tombs, especially around Pyongyang and to the southwest, are undergoing restoration and renovation, nay, total reconstructions – some sites have been spruced up with 'authentic' statues that unfortunately end up being a load of tat, but others are worth seeing.

Of note are the three tombs of Kangso, the Royal Tomb of King Tongmyong and the three tombs in Anak (16km north-northeast of Sinchon and due west of Sariwon). They are all on a list of 63 Koguryo tombs in Pyongyang, Nampo and South Hwanghae, collectively known as 'the complex of Koguryo tombs', that UNESCO designated as World Heritage Sites in 2004, along with several Koguryo forts and remains in northeast China. Such is the prestige of this ancient kingdom that UNESCO's listing was partly ascribed as a bid to force the two communist countries to 'share' their common past and stop rewriting it with a view to getting one over the other.

Of the Anak tombs, number three, that of a provincial king, is notable not only for its paintings and size (seven chambers) but more for a rare inscription that allows the construction to be dated to AD357.

Other sites at Susan-ri, Yaksu-ri and Taechu-ri (in an area around the Kangso tombs, 20km west-southwest of Mangyongdae) can be walked around. The tombs at Anak, Kangso and Tokhung-ri can be entered, but only with some advance preparation and for a price – the downside to the preservation is the associated cost of 'unsealing' the tombs for visitors, and the charge for visits within the tombs was last quoted at €100 per person per tomb.

STEAM TRAINS

Across the top of the West Sea Barrage runs a road and a rail line, along which steam trains travel from Nampo to Cholgwang. Specialist trips for steam train enthusiasts have been operated since the early 1990s. Groups of people standing on bridges watching railway stations and photographing anything that moves can ruffle authorities not used to the sport of 'trainspotting' – although trainspotters in the UK have had a time of it in recent years from paranoid authorities and their security fears, real and imaginary. Groups have gone into the country in this way fairly regularly, but trains are by no means so regular in DPRK, even the ones that don't run on electricity. Interested parties can ask tour operators about such trips.

industrial park between Nampo and Haeju is planned on a similar scale to the Kaesong project. All this industry befell a town that for centuries had eked out a living by fishing, not a bad thing to do with the West Sea, rich in shellfish, sea bream, croakers, lizard fish, prawns, cutlass fish, horse mackerel, squids, flounders and blue crabs, all being hooked, trapped and netted by Koreans, Chinese and Japanese for some time, although this is becoming a bit of an issue such that catching crabs causes bullets to fly. There is also said to be oil under them there sea waters.

At the turn of the 19th century Nampo's location at the Taedong's mouth realised greater significance as the village grew into a naval-trading town. Post-1945 the government of the DPRK directed Nampo's most spectacular urban and industrial growth and in the mid-1980s the gargantuan West Sea Barrage was built.

GETTING THERE AND AWAY Nampo is about a 45-minute drive by bus from Pyongyang, but there are tours where you can cycle much if not all the distance from Pyongyang to Nampo, Kuwol and other locations around the country. There's very little traffic to worry about, nor pollution to choke on. Tour companies may or may not put it on a tour.

WHERE TO STAY AND EAT

🏠 **Ryonggang Hot Spa Hotel** Onchon, 25km northwest of Nampo, 80km from Pyongyang. 7 nicely decked out villas & enough mineral water to bathe in. **$$**

🏠 **Hanggu Hotel** (109 rooms) Waudo recreation ground. **$$–$**
🏠 **Waudo Hotel** Waudo Pleasure Grounds. Serviceable. **$$–$**

WHAT TO SEE AND DO As well as its **Kim Il Sung statue** and its adjacent **revolutionary museum**, sights to see in Nampo now include a tour of the **sea-vessel repair shop** and of late the city's **orphanage** (see box, page 175) has sometimes been open to visitors. The latter is a handsome new building, cheerfully decked out and a visit would include seeing some of the 300 or so resident children in the playroom, and they may put on a performance involving song and, er, wrestling. There's also the **Nampo Glass Works**, built with Chinese money and opened by China's then premier Hu Jintao in 2005, where all of the sexy neon in Pyongyang and elsewhere is produced. Visitors see the whole process from smelting to cutting sheet glass.

The city's other features include the 1970s buildings in **Nampo Sports Village** and **Tae kwon do School**, with its students aged six to 16 showing why you should never pick a fight with a Korean, and the **Waudo Pleasure Grounds** of Wau Islet

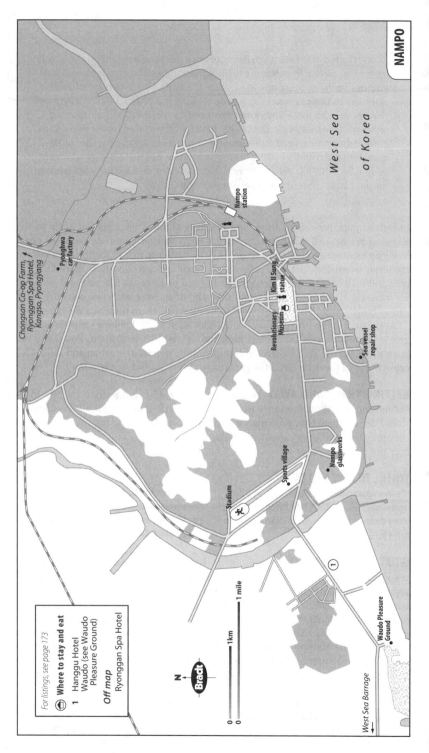

NAMPO

West Sea
of Korea

Nampo station

Pyonghwa
car factory

*Chongsan Co-op Farm,
Ryonggan Spa Hotel,
Kangso, Pyongyang*

Kim Il Sung
statue

Revolutionary
Museum

Sea vessel
repair shop

Nampo
glassworks

Sports village

Stadium

①

Waudo Pleasure
Ground

West Sea Barrage

For listings, see page 173

ⓘ **Where to stay and eat**

1   Hanggu Hotel
        Waudo (see Waudo
        Pleasure Ground)

Off map

        Ryonggan Spa Hotel

N

Bradt

0   1km
0   1 mile

LENDING A HELPING HAND

The Nampo orphanage is the only one in the DPRK that's open to arranged visits from tourists, and it's supported by tour companies like Koryo Tours, but there are many other orphanages across the country that outside organisations and NGOs are working with. NGOs operating in the DPRK range from the world known, such as UNICEF, down to operations with just a handful of volunteers.

At the latter end of the scale for example is the NGO working with the Nampo orphanage, the UK-based Love North Korean Children (*www. lovethechildren.org*), which provides the foodstuffs and the cooking equipment and builds the bakeries to feed orphanages across the DPRK with breads and buns. Nonetheless its aims are high, and already operating in Nampo, Pyongyang and Sariwon, the group aims to have bakeries in 26 cities. Marama Global (*www.maramaglobal.org*) is another group that's been working for years with an orphanage in Wonsan, and they're partnered with the Korean Education Fund (*www.koredufund.org.kp*), a DPRK non-profit organisation aiming to improve the quality of education in North Korea.

Projects range from long-term efforts to revitalise agriculture, to providing medicines, development aid, and educational materials to emergency relief such as housing for victims of typhoons. A great many of these groups are based in the ROK and the US, as well as Europe, Canada, and Australasia, and they mostly divide into secular groups with a humanitarian purpose, to groups of religious origin but whose work in the DPRK is only, and strictly, humanitarian. Many also stress how they do not purchase in country, but bring all their own needs in and oversee their distribution and use to ensure that those who need are those who get.

To name but a very few of the organisations working with orphanages: Mission East (*www.miseast.org/en*) is a Danish NGO that since 2011 has conducted food assistance programmes reaching some 50,000 people in the DPRK, mostly children, in North Pyongan, Kangwon and South Hwanghae provinces, and engaged in reconstruction work following the flood of 2012.

The US-based NGO Good Neighbours (*www.goodneighbors.org*) has a programme of support for orphanages in nine DPRK cities, including Nampo, Pyongyang, Wonsan, Chongjin and Haeju. The Korean Friendship Network (*www.koreanfriendshipnetwork.org*) is a Rotary Club endeavour that has supplied foodstuffs to orphanages around Pyongsong, as one project, and also contributed to the work of ShelterBox (*www.shelterbox.org*), which in 2007 delivered hi-tech tents to villages in North Hwanghae for people rendered homeless by floods.

There is a far more comprehensive (but nowhere near exhaustive) list on page 281. More information about other groups and projects involved in long-term humanitarian, development, emergency aid and business can be found on the excellent Engage DPRK website (*www.engagedprk.org*). An overarching facilitator for such projects is Reah International ('reah' means 'friend') (*www.reah.org*), again Christian in origin, that empowers people through Christ to work in the DPRK. However, be careful not to confuse such groups with a third category, not listed here, that use humanitarian works as a vehicle to enter the country and proselytise.

and Wan Peak. Going west through the city, great plains of solar salt farms (as opposed to mines) roll right out to the point where 6km west of Nampo the **Nampo West Sea Barrage** begins.

The barrage is the main point of any tour, a massive feat of civil engineering, through which all vessels to Pyongyang pass, with the three locks able to take ships up to 50,000 tonnes in size. It was built as a one-fix solution to many problems – to control the tides and allow Nampo port to operate without ships being beached; to prevent periodic large-scale flooding from Nampo all the way to Pyongyang (as happened with fatal consequences as recently as 1969) and protect the farmland by the same token, a critical area of agricultural output for DPRK; and further to that, to revitalise the region's agriculture at one stroke.

This involved reclaiming some 500,000 acres of land for farming from wetlands and lagoons, to back up a 130 square mile/2.7 billion cubic metre reservoir and a 70km canal built to irrigate the farmlands of South Hwanghae with river water now protected from ebbing salination, and not least to provide hydro-electric power to feed large-scale fertiliser factories to feed the farms and increase rice and grain output several-fold.

The barrage opened in 1986, crossing the 8km-wide estuary, costing an equivalent of US$4 billion over its five-year construction, a massive use of resources for the DPRK, and not a few lives from the three KPA divisions employed in building it. The barrage may be indicative of the kind of gambling gigantism that was manifest in the leadership's mindset at the time of its conception and construction, with ever more resources being directed at ever more vast, single projects – the construction of the

CHONGSAN CO-OPERATIVE FARM

It would not do to visit this vital area of agriculture and without seeing **Chongsan co-operative farm**, some 10km outside Nampo back on the road to Pyongyang. It is notable from the road by a large bronze statue of Kim Il Sung standing surrounded by enthused farm folk. This suggests something of the importance of the venue as the location of one of the Great Leader's most inspired moments, developing the Chongsan-ri Spirit and Method, 'a revolutionary work method of Juche created by the President while developing the anti-Japanese guerrilla style of work, the traditional work method of the Worker's Party of Korea, in keeping with the new realities of socialist construction,' as KCNA trumpeted on the 40th anniversary of its conception. More mundanely, what the Chongsan-ri spirit says is society's superiors can best lead the masses if they put the latter's interests first and get down onto the shop floor, or into the fields, and find out what's really going on before giving guidance. It's the essence of on-the-spot guidance, by which Kim Il Sung certainly led by example his entire life. It came to him during a fortnight spent around Chongsan-ri and Kangso county in 1960, as depicted in the mural of him sitting on the floor with farmers, which is itself based on a photo visible at Kumsusan Palace of the Sun. The Chongsan-ri Spirit became part of the Chollima Movement and Juche lore, even being enveloped in the ballet *Come to Chongsan Plain*. Hence, as co-op farms go, Chongsan-ri is pretty impressive, with well-made, sizeable buildings, including a cultural hall and cinema, and with two monuments and a revolutionary museum on site. It's possible to visit a farmer's home and go to a kindergarten class for a show. Check out the snail farm in the greenhouse.

Grand People's Study House and the Juche Tower being other examples. Obviously such vast-scale projects will have vast impacts, not necessarily all of them positive, with the loss of wetlands and the halting of tidal flows impacting on the river and coastal estuary's abilities to cleanse themselves, particularly of industrial pollutants that by and large pipe unchecked into the waters, impacting marine health and fish stocks.

It is not clear the extent to which the barrage has alleviated the DPRK's agricultural problems. It may be reluctantly noted that Nampo has in the past half-decade been a major point of import, along with Haeju, for hundreds of thousands of tonnes of humanitarian foodstuffs and fertiliser, principally supplied from the ROK.

The monument at the barrage's northern entrance celebrates the sacrifice of the KPA and others who built it, and the Pi Islet Pavilion which overlooks the barrage shows a stirring video of its construction.

Otherwise, the **Nampo beach resorts** are well known and liked by Koreans and foreign residents, and it's worth getting an afternoon's frazzling on the sand if dwelling in this part. In addition, or else, you might prefer mineral water to sea water. A charming retreat of little stone lodges near Sindok, 80km from Pyongyang on the Youth Hero Highway, is the **Ryonggang Hot Spa Hotel** providing baths filled with local spring water (albeit salty) that are 'rich in bromine and radon', but it's advised to stay in no longer than 15 minutes, then rinse, then enjoy clams cooked by burning petrol. Other spa sites listed, but of which little is known, include Susan Spa, Chongsan Spa and Lake Thaesang. The town of Kangso has similar mineral springs facilities, and a **bottled water factory** that's known to have been visited, and all providing an elixir of life in contrast with Kangso's other hearth of interest, the Koguryo tombs.

CROSSING THE BARRAGE TO GO SOUTH OF THE TAEDONG

Unryul The southern end of the barrage connects with Unryul County, on the northwest coast of South Hwanghae Province.

Unryul's dominant industry is iron ore extraction and processing, for which the Unryul conveyor belt, almost as long as the sea barrage, was built and is worth a look due to the sheer scale of this great black tongue of rock. In Unryul town, diversion may be made to the **Unryul Revolution Museum**, dedicated to Kim Il Sung's father, Kim Hyong Jik. From there speed onwards to the town of Kwail in the so-named county, where fruit farms cover most of the cultivated land, especially around **Songgok-ri**. The farms and mines crop up amid the shallow, afforested slopes and trickling streams sliding away from the Mount Kuwol range of peaks and hills that commands the district.

MOUNT KUWOL 구월산

38.3°N, 125.2°E, South Hwanghae Province

South-southwest of Nampo, south of the Taedong, is **Kuwolsan**, or Mount Kuwol, a gentle, handsome range of peaks, hills, waterfalls and spas, with a healthy sprinkling of temples and hermitages, roped within a nature reserve covering 110km². Its name is taken from the ninth month of the lunar calendar, when the area's natural blooms are at their most radiant. The mountain and its nature reserve are not that high on tourist itineraries, for foreign tourists at any rate, except for Merrill Newman (see box, page 178), and not all of the sites are accessible, but if the chance comes up then it's worth seeing.

The highest peak is the 954m **Sahwang peak**, followed by **O** at 859m, **Insa** at 688m and then **Inhwang** and **Juga** peaks. Sahwang is looped by the remains of the 5.2km **Kuwol Mountain fort**, built during the Koguryo dynasty (277BC–AD668)

MERRILL NEWMAN

The Mount Kuwol area indirectly came to the world's attention in November 2013 during the detention of the 85-year-old American, Merrill Newman. Newman had visited the DPRK with a friend on a ten-day private tour and had sought to see the Kuwol area, where, it transpired, he had trained anti-communist forces during the Korean War, and since which time the DPRK and the US have not been at peace. Details of this backstory spilled out during his trip, and having this enemy serviceman seeking to tour his old hunting ground and even look up former allies was considered too much to overlook. His final evening involved an unhappy conversation with an unknown Korean who invited himself to his table, then, the next day, as Newman sat on the plane to leave Pyongyang, he was arrested five minutes before take-off and held for several weeks in the Yanggakdo – it took three weeks for his plight to come to the world's attention – and he was only released following the signing of a false confession written in diabolical English and some wading in by US politicians. It was all very unfortunate, but the salutary lesson is, as Newman later admitted, people in the US so surely underestimate how 'not over' the war is for the DPRK. US citizens are welcome, and former service personnel are welcome albeit under certain provisos that must be checked with home governments and tour operators. But all in, don't mention your war record.

and expanded under the Ri (1392–1910). The fortress gates on all but the northern side are still visible. Also around Sahwang is the **Samsong Pleasure Ground**.

The site is sprinkled with relics such as fortresses, temples, historical houses and tombs, related to the early development of Korea as well as to the origins of Buddhism.

The faded beauty of the 9th-century **Woljong Temple**, rebuilt in the 15th century, hides in the southern Jol Valley, east of Asa peak. The restored **Samsong Temple** was originally dedicated to Korea's spiritual founder, Tangun, and during Koryo times the temple added Tangun's father and grandfather to its rolls of reverence.

The mountain of **Sokdamgugok** (nine valleys of pools and rocks) sits on the River Sokdam, 12km north of Haeju. In the Unbyong Valley (namely, the finest among nine valleys) sits the 15th-century Sohyon Academy, where the famous scholar Li Ryul Gok taught, and the names of Sokdamgugok's various peaks and valleys are themed along with the celebration of all things peaceful, quiet and meditative, from the Munsan (best place for reading), Kwan Rock (horsehair hat), Chwilyong (a flower-patterned blind), Chohyop (fishing place) to the Kumtan (stream murmuring like Komungo).

An official nature reserve since the 1970s, Mount Kuwol is supposedly visited by half a million tourists each year, due to its proximity to Pyongyang, but despite being listed as one of the five celebrated mountains of Korea, along with Paektu, Kumgang, Myohyang and Jiri, Kuwol has been an irregular entrant on Western tourists' itineraries this century. In 2003 however it was listed as a UNESCO Biosphere Reserve, mostly to protect a 'typical forest ecosystem of Korea which survived the damages of the Korea War', according to a report from the DPRK State Academy of Sciences. It's an area of interest for its mix of pristine and rehabilitated forest, mostly temperate, broadleaf stuff, *Abies nephrolepis, Picea jezoensis, Eichornia umbellata, Castanea crenata, Pinus koraiensis, Fagara schinifolia*, etc. Its array of ecosystems from 900m-high ranges to wetlands, includes the coastal

Unryul Migratory Birds Reserve estuaries; black-faced spoonbill, Chinese egret and red-crowned crane are found in the wetland dominated by *Suaeda japonica*, *Phragmis communis* and *Carex dispalata*. In the biosphere reserve is also one of the DPRK's most important rice producing areas, although most of that is 'transition area' and therefore open to use. The base is rich in medicinal herbs such as ginseng and *Forsythia ovata*.

HAEJU 해주

38.05°N, 125.45°E, 140km south of Pyongyang, capital of South Hwanghae Province, located on Haeju Bay, Korea's West Sea

In contrast with Nampo's more recent resurgence, Haeju has been in decline after centuries of prominence as a trading port with China and also as a scholars' town of Buddhist learning, in keeping with the fact that in AD983 it was made one of 12 civilian-run regional capitals under the Koryo King Seongjong. Little would interrupt these two strands of the city's business for many of the intervening years up to the late 19th century, whereupon it would become noteworthy to history more by default, being the birthplace of one of the leaders of the 1894 Tonghak rebellion, Kim Gu, and Ahn Chung Gun, the assassin of the Japanese colonial governor Hirobumi Ito in 1909.

In the early 20th century the city's trading position was somewhat sidelined by the building of the Seoul–Sinuiju railway. The area became a hotbed of intra-Korean fighting in the run-up to the Korean War, but things were settled in favour of the North's way of seeing things. Haeju became host to the Kangdon Political Institute, which trained guerrillas and political officers for infiltration and sabotage raids into the ROK, with several thousand troops being trained in activities further south in the months preceding June 1950, although Kim Il Sung reputedly closed the academy in the end as it was being run by a potential rival from South Korea.

What with being just 3km from the 38th parallel, and so part of or proximate to the stalemate battle lines of the late Korean War, Haeju was inevitably going to be in the thick of war when it did break out. It was the first city taken by ROK forces in a counter-attack in June 1950, and thereafter became a major through route for refugees fleeing the conflict from both directions. The city was repeatedly strafed, bombed and shelled by British, US, Australian and Canadian carrier-borne aircraft and ships at various points throughout the Korean War, with tens of thousands killed, mainly civilians.

Post-war, with the DML redrawn more like a wiggly and heavily mined 38th parallel, Haeju found new favour by being the DPRK's only west coast port not to freeze in winter. Industry was added to trade for Haeju with large chemical and cement production facilities built post-war, and it is stated that the city is a noted producer of semi-conductors. The city's airfield is a KPA gig and is where more than a few dodgy operations against the ROK have been launched.

But for the longest time, the city's position on the cusp of the DRPK's breadbasket province of South Hwanghae, and the (once) bounteous West Sea for fish, has meant that much of the city's trade and later industries has been involved in agriculture, fish products, food processing and exports. Indeed these trades had earned the city the moniker of 'city of rice and fish', with rice being markedly cheaper to buy than in other Korean conurbations.

However, Haeju's population has suffered malnutrition from food output being affected by floods and droughts over the years disrupting hydro-power production, transport, industry and farmland, leaving many people on low incomes facing tight

5

food supplies with the resulting higher prices for rice and grain. If the breadbasket around Haeju has only crumbs to show, things must be bad.

There were hopes to rejuvenate Haeju and its industry and give its near quarter of a million inhabitants further employment through Hyundai's proposal to invest in the city's port facilities and build rail links to Haeju, along with a large-scale, ten-year redevelopment of the city and its industries, focusing mainly on textile, shoe and toy manufacture.

The plan was shelved as DPRK–ROK relations soured, but since the Kaesong Industrial Zone reopened in September 2013, Pyongyang has also listed Haeju as a Special Economic Zone.

BLUE CRAB BLUES

In good times and bad, during stand-offs and rapprochements in intra-Korean relations, the West Sea (or Yellow Sea to non-Koreans) has been the venue for some bitter spats between the Korean fishing and naval fleets.

The DMZ division extends into the West Sea by way of the Northern Line Limit, or NLL, as drawn on the map by the UN after the Korean War. As an imperialist construct it's a boundary the DPRK has never accepted; and while the DMZ is tense, at least it's very clear where the borders are. Naval boundaries are somewhat more fluid affairs, and can be inadvertently crossed at the best of times, and such a watery line between two states on the cusp of war is bound to lead to trouble. In 1999, several ROK sailors were wounded and 30-odd DPRK sailors killed when a torpedo boat was sunk in the first armed naval clash between the Koreas since 1953. A ROK navy boat was sunk in 2002 with numerous dead on both sides; the ROK navy fired shots at Northern fishing boats the following year.

Various theories have surrounded the skirmishes, with the West usually blaming the DPRK and claiming the shoot-outs are metaphorical expressions of Pyongyang's dissatisfaction with other issues, like wanting to normalise diplomatic or economic relations between the US and DPRK, or talk about intra-Korean family reunifications. An explanation for the 1999 skirmish was the DPRK military's violent dissatisfaction with the country's leadership for accepting a visit from to Pyongyang by US envoy William Perry. Improved relations with the US would ultimately imperil the need for a large military and begin the great capitalist seduction and corruption (about better US relations, family reunifications, rapprochement with the ROK, anything). An alternative explanation was that Perry was visiting Japan and the ROK to discuss the regional situation, upon which the DPRK sought attention so it shot the place up. Upset over joint US–ROK military exercises was another excuse, compounded by the US having at the time just bombed the Milosevic regime into capitulation, and Pyongyang feared a similar plot was in the offing. All such theories tie into the DPRK finding it only gets the aid it needs to survive when it starts shooting – which seems a suitable response by a government that views sanctions as a form of war.

Not least however is the fact that beneath the waves are hordes of blue crabs, worth tens of thousands of dollars a tonne for sale to Japan and China, and bullets will fly when foreign fishing boats and their backers are taken for crab-stealing pirates getting what they deserve for foraying into a no man's land (or sea).

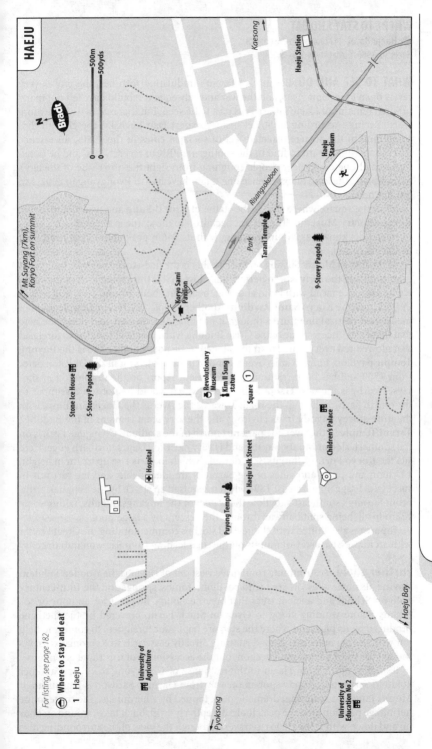

HAEJU

Mt Suyang (7km),
Koryo Fort on summit

Kaesong

Haeju Station

Stone Ice House
5-Storey Pagoda

Noryo Sami
Pavilion

Hospital

Revolutionary
Museum
Kim Il Sung
statue
Square 1

Puyong Temple

Haeju Folk Street

Children's Palace

Risangsokobon

Park

Tarani Temple

9-Storey Pagoda

Haeju
Stadium

University of
Agriculture

Pyoksong

University of
Education No 2

Haeju Bay

500m
500yds

N

Bradt

For listing, see page 182

Where to stay and eat

1 Haeju

⌂ WHERE TO STAY AND EAT

⌂ **Haeju Hotel** (42 rooms) On the edge of
Haeju Sq. 1980s Soviet style. **$$–$**

WHAT TO SEE AND DO Because of Haeju's undulating fortunes, the city is very rarely open to foreign visits, and the war and subsequent rebuild have left not many original remains of Haeju's illustrious past to be seen. But that makes it all the more worth seeing. According to Soviet history expert Dan Levitsky, the city still has something of the austere, isolated feel of socialist cities of the 1980s, an essence that's increasingly hard to find in the southern DPRK in recent years, and he noted that at night he could hear people coughing from right the other side of the city's main square, the kind of experience one might have had in Pyongyang in 2002, say, but not now.

It's in the square where stands the statue of **Kim Il Sung** and its accompanying **Revolutionary Museum**. The distant backdrop to the statue is an impressive series of steep hills known as **Mount Suyang**, with its 946m peak about 7km northwest of Haeju's centre.

At the foot of Mount Suyang on the city side is the **five-storey pagoda**, built from granite during the early Koryo period, and close to it is the gaping arch of the **stone ice house**, once faced with loam and peat, being first built around 1000 and rebuilt in 1735, and the **Koryo Sami Pavilion**. Another temple, the **Haeju Temple**, is often mentioned in local literature although it has long disappeared, and it may be here that there was once a statue of the Great Buddha with a magical stone in its forehead that glowed red every time Japan threatened to invade. Another site is the **Puyong Temple** pavilion, built on stilts over a pond of lilies, the largest in the DPRK; it dates from 1500 and has been restored, a government report on the restoration of sites says. Nearby is the new **Haeju Folk Street**, which would be not too dissimilar to the one in Sariwon just up the road. Towards the river is the **Haeju Stadium**, with the **nine-storey pagoda** in its environs and the very scant remains of the Buddhist **Tarani Temple** in the riverside park just north of the stadium. Changdae Peak is on the southern side of Mount Suyang and is very close to Haeju's northern edge. Here sits the **Koryo Fort**. Within its 8km of walls, which in parts rise up to 7m in height, 14 command posts and gates of the barracks are identifiable, and the fort was in successful usage up to at least 1894 when it repulsed an attack by the Tonghak army. From Suyang's southeast side flow the waters of the **Suyangsan Falls**, falling some 128m in all, being split halfway through the descent by a large pool.

The area is also dotted with statues and slogans commemorating the Great Leader with an impressive array of murals on the road leading from Sariwon into the city

Further afield A 30-minute rural drive west out of Haeju is the wooded **Sokdam Ravine**, its nine valleys littered with pavilions, tombs, springs and the 16th-century **Sohyon School** and ancient trees that breathe clouds. It's great for an hour or so's hiking, before winding along to **Gyenam Stock Farm**, powered by the methane produced by its pigs, and where the staff are happy for foreigners to come and help out with the pig breeding. A road running directly eastwards to Kaesong exists, via the spa towns of Yonan and Paechon, but the accessibility of this route is tenuous.

It's 54km north from Haeju to the resthouse of Chaeryong town, and another 20km to Sariwon. A beauty spot on the way from Haeju to Sariwon is **Jangsusan** or **Mount Jangsu**, a stunning, dramatic peak topped by a hermitage. The route to the hermitage pavilion atop the peak looks deceptively swift, but it takes around an hour up and down with some ridges to traverse, though the view of the surrounding hills and lake is worth it. It was also where the DPRK film *Hong Kil Dong* was filmed, the eponymous hero being a Robin Hood-esque legend, and if you plan ahead maybe the guides could have the film played on the bus.

All in, as Levitsky put it, the region between Sariwon and Haeju is a 'hidden gem' of 'striking beauty', with numerous opportunities for hiking and outdoor exploration, and much more to come.

6

North from Pyongyang: Pyongsong and Mount Myohyang

For maps of the region see pages 154–5 and 188–9.

Kim Il Sung put it succinctly: 'You can see scenic beauty everywhere in our country, but Mount Myohyang 묘향산, or Myohyangsan, is particularly well known from ancient times for its wonderful and exquisite geographical features and idyllic scenery.'

Mount Myohyang is a fabulous pocket of peaks and forested valleys in the centre of the country. Its temperate climate makes it a worthwhile visit in all seasons, although in July the windless slopes make it a humidity trap. Myohyangsan (meaning 'mountain of a single fragrance', which is that of the juniper covering the area) is one of five of Korea's holy mountains, with a famed 1,000-year-old temple at its heart. The DPRK state has reconfirmed the holiness of the area by siting the extraordinary International Friendship Exhibition of Gifts to the Great and Dear Leaders here.

It takes four hours by train from Pyongyang, although the site is most easily and usually accessed by road (assuming the road's in good repair). It's a 160km drive from Pyongyang via Anju, or 150km via Sunchon and Pyongsong 평성, and the latter town is well worth an excursion.

PYONGSONG 평성

Located about 30km northeast of Pyongyang (39°15'N 125°51'E), on one of the routes to Myohyangsan, is the vibrant town of Pyongsong. Until 2012, this bustling conurbation could only be seen by visitors to the DPRK if they'd been bounced from over-booked hotels in Pyongyang. That's since changed and the town is one of the country's newest openings for Western tourists. So new in fact that in 2013 one tourist bus got something of a mystery tour trying to find the hotel, as none of the guides nor driver aboard had been before or knew where it was.

It's a picturesque 40-minute scoot from Pyongyang to Pyongsong, with the road tracking a flat river-plain between steep hills that ebb, encroach and again ebb away. Visitors can see up close the various kinds of farms and rural housing – and as elsewhere, every square inch of soil is cultivated. Near to town one passes a quarry, a rail marshalling yard and increasing numbers of coal trucks, as coal mining figures big in the area's economic activity. Formerly a village called Sainmyon, it was mining that in the aftermath of the Korean War rapidly led it to grow into a town, being renamed Pyongsong in 1964 and becoming the capital of South Pyongan County in 1969. The country's only **coal-mining university** is here, one of a fleet of higher education institutes that also swelled the town's population, and following in the wake of Kim Il Sung University's decampment to Sainmyon during the Korean War. The **DPRK State Academy of Sciences** is here too, and according to the Federation of American Scientists, so is Pyongsong's Atomic Energy Research Center, part of **Pyongsong College of Science**'s nuclear physics department which has some 6,000 associated staff.

These days, nearly a quarter of a million people dwell in what's a significant trading town, with wholesale and farmers' markets that developed out of alley markets all doing determinedly well, despite big bods sometimes fearing that self-interest augers the end of the common good. DPRK observer Andrei Lankov has said Pyongsong has a 'rather sophisticated infrastructure' around its wholesale markets, with many privately owned trucks and storage facilities used by thousands of traders, dealing in all things from lady's dainties to televisions, foodstuffs and money. There's a lot of construction going on among the city's tall and not unhandsome apartment blocks, including a schoolchildren's palace overlooking Pyongsong Park, and there are more buses and lorries rolling around than one sees elsewhere. In warm weather the town bustles with people on bicycles, oldies and young milling and chilling, skating, and congregating at the numerous street kiosks or in alley markets. Some play in the stepped river that runs right through the town, others wash their clothes in it. Still, the rusty floodlight towers of the football stadium lack any lights.

WHERE TO STAY The recently renovated **Jangjusan Hotel ($$)** sits in the centre of the city, on the southern side of the river running east-west through the town. It allows all nationalities, stocks foreign beers and has an outside bar where Kim Il Sung smiles approvingly over all-night revelry. There's a tantalising view just through the hotel gates and over the water of a colourfully lit main drag and floating bar.

WHAT TO SEE AND DO On any itinerary should be the stone expanse of **Pyongsong Square**, its statue of **Kim Il Sung** first put up in 1963 then redone in 1993, and flanked to the left by a large **revolutionary museum**.

Otherwise, there's a bevy of sites to the north of the city. Going north from the roundabout at the city's east end where one enters from Pyongyang, the **Kim Jong Suk Higher Middle School** for gifted children (some 800 of them) is about 2.2km along the road. Named after Kim Jong Il's mother, the school's highlights include its regularly updated wall charts of who's top of the class and who's flop of the class, pupils using the country's intranet, and the solar panels in the school's large vegetable garden. Outside is a statue of the number '5', the top mark in DPRK schools, and a hare and tortoise (in Adidas shorts no less!) statue that may elicit an interesting take on the well-known tale. Older pupils may be seen taking driving lessons in a lorry on the basketball field.

Visitors may be invited to observe a class, then some will be 'volunteered' to speak to the students, so beware – have something to say, and be in a state to say it! Visitor Matias Sueldo wrote of a visit to a geography class being taught in English: 'The teacher came to our group, grabbed my hand, and led me to the front. I didn't know much about the country at hand, the West Indies, but offered to discuss the US or Argentina (where I had lived during high school). Not surprisingly, the students asked me about Argentina. It took me a few minutes to warm up, but soon I found my professorial footing and led what I hope was an enjoyable 15–20 minutes of discussion with the students. I generally love teaching, but given that it's such a closed country it was really a unique experience to be able to teach North Korean students. I think it embodies a lot of the "positive interaction" that you and the other tour leaders hope that tourism will bring to North Korea. It was an incredible experience and something I will never forget.'

6

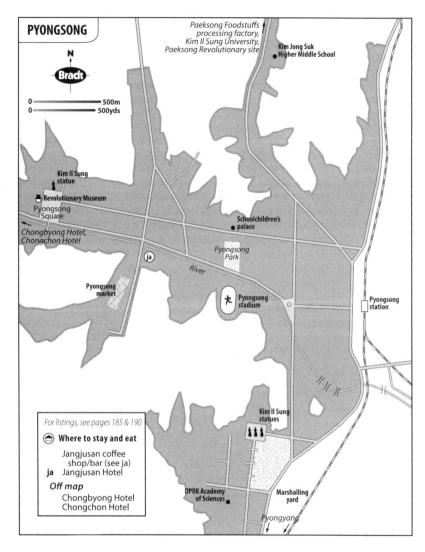

PYONGSONG

N

Bradt

| 0 | 500m |
| 0 | 500yds |

Paeksong Foodstuffs
processing factory,
Kim Il Sung University,
Paeksong Revolutionary site

Kim Jong Suk
Higher Middle School

Kim Il Sung
statue

Revolutionary Museum

Pyongsong
Square

Chongbyong Hotel,
Chongchon Hotel

Schoolchildren's
palace

Pyongsong
Park

River

(ja)

Pyongsong
market

Pyongsong
stadium

Pyongsong
station

For listings, see pages 185 & 190

Where to stay and eat

Jangjusan coffee
shop/bar (see ja)
ja Jangjusan Hotel

Off map
Chongbyong Hotel
Chongchon Hotel

Kim Il Sung
statues

DPRK Academy
of Sciences

Marshalling
yard

Pyongyang

Back on the road going north across flat farmland, it's another 5km to a fork, go left, then 1.4km further along just before a river crossing turn left going west onto a road hedged in by hills. It's a road so quiet that farm workers picnic in the middle of it and look at your approaching tour bus like you're the fools. Another 2km later is the **Paeksong Foodstuffs processing factory**, where pickles, soju and cookies are made. Some groups have visited when it's in full production, while others have found it's idle because it's maintenance day, or lunchtime, or lunchtime on maintenance day. This has sparked debate about whether it's really a functioning factory or a Potemkin factory, or indeed, whether visitors are too cynical and quick to damn. Overall, it's a factory set in fields, miles outside a town really better known for trading, mining and education. It was built on Kim Jong Il's orders in 2009, being situated on the way to an important revolutionary site, and for that it may simply be an under-used factory born of a well-intentioned but ill-conceived idea.

Then 2km further west along the road as the valley closes in on itself is the **Paeksong (white pine tree) Revolutionary Site** where **Kim Il Sung University** decamped from Pyongyang during the Korean War, with up to 1,000 students across nine faculties. This hidden academic base has a monument kept under CCTV guard and a few exceedingly well-preserved teaching huts and dormitories from those heady days, with open wiring feeding the light bulbs, as well as the overgrown Aztec-ish remains of a large auditorium. Much is made of Kim Il Sung's visit here in 1952 at the time of his 40th birthday, when he decreed it should produce people trained to work in government.

Students of DPRK cinema should also recognise the well-preserved **Anguk Buddhist temple** on Mount Pongnin, which dates from AD503 and was rebuilt in 1400 and the late 18th century. It survived the war and has become a key film-shoot location. The Taeungjon hall, or 'hall of Great Enlightenment', dates from 1785 and is one of the few two-tiered temple halls in Korea and the largest one in North Korea. 'It was used for the propaganda of Buddhism at that time,' as KCNA puts it. The signboard of the hall is said to have been painted by King Sunjo of the Ri. On the site a fabulously ornately painted Thaephyong Pavilion, or 'pavilion of perfect peace', also stands, and a nine-storey stone pagoda engraved with lotus flowers.

The town's substantial wholesale and farmers' markets have yet to appear on any tourist itinerary, although more can be read about their recent adventures on www.nkeconwatch.com. The work of the Korean Friendship Network (*www.koreanfriendshipnetwork.org*) with orphanages is also worth looking up online. But with tourism now having a toehold, and the local authorities seemingly plugged into tourism's potential, sites like the **schoolchildren's palace**, the **Ponghak brewery**, **Taedonggang textile factory**, **artificial leather factory** and others are lining up for future visits, with a lot more scope for exploration to come.

Another 27km north from Pyongsong towards Myohyangsan is **Sunchon**, a manufacturing town with a population of 430,000, and notable for the local ore that's mined, the sizeable cement works, a fertiliser factory and a plant producing Vinalon fabric (see page 218). The longer but better road goes via Anju, another major coal-mining town with a population just under a quarter of a million. In its environs are the **Paekchang Pavilion** and the nearby **Namhung Youth Chemical Complex** on the River Chungchon, which the road follows for a long way. Either way, both the Anju and the Pyongchong roads converge at Kaechon and go through Kujang. Where the River Myohyang meets the River Chongchon, there is a sharp turn-off (to avoid a sharp finish to the road) towards Hyangsan town that is the gate to Sangwon Valley, though the town has little else to say for itself. Eight kilometres past Hyangsan Barrage is the pyramidal Hyangsan Hotel and the valley proper for Myohyangsan begins.

MYOHYANGSAN 묘향산

40.05°N, 126.2°E; 150km north of Pyongyang. Chagang, North and South Pyongan provinces meet around it.

Myohyangsan, or Mount Myohyang, is like a wet hand resting on a table, with four valleys running up between the fingers and thumb to the peaks on the knuckles. The River Myohyang runs along the fingertips towards the River Chongchun, and from the road tracing the river begin all the valley walks, some taking a morning, some all day. Myohyangsan features on many tours of the DPRK and is really not to be missed.

FLORA AND FAUNA Wild goat, musk deer, hare, badger, racoon, wild boar and flying squirrels occupy these parts, and leopards and bears occasionally forage in the

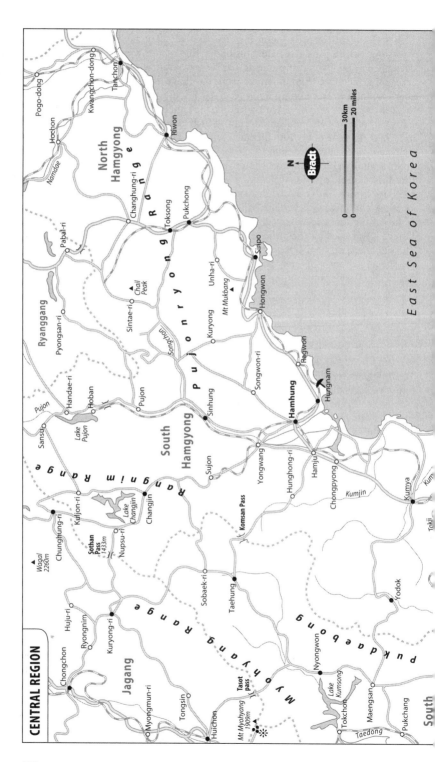

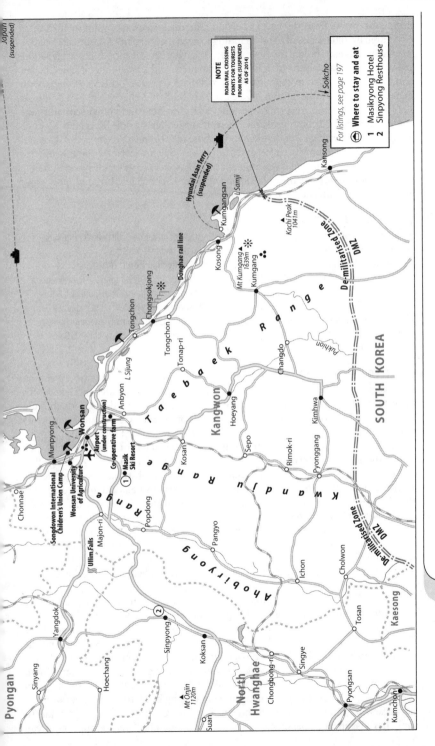

NOTE
ROAD/RAIL CROSSING
POINTS FOR TOURISTS
FROM ROK (SUSPENDED)
AS OF 2014)

For listings, see page 197
Where to stay and eat
1 Masikryong Hotel
2 Sinpyong Resthouse

Sokcho

Kansong

Hyundai Asan ferry
(suspended)

Kumgangsan

Samji

Kachi Peak
1041m

Demilitarised Zone

DMZ

Kosong

Mt Kumgang
1639m

Kumgang

SOUTH KOREA

Donghae rail line

Chongsokjong

Tongchon

Tongchon-ri

Changdo

Pukhon

Japan
(suspended)

L Sijung

Tonap-ri

Anbyon

T a e b a e k   R a n g e

Kangwon

Hoeyang

Sepo

Rimok-ri

Kimhwa

Pyonggang

Munpyong

Wonsan

Airport
(under construction)

Cooperative farm

Masik
Ski Resort

Kosan

Songdowon International
Children's Union Camp

Wonsan University
of Agriculture

Chonnae

K w a n d j u   R a n g e

Popdong

Pangyo

Ichon

Cholwon

De-militarised Zone

DMZ

Ullim Falls

Majon-ri

A h o b i r y o n g

Yangdok

Sinyang

Hoechang

Sinpyong

Koksan

Mt Onjin
1120m

Chongbong-ri

Singye

Tosan

Kaesong

Pyongsan

Kumchon

North
Hwanghae

Suan

Pyongan

deciduous forests from the valleys beyond. The thick tree canopy, up to 1,000m, is structured by 200 species of trees, including Korean maple, many Asiatic oaks, pakdal, Aceraceae, Korean spindle tree, ash, agaric, Asian hazelnut, Chinese sumac, Japanese red pine and Asian white birch. Bark-climbing fern and a multitude of moss, lichen and bryophytes thrive in the humid microclimate, as do 460 species of herb, with medicinal poppy and aconitum. Azalea, apricot and wild cherry blossom bombard the valley with colour in spring, and magnolia, clove tree and guinguecostatus take over in summer. Bluebird, grosbeak, Korean crested-lark, oriole, Korean scops owl, goldfinch, grey wagtail, woodpecker and cuckoo take in the scene from the skies and char, silver fish, rainbow trout, eel and Moroccan oxycephalus view from the streams. In 2009 UNESCO named Myohyangsan as a biosphere reserve, citing 30 endemic plant species, 16 globally threatened plant species, 12 endangered animal species and an array of medicinal herbs as all growing here.

⌂ WHERE TO STAY AND EAT

⌂ **Hyangsan Hotel** [map page 194] (228 rooms) 5km from Hyangsan town on the Myohyang River. 15-storey pyramid, fully renovated with works finished in 2012, kitting it out with a gym, sauna, spas & an Olympic-size swimming pool, as well as the usual bar, billiards & karaoke, & it is truly luxurious such that the guides call it '6-star' – tongue in cheek, mind, with all manner of amusements, although the revolving restaurant (of course!) still doesn't quite succeed with the night views. **$$$**

⌂ **Chongchon Hotel** [map pages 188–9] (33 rooms) 5mins by car from the railway station. Distinguished by Neo-Korean grandeur. **$$**

⌂ **Chongbyong Hotel** [map pages 188–9] (22 rooms) 15mins from Myohyangsan railway station by car. Small & cosy looking. **$$–$**

WHAT TO SEE AND DO Within the same tongue of land where the Hyangsan Hotel sits is the Myohyangsan Children's Camp, which Kim Jong Un visited with his wife in May 2013. Hysterical children, once they'd calmed down enough, sang 'songs including "We are the Happiest in the World," and "General to Front while Children to Camps", according to KCNA. Assuming you don't receive so rapturous a reception, you pass the camp to go up the valley, and 1km from the hotel, just across the River Myohyang, are two huge traditional Korean-style buildings that serve as the fronts to the **International Friendship Exhibitions**, dedicated to the world's gifts for the Great Leaders and kept in cavernous halls burrowed deep into the hillsides. On the left of a classical edifice is Kim Il Sung's building, and the right one is for Kim Jong Il. From the moment you see the guards with their silver-plated machine guns, be on your best behaviour, and cast your gaze upon the concrete beams and rafters decorated with kimilsungia and azaleas. You may (with gloved hands) be allowed to open the four-tonne, bronze-coloured doors of the Kim Il Sung exhibition, doors that open so easily it 'makes you feel mysterious', according to local lore.

Inside, it's hats off, cameras into a kiosk (like Kumsusan Palace of the Sun, it's no photos and no negotiation) and baggy cloth socks covering your shoes as you pad around the exhibition's 100 rooms. It contains 71,000 gifts of homage to the Great Leader, starting with a large room with his statue and a map showing the country and 'rank' of the gifts. This is a holy of holies room, and you will be asked to bow before the figure of Kim Il Sung, positioned coming down a path from Mount Paektu to greet you, so that's what you do. In this room are the most treasured of the gifts and tributes given in honour of Kim Il Sung by global dignitaries over the decades, with some bequeathed by no less than Billy Graham. Then, off corridors so long they disappear by perspective into the distance, and between groups of Korean tourists who swiftly appear and disappear from view like apparitions, you tour long, windowless rooms of gifts, categorised by continent and arranged chronologically. Time lights buzz on and off from room to room, as you marvel at Mao's and Stalin's railway carriages (Mao pays homage to Kim Il Sung!), a stuffed crocodile drinks' tray holder, fossil-topped tables, Kalashnikov-shaped vodka bottles, gold tanks. It's a pantheon of extraordinary gifts and knick-knacks from lost worlds of politics and style. This enormous collection is like a vast collage of gifts charting the chronology and reach of DPRK foreign relations, as gifts from some countries begin and finish as friendly regimes come and go. By the early 1990s it's observable how the gifts to Kim Il Sung become more discreet, but by the late 1990s improved relations with the ROK saw Kim Jong Il blessed with some excellent consumer durables among 40,000 other gifts.

Crossing the river, it's some 4km left to the Hyangsan, or a few hundred metres right into the Sangwon Valley to find the historically holy **Pohyon Temple**. The Pohyon Temple was founded in 1042 by the monk Kwanghwak, and was named after the saint that guards the morals of Buddha. Half of its original 24 buildings were levelled during the Korean War. Prior to then, the temple housed 60 monks, a fifth of whom were students. Substantially fewer monks await as you enter into Pohyon through the 14th-century Jogye Gate. Beyond this sits a monument to Kwanghwak and another monk, Thamil, founder of the Ansim Temple, and embedded among 1,200 characters relating their lives are bits of bomb shrapnel.

You then have your sins cleansed as you pass through the Haethal Gate that marks the crossing from the mortal into the Buddhist world. The Bodhisattvas of Pohyon (the moral guardian) and Munsu (the guardian of wisdom) inhabit this gate. Four guardians of the Buddha check you for heathen status as you cross through the final, largest gate, Chonwang, dating from 1042. Beyond is the courtyard of Manse Pavilion with its nine-storey pagoda, 6m of granite and with its lotus-covered pedestal indicating its Koryo heritage. In Manse were kept the one-tonne bell and drums struck for prayer every morning. Behind Manse is the Koryo-dated octagonal 13-storey pagoda, nearly 9m tall, and there sits Taeung Hall, Pohyon's main temple room. This was the grandest building from 1042 to be destroyed during the war. It was rebuilt with its stunning paintings and carved detailing.

Decades ago, at around 03.00, the valley would shake with the reverberations of the temple gong being struck in the darkness. This was the first call to prayer of the day, and would be overlapped by the throaty chimes of the bell that hung in Manse Pavilion. The monks striking these instruments sang Buddhist hymns in low, monotonous incantations. The one beating the gong would move to striking the large bell, then the drum and then a large wooden fish before leaving the temple to join a score of monks in another hall who had congregated in the passing half-hour. Lights burnt before the altar, and monks, some dressed in black and others in white, sat cross-legged in a semicircle, intoning hymns in high-pitched voices. They then stood and raised their hands in prayer to the Buddha, bowing and kneeling so their foreheads touched the floor, repeating this as they filed to another altar before resuming their seating and their prayer. The whole sequence would be repeated several times a day.

Next appears **Manse Hall**, a residential building originally built under the Ri and rebuilt in 1875, either for the messengers or the head of Pohyon Temple. The **Kwanum Hall** is an original Pohyon edifice and in this heated setting was most Buddhist doctrine taught. The 1794 **Suchung Temple** commemorates the Army of Righteous Volunteers who fought in the Imjin War against Hideyoshi, with the great priests Samyongdang, Choyong and Sosan, the leader of tens of thousands of monk soldiers that liberated Pyongyang. Every spring and autumn, memorial services are held here to their memory.

On the far side of the temple complex is the newly built, traditionally styled archive for the 80,000 blocks of the Tripitaka, a massive containment of Buddhist scripture

WELCOME FRIENDS, AND NOT

The room in the Friendship Exhibition where Kim Il Sung's statue stands is a holy site, a Pharaoh's tomb where the most important gifts are kept. Given the regime's antipathy to Christianity, it is all the more surprising that a fine eagle on display was given by the Reverend Billy Graham, the righteous conservative American evangelists' evangelist and possibly epitomising the invasive American missionary Christianity that the DPRK state would react so virulently against. Graham claimed that in 1950 it was he who had advised President Truman to involve the US in repelling communism in Korea, amid fears for the fate of the Church there. But based on visits to the DPRK and meetings with Kim Il Sung in 1992 and 1994, he changed his view, finding Kim to be 'very warm and friendly', and said he had 'learned to appreciate Korea's long struggle to preserve its national sovereignty', particularly against Japan. Kim was indeed a 'different kind of communist', he later said.

In 1994 Graham delivered a message from the Pope, preached at Pyongyang's Pongsu Church, and told students at Kim Il Sung University he believed 'true religion has a legitimate place in modern society and why I believe Christ has a message for the people of the DPRK', saying 'Christians – although often a minority – make good citizens and have a positive effect on their societies' (see www. billygraham.org).

Bold words, and his second visit helped quell tensions bubbling out of the DPRK's then-suspected nuclear programme, which was cooking up a possible military altercation with the US.

Maybe Kim's receptiveness to Graham isn't so surprising as the former was brought up as a Presbyterian. Just as Graham's stance towards the DPRK softened with age, so maybe Kim saw his own end coming and something within him floated to the surface – he died just weeks after Graham's second visit. But the Grahams still came. Graham's wife Ruth visited in 1997, 60 years after she'd left the city where she'd lived. She spoke at Pongsu Church and dined with foreign minister Kim Yong Nam. And Graham senior's son Franklin, also a preacher, visited in 2000 and 2008 as part of the Billy Graham Evangelistic Association, preaching at Pongsu and visiting hospitals, with aid coming from the Samaritan's Purse organisation.

Kim Il Sung hosted South Korean evangelists as well as Americans. In December 1991, he had over the founder of the South Korean Unification Church, the Reverend Sun Myung Moon, and met him 'with a bear hug', according to Moon's account (*www.tparents.org/library/unification/books/40years/40-5-19.htm*). For Moon, the visit 'encapsulated his life's work' to return to North Korea, where he was born, and later persecuted, imprisoned and tortured from 1948 to 1950 for his beliefs, before escaping south. But Moon's mission was 'to forgive, love and unite'. Despite North Korean officials seemingly seeking to upset him, slashing his allowed entourage at the very last minute and meddling with plans to meet up with family members not seen for over 40 years, Reverend Moon later wrote: 'As I set foot in Pyongyang, my heart was as clear as the autumn sky. I did not feel and literature from the Koryo and Ri dynasties and considered a world treasure. The first books of Buddhist scriptures, 6,000 volumes, were made in the 10th century, followed by another 4,770 volumes. All the prints and printing blocks were destroyed in 1231 during the Liao occupation. Exiling itself to Kanghwa Island from 1236 to 1251, the Koryo court spent its time productively, remaking the entire

that I was entering the house of my enemy, but rather that I was returning to my hometown to visit the house of my brother.'

And the trip went down a storm. His speech was front-page news in the North Korean press, with all references to God kept in, he was offered first rights to develop Kumgangsan as a tourist area, family reunion facilities were promised (and delivered), and even his birthplace was agreed to be preserved as a shrine (and it is – it's near Jongsu, between Pyongyang and Sinuiju).

Aside from these high-level rapprochements between Christian leaders and Pyongyang, religious groups of all creeds have been behind many lesser-reported diplomatic and aid efforts going into the DPRK, working at many levels.

Many Christian groups do vital humanitarian work, solely for the love of man, from the Lighthouse Foundation (I give the website address to avoid confusion with other similarly titled groups worldwide: www.thelighthousefoundation.com), the Wheat Mission Ministry and Campus Crusade for Christ Korea, with work ranging from directly supplying powdered milk to orphanages to supporting medical teams working for free in the DPRK.

There are other organisations who believe all the North needs is a healthy dose of Christ's love. From 2002 the issue of the DPRK's nuclear program flared up again, with another half-decade of threats, breast beating and stomping around by all sides. Enthusiastic South Korean church leaders and businessmen concluded that peace could come from Christ's Word, and sought to send another American preacher to Pyongyang in 2007 to hold Mass for 15,000 believers (as well as incidentally marking the 100th anniversary of the 1907 Pyongyang Revival; see box, pages 70–1). But the Mass was never held, and the nuclear situation rumbles on – not that the former would have solved the latter.

There are also Christian groups more interested in saving souls than saving lives, seeking to convert people by tying copies of the Gospels to balloons and floating them across the DMZ (see www.billionbibles.org), or by brave souls who risk their lives to save the souls, but risk the lives, of people in the DPRK. In November 2012, South Korean-born US citizen Kenneth Bae, when leading a group in Rajin for his China-based company Nations Tour, was arrested and charged with numerous offences under the umbrella issue of 'hostile acts against the Republic', and sentenced to 15 years hard labour. None of the charges directly related to proselytising, but Bae had, at least until 2011, been working as a Christian missionary with the Youth With A Mission group, and as NK News reported, Bae had noted on a Korean church website he and others were preparing 'to spread the gospel from Pyongyang to Jerusalem', and set up a 'new base' in China for missionary works in the DPRK.

This is a high-profile detainee who, by October 2013, was in such poor health he'd lost 50lb in weight. Extrapolate from that how Korean Christians in the DPRK might fare. Nonetheless, for many more missionaries, this only spurs them on all the more.

6

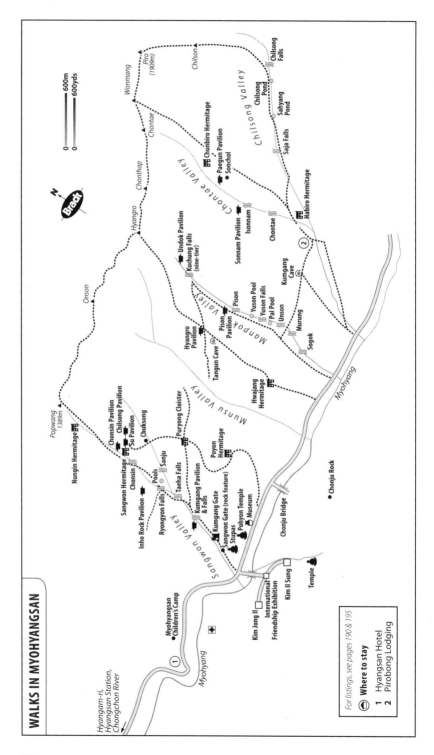

WALKS IN MYOHYANGSAN

Hyangam-ri,
Hyangsan Station,
Chongchon River

Myohyang

Myohyangsan
Children's Camp

Popwang
1389m

Nungin Hermitage

Onson

Sangwon Hermitage
Chonsin
Chonsin Pavilion
Chilsong Pavilion
Su Pavilion
Chuksong
Sanju
Pools

Inho Rock Pavilion
Ryongyon Falls
Taeha Falls
Puryong Cloister

Kumgang Pavilion & Falls
Kumgang Gate
Sangwon Gate (rock feature)
Stupas
Pohyon Temple
Museum

Poyon Hermitage

Munsu Valley

Hwajang Hermitage

Tangun Cave
Hyangro Pavilion

Manpok Valley

Pison Pavilion
Pison
Yuson Pool
Yuson Falls
Pal Pool
Unson
Murung
Sogok
Kumgang Cave

Kuchung Falls (nine-tier)
Undok Pavilion

Hyangro

Hyangthap

Chonthap

Chontae
Wonmang

Chunbiro Hermitage
Paegun Pavilion
Sonchol

Sonnam Pavilion
Isonnam

Chontae

Habiro Hermitage

Piro (1909m)

Chilson

Chilsong Valley

Chilsong Falls
Chilsong Falls
Chilsong Pond
Sahyang Pond
Saja Falls

Myohyang

Chonju Rock

Chonju Bridge

Kim Jong Il
International
Friendship Exhibition
Kim Il Sung

Temple

For listings, see pages 190 & 195

Where to stay
1 Hyangsan Hotel
2 Pirobong Lodging

0 ———— 600m
0 ———— 600yds

Bradt

N

text in 80,000 blocks of magnolia, pakdal and birchwood. Each block measures 50 by 23 by 4cm with 22 lines of 14 letters per line, with a lacquer protection. Scholars come from far and wide to review the blocks and the scriptures. Nearby is the Bell House and Korea's largest bell at seven tonnes.

Hiking Three hikes can be done in one day or less: up the Sangwon Valley, up the Manpok Valley and up to Piro Peak. The Sangwon Valley route totals 14km and starts a little way west of the Pohyon, at the monstrous mushroom shapes of stupas in the monks' graveyard.

Sangwon Valley Near the westernmost stupa is the large rock of Sangwon Gateway, which you pass under towards the collided rocks of Kumgang Gate. Past here is the Kumgang Pavilion overlooking Kumgang Falls, and 1km on are the misty Taeha Falls. It's only half as far again to the spectacular Ryongyong Falls, cascading 84m from the Ryong (dragon) pool, preceding the Sanju Falls and Pavilion. Inho rock sits up to the left of Ryongyong Falls, and the pavilion up there has great views. Carry on up to the stepped Chonsin Falls (86m) that overlook the charming Koryo-era Sangwon Hermitage (rebuilt in 1580). The Su Pavilion here has the legendary milk of Buddha that cures all ills. Walking 2km onwards, rising 500m, you come to Nungin Hermitage, the highest in Myohyang at 1,000m, rebuilt in 1780. Chilsong Pavilion and Chonsin Pavilion are located very close to Sangwon Hermitage. Then it's only another 1km to Popwang Peak at 1,389m. From here it's possible to trace the knuckled ridge about 10km to Piro Peak, a three-hour jaunt but watch the winds.

Coming straight down from Popwang, from the back of Sangwon Hermitage is the Chuksong Temple, built in 1875. A 2km diversion tumbles down to the Puryong Cloister and its massive sweeping eaves dating from 1700. From Puryong is a path back to Kumgang Pavilion, about 800m away, and another path taking a more direct route down to the valley floor, passing the Poyon Hermitage on the way.

Manpok Valley Roughly 4km from the Hyangsan Hotel along the River Myohyang is Manpok Valley, with a 6km round trip drenched in waterfalls. First, 500m along the way is the Sogok (prelude) Falls that prelude the valley's 'symphony of falls'. It's then 250m to Murung Falls, where eight brothers used to rest here after collecting firewood. On to Unson Falls, then the Pal pools where fairies used to frolic. Onwards to a bridge spanning the 66m Yuson Falls (fed by the Yuson Pool above them) that break from a sheer slope amid the trees into eight pools. A steel handrail goes up to the highly protrusive Changes Rock, and it's 300m to the twin Pison Falls that drop some 46m. Then past Pison Rock and Pison Pavilion, it's 1km to Kuchung (Nine-Tier) Falls and Undok Pavilion. Seven hundred metres down west of here is Hynagno Pavilion and the nearby Tangun Grotto, where legend says was born the founder of Korea, Tangun. Down from there appears the 30m-wide Mujigae (rainbow) rock, a rainbow that the fairies rode down to earth. It's 2km downhill to the Koryo Temple of Hwajang Hermitage, and then you're back on the road.

Piro peak A third hike goes up to Myohyang's highest peak, the 1,909m Piro Peak. Starting 5.5km from the Hyangsan, it's 9km up the Chontae and Chilsong valleys and along to Piro, with stunning views from the knuckled ridge leading to it.

First, past **Pirobong Lodging** for travellers, it's 2km up to Habiro Hermitage, originally 16th century (rebuilt in 1882), where the Chontae Valley and Chilsong Valley streams meet. From here are two routes, one going directly to Piro Peak up Chilsong Valley, the other up Chontae Valley to Wonmang Peak and along.

Chontae Valley Up Chontae, it's 400m to Chontae Falls and 200m more to Isonnam Falls, then the three-pillared Sonnam Pavilion. Paegun Pavilion sits at 1,200m, 2km from Habiro, and nearby is the heavenly spa of the 'sachol' (drinkable) spring. Behind Chunbiro Hermitage is Paegun Rock, affording a bird's-eye view. Alpine flora found here include thuja, sabina (*Sargentii nakai*) and cloves. Wonmang rock is 2km up, at 1,825m, third to Piro and Chilsong peaks.

Chilsong Valley Up Chilsong Valley, it's 2km to Saja Falls and another 2km to Chilsong Falls, and then 6km to Piro Peak, from which point the whole world is yours and on the finest days the West Sea of Korea can be seen.

Ryongmun and Paengryong caves
Ryongmun Cave is an amazing grotto of cavernous halls with vaults soaring 40m, populated by stalactites and stalagmites and separated by long pools. Discovered in the 8th century, it's been used as a hiding place for refugees evading the numerous wars that have swept the peninsula (hence the many marked fireplaces), and to stash Buddhist images and other treasures from greedy local chieftains. A lone Buddhist monk spent 18 months down here among the bear skeletons. In the rainy season, the waters rise to make pools big enough for boats to traverse over long distances. It's 2km all the way through, and is situated 30km east of Hyangsan town, 1.5km from Unhung-ri. Seventeen kilometres further east, 5km beyond Taephung-ri, is Paengryong Cave, smaller but no less full of giddyingly weird limestone protrusions and damp chambers populated by damp dwelling spirits.

7

East Coast Central: Pyongyang to Wonsan

For a map of the region see pages 188–9.

The 3½-hour drive from Pyongyang to Wonsan 원산 (via Koksan) takes in a handful of sites. **King Tongmyong**, founder of the Koryo Kingdom, has his reconstructed tomb 25km from Pyongyang, and 15km further on you pass the **Hugu-ri**, with early Palaeolithic remains and a nice cave.

As the road batters the suspension it winds and coils up tighter and tighter round conical hillsides, until it breaks out onto a large, lush plateau hemmed in by slopes. About 110km from Pyongyang, **Sinphyong Resthouse** appears on the shore of a small reservoir, walled in by hills that in autumn become canopied by blazing red maple trees. There's a restaurant, a guesthouse and a shop, and great vat of snake wine, a local speciality renowned for its positive qualities for your appetite and enabling men to men to 'puff their hoods' like a cobra, although its potency can as easily render them unconscious and incapable of any ardour whatsoever.

The road continues through a series of impressively long tunnels (one of note is the 4km Rainbow tunnel), the interiors clouded with dust and vapour from seeping water, and into steep-sided valleys. About 35km east of Wonsan (as the road goes) is a turning to **Ullim Falls**, located some 8km north of the highway down a very steep and twisted road hewn off the hillside. About 1km from the falls is a car park with a map depicting a considerable range of possible walks in the area, although you'll likely just follow the stream uphill past a substantial tea house to the falls themselves. It's a lovely and very welcome stop-off point, pretty popular with locals, and you can swim in the attractive shallow pool below the falls.

For winter visitors, just south of the highway about 20km from Wonsan is the new and controversial Masik Pass ski resort. In 2013 its construction became a world media event as the resort was denied a ski lift by Western manufacturers not wanting to breach UN sanctions on luxury goods. So the Chinese supplied them instead and the Koreans thereby finished the project in Masikryong speed to open it on 1 January 2014. The resort's nine ski runs vary between 2km and 5km. Accommodation is at the 120-room **Masikryong Pass Hotel ($$)**, with its 25m pool, cafés, bars, restaurants, steam room, sauna, and internet at US$0.20 a minute.

Neither the falls nor the resort are far from the east coast, and soon enough from the highway the Korean East Sea comes into sight and you sweep into **Wonsan**.

WONSAN 원산

39.1°N, 127.28°E, 200km east of Pyongyang, capital of Kangwon Province, Gulf of East Korea
With a population of 331,000, Wonsan is at the centre of this well-populated strip of coast and is the connecting hub from Pyongyang northwards to Hamhung city and

acts as the gateway to the mountains of Kumgangsan in the south. The city's tall, wide boulevards branch like spokes from the hub of a large roundabout speared by a stellae which commemorates the dearly departed Kim Il Sung and Kim Jong Il, and the roads head off to big open spaces. It is a handsome, tidied reflection of the hills and beaches surrounding the city and the sea breeze blows coolly through it all, while the surrounding land is the most fertile in the province, and under the soil, gold is mined.

As the Kangwon provincial capital, Wonsan was built as a major port for trading goods with Russia, China and, up to a few years ago, Japan – although the stillness of the harbour's waters suggests little trade is going on now, and you may see the ferry that once plied to Niigata and back, all moribund as it's moored up at the dockside. Still, something's improved in the last few years, at least as is suggested by the army of tall white tower blocks standing sentinel on the city's central hill now brilliantly lit at night.

Served by ten universities and colleges, Wonsan's industries also include fishing, rice processing, oil refining and brewing (particularly rice wine), and the manufacture of ships, locomotives, textiles and chemicals. Since the 19th century, the city's been well known for its leather and fur goods. Wonsan's connections to the forested, mountainous north meant it was the first point for many hunters, whose appetites for game were provoked by the large bear and tiger skins treated and traded through the city.

Hunters now may be seeking business opportunities, as the talk from on high is the city's future lies in hi-tech industries and tourism. In 2012 the Institute for Far Eastern Studies reported that the DPRK had announced a ten-year, US$10 billion plan for ten million tourists a year to come to Kumgang, with a special economic zone in Tongchon County between Wonsan and Kumgangsan being built with IT, electronics and auto factories, amid golf and marine resorts, and all served by a new million-person city. The highways from Pyongyang–Wonsan–Mount Kumgang would be revamped, as would Wonsan's airport with links to 18 international cities. A new land route would link Dandong to Kumgang, new sea routes would link Kumgang to Japan, Russia and the ROK, and travellers could sail from Rajin-Sonbong to Kumgang via Wonsan, or go by train from Wonsan.

The plan revived much of what had been planned with South Korean investment, before the 2008 shooting (see box, page 46) saw the end of all that. But in May 2013 Wonsan was designated as a new economic development zone open for foreign investment, and there are new hotels serving summer visitors to the city's beaches on the Kalma Peninsula while former Korean People's Army residences are being converted to civilian use. Winter travellers can now visit the Masik ski resort in Ryongjo-ri, Popdong County, just outside Wonsan. Blueprints exist for a US$200 million plan to rebuild Wonsan airport for international traffic, as NK News reported. Maybe all the talk of big things is becoming real.

HISTORY The city has existed here since the early Koguryo period, was named Wonsan under the Koryo, and for centuries was a trading settlement with incoming junks anchoring in its natural harbour.

By the 1880s, Wonsan was one of three ports being run by the Japanese (who called it Gensan) and had around 15,000 inhabitants, with two small settlements, one for the 700 Japanese residing in the city along with their own police force, and the other for other foreigners, mainly French, Russian and British. There was also a small Chinese population, filling minor official and entrepreneurial roles, selling imported goods and staffing their own small police force as a counter to the

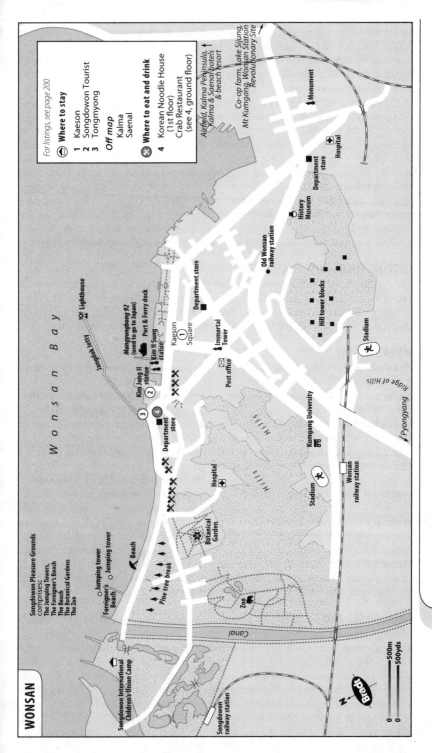

WONSAN

Songdown Pleasure Grounds
comprises:
The Jumping Towers,
The Foreigner's Beach
The Beach
The Botanical Gardens
The Zoo

For listings, see page 200

Where to stay
1 Kaeson
2 Songdowon Tourist
3 Tongmyong

Off map
Kalma
Saenal

Where to eat and drink
4 Korean Noodle House
(1st floor)
Crab Restaurant
(see 4, ground floor)

Songdowon International
Children's Union Camp

Songdowon
railway station

Canal

Zoo

Botanical
Garden

Jumping tower
Foreigner's   Jumping tower
Beach.   Beach

Pine tree break

Hospital

Department
store

Lighthouse

Janglok Jetty

Wonsan Bay

Kim Jong Il
statue

Kim Il Sung
statue

Mangyongbong 92
(used to go to Japan)
Port & Ferry dock

Department store

Kaeson
Square

Immortal
Tower

Post office

HILLS

HILLS

Stadium

Kumgang University

Wonsan
railway station

Stadium

Ridge of Hills

Pyongyang

Airfield, Kalma Peninsula,
Lake Sijung,
Mt Kumgang, Wonsan Station
Kalma & Saenal hotels
& beach resort

Co-op farm, Lake Sijung,
Mt Kumgang, Wonsan Station
Revolutionary Site

Monument

Hospital

Department
store

History
Museum

Old Wonsan
railway station

Hill tower blocks

N

Bradt

0   500m
0   500yds

Japanese. As the Chinese and Japanese both ran the country, Captain Cavendish couldn't tell 'which race the inhabitants hate most' (see page 278).

It was under Japanese colonialism that Wonsan underwent unprecedented urban growth, as its role in exporting commodities to Japan grew and the city's major industries were founded for producing and shipping cheap manufactures to Japan, and a railroad hub for Japanese goods and men into Korea. These same port and shipping facilities made Wonsan ideal as a Japanese navy operations base during World War II. Five years after that conflict's end, US marines landed here to a reception of South Korean soldiers as the UN forces pushed back the Korean People's Army in late 1950, but the city was retaken by the North in the coming winter with the UN undertaking a considerable evacuation out of the port. Then from 16 February 1951 to 27 July 1953 saw the longest naval blockade in modern history occured as the US navy bombed and shelled the city into little more than a map reference for the North Koreans to retake in ground fighting. All that you see has been built since then. Wonsan was where the USS *Pueblo* was taken in 1968 and where it was moored for decades as a museum, before being moved to Pyongyang.

GETTING THERE AND AWAY From Pyongyang, it's a 3½-hour drive, or these days one can do the very scenic train ride. The ferry connection with Rason has yet to be firmly established, and the same is true for any Wonsan–Kumgang ferry. The ferry to Japan, which wasn't really for non-Koreans, no longer runs. All connections with the ROK now lie buried under dunes of dust on a rotting shelf somewhere.

WHERE TO STAY

⌂ **Kalma Hotel** (94 rooms) On Kalma Peninsula. Rooms from deluxe, 1st, 2nd & 3rd class across 2 blocks. Deluxe rooms have their own saunas, 1st class have jacuzzis, & all rooms except 3rd class have the complete works of Kim Il Sung. Both blocks have banquet halls, restaurants, bars, billiards & ping-pong. **$$$–$$**

⌂ **Saenal Hotel** Features billiards, ping-pong, restaurants, a meeting room & a banquet hall, room for over 200 guests on 18 floors. **$$$–$$**

⌂ **Kaeson Hotel** (164 rooms) On the seashore opposite Haean Square. **$$**

⌂ **Tongmyong Hotel** (44 rooms) Serviceable & unusually designed hotel at the base of the Jangdok jetty, with a brilliant undersea fantasy sculpture in the lobby. Bookshop, billiard bar upstairs, but don't trip on the cables on the balcony! **$$**

⌂ **Songdowon Tourist Hotel** (194 rooms) Songdowon pleasure grounds, not often visited. **$**

WHERE TO EAT AND DRINK The seafront roads running on both sides of the Tongmyong Hotel are lined with restaurants. Recommended are two places right opposite the Tongmyong: there is a large-eaved building named **Korean Noodle House** with stairs going up, but at the car-park level is a doorway going into a much smaller, cosier place with two rooms, one with baking *ondol* heating. Here a slap-up steamed crab feast for four is about €30. Arrange in advance.

WHAT TO SEE AND DO Wonsan's concrete cityscape is bolted to a backdrop of steep hills that screen in the natural harbour and give the city its name of 'Folding Screen'. The high-rises that launch out of the main hill overlooking the city resemble the Chongsokjon rock formations further south down the coast. Many a morning these high-rises seem to be rising up out of a mist covering the lower city. Wonsan's port proper is bracketed by the **Songdowon** pleasure grounds to the north and the southern Kalma Peninsula resort of **Myongsasimni** and its 4km of beaches.

Start out at Jangdok jetty, which spurs out from next to the Tongmyong Hotel, where you'll likely stay. In the right weather, locals gather at the jetty and the surrounding waterfront to picnic or have barbecues going long into the evening. By day, the jetty is lined with folk fishing or harvesting and hammering open molluscs – some for sale on little stalls which your guide might be able to buy. Making the 1.2km stroll along the jetty to the lighthouse at the end earns the reward of a grand view of Wonsan from the sea.

Just northwest of the jetty are the **Songdowon pleasure grounds**, a long sandy, segregated beach with locals hurling themselves from diving towers, the beach backed by a gamut of restaurants and a windbreak of pine trees. Some of them are over 700 years old, and behind them hides a **zoo** and **botanical gardens** (with stores of kimilsungia and Kimjongilia – see box, page 146) that make for a good half-hour's ambling around. Kim Il Sung once commented on one of the trees, requiring it to be fenced off and now forever commented upon. The woodlands also shroud a mudbath centre with treatments, including being pampered with electric plates. Locals picnic and dance in the clearings amid the pine trees. An aged canal abruptly cuts the windbreak and the beach, across which is **Songdowon International Children's Union Camp**. It's a nice three-star hotel built in 1993 with lots of activities and events for up to 1,200 children, but don't visit unless children are there or you're essentially going around an empty hotel. It is truly international, children from the world over can come, and interested parents can ask tour operators about dispatching their kids to the DPRK for a summer fortnight.

Back along the quay are supposedly boats that can do small trips of the coast down to Tongchok, but this hasn't been verified. Following the coast north beyond Songdowon is a neighbourhood pretty much reserved for the great and the good, which doesn't include tourists. The waterfront running southeast of the Jangdok jetty, beyond the two hotels, is the main point of embarkation for passenger ships, and some loading of cargo ships goes on, but the latter activity, if it happens at all, happens in a cargo port further along. These vessels break up the sea view from the long, wide park that runs all along this waterfront, dominated at the northwest end by statues of the Great and Dear Leaders (the latter were added in 2013), and a formal series of geometric paths and junctions grid down to the other end, dotted with small pavilions and statues. The broad plaza of Haean Square fronts onto this park.

Further in town, at the foot of the central hill is **Wonsan Station Revolutionary Site**. This reconstruction of the city's old Japanese-built railway station and Tongyang (Orient) guesthouse is where Kim Il Sung stayed over 18–20 September 1945, as on his way to liberate Pyongyang he stopped off to meet local guerrilla leaders and discuss 'the three tasks of building the Party, the state and the army', as KCNA put it. The guesthouse and station hall, flattened during the Korean War, were rebuilt in 1975. What survived were the Japanese-built steam train (but don't touch it – you'll get greasy hands) and the Korean-built carriage that took him to Pyongyang (third class, he was down with the proles). Both are housed in the furthest building.

About 2km due south of the Tongmyong Hotel (as the crow flies) are burial mounds, behind Ai Su Dok University, but not much about them is known. They could be part of the Old Castle of Tokungen which holds the tomb of the founder of the Chosun dynasty. The road heading southeast, which you'll take if going on to Kumgang or the co-operative farm just out of town, will also pass an obelisk high on a hill just over 3km southwest of the hotel. Anyone is welcome to identify this structure as well as visit the rumoured 'experimental station for marine products'.

There is also the Kalma Peninsula, which either resembles a bone or a chicken head; anyway this outcropping of land makes up the eastern wall of Wonsan Bay. Local tourist maps have placed a line of beaches along its bay side, as this book did in its first edition; however, further research involving Google Earth showed there were no beaches on the port side of the peninsula, but there was (and is) a substantial airfield, home to various KPA MiGs, protecting a complex of large, palatial buildings dotted towards its bird-headed end. This might suggest it's not the greatest place to sunbathe after all, but there is also a lovely long beach with pristine white sands on the peninsula's east side, a resort now open (upon payment) to guests at the newly opened Kalma Hotel. Punters can hire inflatable boats or play volleyball.

AROUND WONSAN About 6km north of the city centre along Asian Highway 6 towards Hamhung is the **Wonsan University of Agriculture**, a leafy campus with students in white shirts, red ties and berets bounding down corridors decorated with beautiful paintings of botanical subjects and tanks smashing up American imperialists. The rooms need renovating, lightbulbs and toilet paper are missing, but new strains of crops thrive in the gleaming new greenhouses donated by Kim Jong Il, who placed great importance on the institute's ability to reform the DPRK's agriculture.

But the main, pre-war brick building with its round-arched windows is only half of what was built when the place was originally the Tokwon Abbey of St Benedict. This was founded by a group of German St Ottilien missionaries who landed in Seoul in 1909, and despite the Japanese spread God's Word right into Manchuria. The Tokwon mission had flourished into an abbey in 1927, evidenced by an impressive Italianate-style church. However in May 1949, a little more than 3½ years after Kim Il Sung convened with the many in Pyongyang, something of a pre-wrath rapture was wrought upon the abbey. Some of the few survivors set up a new monastery in the South, or repatriated back to Germany in 1954. Nonetheless, the Catholic Church still claims the Territorial Abbacy of Tokwon.

About 6km further northwest is the small town of Munpyung, still famed for its lead smelter, a 1930s-built relic of the Japanese occupation. Slag heaps dominate the horizon: behind its imposing gateway, the ageing factory employs around 1,800 people and produces lead bullion for use in the local battery industry and for export to China.

Going just under 8km southeast of Wonsan down Asian Highway 6 gets you to the **co-operative farm**, which is well worth a look. Cross the last bridge on the edge of Wonsan, turn right, then turn left at the next big stele 6km later. This idyll of rustic harmony and model of co-operative farming (see box opposite) has been frequented by Kim Il Sung and Kim Jong Il, which suggests why it's on the tour map.

Things have improved now to the point where locals no longer smoke cigarettes made from rolled newspaper. As with other model farms, visitors have been allowed to 'drop in' on a farmer's household to meet some very well-mannered children, although their songs may be interrupted by broadcasts from the radio high up the wall. This may be your only chance to visit a house of this kind in the country, and these are good quality, well-made houses, shown by their tiled roofs – no thatched roofs here.

In olden days houses used to have wooden chimneys wrapped in thatch, but the air from the stove would have lost all sparks as it was piped under the floor in the *ondol* heating. Many of the poorest rural dwellings didn't have raised floors for *ondol*, and were built on the earth, so were notoriously dirty. Cattle and pigs were brought in to protect them from tigers, and the floors were veritable bug farms, such that travellers would barricade themselves in with fresh straw, hoping this would prove impenetrable to bugs during the night.

Rest assured little of the above still applies today, although if the single-storey houses are not made of concrete blocks, they may still be built as they were from

Co-operatives are units of up to 300 households that jointly own and run the land. Each co-op is controlled at the *kun* (prefecture) level, that sets output targets to be met by the co-op. Produce is traded and sold for external goods like tractors and fertiliser. In the co-op the farmers own their own houses but work in units on the land, in specialised work teams, like the rice-work team, or the cow-work team. Similarly assigned teams can compete for speed and output, with results posted up in the village square so all can see who's leading and by how much. At the end of the crop cycle or year, those more than fulfilling their targets are rewarded in cash and kind, those failing lose payments.

Each day, members of co-ops gather at around 08.30 after a signal bell to receive instructions for the day's tasks. Lunch is at noon, held at home or in the communal hall, with dancing and music groups. During the ten-minute breaks per hour are 'news reading meetings'. At each day's end the work is evaluated and points are put in farmers' Labour Notebooks according to the work done. This ultimately affects their level of pay. They then go to the communal bath-house, cinema, political meeting or home, unless they're needed for other 'voluntary' tasks of irrigation building or factory work; otherwise they tend to their own plots. Farmers have small private plots for bees, pigs, chickens and rabbits, which can be sold. This element of private ownership differentiated the DPRK's collectivisation programme from China's that happened almost concurrently in the 1950s, for China had much greater emphasis on communal living and state ownership. Where surplus has allowed, in recent years there has been an increasing number of farmers' markets appearing across the country, as a private supplement to state rations. However, with regard to the problems of food supply still afflicting the country, the number of farmers' markets remains limited.

clay brick coated with cement, with gardens fenced in by split bamboo. If you are invited into one (and take off your shoes on entering!) there's an obvious lack of furniture, beyond the shelves and cupboards against the wall. Very little clutters the smooth, lacquer-papered floor, except a low table and floor cushions brought out for eating meals. As you sit and notice the heated floor, don't forget not to point your soles at anyone. These houses often have no more than three rooms, including the bedroom and kitchen, so the third room is multi-purpose, for entertaining, studying, eating, and listening to the announcements from the radio. Two gleaming pictures of the Great Leaders will hang high somewhere. The rooms are not divided by doors but maybe by screens. In the kitchen you'll see large earthenware pots for *kimchi* and holding dry comestibles. Having been duly entertained by the wife and her children, it should be time to bid farewell and get back on the way to Kumgang.

8

Wonsan to Mount Kumgang, or Kumgangsan

For a map of the region see pages 188–9.

The drive from Wonsan to the resort at Outer Kumgang is over 100km along a scenic coastal route. The road sails alongside the railway across a green sea of paddies before tacking right onto the shoreline, racing the electric fence all the way to the DMZ. *En route* there are many modern stelae on the roadsides, the inscriptions of which the guides can translate, and cranes keeping an eye over the fields and lakes.

Around 37km from Wonsan is **Tongjong Lake**, formerly a seawater bay, and the beach of Chona port. Ten kilometres further south is **Lake Sijung**, which the road and railway keep separate from the sea. On the lake's shore is a small, very hot **guesthouse** specialising in mud treatment and massage. The mud at the bottom of the lake is formed by a rich, thick layer of rotting things that may well contain the carcasses of carp, sardine, mullet, lobster, clam, abalone, eel and snakefish that otherwise harass the rowing boats floating from the guesthouse. This mud is heated up and packed onto your body so that its nutrients may seep in and sooth your inner ills. It also pongs and can be too well heated, but a soak in the stuff helps cure numerous skin complaints, bronchitis and heart trouble. Although the bedrooms can become like ovens at night, it is a tranquil, pleasant place to stay with a good little restaurant and a bar more or less willing to sell alcohol late into the night.

The guesthouse is 1km north of a beach that's entered through a reception pavilion that provides towels and showers for a nominal fee and sells trinkets and quality booze (it's an area popular with Russians). The little islets dotted along it can almost be walked to across the beach's long shallows, in which the holidaying Koreans scour for shellfish. If you meet any Russians and they hospitably offer you a drink, agree to it. Around 50km from Wonsan is the port town of Tongchon, which for now has little to excite the visitor (this may change – see page 198), but is adjacent to the beautifully geometric **Chongsokjong rocks** that protrude from the sea like great teeth. Another 42km along is Kosong, the last major town before Mount Kumgang 금강산.

KUMGANG FLORA AND FAUNA

Four hundred species of butterfly flit through the steep, forested slopes of Kumgang. Of the dozens of animal species in these mountains are musk deer, roe deer, antelope, bear, wild boar and flying squirrel. Flying in and around are kingfisher, yellow fisher, pied wagtail, pheasant, black-naped oriole, migratory grosbeak, Korean scops owl, cuckoo, wild geese, heron and gulls apuses. The streams hold carp, trout, salmon, and ten species of batrachians, including the bell-toad. The area ranges from deciduous to lower alpine forests, in which are stashed some

1,200 plant species, from bamboo to fir, oak, chestnut, hawthorn and varieties of maple and pine, thuja, Sabina chinensis, mountain cranberry and blueberry. The mossy ground is shielded with azalea, yellow clematis, primulas and lilies; Japanese red pine and herbaceous fern protrude from the cracked cliffs. Local species to be spotted include Kumgang stephanandra and Kumgang bellflower. Indeed, botanists to these parts are warned by the local tourist information agency: 'There are some plants that will attract you. If you fail to see them, you will regret for your lifetime.'

KUMGANGSAN 금강산

38.45°N, 128.1°E; 108km south of Wonsan, Kangwon Province, near to the DMZ and East Korea Sea

Mount Kumgang is situated in the northern part of the Thaebaek mountain range on Korea's central-eastern coast, and covers an area of some 40km east–west and 60km north–south. Kumgangsan in Korean, or Mount Kumgang, means 'diamond mountain', so called as the granite peaks and hillsides glitter in the sunlight, but they have had different names in each season, being the Pongnae Mountains ('spirits enjoy visiting') in summer, Phungak ('variety of views') in autumn and Kaegol Mountains ('snow sided') in winter. The highest is Piro Peak at 1,639m and another dozen touch over 1,500m, with a hundred or so over 1,000m and peaks as sharp as 'the tips of paint brushes' – although there may be fewer than the commonly cited 12,000 peaks.

Kumgang's been considered sacred for millennia. 'Buddhism,' wrote Isabella Bishop in *Korea and Her Neighbours*, 'which possesses itself of the fairest spots of nature, fixed itself in this romantic seclusion as early as the 6th century.' Access was through Tan Pa Ryong (since renamed) that means 'cropped hair pass', a Rubicon for anyone seeking a life of Buddhist solace. In feudal Korea, bachelors had heavy braids of hair, married men's hair was coiled into a top-knot, but monks, unencumbered by considerations of marital status, shaved all their hair off. The town of Choanjri once housed a great concentration of 16 temples and halls dating from the 6th century. Even by the late 19th century, when Buddhism had long fallen from official (and therefore financial) favour and most Koreans were succumbing to Christianity, 45 monasteries, nunneries and shrines were counted in the area. Thirty-two remained pre-World War II, but today fewer than a handful remain in use.

However, tourists have long been filling out the space left by thinning pilgrims. Cavendish observed in 1887 that:

> The Koreans are great lovers of nature and admirers of scenery, and are also great pedestrians; they – that is, the men, who always seem to have plenty of time to kill – often make pilgrimages to places whence a fine view may be obtained … annually they [Diamond Mountains] are visited by hundreds of Koreans.

The Japanese turned the area into a park, and today Kumgang's spiritual splendour has allowed it to be the only place in the DPRK that South Koreans could visit, until this was restricted in 2008. Kumgang is divided into three areas, Inner, Outer and the Sea of Kumgang, with 22 subdivisions within it and so many different routes of peaks, pools, lakes, waterfalls and temples to follow that a serious walker would need a week to cover the place.

Kumgang's proximity to the border with the ROK led to the area to being closed off for most of the Cold War, with its tourists and Buddhist pilgrims replaced with soldiers. The area has only become accessible to tourists since the late 1990s, and initially this was restricted to Outer Kumgang and the Sea of Kumgang. Inner

Kumgang was even more restricted. The gates to Inner Kumgang creaked open to Westerners for the first time in decades in the early noughties, when one man made a fleeting visit:

Taking the road in from the east coast, we were soon in a shallow valley, with sheer granite hillside either side, our Volvo grumbling along a grotty track of dust and rubble, hewn from a hillside with a stream trickling past the other way.

We were the only passengers on this road, as it snaked into higher passes, tighter turns, thicker foliage and into breezier expanses. In three hours I only saw one single truck, laden with workers, hammer past us, at a junction where our car had decided to give up for a while, having shaken some important parts of itself loose.

While my driver and two guides worked on the car, I spied nearby a thin dirt track, closely shielded with trees with interlocking branches clasping overhead, and atop the track, about 150m away, I could see a gateway to some kind of village. My guides otherwise engaged, I wandered up this track, waving my camera around as if photographing the butterflies. Only a few metres short of this village, one of my guides somehow had quickly but silently legged up behind me and strongly indicated with his hand that we should go back to the car. Noting his silence, I looked at him quizzically, trying to impart with my face a message of innocent 'what's the problem?' He nodded past me to the village gates, to where I looked and suddenly spied a good half-dozen big green army trucks shielded by foliage. I realised this was possibly the most inhospitable place on earth to a wandering foreigner with camera and I sped down the track with the guide.

The car fixed, we continued and came atop a kind of plateau, flanked by tall, more sheer rock formations rising sharply from the edges of flat fields with a few farmers here and there, where maize grew in ditches, and in the distance the higher peaks of Kumgang could be seen lazily lifting their noses up into the clouds. In these hillsides were many small triangular entrances which my guides said were mines – possibly gold, they weren't sure.

I lost count of the number of checkpoints we went through, the final one being amid a copse of pine trees (we were high up by then) and taking a good 15 minutes. Then it was a final climb up over a ridge and into a valley walled with sharp pointed pale grey granite festooned with lush greenery and breathing mist. My guides told me it was the first time a British man had been there in 60 years, and their first time there as well – we all cheered.

Still there was no-one else around.

Later as we visited a temple I received some opprobrium from the Western tour leader for antagonising a cicada then swatting it with my hat in the presence of the temple's chief monk, something my Korean guides found hysterical.

Access to Inner Kumgang from the DPRK side remains intermittent while Outer Kumgang and Sea of Kumgang are as open as the Hyundai resort that occupies them. The resort was to absorb Inner Kumgang, but the plan went south along with the Hyundai's plans to expand the resort all the way up to Wonsan.

However, with the DPRK having confiscated and reopened the resort, there are now land and, in theory, sea routes from the DPRK into Kumgangsan.

HYUNDAI KUMGANGSAN TOURIST RESORT The tourist complex built at Kumgang by Hyundai Asan, the firm also behind the Kaesong Industrial Zone (see box, pages 160–1), is like nothing seen in DPRK ever. The resort, called Onjeong gak, has had $350 million from Hyundai for sprucing up the old buildings and adding a sparkling fleet of first-class hotels, bungalows, chalets, yurts and caravan parks dotted among restaurants and facilities for all seasons, including cinemas and sledging (in winter) and jet-skiing (in summer). There is also a small hospital, a Family Mart shop, duty-free shops and more. It was built as a zone apart in luxury (now, so much tumbleweed), and administratively, too, set apart from its host Kangwon Province in 2002 and designated the self-administered Kumgangsan Tourist Region, over 500km^2 in size. The benefits were many-fold, as DPRK got a levy out of the profits from the resort, and the supply of North Korean construction materials, men and hotel service personnel drew hundreds of millions of dollars in cash into the DPRK. In addition a few merry little 'private' enterprises were set up, from guides to hawkers of fruitmeats and teas to tourists, a prospect that brought in sellers from beyond the mountains.

The giant paintings, inscriptions, plaques and mosaics of the Great and Dear Leaders are still marked around the site, although there are slight accommodations to the sensitivities of South Korean visitors – whereas a painting of the Great and Dear Leaders welcomes visitors into hotels across the DPRK, the massive painting in the Hotel Kumgangsan shows only Mount Paektu. Tourists had to wear ID tags at all times, follow guided itineraries and endure proscriptions to movement and photography much like elsewhere in the country. That said, the visitors, shuttling along a well-made road lined with tall, green metal fences, could still see up close the more traditional existence of the DPRK population working the fields, or in greenhouses growing food for the hotels.

Tourists from the ROK started visiting Kumgangsan in 1998, rapidly rising from 15,000 to average almost quarter of a million a year, with the million-visitor mark passed in mid 2005 and capacity expanded to take 400,000 visitors a year. Special weekend tour packages were introduced in 2006 for foreigners to sail from the South and stay in Kumgangsan, with entertainment from the Pyongyang Moranbong Acrobatic Troupe. Plans were also afoot to build similar resorts at Mount Myohyang and Mount Paektu. Whereas Southern tourist buses once could only ginger up to the DMZ for passengers to peer across the border, a road was built right through the DMZ and became a regular route for daytrippers. A rail link for tourists was also in development.

It was all going so well. Then in July 2008, a KPA soldier shot dead a 53-year-old South Korean woman, Park Wang Ja, who'd wandered off a golf course. All tours were suspended, and have remained so, with North–South relations further rocked by the sinking of the ROK's *Chenoan* and the shelling of the Yeonpyong Islands (see page 47). In 2010, the DPRK confiscated the resort and said it would bring in tourists overland from Pyongyang or by boat from Rason. This understandably seriously irritated the South Korean government and Hyundai, who, along with their considerable investment into the resort, had agreed to a 50-year exclusivity deal regarding rights of access, the protection of assets and disputes being settled through negotiation. All that was ignored. In August 2011, the *Man Gyong Bong* cruise ship, that used to sail regularly to Japan but was banned in 2006 following missile tests by North Korea, took a load of visitors, mainly Chinese with a handful of Westerners, from Rajin port to Kumgangsan. Some months later the Singapore-registered cruise liner, the *Royale Star*, with a capacity for 800 passengers, was also planned to ply the same 20-hour-leg route on a monthly basis, from spring to autumn, with Westerners and East Asian tourists aboard. However, at the time of writing such plans were still on the drawing board. Visitors have also bussed overland within the DPRK into Kumgangsan, albeit in numbers way below the heights reached by South Koreans and the 100,000 visitors hoped for by the DPRK, and the closed duty-free shops and largely empty areas make it something of a ghost town. Still, the DPRK also seeks investment from hotel and tourist firms in China, particularly from the large numbers of ethnic Koreans prospering in Jilin, Heilongjiang and Yanbian, and some positive noises have been heard. Nonetheless, investors might rightly think their investments are only as safe as Hyundai's, and the DPRK must learn it's no way to do business.

The closure of the site to South Koreans also betrays the resort's achievement as a harbinger of peace, prosperity and co-operation between North and South. Tourists coming from the South Korean port of Sokcho by ship would alight at Kumgang through a port that had been converted from use as a DPRK naval base. Visitors could also play golf on a course converted out of an artillery range. Building a tourist bus route through the DMZ denoted how good intra-Korean relations had become if neither side thought the other might suddenly send their tanks through this gap in the world's most fortified frontier.

For all that, however, tourism invariably destroys the 'local', which in the DPRK context may be no bad thing, but once pristine and gloriously empty areas become filled with people seeking those qualities that their very presence destroys. Meanwhile the Hyundai complex is almost like a gilded cage in a prison state. With the holiday camp and tourists replacing army camps and troops, some physical and cultural barriers are broken down, but thrown into sharp relief are other more deep-seated barriers between the DPRK, its Southern brethren and the world beyond.

If or when the resort reopens to ROK visitors, the restrictions about laptops, mobile phones, cameras, camcorders and binoculars would be the same as for coming into Pyongyang (see page 83) – but assume nothing and check with whoever is running such tours. It was the case that Westerners leaving the ROK at Goseong went through a 'foreigner' queue and ended up on a bus that was 'theirs' for the whole tour. Re-entry permits to the ROK were not required for these excursions, because travellers were not actually leaving Korea at all – instead, resort travellers got a temporary 'passport' containing their passport info, a debit card for use in the resort, and a filled embarkation card, all carried in a plastic sheath worn around the neck at all times, which they'd lose on pain of a fine. Photography was highly limited and criticism of the DPRK leadership banned, as well as trying to buy locals' Kim pins, among other things. Shame they didn't add that visitors should not stray off golf courses.

Getting there and away   From the DPRK side, it's a 3½-hour drive from Wonsan to the Hyundai Asan resort.

Tales of the *Man Gyong Bong* or the *Royale Star* ships coming south from Rason remain fiction. Check with your tour operator to see if this route is operating.

Access from the ROK – by ship or by bus – is suspended at the time of writing (2014) and will remain so for the foreseeable future. Should they ever resume, they may be based on what went before, ie: tour reservations had to be made at least ten days in advance, with the usual restrictions applied on what could or could not be taken into the DPRK. Information for coming by ferry was at www.hyundai-asan. com or you could try the general number (↘ +82 2 3669 3000). Hyundai also did the road tours and there were bus tours from Seoul to Kumgang that took seven hours, including a break at Hwajinpo resthouse and crossing the DMZ. Details were accessible through www.mountkumgang.com but that website is now defunct.

Where to stay   Despite all of the hotels, chalets, caravans and yurts, since the resort's confiscation, the choice of accommodation is much reduced and will most likely be the Kumgangsan Hotel.

Kumgang (173 rooms) Previously the 'Kim Jong Suk Recreational Centre', refurbished to be Luxurious & lit up like a Christmas tree at night. **$$$$**

Kumgangsan Hotel (240 rooms) Onjong-ri, Kosong. Opened in 1958 but revamped since. There are also a few bungalows. Facilities include internet access (not cheap), souvenir shop, billiards, a dance floor, a nice open bar beneath the stairwell serving the same beer as found in the Yanggakdo, & a bathhouse that derives hot water from a spring. **$$$**

Hotel Haekumgang (157 rooms) This giant floating Connect 4 game hotel moored off the Sea of Kumgang is currently closed. **$$$–$$**

Kumgang Family Beach Hotel (97 rooms) Currently closed. **$$$–$$**

Where to eat and drink Aside from the eateries in the hotels the following are scattered across the resort, although with the total dearth of South Korean visitors at the time of writing, these gaffs are highly unlikely to be open.

Kosung Seafood Restaurant Fresh *sashimi* among others, overlooking Kosung harbour.

Mokrangwan A folk restaurant serving traditional North Korean specialities with a view of Kuryong Falls. Cold noodles, mixed vegetable rice & bean curd.

Tanpung Restaurant One of the original restaurants, shaped like a key, on Samil Lagoon.

What to see and do Politicking aside, Kumgangsan is a massive area of outstanding natural beauty that's best seen on foot. The following outlines of walks and tours in the three main areas of Kumgangsan are the most 'usual' but are not exhaustive.

Inner Kumgang The long road towards Inner Kumgang from Kumgang town (Kumgang Province seat) hugs the hillside as it wiggles higher and higher up a very spacious valley dotted with new pavilions marking viewing points. A long, lush plateau stretches out, flanked by vertical cliffs with mines burrowed into their bases. The road quality deteriorates as it descends from the plateau past the hamlet of Naegang-ri, 10km from Kumgang, into a copse of trees and the final checkpoint. Herein its dirt tracks crudely cut from the sheer cliffs battle with foliage and it's a slow final climb and descent through thick greenery, but spectacular peaks flit into view, locked in frozen battle with the tentacles of tree roots and ivy. Eventually you pass the **Naegumgang Resthouse**, and the road forks. Right goes past the Okgyong pond, for 2km to Monggyong Rock, like a great split mirror 90m high. In legend it read the minds and showed the sins of those who saw it. Two caves emerge further on, and then the path splits as the stream splits. The right fork goes to Ryongwon Hermitage, south of Jijang Peak, and continues for 4km to Paekma Peak. The left fork goes around Jijang Peak's north side and takes in a series of waterfalls *en route* to the Mun, Jungmyong and Tabu pagodas. However, this is quite a trek.

Back at the main road from Naegang-ri, the road snakes along, hugging the stream, past the three-storey, 7th-century pagoda of Jangan Temple, one of the four major temples of Mount Kumgang. Continuing north past Ul Pond, 3.5km from Naegang-ri, is the Sambul Bridge which is the diversion of Sambul Rock. The latter is covered with three large and 60 small Buddhist images dating from the last century of the Koryo Kingdom. Legend has it that the images were carved by two monks, named Raio and Kinko, who were bitter rivals and challenged each other to carve the greatest Buddha. The loser would have to commit suicide, and the locals thought Raio's three big Buddhas were better than Kinko's 60 small ones, so Kinko threw himself into the river nearby. It's at this bridge that a track loops east-southeast to the paths around Sibwang and Jijang peaks.

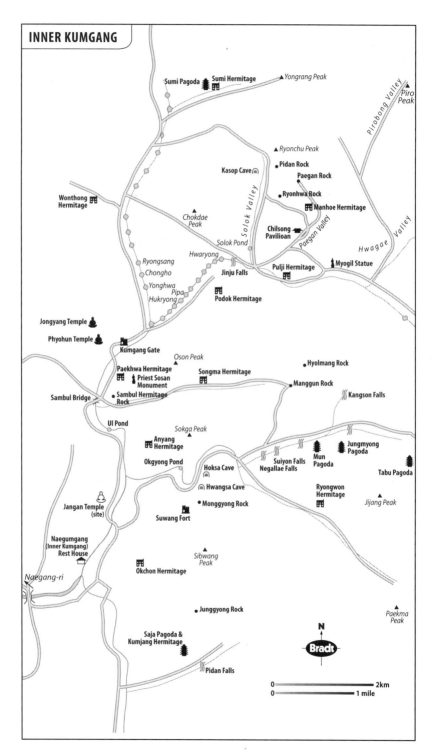

INNER KUMGANG

Sumi Pagoda · Sumi Hermitage

▲ Yongrang Peak

Pirobong Valley

▲ Piro Peak

▲ Ryonchu Peak

Kasop Cave · Pidan Rock

Paegan Rock

· Ryonhwa Rock

Manhoe Hermitage

Wonthong Hermitage

▲ Chokdae Peak

Solok Valley

Chilsong Pavilioan

Paegan Valley

Hwagae Valley

Solok Pond

Hwaryong

Myogil Statue

Ryongsang
Chongho
Yonghwa   Pipa
Hukryong

Jinju Falls

Pulji Hermitage

Jongyang Temple

Podok Hermitage

Phyohun Temple

Kumgang Gate

▲ Oson Peak

Hyolmang Rock

Paekhwa Hermitage
Priest Sosan Monument

Songma Hermitage

Manggun Rock

Kangson Falls

Sambul Bridge · Sambul Hermitage Rock

Ul Pond

▲ Sokga Peak

Anyang Hermitage

Okgyong Pond

Hoksa Cave

Suiyon Falls
Negallae Falls

Mun Pagoda

Jungmyong Pagoda

Tabu Pagoda

Hwangsa Cave

Ryongwon Hermitage

▲ Jijang Peak

Jangan Temple (site)

· Monggyong Rock

Suwang Fort

Naegumgang (Inner Kumgang) Rest House

▲ Sibwang Peak

Naegang-ri

Okchon Hermitage

· Junggyong Rock

▲ Paekma Peak

Saja Pagoda & Kumjang Hermitage

N

Bradt

Pidan Falls

0 ————— 2km
0 ————— 1 mile

Staying on the main track going north, you pass a monument erected in 1632 to the great Buddhist priest Sosan, a local who valiantly led monk-soldiers against Hideyoshi's invaders in the late 16th century. On the right is the Paekhwa Hermitage. Then, round a bend and over a bridge is Phyohun Temple, first built in the 670s under the Koguryo was for centuries one of the largest temples in the area, with 50 monks. Hideyoshi's mob destroyed it and the Korean War flattened it again, but the rebuilt temple is still technically active.

A hundred metres from here is the 'valley of ten thousand waterfalls', as marked by a 16th-century calligrapher who wrote 'Kumgangsan and Manphok Valley' just below the large Kumgang rock. The graffiti are actually the names of visiting dignitaries carved in Chinese script by the monks in thanks for their patronage, and here the valley splits.

Strolling up the right valley, bathe your feet in the dark-blue Hukryong Pool and listen out for the mandolin sounds of Pipa pond, if not for the hiss of the flaming dragon in Hwaryong Pool.

Beyond a flimsy-looking suspension bridge, the lowly turret of Podok Hermitage appears high up a cliff side, perched precariously atop a brass pole. Podok was built in AD627 under the Koguryo and solitary monks would inhabit the site for their monastic lives of devotion to Buddha, looking down into the ravine through a hole in the floor. Be careful that you are not so overwhelmed by the beauty of the monks' solace that you kill yourself, as one foreign visitor is fabled to have done, or at least see the Jinju Falls first, just beyond Podok.

Alternatively, back at the graffiti, take the left valley up past a series of ponds. Continuing north the path cuts right (east) to circle Chokdae Peak, or continue on to Sumi Pagoda and Sumi Hermitage beneath Yongrang Peak. A complex network of converging valleys make the paths loop and double back to surround a wealth of rocks, peaks, pavilions and hermitages, known as **Paegundae district**. The path almost loops back to the Podok Hermitage. Paegun Valley has good views of Inner Kumgang, but its main attraction is the sliced buttresses of Paegun Rock, from where the clouds scatter in the morning and return in the evening to play with the cranes. Pobki Peak along here is heavily inscribed, before Junghyangsong, which translates as a 'rampart of smoke from a million incense sticks'. Here also is Kumgang's finest spring of water. Solok Valley has good views from Ryonhwa Rock, Ryonchu Peak with its cactus-shaped crown and the sensuously smooth Pidan Rock.

The final gulley in this knot of valleys is the fabulous **Hwagae Valley**, with its climbing, winding paths that pass the extraordinary Myogil Statue, a huge 15m Buddha carved into a rock. It's thought that the victorious monk Raio completed it as a sculpture of honour in late Koryo. The 7th-century Manhoe Monastery is nearby and it's 4km up through the Pirobong Valley to Kumgang's highest point, the 1,639m Piro Peak, where you're some 8km from Phyohun Temple.

Sea of Kumgang Just inland from the spectacular rock formations that dot the coast is Samil Lagoon or 'three-day' lagoon, where a king stopped for a rest and stayed three days, captivated by its beauty. The bus goes west out of the Kumgangsan resort down Asian Highway 6 for about 9km and crosses the rail line by a checkpoint and mural. From where the bus stops, it's a five-minute jaunt up through woods to the Chungsong Pavilion which has a fine view of the lake and from where you can hop down to a red suspension bridge. The **Tanphung** (maple) **Restaurant** is nearby, and anyone who goes can write in and tell us what it's like.

A two-tone, orangey-brown hotel in the western part of the resort that's passed on the way to the lake is is where reunions of families divided since the Korean War have sporadically taken place. One cannot begin to imagine the joy but moreso the profound sorrow that's unleashed within.

Outer Kumgang The **Kumgangsan Hotel** is a juncture for many hikes. It's 300m from the Kumgangsan Spa, the silica-imbued water of which simmers nicely between 37°C and 44°C and is good for hypertension and heart troubles. Nothing gets the blood going like a bit of revolutionary fervour, however, and you could find yourself being lured into the **Kumgangsan Revolutionary Museum**. Alternatively, get your boots on and head for the hills.

Sujong Peak Sujong Peak, a good place to watch the sunrise cast its net of mist over the mountains, is 3km northwest from Kumgangsan Hotel. From the hotel, cross the Onjong stream towards the Kumgangsan hot springs, behind which is a track that's an hour's hike up the Sujong Valley to Sujong and Pari peaks. First is a small drinking spring, and then follow 30m and 100m 'seasonal' waterfalls. Beyond a stone gate is the roundish flat rock of Kangson where the fairies used to come. Look out for three rocks, shaped like a turtle, a flying pigeon and a man in bed.

The trail forks towards a suspension bridge that leads to an 'observatory' beneath the ridge on which sits Sunjong Peak, like a cluster of artichokes. From here the sea can be seen. The right fork goes to the hollows and water of Kumgang Cave, then the ridge goes right to the smooth dome of Pari Peak, like an upturned bowl.

The Onjong stream flows from west to east through Onjong-ri, passing the Kumgangsan and Onjong hotels on the way. A road follows the stream. Along the road due west away from Onjong-ri, the Sujong Peak area is on the right, Singye Valley is away on the left, and Hanha and Manmulsang valleys lie ahead. Hanha (cold fog) Valley is the broadest valley in Mount Kumgang and it splits into many sub-valleys between peaks. Sanggwanum Peak (1,227m) aligns with the other oddly shaped peaks of Nunggot Rock, Kom Rock and Tol Gate.

Kom Rock resembles a bear with its paw raised against the cliff. This bear once mistook the gemstones in the stream below for acorns, but got stuck on the way down to get them. It's near the Onjong's Munju Pond and Munju Bridge, a couple of hundred metres from the 43m-high Kwanum Falls also on the left or south of the stream.

About 10km west from the Kumgangsan hotel lies the Mansang Pavilion, the start of an odd walk of curious boulders. First is Samson Rock, like three spirits, then Kwimyon Rock, the figure of a goblin or a massive petrified tree. Look out for the 'man on seven rocks' and those resembling eagles, bears and tortoises. It's a steep, sharp path up Jolbu ('axe chop') rock to Ansim ('saddle') rock.

Fork right 100m to the spring of 'Forget stick' (*mangjang*), whose rejuvenating waters are said to make the old forget their sticks. Then it's a climb to Kumgang's highest gate, Chonil ('sky') Gate, to see over Chonson Rock, which doubled as an observatory. From here you can see the weird, smashed white glass face of Manmulsang. Look out for the Samsong Hermitage and the looming peak of Sandung. An offshoot from the track goes northeast and then divides, the right fork looping back to the main road, the left continuing for a good few kilometres to Chonpok Valley, with its series of falls, odd rocks and caves.

Sejon Peak A different road heads due south of Onjong-ri and then bends westwards. Take it through Sulginomi Pass where the egg-shaped rock appears on the left. About 1.5km beyond the bend in the road a short cut from Kumgangsan Hotel appears, joining just where sits one of Kumgang's oldest temples, Singye, that dates from 519.

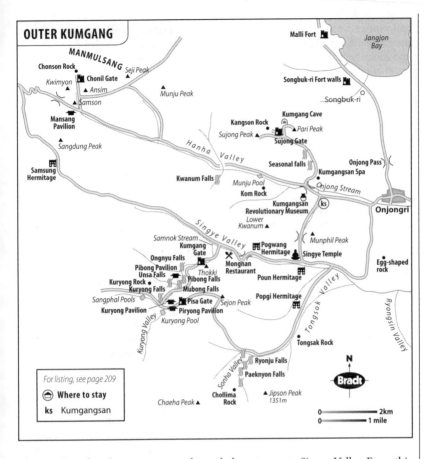

For listing, see page 209

⊜ Where to stay
ks Kumgangsan

The temple and its three-storey pagoda mark the entrance to Singye Valley. From this pagoda are brief excursions up to Munphil and Lower Kwanum peaks, flanking the path going north to the Kumgangsan. From the main road, two paths loop southwards and converge on Sejon Peak. The first route starts a few hundred metres east of Singye Temple, going up the shallow Tongsak Valley on a very pretty jaunt of mild exertion. Tongsak holds the shaking Tongsak Rock that weighs tonnes and shivers with the lightest prod. It leads into Sonha Valley with its Ryonju and Paeknyon waterfalls and where sits the Kobuk (turtle) Rock, a turtle that stretched its neck to drink water but was so captivated by the falls it turned to stone. From Ryonju, look southwards to the 1,351m Jipson Peak, Kumgang's sharpest point, high on the northern range with the cloud-shrouded Chaeha Peak to the west, and the Chollima Rock (like Pyongyang's statue) between them. The path from Ryonju carries on westwards along a ridge to Sejon Peak.

East of Jipson Peak is the 4km Ryongsin Valley, a track around waterfalls and pools, including the 7m-deep Jonju Pool and 8m-deep Ryongyon Pool. In south Ryongsin Valley is Palyon Valley with a stone-arch rainbow bridge, and the 8th-century Palyon Temple beside it.

A **second route** to Sejon Peak starts some 2km further west along Singye Valley from Singye Temple. Going west, Pogwang Hermitage appears on the right, and you cross a bridge, and come to **Mongnan Restaurant**, plonked onto the stream and with an outdoor draught-beer bar. It is a good place to refuel, and be amused by the model frog jazz band. The road, now a track, forks to the south, whence Ongnyu and Kuryong valleys extend like a twig from a branch from a tree, each littered with waterfalls and pools going up to Sejon Peak, about 4km from the restaurant.

The Samnok stream trickles from Ongnyu ('clear water') Valley, so you follow it up and south, past the Thokki ('tortoise') Rock on the left. Sliding through the eye of Kumgang Gate seals your presence in the valley. Look for the flower-like Chonha rock. Ongnyu Falls channel through flat-sided trenches to the 6m-deep Ongnyu Pond, over a bridge and 200m more past Ryonju Rock and Falls, then the spectacular Pibong Falls ('Phoenix Falls', from the swirling mists) tumble 140m down what looks like a thousand broken dinner plates and past Mubung Falls.

From the Pibong Pavilion, Unsa ('silver string') Falls are next as you continue upwards towards Kuryong ('nine dragons') Pavilion, stacked onto the hillside of Kuryong Valley, where someone enterprising may be waiting with drinks to sell. From here is a fine view of the 74m-high Kuryong Falls that cascade out from a beautiful parabolic curve of rock into Kuryong Pool, and is one of Korea's largest falls. Nine dragons reportedly live in the 13m-deep pool at the base of the falls, defending Kumgang from interlopers.

Going beyond this pavilion may not be possible, but if it is, the path continues from here to Yondam Bridge and traverses 700m of rocky cliff and ladders to arrive at Kuryong Rock to view the eight large green Sangphal pools, noted as bathing spots for good spirits. That said, the mountains are something of a sacred site and the water out of the mountains is ultimately drinking water, so guides may well prohibit any swimming. Sneak through Pisa Gate and nothing but a ridge-hike remains until you get the grand overview from Sejon Peak, now reached from both sides.

Further possibilities Outer Kumgang has Songrim district, which has Songrim Cave and Songrim Hermitage, but be careful! 'If you are enthralled by the views, you are liable to get behind from your companions.' Unsudae district is the site of the 9th-century Yujom Temple; Kumgang's largest, it was destroyed by US bombers and only the foundations remain. Chonbuldong district is in the Chonbul stream basin in east Manmulsang district, with the 1,000 Buddha-shaped rocks of Mount Chonbul, and Sonam, Chonpok and Chonbul valleys.

9

East Coast to Tanchon 단천

With Robin Paxton. For a map of the region see pages 188–9.

HAMHUNG 함흥

39.5°N, 127.35°E; 110km north of Wonsan, South Hamgyong Province

Hamhung is North Korea's second city. The birthplace of the founder of Korea's Ri dynasty and the site of a famous battle during the Korean War, Hamhung has since developed into a spacious industrial city of around 750,000 inhabitants. The city is located close to the northern end of Hamhung Bay and is served by the nearby port of **Hungnam**, one of the country's largest export centres.

Hamhung is renowned as a heavy engineering centre and is home to 30% of the DPRK's industrial capacity, producing machinery, trucks, metals, and fertiliser out of the enormous Hungnam ammonium fertiliser plant, the largest in the DPRK.

Relative to other cities in the region, Hamhung is bustling with activity. Though there are few cars, cyclists tear along the pavements and pedestrians stroll past the grandiose theatre building. The occasional street vendor does a brisk trade by the roadside and there is some construction work going on.

Hamhung also boasts a proud academic tradition. The city's branch of the Academy of Sciences is particularly strong in the field of chemical research, having developed the Juche fabric known as Vinalon, which is produced at the February 8 Vinalon textile complex. However, this well-publicised expertise has given rise to suspicions among Western intelligence sources that the city is also a potential centre for chemical weapons production.

HISTORY A settlement at Hamhung dates from at least the 12th century AD. A walled city around Mount Tonghung is believed to have been built in 1108. The ancient city is possibly the birthplace of the founder of the Ri dynasty, Ri Song Gye, which ruled Korea from the late 14th century until Japanese occupation in 1910.

The Hamhung/Hungnam area was also the site of a major battle during the Korean War. Twice in 1950 the city was evacuated, as US and South Korean troops took it in October before being driven out by advancing Chinese-backed North Korean troops in December. Hamhung's development into a major industrial centre has occurred largely since the independence of the DPRK. There are many small hydro-electric projects dotted in the hills around the city, and burial mounds from the second Arduous March (see box, pages 248–9). Much of the architecture is in the post-war style and Kim Il Sung was a frequent visitor to the city, which is marked by monuments to the Great Leader.

> **WHEN TO GO**
>
> The most favourable seasons are spring and autumn, when the climate is cool and dry. Summer can be hot and rainy.

GETTING THERE AND AWAY From Pyongyang, it's the same road as to Wonsan (three hours or so, stopping at Lake Sinpyong and maybe taking lunch at Ullim Falls), then another three hours from there to Hamhung, driving up high into the hills and traversing open plateaux of farmland.

The road surface deteriorates going north from Wonsan and has to wind through mountain terrain. The landscape to the immediate north of Hamhung is flatter, where the road traverses the Hamhung plain. Hamhung is also accessible by train from Pyongyang. The east coast rail line from Wonsan to the Russian border passes through the city and now features on tour options.

WHERE TO STAY AND EAT

Majon Beach Resort (108 rooms) Majondong, Hungnam District. Located by the beach, around 25km east along the coast from Hamhung itself, the resort has a newish hotel, built in 2009, with a restaurant, shop, billiards, pool & a row of a dozen badly numbered villas along a path that leads to another restaurant & a bar. Sea views & bathing facilities. **$$$-$$**

Sin Hung San Hotel (76 rooms) Tonghungsan District, Hamhung. The hotel is located on Hamhung's main thoroughfare, close to Mount Tonghung & still (at time of writing) is a fine albeit faded example of Soviet-era finery & ostentatious décor. There is a large car park at the front. A 1st-floor restaurant serves basic Korean food, & a smoke-filled billiard hall & bar on the ground floor & which, as a speciality, serves cold noodles that one visitor said was 'like eating sunlight'. The hotel is next door to a large restaurant built in traditional Korean style. **$$$-$$**

WHAT TO SEE AND DO If you're coming to Hamhung from the south from Wonsan (along Asian Highway 6) you'll cross what is in effect the city's eastern entrance, the **Songchon River Bridge**, a wide low-level span across the eponymous river estuary as it flattens out towards Korea's East Sea. This bridge was destroyed and rebuilt several times during the Korean War.

The road straightens into Hamhung proper and on the northwest side is a crisply tended manmade hill topped by statues to Kim Il Sung and Kim Jong Il. There are good views of the river and the city up here. Next along the road is the obligatory **Kim Il Sung Revolutionary Museum**. Some 600m due north of the statues, along a crooked wooded path, lie an old **temple** and the **Monument Zoo**, although little is known about either. Back on the main road, moving further northeast, pass **Sin Hung San Hotel**, where one might take in some fine cold noodles, takes you to the city's **main square**, which in the finest North Korean tradition is as vast and empty as the main squares in other cities, but this one is nonetheless utterly dominated by the sun-eclipsing brutalist grey edifice that is **Hamhung Theatre**. The theatre opened in 1984 and hosts various cultural performances. The building is said to contain around 800 rooms and the sheer enormity of the place, fully fronted by heavy mahogany doors and bedecked within by grey marble, apparently even succeeded in surprising dignitaries from Russia when taken to see it, who maybe wondered where the money came from and who was going to pack it out for performances.

The square is cut through by the broad road heading southeast towards Hamhung station (from where visitors may now arrive by train). Beware of the traffic of cars and tractors along this road, while from the square's northeast rear, beyond the stelae unfolds **Hamhung Youth Park** that flanks the city stadium.

On the northern end of Hamhung is **Mount Tonghung**, a 319m hill that offers good views of the city. It is home to several temples, including the **Kuchon Temple** and the **Sonhwa Hall**. The buildings and city walls are believed to date from the early 12th century, though most of what is standing today has been rebuilt more than once.

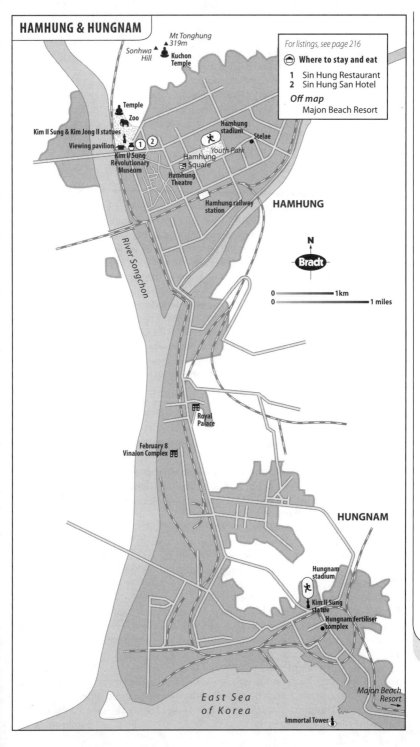

HAMHUNG & HUNGNAM

Mt Tonghung
▲319m
Sonhwa Hill ▲
Kuchon Temple

Temple
Zoo
Kim Il Sung & Kim Jong Il statues
Viewing pavilion
Kim Il Sung Revolutionary Museum
Hamhung Square
Hamhung Theatre
Hamhung stadium
Stelae
Youth Park

Hamhung railway station

HAMHUNG

For listings, see page 216
⊜ **Where to stay and eat**
1   Sin Hung Restaurant
2   Sin Hung San Hotel
Off map
    Majon Beach Resort

N

Bradt

0 ————————— 1km
0 ————————— 1 miles

River Songchon

🎋 **Royal Palace**

February 8 Vinalon Complex 🎋

HUNGNAM

Hungnam stadium
Kim Il Sung statue
Hungnam fertiliser complex

East Sea of Korea

Majon Beach Resort

Immortal Tower

HUNGNAM 흥남

Going downriver from Hamhung about 9km gets one to the industrial port city of **Hungnam**. Nestled off the raised road just about halfway between the two cities is the **royal palace** where the Ri dynasty's founder Ri Song Gye came to live following his abdication from the throne. Despite having founded the Ri, local lore doesn't rate him highly, possibly for his proclivity for having lots of courtesans. The main buildings were finished in 1398, but were destroyed by Hideyoshi's forces and rebuilt in 1610 – all slots, no nails – before the Korean War came and did some damage. Visitors seeking longevity may get to touch the crazy 450-year-old pine tree, and it's a very romantic venue under moonlight or on a torchlit tour of the place.

WHAT TO SEE AND DO Almost opposite the palace across the road is another site that's hovering on the fringe of tour itineraries, the vast **February 8 Vinalon** chemical complex, with a capacity to produce 50,000 tonnes per annum of the manmade fabric, and 10,000 tonnes of Movilon, another manmade fabric lost on most of the world. Vinalon is the DPRK's indigenous equivalent of nylon, from which a great deal of clothing and textile goods is made. Dr Lee Seung Ki developed the fibre in 1939 out of a polyvinyl alcohol from limestone and anthracite coal, and when he defected to the DPRK he took the formula with him, with the production of Vinalon beginning in 1954. The problem with nylon is the DPRK lacks the oil from whose by-products nylon is made, but the country's abundant in the limestone and anthracite that make Vinalon. Because the DPRK is entirely self-sufficient in the stuff (to the point of being the world's sole producer) it's also known as Juche fabric. Vinalon is durable and heat resistant, but hasn't caught on beyond the DPRK (the ROK briefly made some quantities in the 1960s) as it's relatively difficult and costly to produce in terms of energy.

The complex (its date denoting the foundation of the KPA, which presumably wears a lot of the stuff) started producing fabrics in 1961, and has since expanded to produce other chemical things, the output of 10,000 workers, thankful for their jobs after the plant was upgraded and reopened in 2010 following 16 years of being mothballed.

Right down on the waterfront is the **Hungnam Fertiliser Complex**, visible from a way away with its towering chimney belching out bright yellow smoke. 'Fertiliser is rice, rice is socialism,' as Kim Il Sung said. With the plant's capacity to produce 40% of the country's fertiliser, we can appreciate the importance of the complex not only to the DPRK's development, having been deemed central to the country's process towards industrialisation, but also its survival. The plant was originally built and destroyed by the Japanese, then rebuilt, then destroyed during the Korean War, then rebuilt. The fertiliser is produced from gasified anthracite, a process that's still a source of pride. As the museum tells it through its dozen-plus rooms, the Kims visited the plant often and toured Chinese and Russian leaders around it. Kim Il Sung's desk, chair and even his spoon are lovingly preserved. When you are taken to the main generator hall, with its machinery, dials and levers from another era, consider the opulence of the museum and the long, long panels outside dedicated to the Kims. The generator hall has two very fine propaganda posters within, and the plant has many impressive posters and slogans across it. An incongruous item may be a tiny duck farm on the go just outside the hall's entrance. A final note for smokers: do not light up even if you see workers having a crafty one.

The port of Hungnam has vintage freighters and fishing vessels aplenty, and you can see the towering stelae to the Leaders atop an island about half a mile out to sea, like a birthday cake. Going northeast from here along the coast is the **Majon Beach Resort** (see details on page 216), a fabulous sandy beach with shallow waters, a drop down from a large hotel building and a string of two-storey villas with comfortable en-suite rooms. Meals at the hotel are fine, with local seafood. Aid agencies and NGOs work out of the resort, so there will probably be some foreign company if you stay there. The beach seems swimmable by day and hosts beach parties in the evening, and at night you'll see the glow of fishing-boat lights on the horizon. Korean People's Army guards do patrol the beach but they're not out to get anyone. However, this author does recommend that guests don't get ridiculously drunk, take over someone else's hotel room, try and fight everyone, then run naked to the beach, resisting all efforts by AK-47-equipped guards, guides and tourists to restrain them.

To further understand the importance of agriculture to the country and the changes it has undergone in recent years, a trip may be made to the 600ha **Gongbong Model Village**, home to 1,500 people. This farm's claim to fame is that it was the first in the country to introduce double cropping begun in 1998, with fields alternating output from soybean, potatoes and vegetables to rice (which surely must need a lot of fertiliser to stop the soil being exhausted). The top farmers are heralded at the farm's museum. There's a stableyard full of tractors, some of serious Soviet vintage, and a visit may be made to a farming family's house, with their name posted on the outside – and please remember, it *is* their home, so be respectful.

TANCHON 단천

40.28°N, 128.55°E, 150km northeast of Hamhung, capital of South Hamgyong Province
When the river in Tanchon runs grey, say local residents, it's a sure sign that the lead and zinc mines further upstream are in full swing. This bodes ill for any remaining marine life, though is a boost to the industrial needs of the northeastern port city. Environmentalists baulk at the metallic content of the Pukdae River as it drains into Korea's East Sea but Tanchon has taken a prominent position in the national economy following the construction of a zinc smelter and magnesia plant on the coast.

Tanchon is one of several major ports along the eastern Korean coastline. The city lies in the delta of the Pukdae River, below the imposing foothills of the Paektu mountain range. The city's uniform white apartment blocks give way to more ramshackle, rural housing closer to the coast, where oxen haul carts along the road from the nearby fields. Tanchon is also a regional agricultural centre, though like other parts of the country it has been affected by droughts over the years.

A long, straight road runs from the city centre across sandbanks and the river delta to the zinc smelter and magnesia works. The approach to the plants is marked by a string of prominent letters, proclaiming: 'Long Live the Dear Leader Kim Jong Il, Sun of the 21st Century!' At shift's beginning and end, the road is packed with workers in brown overalls cycling to and from the factories.

The city is also a useful stop-off point for travellers to the far northeast of the DPRK. World Food Programme convoys plying the Pyongyang–Chongjin aid route often spend the night in Tanchon, grateful for the respite from the treacherous, winding roads.

HISTORY Though an important eastern port of the DRPK, Tanchon is traditionally behind Wonsan, Hungnam, Chongjin and Rajin in the pecking order. Its prominence has grown since the flat stretch of land between the town and the coast was selected by Kim Il Sung himself as the site of a new zinc smelter in the early 1980s.

Smelting began in 1985, using ore from the Komdok mining complex some 80km inland. A brand-new magnesia plant followed in 1997, fed by magnesite ore from Ryongyang, with the area reckoned by the DPRK at least to have deposits of 5.4 billion tonnes. The zinc plant has been upgraded, as have the city's port facilities with a view to not only increasing exports of raw material zinc and magnesium to China, but also to produce magnesite finished products.

GETTING THERE AND AWAY Tanchon's accessibility to visitors is more patchy than other sites in the DPRK, but in any case it is on the main rail route linking Wonsan with the Chinese/Russian border. A branch line runs the 80km inland to Komdok.

By road, the city is a five-hour drive from Hamhung and around eight hours from Wonsan. The road between Hamhung and Tanchon is a winding two-lane dust track, extremely scenic in parts as it flirts with the East Korea Sea before disappearing back into the mountains. The route is certainly not conducive to high-speed travel.

WHERE TO STAY AND EAT Accommodation is available in a hilltop **hostel** situated around 2km from Tanchon itself among well-tended gardens. The hostel's VIP suite offers a double room with desk, fridge, deckchairs and some startling colour schemes. The en-suite bathroom has running water only periodically and there is no hot water. Also attached to the suite is a spacious meeting room decorated with several photographic portraits of Kim Il Sung.

Meals are served in a **cafeteria** housed in an adjacent building. The range of food is substantial and the dining room boasts a fresco of the Tanchon shoreline across one entire wall.

WHAT TO SEE AND DO
Kim Il Sung and Kim Jong Il murals
Like every town in the DPRK, Tanchon displays extracts from Kim Il Sung's and Kim Jong Il's writings on large, stone walls. In Tanchon, the monuments can be found in a courtyard set slightly back from the main avenue through the town's modern housing.

Tanchon Zinc Smelter
This is another fixture, its huge red gate and heroic picture of Kim Il Sung and his subjects welcoming visitors to the plant, opened in 1985 and now employing around 2,300 people.

Riwon
The attractive town of Riwon nestles at the end of a river valley, only 40km south of Tanchon. The town is a fishing centre and is home to a high concentration of naval officers. It hugs the coastline of Riwon Bay, where the road from the south dips to sea level before climbing inland into the mountains again. The east coast railroad skirts the western edge of town.

KOMDOK

41.05°N, 128.55°E, South Hamgyong Province, 80km northwest of Tanchon

Komdok is a mining town planted around 600m above sea level at the end of a valley in the Paektusan range, and is reputedly revered throughout the DPRK as the country's leading source of several metallurgical ores, primarily lead, zinc and silver.

The town's name translates roughly as 'Spider Plateau', as maps of the area show eight major mine shafts feeling their way outwards from it, like an arachnid. Komdok also forms part of the 'Precious Mountain' area that encompasses the adjacent Ryongyang mining centre, the DPRK's primary source of magnesite ore.

The name stems from an age-old eulogy attributed to Kim Il Sung about the mineral wealth held within the mountain. There are 7,000 lead and zinc miners in Komdok, living with their families in homes haphazardly cascading up the hillside, and many of these miners work at the Ryongyang magnesite mine. A single-track tarmac road climbs up the valley side to an isolated ore processing plant at 1,200m above sea level, offering a breathtaking panorama of the valley and town below.

The town is also close to the source of the Pukdae River, though its waters often run milky-grey rather than blue. At times, up to 10% of the lead concentrate produced on site is believed to escape into the river so pity anyone going in there. Agriculture is limited, though potatoes are grown in small plots of land on the hillsides above the town.

Komdok suffered heavily in the disastrous floods of the mid-1990s, and bouts of heavy rains since, causing widespread damage to the town, the mines and transport links. However, the town's industrial facilities have had some modernisation and flushed Komdok's residents with renewed pride in their exulted work.

HISTORY The site was first mined in the 14th century, though silver was discovered in the area as early as the 10th century AD. There are two major mining complexes at Komdok, the Ryongyang mine which produces magnesite ore, and Komdok's seven mines and three processing complexes which produce almost half of the DPRK's lead and zinc, and silver as a by-product. The Komdok complex has been in operation since 1946, albeit with periodic stoppages along the way, and has mined over a hundred million tonnes of ore, with three times that estimated to still be underground. Kim Il Sung visited Komdok in 1961 and 1984, and during the latter visit he supervised the opening of the third ore processing plant high on the mountainside. Outside the plant's main entrance is a billboard depicting the Great Leader's exact route that time and his words, including the immortal line that the factory resembled a 'sea of machinery'.

The most celebrated visit, however, was that of Kim Jong Il in July 1975, who ventured inside the main mine shaft and expressed horror that workers were spending up to 14 consecutive days underground so as to surpass production targets by as much as 150%. Rusting railway cars still protrude from the river further downstream in grim tribute to the succession of heavy floods that have hit the area in recent decades, and which have stymied investments to double the output of lead and zinc to 14 million tonnes per annum to sell to China. In June 2013, DPRK cabinet premier Pak Pong Ju visited the area to focus on 'work for preventing damage in rainy season', underscoring the area's economic importance.

GETTING THERE AND AWAY The spectacular 80km mountain road from Tanchon to Komdok takes about three hours by car, following the Pukdae River and passing through a mountainside settlement producing phosphorous. Several cartoonlike stone sculptures of animals appear along this road. There is no regular bus service and the trains are mainly for freight.

WHERE TO STAY AND EAT There is accommodation available in the hostel (**$$–$**), which is also part of the Komdok mining complex's

WHEN TO GO

April to June and September to October are the best months to visit. Winter temperatures fall well below freezing and nights are cold all year round. July and August can be rainy.

headquarters, overlooking the central square. Hot running water is available on request for one hour per morning. There's a sauna in the basement.

WHAT TO SEE AND DO The **central square** is the town's main focus, through which practically the entire adult male population treks in the morning towards the mine, and around times of national celebration they are hailed along the way by the town's womenfolk, singing songs of reaching production targets. A huge fresco at one end depicts Kim Il Sung in hat and trench coat, flocked by the enthusiastic womenfolk of the town, and the other shows a young Kim Jong Il in a dazzling white coat, holding court with the miners deep underground. Kim Il Sung's writings are carved in red along another side of the square. A bridge leads off from the square towards the stone obelisk inscribed with the words of Kim Il Sung, and from there it's a small climb to the entrance of the main mine shaft.

Komdok Museum of Mining The museum is housed in the lower storey of a medium-rise building near the central square with 'Juche' 주체 out front. There is a lot of memorabilia from Kim Jong Il's visit in 1975, ranging from his wicker helmet to the mining car, replete with red-and-cream upholstery, in which he travelled into the mountain. The museum also houses an interesting scaled-down model of the Komdok mining complex, viewed as a cross-section of the mountain and replete with a model train buzzing along the set.

Underground Mining Museum The train journey into the main mining shaft takes around 35 minutes, barring any derailments (which are more inconvenient than perilous given the slow rattle at which the train travels). Down below is a small shrine dedicated to the Dear Leader's first visit, comprising of a whitewashed, lampshade-less single-bulb room where he sat and talked during his several hours underground in 1975, with his small wooden desk and chair still preserved and untouched. Outside this shrine are socialist artwork and reproductions of workers' bulletins from that time, with one telling of the miner who worked a 14-day unbroken spell to exceed production targets by 150%, leading Kim Jong Il to decree that all miners must return above ground at shift's end.

Number 3 Ore Processing Plant Built in the early 1980s, the plant is the newest building within the mining complex. The journey to the plant rises to 600m and affords great views of Komdok, and there are a number of small, attractive cartoon carvings: a cow heading a football, a bear drinking from a bottle and a rabbit downhill skiing.

10

Northernmost Corner

Travelling to Chongjin 청진시 has commonly involved flying in to the small town of Orang with its single slab-strip airport, lined with rows of old MiGs and maize, and a perfunctory 'terminal' with plush chairs and an allotment over which an aerial battle is depicted in punched metal. Orang itself is very dusty and low key, with an odd sense of resembling a central American frontier town.

It's a seriously bumpy but picturesque 90-minute drive northwards from Orang to Chongjin, first past the beautifully blue sea with a mere handful of small fishing boats visible through the electric fence that runs along the coast. The road then tracks along a flat riverbed amid shallow hills before climbing and winding up, down and around hills. If you've come from Paektusan you may tell there is a seasonal difference in foliage. This part of the world is still very infrequently visited by anybody and one quite quickly gets the sense of being in the hinterland. The bus fleet is notably older than the capital's, decorated almost like a boudoir with pelmets and lacy curtains. Passengers are very much under the watchful gaze of the driver, employed by the more conservative Chilbosan division of the Korea International Travel Company (KITC), which has much tighter rules on photography. He'll pound the vehicle along roads of pedestrians, bicycles, bullock-drawn carts and open-back trucks rammed with people stuffed hideously close to horrendously choking pots of hot pitch, on-board refineries that fuel the lorries and asphyxiate the passengers. Crops chop all the way up the hillsides, while men and women haul rocks and lumber as they repair the roads and railways. Younger women's heads are adorned with bowls and bags. Pavements are for drying corn, balconies are for drying peppers, cottage roofs are for growing pumpkins, indeed entire villages lie camouflaged under webs of pumpkins. Railways with sleepers like crooked and rotten teeth are so underused that farmers herd their goats and geese on the tracks, while pedestrians roll their bikes along them, with white shelter boxes built onto bridges to cope with this extra-curricular traffic.

Sights of note on the way north include the town of **Kyongsong** 경성 35km from Chongjin, seat of its namesake county that's known mainly for its ceramics, fishing and hot springs. **Kyongsong Onpho**, 12km northwest of Kyongsong's capital, features an excellent health resort, with the Onpho Resthouse where the spa waters, rising up from some 500m underground, are naturally heated up to 57°C. The waters are high in radon content and can treat neuralgia, arthritis and gynecopathy, while the spa 'draws a large number of people for its good curative effect', as it has for hundreds of years, according to KCNA. **Kyongsong Spa** lies in Haonpho-ri, 2km from the county seat, with spa and sand baths, and there are spas in nearby Songjong and Posan. The Koryo-built **Fort of Kyongsong Seat** is 1km northeast of Kyongsong, and was rebuilt and enlarged between 1616 and 1672 under the Ri. The **Kyongsong Nam Gate** has been rebuilt many times. It is possible to go along the beach and coast.

NORTHEASTERN REGION

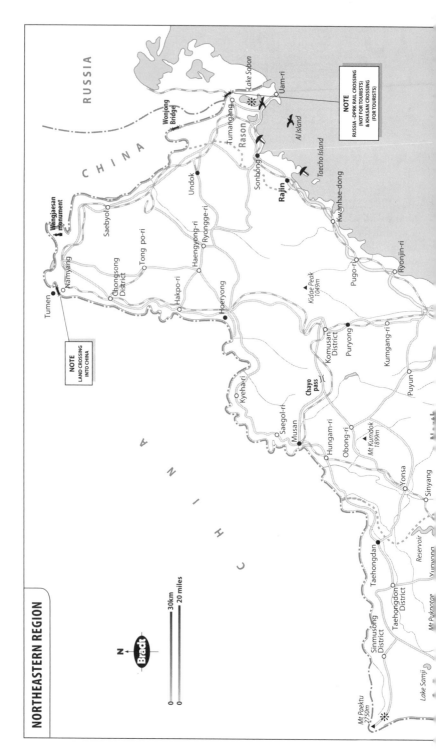

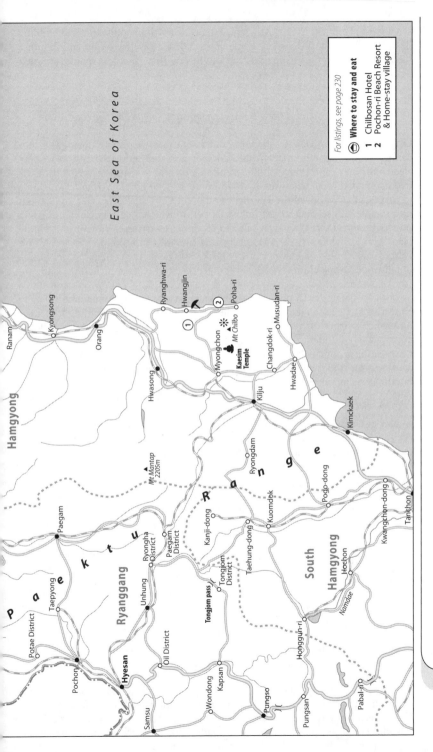

East Sea of Korea

For listings, see page 230

Where to stay and eat
1 Chilbosan Hotel
2 Pochon-ri Beach Resort
& Home-stay village

Hamgyong

Ranam

Kyongsong

Orang

Ryanghwa-ri

Hwangjin

Poha-ri

Myongchon

Mt Chilbo

Kaesim Temple

Changdok-ri

Musudan-ri

Hwasong

Hwadae

Kilju

Kimchaek

Mt Mantap
2205m

Ryongdam

R   a   n   g   e

Pogo-dong

Paegam

Kanji-dong

Kuomdek

Ryongha
District

Paegam
District

Tongjom
District

Taehung-dong

Tanchon

Kwangchon-dong

P   a   e   k   t   u

Taepyong

Unhung

Ryanggang

Tongjom pass

South

Hamgyong

Hochon

Namdae

Potae District

Oil District

Wondong

Kapsan

Honggun-ri

Pungsan

Pochon

Hyesan

Pungso

Pabal-ri

Samsu

Closer to Chongjin is Sing Am, which opposite a striking pink, turreted building has a temple yet to be visited, while some 17km away from Chongjin another temple stands over the rail line, waiting for visitors. Then Chongjin looms into view.

CHONGJIN 청진

41.45°N, 129.45°E; Capital of North Hamgyong Province, Korean East Sea coast, 81km south of Rajin

Originally a fishing village, Chongjin underwent massive growth during the 20th century as the Japanese made it into a major port and industrial city, producing steel, machinery and chemical fibres, building its grid of roads to serve those ends and its population of what was, by 1945, some 300,000 people. Around two-thirds of that number survived the US shells and bombs of the Korean War, to blossom into the DPRK's second-largest industrial city, to which it still has something of a pungent claim. There is an array of factories, mills, towering chimneys and spindly black cranes, while its 627,000 inhabitants live in a mix of spaciously laid-out concrete apartment blocks, or densely packed single-storey cottages under forests of tall wooden-box chimneys. The overall feel of most of these structures is they're from a past era.

The City of Iron, as Chongjin's been nicknamed for its six million tonne-capacity Kim Chaek No 1 Iron and Steel Complex, is rusty, and for all its output it's telling how much a city of such importance to the DPRK's industrial economy has suffered energy-starved underactivity and investment in recent years. Like Pyongyang, the heavy smog is actually mist drawing in from the hills. Still, there is a fair amount construction and renovation work going on, ranging from several large new buildings rising up around the main square to tower-block residents precariously repainting the walls outside their windows in colours as bright as the little kiosks that dot the roads. The large open areas between the tower blocks are not spaces to play but areas to grow crops, like every other spare square inch in the country, reminding one of the reality of the situation that jars in juxtaposition to the murals of the beaming Great and Dear Leaders that flank the roads.

Despite being a port where foodstuffs could simply be floated in, Chongjin suffered badly in the 1990s famine and was the location for much of the worst that's reported by Barbara Demick (see page 275). Wonder to yourself what the soil of the surrounding hills contains. Out of such hardship, many of the city's dwellers undertook what would develop into a substantial basis of individual entrepreneurialism. Despite strong guidance from on high that they should desist from such business and revert to more orthodox means of surviving, the locals have since vigorously and successfully defended their ways. From survival to revival, there's Chinese investment to renovate and expand the city port's cargo-bearing capacity to seven million tonnes a year, a rare sign of optimism about the future fortunes of the city and the country, but then China and Russia aren't far away. There's long been enough by way of foreign ships, crews and delegates coming here to keep Chinese and Russian consulates in the city open.

Outsiders coming into the city from the south will note how augmented the city's spaciousness is by the emptiness of the long, six-lane No 1 road that strips into town, tracing alongside the only tram system outside of Pyongyang, with its straight rails chivvying the trams around the long bends. Passing on the left an extraordinarily long conveyor complex, on the southeast side one can glimpse the Kim Chaek No 1 Iron and Steel Complex, and the spilling of heavy fumes from the adjacent power plant into the road might hopefully suggest the plant's 25,000

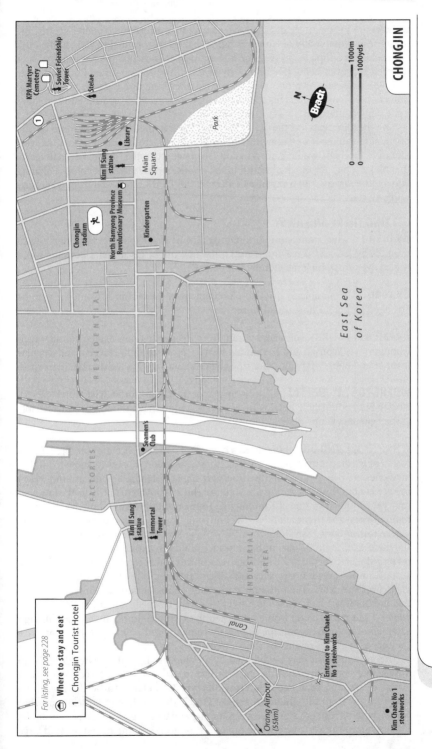

For listing, see page 228

Where to stay and eat

1 Chongjin Tourist Hotel

CHONGJIN

KPA Martyrs' Cemetery
Soviet Friendship Tower
Stelae

Library

Kim Il Sung statue

Main Square

Park

North Hamyong Province Revolutionary Museum

Chongjin stadium

Kindergarten

RESIDENTIAL

East Sea of Korea

FACTORIES

Seamen's Club

Kim Il Sung statue
Immortal Tower

INDUSTRIAL AREA

Canal

Orang Airport (55km)

Entrance to Kim Chaek No 1 steelworks

Kim Chaek No 1 steelworks

0 ————— 1000m
0 ————— 1000yds

N

Bradt

workers are productively engaged. It's named after a resistance fighter against the Japanese and major ally of Kim Il Sung, but who was executed in 1951 at the rank of general for failing to prevent the US landings at Incheon. His honour was later restored however, being posthumously awarded the National Reunification Prize in 1998, his home town of Songjin renamed after him, and likewise a technology university in Pyongyang. He's one of the very few outside of the Kim family to have a site named after him.

Now heading east-northeast, as the road crosses the river you can see on the north side the massive Chongjin Chemical Fibres factory, which among its least offensive products would rank Vinalon (see page 218), the 'Juche material' fabric that makes up much of what's shorn in the DPRK. Swiftly after that comes Pohanng Square, the massive open expanse that centres all DPRK cities, and from where any tour will start.

GETTING THERE AND AWAY

By plane Flying from Samijon to Orang airport is a 45-minute prop flight or 20 minutes by jet, and if leaving from Orang one might get a metal detector wand waved over you which they ignore if it beeps.

By road It is possible to drive to Chongjin from Rason but it would have to be arranged with your hosts in advance.

By rail Cross-DPRK sojourns by train from Pyongyang now extend all the way to Chongjin, via Wonsan and Hamhung. Regular cross-country travel by rail is a new frontier and offers a far smoother ride and different views to those taken in by road.

WHERE TO STAY AND EAT Visitors can stay at the **Chongjin Tourist Hotel ($$-$)**, a basic but comfortable hotel with a brewery and sauna, and there's food available at the Seamen's Club.

WHAT TO SEE AND DO Chongjin as a city is still quite a new entrant to the DPRK's roster of regular tourist venues, with a sparse selection of sites to show for it, but new ones are being added all the time. Starting at Pohanng Square, around which many new buildings are going up, you find the 25-foot statue of **Kim Il Sung** that may yet be joined by one of Kim Jong Il. To the right of the monument is the city's main **library**, and to the left is **North Hamyong Province Revolutionary Museum**, where Kim Il Sung, Kim Jong Il and Kim Jong Suk were frequent visitors. Indeed the main exhibit on display in the entrance hall is an extraordinary topographical map of the area, bedecked with hundreds of tiny lights marking all of the statues, secret camps, revolutionary sites and all else relating to the three Kims' work and visits over the years. The museum is arguably almost a museum of their visits. A major exhibit is a hall with slogan trees that were rescued from local forest fires in 1998 – 17 brave men and women lost their lives while fighting these fires, although the memorial to them and the dubiously romanticised painting of their fate says they gave their lives saving the slogan trees.

The museum visit may be followed by an uphill walk to the **Soviet Friendship Tower** that commemorates the city's liberation from Japanese forces by the Red Army, with the **Korean People's Army Martyrs' Cemetery** nearby. Both are just a stone's throw from the **Chongjin Tourist Hotel**. The two-halved hostel is basic but comfy, with its restaurant staff serving singing and dancing as well as beer from the on-site micro-brewery, where one can while away an evening drinking amid large steel brewing tanks at €0.40 a cup! A sauna can be fired up with enough notice, but for sure an excellent sauna and steam room and cold pool for dousing can be found at the **Seamen's Club**, with soap scrub pads and towel all provided for CNY20. Other amusements at the club include karaoke, a gym, pool tables, bar and cold noodles, and the possible company of Chinese and Russian ship crews.

A frequent listing is a tour of a primary school where the children put on a show. Passing the spinning rocket ride and Ferris wheel in the playground and the gaudy painted fruits and images of Taedonggang rockets on the wall is a room dominated by a large model of where the Eternal President grew up, surrounded by little chairs. After that visitors are treated to a technically excellent show of song and dance, with numbers from traditional Korean folklore to jazzy guitar and classical cello sets, performed by children in amazing outfits of billowing blouses and brilliant silver-sequinned jackets. Rewards for the performers can be bought from the Tourist Hotel shop, well supplied as it is with confectionary, ceramic souvenirs and car parts.

CHILBOSAN 칠보산

Chongjin is the nearest city to the real jewels in the crown of north Hamgyong's coast: Chilbosan, or the **Chilbo Mountains**. The name Chilbo means 'seven buried treasures', which must include the magma that made the area. It's a volcanic area formed one million years ago from lava blasting out of the nearby Paektu and Hamgyong ranges, and such activity has been recorded as late as the 3rd and 4th centuries AD. The igneous rock that structures the area has been carved by wind and rain into the most fantastic peaks and valleys, with suspended rocks hanging over vertiginous hillsides, and these scars in the earth's crust seep spa water but are healed with the greenery that the rich soil and diverse climate support. In a similar way to Mount Kumgang, Chilbo is divided into three districts, Inner, Outer and Sea, covering 250km² and lorded over by the 1,103m Sangmae Peak – although the peak securing the most attention is Chonbul Peak at 659m.

From Chongjin to Chilbosan is a long and dusty ride south, at least four hours, along a pot-holed road that snakes across river plains of paddies, then ascends into the hills, verges lined with purple cosmo flowers, pounding through orderly villages dominated by grand Party buildings and immortal towers, towns marked by murals and hillsides strapped with slogans. For all the familiarity of the décor, however, this is the North Korean outback, or that's how the guides from Pyongyang sometimes see it.

A stopping point some 2½ hours in comes at the brow of a hill where there is a concrete car ramp for fixing bust vehicles and a poster suggesting everyone should plant trees. Innumerable compact collections of cottages flit past until around three hours the road rises and you're looking at rock face one side or across deep, heavily foliaged ravines the other, there being few enough people in these parts to have left the trees standing. Many increasingly tight turns and desperate feats of braking later, and you're in the heart of Chilbosan, where the locals are notably friendly in this fabulously pristine environment.

WILDLIFE Sea, fresh water, deep ravines, dense forests and barren, lofty pinnacles offer ideal habitats across the spectrum of fauna. Of 250 known species, wild boar, black long-haired pigs, leopards, wildcats, mountain squirrels and ground squirrel vie for space among the pine, azalea and maple trees alongside roe deer, bears, badgers, weasels and hedgehogs. A hundred bird species have been identified as

Northernmost Corner CHILBOSAN

All over the countryside are huge slogans carved with massive characters along hillsides, ridges and in fields that usually end in an exclamation mark, and it passes the time to get translations off the guides. A selection is as follows: Long live the great Juche idea! Let us learn by example from Kim Jong Il's patriotism! Let us carry out the last instruction of Kim Il Sung! Let's turn out as one to build a prosperous country! Let us safeguard the respected leader Kim Jong Un at the cost of our own lives!

In 2013 the slogans around Paektusan mostly related to Kim Jong Il, whereas around Chongjin they were about Kim Jong Un. Does this mean some Party units are more forward-looking than others?

resident to the area, with scores more migrating by the season, including nuthatch, tree-creeper, coal tit, great tit, marsh tit, long-tailed tit, golden crest, rose finch, blue magpie, hazel grouse, wrens, pheasants, magpies, carrion crows, turtle doves, jays, eagles, sparrowhawks, kestrels, blue tails, hawk owls, wagtails (pied and grey), starlings, red-tailed thrushes, Baer's pochard and Oriental storks. Stickleback, dace and loach start the list of a score of fish species found in Chilbo's waters.

GETTING THERE AND AWAY Chilbosan is at least four hours' drive by tourist bus or tour car from Chongjin or three hours from Orang.

WHERE TO STAY The **Chilbosan Hotel ($$)** is a single-storey collation of villas in the thick of the inner Chilbo valleys. It doesn't have much electricity but it's serviceable and where US tourists get billeted. Set a short way from Pochon-ri Beach is a newly built village of '**homestays**' **($$)**, two-storey homes in which guests stay and spend an evening conversing with their hosts, so have a phrasebook and soju (and some other offering) handy! A large wall switch turns off the *ondol* floor heating so you don't bake at night, and unfortunately sneaking down to the beach after dark isn't on. These houses are above the normal standard of living, but they're homes nonetheless and you are guests. The area receives WFP aid, which says a lot about why they'd want to put up random strangers in their house, and the accommodation is pre-arranged as part of tours. Americans can't stay at the homestays and will probably be billeted at the Chilbosan Hotel.

WHAT TO SEE AND DO Chilbo itself is a triangular mass of rocky hills and outcrops that fan out to the sea. Chilbo Peak is shrouded in a flowing cloak of volcanic ridges, valleys and peaks that face seaward. Good long walks are arrangeable, but not mountain climbing. It is also possible to get to a thermal spa in the Chilbo Mountains. Of the three districts, Inner Chilbo is the furthest pocket from the sea and, it seems, has the most sites to offer.

Inner Chilbo Stumpy mountain ranges of red and brown sandstone, resembling the finer points of the Grand Canyon, tower up out of valleys held together by forests of evergreen pine trees, tender azaleas and maples and make Inner Chilbo a truly spectacular place to spend an afternoon or some days. Seek out the bizarre cluster of mushrooms that constitutes Pae Rock, and the samples of streamlined strata held aloft on Nongbu Rock, looked down on by craggy Kumgang Rock. Suri Peak is frozen mid-launch from a silo of trees, Pubu Rock is a gallery of stone monks. Thajong and Hwaebul rocks are the mace and axe-shaped formations that dominate their locale.

The main non-natural site in these parts is **Kaesim Temple** on Mount Pothak, located about 1½km up from the turning where a mural commemorates Kim Jong Il. Built in 826, the temple is notable for being one of the few sites that dates from the Palhae dynasty. It comprises the Taeung Hall, Hyangdo Pavilion, east and west monasteries and Sansin Pavilion, containing much original artwork, centuries' old Buddha statues and amazing dragons in the pavilion's eaves since its reconstruction in 1784, from when dates the temple's bronze bell and the chestnut tree that grows in front of the temple. The surrounding hill in which the temple is nestled, shielded from the wind but never in shadow, is described by those in monk's garb as 'feminine', and there is a large wooden pestle-and-mortar creature that 'helps with fertility', upon which a woman may sit but at risk of sliding down its polished bum and onto its tail (apparently a Russian visitor tried this). Whether this anecdote was related to Kim Jong Il in his visits in 1996 and 2001 isn't known.

Outer Chilbo   Inner Chilbo is cupped from the ravages of the sea by the fortress hills of Outer Chilbo. The finest area is the Manmulsang district, with its dense forests crowding over its congregation of waterfalls and pools. On the trekking trails keep a lookout for the lofty Samson rocks and the military precision of the Chonyu Rock. A finger of rock just touches an opposite pillar to make Kangson Gate, through which can be seen the Sea of Chilbo.

Sea of Chilbo   Hwangjin-ri is a village at the northern end of the Sea of Chilbo, and sits in the shadow of Chonyu Rock, guarding the entrance to Hwangjin Valley where the Hwangjin Spa Sanatorium is located. Pochon, Onsupyong and Taho are other **spa sites** located around Chilbo. A path stretches southwards along the Chilbo coast for about 30km, starting in Hwangjin-ri. The attractions of hermitages and strange rock formations flank the path as it picks through the villages of Pochon-ri, Phoha-ri and Mokjin-ri. These villages are the hubs of the local farms visible from inside Chilbo, and the local people are seemingly steeped in a very traditional rural life.

Going south from Hwangjin, the path passes the rocky outcrop with the Sinbu Hermitage, adjacent to Sol Islet. A few kilometres to the south is another raft of rocks with the Tongmun Hermitage and Pochon-ri. Following the river east inland takes you to Inner Chilbo, but a rivulet goes north to Nojok Peak, and the Chotjik and Ryukdan waterfalls descend a worn staircase of rock, between evergreen pine trees holding onto sheer cliffs. Back on the path going south, look for Mujigae Rock and Tal Gate on the way to Phoha-ri, some hours' walk away. Beyond Phoha-ri on the coast appears the dramatic Khokkiri Rock and before the bizarre Unmandae Cape is Roga Valley. In here is a series of waterfalls, and this crevice, effectively the southernmost feature of the Sea of Chilbo, is itself worth an afternoon's scouting and the beautiful scenery of the curious rocks in the Sea of Chilbo throws visitors into a trance. It is unlikely you will be going far south of the Chilbosan area, however. On the coastal outcrop down that way is the missile-testing zone where the KPA has tested and launched its infamous Taepodong missiles, and east of Chilbosan National Park is where some big bangs have been heard coming from deep beneath the ground. It says a lot about the area's remoteness. There's a lovely beach to stroll along and possibly have a beach party.

One thing to note for visitors billeted at the Chilbosan Hotel is that while it's only about 12km by road from there to the beach and a few more to the homestays, if you're thinking of toing and froing it's still a long drive along tight roads that are pitch black at night, and probably at the end of a far longer and tortuous drive. Consider the driver.

RAJIN 라진 AND SONBONG 선봉, COLLECTIVELY KNOWN AS RASON 라선

42°20'24"N 130°23'23"E (Rajin); 42°21'N 130°24'E (Sonbong); North Hamgyong Province, bordering China and Russia

North from Chongjin along the coast – and now accessible by road from that city – is the DPRK's northeastern-most corner where lie the two cities of Rajin and Sonbong, cities whose names have been collectively wed to name the area **Rason Free Trade Zone**. This is frontier country in many senses: as the area where the DPRK has borders with China and Russia; as a Special Economic Zone, it's a somewhat autonomously-run enclave of development and experiment for capitalist – and foreign – ways of doing business; for the contrast between the industrial developments and the still beautifully pristine natural landscapes in and around the zone; and that so, so few Westerners visit here at all. The area's distance from Pyongyang and the different ways of doing things amid swathes of untouched land give this place a unique frisson.

The 750km² Rason area was dedicated in 1991 as a foreign investment zone and prospective hub of investment, industry and export by road, rail and sea to Russia, China and wherever the Pacific can take it. Two-thirds of the region's people inhabit Rajin and Sonbong, many working in Rajin's general trade port, Sonbong's oil processing refineries and the iron, magnesium, uranium and ceramics industries on the cities' outskirts. Since its inception, the bias has been more to promote the area for industry instead of tourism, but the zone's development has taken time. Doing business with the DPRK is a fine art, and the forested hills and wetlands, lakes and the Tuman River delta within the Rason Zone still host such an abundance of wildlife. The 150km-long coast running down to Mount Chilbo chops from stretches of sandy beaches in lazy bays to dramatic cliffs and rock outlets engineered by Vulcan, the Roman god of fire. Winter along this part of Korea's East Sea is cold and windy and temperatures can fall to -10°C, while August peaks the summer's warmth at 25°C.

For now, Rajin is not an unpleasant town. Its wide tree-lined boulevards are well kept and, like the buildings, it's all well lit at night and everything is on a human scale. Over the years there have been many carloads of investors brought in to discuss theories, plans and maps to point at regarding Rason's development, and there is a fantastic, almost ethereal computer graphic video on NKEconomy Watch (*www.nkeconwatch.com*) outlining the most amazing plans for the city's redevelopment. But one wonders if sooner rather than later the zone may come into its own, and its current not inconsiderable accompaniment of 150 companies from 20 countries could soon seem like small fry.

As of 2013, the Russians are working on completing a 54km rail link down via Khasan to Rajin as part of a bigger plan to link the Trans-Siberian railway to a Trans-Korea line down to South Korea. This would take goods from both Koreas, Japan and China (these east Asian countries producing a quarter of the world's GDP) all the way to Europe via Russia, in a third of the time it takes by ship via the storm-laden waters of the Indian Ocean, the pirates off Somalia, and the Suez Canal under a tumultuous Egypt. Russia also seeks to pipe gas and ship coal to both Koreas, while the ROK and Russia have their own plans to build a large industrial and chemical complex and zone in Rason. Russia's border with the DPRK comes from its purchase of the coastal strip off China in 1860, a deal that cut China off from the coast in this region – and China's northeast industries need a seaport to export from (coal from Jilin already exports through Rason). So it's Chinese money that's rebuilt the bridge from Wonjong and it could be billions more in dollars from China that expand Rajin's port cargo capacity from three million tonnes per annum to 100 million tonnes by 2030.

The area's population may have grown fivefold to one million by then, including not a few score thousand Chinese. Tourism is also being beefed up and will benefit from better road and rail links. A regular rail link has been plotted from Rajin to Mount Paektu, taking travellers coming in on cruise ships from the ROK's Sokcho (to name but one source of tourists), and avoiding the long-winded, multi-visa ROK–Russia–China route. But don't hold your breath.

WILDLIFE Before the world goes mad in Rason, though, there's much wildlife to savour. The variety of the landscape, with its forested hills falling into the sea and the Tuman River delta wetlands, makes it home to a similarly wide variety of waterfowl and migratory birds; the area is considered by experts as a key staging post in this part of Asia for long-range birds. At the northern end of Rason is a series of shallow lagoons, including Korea's largest, the 1m-deep, 41km-round **Lagoon Sonbong**. These are home to tens of thousands of ducks, while crane types known around here are red-crowned, white-naped, Siberian and hooded. Baikal teal and Baer's pochard breed here, too.

In Rason Bay is the **Al Some (Egg Island) Bird Sanctuary**, which is the main home for 100,000 seabirds, including Temminck's cormorants, common and spectacled guillemots, ancient murrelets and white-winged scoter. Other birds spotted in these parts include widgeons, tufted ducks, gargany, common teal, mallard, pintail, shovelers, mandarin duck, grey and white heron, snipe, dusty redshanks, sandpipers, quail, pheasant, harrier, osprey, kite, sparrowhawks, tit-larks, wagtails, skylarks, and eagle owl, red-throated and arctic divers, black and red-necked grebes, and many types of egret and goose. A comprehensive guide to the birdlife of the Rason zone, by Dr Philip Edwards, Nicholas Pertwee and Peter Garland, is printed in the *Journal of the Korean Ornithological Society*. Also in Sonbong Bay is the **Uam Seal Sanctuary**, reachable by boat.

Up in the Rason hills dwell bear, wild boar, racoon, fox and musk rat, ground squirrels and hare. Two-thirds of Rason's surrounding land is forested hills and mountains, on which grow Korean pine, larch, oak, maple, fir, spruce and birch, although local needs for firewood have had a notable effect on the forests.

GETTING THERE AND AWAY International tourists need a letter of invitation to visit Rason – not technically a visa, but still requiring a process of application from the Rason City Tourism Administration (minimum three days' processing), together with a passport valid for one year after entry to the Rajin-Sonbong Zone, emailed copies of relevant passport pages, a curriculum vitae with contact details, and an itinerary. But for all of that you get a DPRK stamp on the paper (unless you're American or Japanese).

The most practical way to get to Rason is by road from China, on tours either by bus or in 4x4s, organised by your hosts, be they a tourist company or prospective business partner. The Quanhe/Wonjong Bridge across the Tuman River in Wonjong is in the zone's northwestern corner. It's three hours by car from Yanji to Quanhe, and 90 minutes' drive from Wonjong to Rajin. In early 2013 the option of coming

10

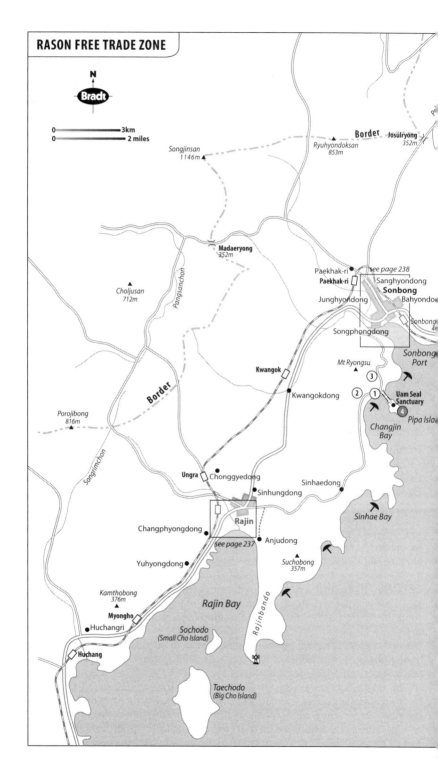

RASON FREE TRADE ZONE

N

Bradt

0 ———— 3km
0 ———— 2 miles

Songjinsan
1146m ▲

Border Josülryong
352m

Ryuhyondoksan
853m ▲

Madaeryong
352m ▲

Paekhak-ri ●   *see page 238*
Paekhak-ri ☐   Sanghyondong
            Sonbong
Junghyondong   Bahyondo●

Choljusan
712m ▲

Pangsanchon

Songphongdong   *Sonbong*
                4

Sonbong
Port

Mt Ryongsu
Kwangok ☐   ③

Border   Kwangokdong   ② ① **Uam Seal**
                    Sanctuary
Porojibong   ④
816m ▲   *Pipa Isla*
                Changjin
                Bay

Songrimchon

Ungra ☐ Chonggyedong   Sinhaedong ●

            Sinhungdong
                    Sinhae Bay

        Rajin

Changphyongdong ●   *see page 237*   Anjudong ●

Yuhyongdong ●   *Suchobong*
                357m ▲

Kamthobong   *Rajin Bay*
376m ▲   *Rajinbando*

Myongho ☐
● Huchangri

☐ **Huchang**

            Sochodo
            (Small Cho Island)

            Taechodo
            (Big Cho Island)

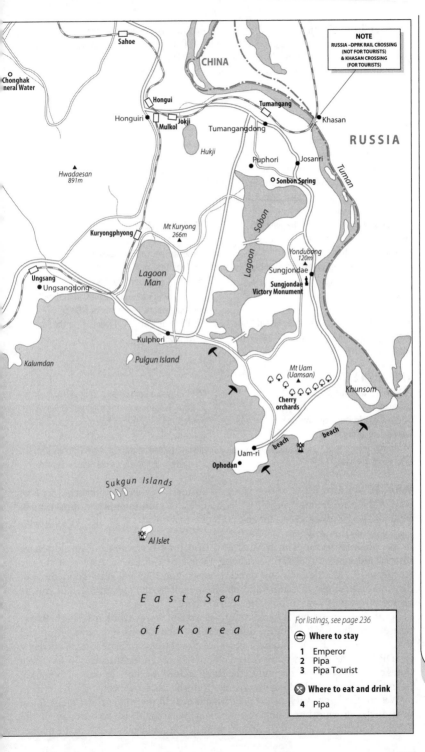

NOTE
RUSSIA –DPRK RAIL CROSSING
(NOT FOR TOURISTS)
& KHASAN CROSSING
(FOR TOURISTS)

CHINA

RUSSIA

Sahoe

Chonghak
neral Water

Hongui

Honguiri
Mulkol
Jokji

Tumangang

Khasan

Tumangangdong

Hukji

Puphori

Josanri

Sonbon Spring

Tuman

Hwadaesan
891m

Sobon

Mt Kuryong
266m

Kuryongphyong

Lagoon

Yondubong
120m

Sungjondae

Lagoon
Man

Sungjondae
Victory Monument

Ungsang
Ungsangdong

Kulphori

Pulgun Island

Mt Uam
(Uamsan)

Khunsom

Kalumdan

Cherry
orchards

beach

beach

Uam-ri

Ophodan

Sukgun Islands

Al Islet

East Sea
of Korea

For listings, see page 236

🏠 Where to stay

1   Emperor
2   Pipa
3   Pipa Tourist

❌ Where to eat and drink

4   Pipa

10

to Rason from Chongjin arose, which is a distance of around 95km by road down the coast. Chongjin is now accessible by train from Pyongyang via Wonsan, or by plane to Orang airport and then bus (see page 228).

In summer, a charter train runs from China's Tuman city to Rajin (currently for Chinese tourists only). Travellers can also get the train from Khasan in Russia to Tumangang and then be driven to Rason.

🏠 **WHERE TO STAY** Rason's tourism facilities are being revamped by the DPRK and Yanbian region's tourist authorities, helping to guide welcome investment into restaurants, hotels and taxi services. Aside from the below options, there is also the **Chu Jin Hotel** right on the beach with a great restaurant offering seafood plus a bar and billiards. The five-star **Emperor Hotel** is on the Pipa Beach and island resort, midway-ish between Rajin and Sonbong.

🏠 **Dongmingsan Hotel** On the peninsula, southeast of Rajin. A new Chinese hotel with a great view of the bay. **$$$**

🏠 **Rajin Hotel** (98 rooms) Large, white, modern building on eastern shore of Rajin Bay. Karaoke, sauna, massage, pool tables, revolving restaurant. **$$$**

🏠 **Pipa Hotel** (36 rooms) At the foot of Mount Ryongsu. Hotel with 4 guesthouses. Karaoke. Low level, quite pretty. **$$**

🏠 **Namsan Hotel** (30 rooms) In the heart of Rajin on the city square. Clean, originally built to house Japanese officers. **$$–$**

🏠 **Pipa Tourist Hotel** On the seashore near the Pipa Hotel. Can sleep 200. **$$–$**

🏠 **Sonbong Hotel** (52 rooms) In the heart of Sonbong County. Grey barracks. **$$–$**

🏠 **Uamsan Hotel** (24 rooms) Near the Sonbong Hotel. **$$–$**

✖ **WHERE TO EAT AND DRINK**

✖ **KITC Restaurant** Opposite the Foreign Language bookshop.

✖ **New World** Russian-signed restaurant with a few Russian dishes.

✖ **Mongolian Hotpot** Guests can stir-fry their food over a hotplate.

✖ **Phalgyong Restaurant** Central Rajin

✖ **Pipa Restaurant** On the far side of Pipa Islet, overlooking the bay. Pipa Islet connects by a bridge to the mainland. The restaurant is known for grilling seafood food at the table. Octopus soup is a speciality round here – do not refuse if served.

WHAT TO SEE AND DO Rason's business is business. Beyond the inevitable array of sites of the 'Kim Il Sung Was Here' ilk, manifest in **monuments** and **museums** in both cities, visitors can see a lot else going on that departs from the revolutionary way of doing things.

Just adjacent to the **Kim Il Sung and Kim Jong Il statues** and revolutionary history museum is the **Rajin-Sonbong House of Culture**, a 1,500-seat theatre frequented by martial arts and dance troupes, and they put on a good show of displays, folk songs, marching and children exulting the joys of life, and can be visited on arrangement through the tourist board.

South from the statues is Rajin's impressive seven-storey **Golden Triangle Bank,** where they pour forth about the differences between Rason's economic set-up and that of the rest of the DPRK, and visitors are also able to exchange foreign currency for DPRK won, the only place in the country they can legitimately do so. These notes can then be spent on a visit to the **Rajin indoor market**, the only such market open to foreigners and selling everything from clams to spanners.

West of the bank is Rajin's art gallery, and next to the stadium is a greenhouse dedicated to growing kimilsungia flowers, which one could visit before taking in the Foreign Language School. If these don't appeal, one could get food from the market

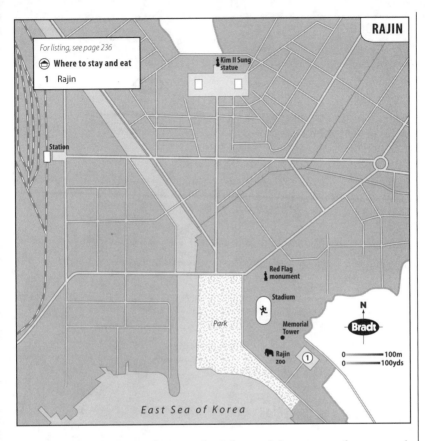

For listing, see page 236

⊖ **Where to stay and eat**
1 Rajin

Kim Il Sung statue

Station

Red Flag monument

Stadium

Park

Memorial Tower

Rajin zoo

N

Bradt

0 ———— 100m
0 ———— 100yds

East Sea of Korea

and books from the **foreign language bookshop** and then get out of town to seek **slogan-bearing trees** on a hike around **Shahyangsan** ('Musk deer mountain') or to visit the revolutionary **Haeyang Village** and visit a farmer's house. Or go picnic along the bays and islands of Rason's coast. Probably not unfortunately, the city's zoo is gone, while in its place is now an international communications centre and foreigners' clinic and a small casino. The area is also blessed with beaches and capes that are clean and clear locations to relax along, with all forms of watersports, and the whole Rason area is fenced in by a series of hills. Rajin's beaches include the headland to Taecho Island, Chujin, Sinhae-ri and Pipa Islet. Going on a boat to see the seals of Pipa is CNY100 extra.

Rason is an industrial and enterprise zone open to foreign interests, and not only can the city's main cargo port be visited, but so can several factories, including **Taehung Trading Company's seafood processing factory**, located in a bay about 7.5km due northeast of Rajin city. This is quite a substantial self-contained complex, big enough for its own **Immortal Tower** and **Kim Il Sung Study Centre**, that somehow relate to the seafood hauled directly out of rusted boats at the pier or massive water tanks of molluscs, all being gutted, filleted and shelled in large halls of pink-clad women, and dispatched by truck. Try and sample some of the mushroom plant produced at the plant. In these parts is the less productive US–Korean joint-venture **shoe factory**, and less of a drag is the **Sinhung cigarette factory**.

10

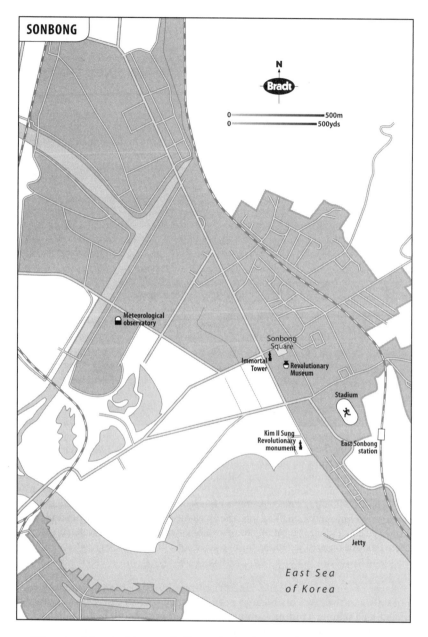

SONBONG

N
Bradt

0 ———————— 500m
0 ———————— 500yds

Meteorological
observatory

Sonbong
Square

Immortal
Tower

Revolutionary
Museum

Stadium

Kim Il Sung
Revolutionary
monument

East Sonbong
station

Jetty

*East Sea
of Korea*

Of greater historical interest in Rason is the **Sungjondae Victory Monument** to General Ri Song Sin, the builder of the Turtle ships that did so much to stymie the Japanese invaders of old. Further down the list of salubrious sites is the Great Cake that is the Emperor Hotel, which hosts the Haeyang ('Ocean') casino. This is where Chinese come to squander hundreds of millions of CNY a year on baccarat, roulette or slot machines, with Chinese government and Party officials among the none-too-sharps, and in 2005 it was closed amid a scandalous rumour that one big gun from Yanbian had blown nearly half a million dollars in public and borrowed funds, before going on the lag. Outrage brought down the house later that year, but it's since reopened.

On the way to Sonbong, you can see the vast, disused **Sungri Chemical Complex**, which sits about halfway between the town and Rajin, opposite Kwangokdong station. In Sonbong itself, highlights include the **Sonbong Kindergarten**, where robust toddlers, brought up amid artwork of woodland animals garbed in khaki filling imperialists full of lead and statues in a garden of tanks, give shows exulting the virtues of all things revolutionary. Otherwise some conversation and sports' activity may be had in a trip to Sonbong **Middle School**.

Dominating the skyline down by the docks is the never-used **June 16 Thermal Power Station**, notable for having been built to burn the heavy fuel oil promised by the US under the KEDO programme (see page 40), which sought to dismantle the DPRK's nuclear plants in return first for fuel oil and then for light water reactors. None of it came to pass. A Chinese-owned **Sonbong textile factory** (things have moved on such that China is outsourcing its textiles manufacturing) has rows and rows of North Korean seamstresses brrring and buzzing away on their flower-adorned sewing stations, working 'without a rest' as the posters say, producing items of attire by the million that are magically labelled 'Made in China'. Aside from the **meteorological observatory** that no-one visits, Sonbong port has a **revolutionary site** dedicated to a visit by Kim Il Sung. And there's a **revolutionary museum** too.

Sonbong has Unsang and, right on the final eastern-most tip of the DPRK's north coast, the village of Uam-ri. From Uam-ri it's easy to access the cherry orchards surrounding the base of Mount Uam, the northernmost hill in Rason's natural frontier. Mount Uam is flanked by the Korean East Sea and the wetland lagoons of the Tuman River, in which the ancient Kulpho ruins are found. Those of a more spiritual inclination may want to look up the goat farm in Rason that was founded by Krahun Tours, a Yanji-based company that forays into the area, but that's up to visitors to arrange with them.

Beyond Sonbong, a road runs from Uam along the Tuman River to other historic fortresses in the town of **Tumangang** 두만강, situated right where the borders of the DPRK, China and Russia meet, and one of the handful of land-crossing points into North Korea. From this town one can view Russia and China, and continue north along the river until you arrive in the sweet briar fields and jigsaw river bends around **Wonjong** (where Kenneth Bae came unstuck; see page 193), 25km due north of Sonbong, another land-crossing point, with more and more Chinese visitors (among others) trundling across the renovated bridge into the Rason area.

HOERYONG 회령

42°26'N 129°45'E, North Hamgyong province
One of the very, very few overland points that Westerners are able to cross and probe into the DPRK is Namyang 남양, North Hamgyong, just over the Tuman River from China's Jilin Province. Crossing the long, lonely bridge over the river had for a long time only been open to Chinese and Korean traders, but as more Chinese tourists have come across on day trips, now Westerners can come too, with their likely destination being Hoeryong town.

From Namyang's passport and customs control, it's a 20-minute drive into Onsong County to the beflamed obelisk and sculptures that comprise the Wangjaesan Monument. This was built in 1975 on the 40th anniversary of the

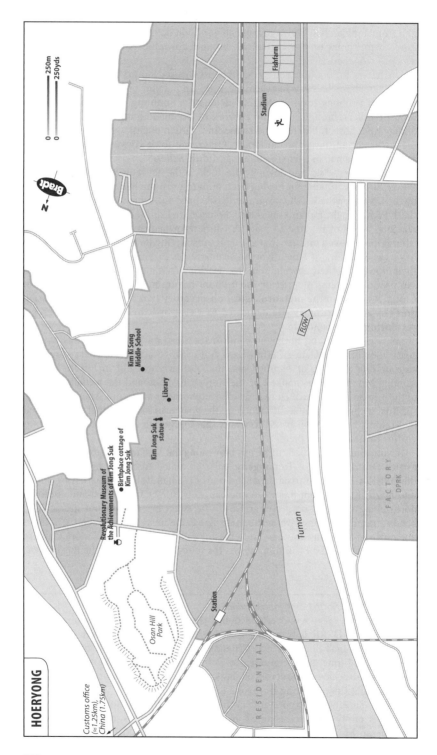

HOERYONG

Customs office
(=1.25km),
China (1.75km)

Revolutionary Museum of
the Achievements of Kim Jong Suk
Birthplace cottage of
Kim Jong Suk

Osan Hill
Park

Kim Jong Suk
statue

library

Kim Ki Song
Middle School

Station

RESIDENTIAL

Tuman

FLOW

FACTORY
DPRK

Stadium

Fishfarm

N

Bradt

0   250m
0   250yds

240

Kim Jong Suk was the first wife of Kim Il Sung, the mother of Kim Jong Il and his siblings, the third of the departed Kims, and she has had an increasingly raised profile in recent years. She's presented as the 'sacred mother of the revolution' and 'Mother of Paektu', a maternal, proto-feminist figure, equally adept in the political wheeling and dealing of pre-war Korea and providing counsel to Kim Il Sung as in preparing great meals for his allies, as well as being able to ride horses, sew, shoot and engage in guerrilla warfare with vigour. Sometimes all such traits are shown at once – Pyongyang's railway museum has a mural depicting her in the snowy forests of Paektusan, firing a pistol at Japanese troops while holding the toddler Kim Jong Il to her breast.

She was officially born on 24 December 1917 in Hoeryong 'into a patriotic and revolutionary family', as KCNA says, with a childhood defined by hard farming graft, murderous injustice at the hands of the Japanese and fighting back with ardour. 'She had to learn to pick herbs, glean and weed with a hoe, the handle of which was stained with her mother's sweat.' A landowner enslaved her sister and beat up and evicted Kim Jong Suk and her mother. They followed her penurious father to Manchuria, where he died, and her mother and brother died brutal deaths at the hands of the Japanese, the latter dying heroically to protect 'Kim Il Sung's Juche-oriented revolutionary line'. Suk had already taken inspiration via nocturnal study from Kim Il Sung's words, and joining the Children's Vanguard she opted not the stooge liquidation or slogan-shouting squads, but instead specialised in propaganda and inciting Koreans to rise up against the Japanese imperialists. She progressed to becoming a hardened guerrilla soldier, joining Kim Il Sung's partisans and working with the Great Leader, a slow romance burning away, while engaging in spying and scouting missions before being captured by the Japanese and incarcerated for 18 gruelling months. Released in 1937, and resuming her soldiering, she married Kim Il Sung in 1940, fighting, bearing children and running camp until liberation in 1945.

There are many tales told and sung of her life and deeds, eg: in the anthology *Mother and Song* or the Foreign Languages Publishing House's book *Kim Jong Suk Biography* which tells of an inspection she made in 1947 to the Pyongyang Silk Mill, where the workers, including young girls, toiled without protection in mightily dangerous conditions. In empathy with a young girl she was consoling for her sorry plight, Kim thrust her hands into the 80°C waters used for boiling cocoons, then scolded officials that the liberation was supposed to have ended this kind of skin-shredding work. She ordered them to start taking an interest in the welfare of the orphans working there, and as for the Japanese-era barbed wire around the plant, 'We fought tenaciously in the mountains in order to pull down such fetters as that fence, didn't we! Let us throw away the barbed wire and pull down the fences to treat the aching wounds in the hearts of our women.' Her husband duly followed just days later to give on-the-spot guidance at the factory and provide various sundries, suggesting she'd put a flea in his ear as well.

She died on 22 September 1949 due to complications from childbirth, and it is her grave in Pyongyang's Revolutionary Martyrs' Cemetery that is given pride of place. Many women's organisations celebrate her birthday and on that day North Koreans visit her grave.

Wangjaesan Conference, whence Kim Il Sung advanced his guerrilla force into Korea to fight occupying Japanese troops, and the monument is flanked by smaller sculptures depicting anti-Japanese guerrillas and their supporters, many of whom came from nearby Onsong town.

Driving for another 90 minutes from there along a winding, hilly road, snow-covered for as long as it's cold, closely tracking the Tuman River border between the DPRK and China (still within mobile phone range!), one eventually arrives in the riverside slab of a town that is Hoeryong. The city was founded as one of six fortress towns in the 15th century by King Sejong the Great to defend against the Jurchen in China, then over the years became better known for its assets listed as the 'Three Beautifuls' – beautiful women, beautiful apricots and beautiful earthenware, before the industries of mining, machinery and paper added themselves to that alluring roster. Since the late noughties (it was designated as a model city in 2009) it's also involved tourism (principally for Chinese tourists coming over the bridge from Sanhe town, right across the river), with military construction units upgrading the railway station and building apartment blocks, commercial premises and a food court, constructed on Kim Jong Il's order to provide 'high quality dishes at reasonable prices' – although at first, reasonable proved at odds with the ability to cover costs and stay in business. Prices are now reasonably many times what they were.

WHAT TO SEE AND DO There's a grand view of the city and China from the heights of **Osan Hill Park**, and the **Kim Ki Song Middle School** has a room filled with stuffed animals donated by the leaders over the years. Kim Ki Song was the brother of Kim Jong Suk, the first wife of Kim Il Sung and the mother of Kim Jong Il, his brother Kim Pyong Il and sister Kim Kyong Hui (widow of Jang Song Thaek). Hoeryong is Kim Jong Suk's place of birth and this is what marks the town on the tourist trail, and why it's a **bronze statue** of her that dominates the town, flanked by a **library**, and very like Mangyongdae in Pyongyang, her **birthplace cottage** is preserved and can be visited, as well as the **Revolutionary Museum of the Achievements of Kim Jong Suk**.

11

Mount Paektu/
Paektusan 백두산

42°N, 128°E; in the northwestern part of Samjiyon County,
Ryanggang (two rivers) Province, the border with China. Northern end of Paektu range.
Janggan Peak on Mount Paektu reaches 2,750m above sea level. For a map of the region
see pages 224–5.

The Tuman and Yalu rivers dividing Korea and China source from one mountain, Mount Paektu. This volcanic mass of frozen lava smashed out from the wide, elevated planes of dense forest and bogs surrounding it over a million years ago, and has a powerful spiritual symbolism for the Korean people, as indicated in the local tourist literature:

> When children begin to study language, they are taught to sing song of Mount Paektu and when they begin to draw a picture, they make a picture of the spirit of Mount Paektu. When they attain the age of discretion, they visit Mount Paektu, because they know their real mind by reflecting it on Lake Chon and when their hair turns grey, they climb Mount Paektu with a desire to be reborn as a youth and live a long life. Those that leave the motherland in a state of sorrow for lack of a nation return to visit Mount Paektu first of all.

Paektu is the backdrop for many of the almighty mosaics and paintings seen across Korea, and its significance for all Koreans is evinced by the dominance of South Koreans in the thriving tourist industry on the Chinese side of the mountain. Paektusan means 'white-topped mountain', as it's streaked in pumice and usually crowned with snow. It sits in an extensive lava area of its own doing, and hasn't stopped adding to it.

There was a massive eruption in AD940. Pumice showered the area and lava flowed many times in the 12th century; the last known eruption was in 1903. In 2002 to 2005 there were concerns about another eruption, as seismicity picked up and the volcano inflated. Many feared it would go off, impacting the Chinese and Korean economies (it's also only 70km from the DPRK's underground nuclear test site, and as those blasts increase in size, so do concerns that one of them will set off the volcano). Those rumblings came to naught, but a positive development is greater international volcanic co-operation, as in 2013 when US–UK scientists were deployed to Paektu to work with Korean scientists in assessing the volcano's mood.

The harsh terrain around the mountain, high barren rock beset by bitter winters, its remoteness, and not least its propensity still to go off, have meant Paektu's environs have remained sparsely populated and sparsely defended for centuries; across its porous border cattle herders, trappers, hunters and loggers pass back and forth. These occupations survive today alongside the slither of a tourist industry that accommodates 'tens of thousands every year' and activities and jaunts by KPA units. The locals are also exceedingly friendly and warm, highly welcome in such beautifully serene desolation.

Koreans once believed that dire punishment befell anyone intruding on the seclusion of the resident spirit, as Captain Cavendish's companion H E Goold-Adams found out when hunting on the lower slopes in the 1880s:

> Before we could sit down to our magnificent repast, the spirit whose domain we were invading had to be propriated; for this purpose rice had been brought (otherwise difficult to cook properly at altitude). A miserable little pinch was cooked, spread out on the trunk of a fallen tree, and allowed to remain there for a quarter of an hour or so until half cold; my men in the meantime (though professed Buddhists) standing in front, muttering, shaking their hands in the Chinese fashion, and now and then expectorating. Their incantations finished, the rice was brought back to the fireside and solemnly eaten. They explained to me that the spirit being such, could not eat rice, and only required the smell, so there could be no harm in their consuming this tiny luxury ... At a later juncture I had to fire both barrels of my shot-gun in the air to appease the spirit.

A more modern mythology has been built around the Great Leader's exploits here, for officially this is where he was based from 1937 to 1943. With mercurial powers, he led his forces into thousands of victorious battles against the Japanese at '200-ri at a stretch to annihilate the Japanese punitive troops and mowed down all the enemy force', a feat the enemy thought only possible through 'the art of land contraction'. Another time before the liberation the Japanese forces surrounded the mountain where hid a small KPA unit led by Kim Il Sung. A ferocious battle raged all night but, next day, only dead Japanese were found, and not one single guerrilla. The Japanese had been fighting among themselves! This positively spooky occurrence finally scared all the Japanese away. Numerous secret camps and battlegrounds have been rediscovered since the 1970s, with more sites being found all the time, and are on public show. For all the mythologising, Kim Il Sung's book *With the Century* provides a much more down-to-earth account of the years of battling the Japanese around Paektu, and is a good insight into the lives and livelihoods and turmoil of life at war with the colonial power during the appallingly desperate period during the 1920s and 1930s.

The average temperature on the mountain is -8°C, the highest being 18°C and the lowest recorded -47°C; Korea's coldest area. The weather changes quickly, some say four times a day, others say four times an hour. The wind is always strong, as the Paektu range striding northwards into China provides the battleground for warm air from the mainland blowing into a barrage of cold. As a result, much of the flora has a distinctive 'blown' shape to it. The freeze begins in September and thaws from late May. Around 2,500mm of rain comes each year, mainly in July. Snow starts falling from early September until mid-June. The harshness of the weather effectively rules out any winter visits, although the scenery is at its most icily barren and empty then, but in spring and summer liquid emerald erupts from the hills and carries down currents of flowers, washing across the area's meadows and valleys.

Within Paektu's thorny crown of petrified lava is cupped the world's highest mountain lake, Lake Chon ('Heaven Lake'). Lake Chon used to be known as Ryongdam or Ryongwangthaek because dragons were thought to live there. Snips of alpine meadow and birch trees cling on to the sheer cliffs of young, crumbling pumice that make the crater like a marbled bowl, filled with an eerily blue water. Should a hurricane be raging around you, the absolute stillness and intense blueness of the lake in its grey-white bowl becomes even more prominent. The surface of Lake Chon is at 2,190m, covers an area of 9.16km², and has a depth of 384m, making it the deepest mountain lake in the world. Supplied by rain and underground springs, its volume is 1,955 million cubic metres. A local guidebook handily points out that should you ever try to empty Lake Chon, get a pump discharging faster than $1m^3$ per second, because that'll take 60 years. The lake's surface ice freezes to 4m thick, and its water temperature never rises above 6°C, so good luck to the hardy ones wading into it.

FLORA AND FAUNA

Broadleaf and needle-leaf forests smother the plains and valleys up to 2,000m, whereupon alpine grass then makes a belt around Paektusan. The road going up takes in a cross section of the different flora and fauna of rising altitude, from the temperate lowlands to the tundra highlands. Most of the species around the lake are thought to have arrived in the last 200 years – including Western hunters. Goold-Adams hunted for tigers reportedly over 4m in length, and leopards nearly 3m long. Not so long ago, every third or fourth village north of Wonsan would reportedly be under siege from tigers who took to raiding houses when snow covered their usual hunting grounds. Wild boar provided easier pickings, which the locals considered pests anyway as the boars snaffled their crops at night. Fauna seen here in more recent times have still included Korean tiger, leopard, lynx, wild boar, deer (including musk deer and Paektusan deer), and at Motojondo (about 50km north of Paektu on the Korean side) black and brown bear, moose, squirrel, field mouse, with wild pig, beaver and sable.

The landscape houses over 200 species of flora, including bracken, blueberry, *Abies nephrolepis*, and 20 species of edible wild vegetables. Blue oval berries (*Lonicera edulis*), evergreen rhododendron, lilies, white angelica, and a hundred or so medicinal plants thrive among the lowland birch and larch trees, and the treeline is finished off at its height by eastern Siberian and Khinghan fir. In the meadowlands are found trollius, blue-violet (*Veronica verticillata*), alpine papaver and red *Lychnis fulgens*. Spying the land from the sky are black cock, pheasant, nightjar, quail, broad-billed roller, black grouse, hazel grouse, woodpecker and hedge sparrow. Lake Samji has Samjian crucian carp, red carp and char carp.

GETTING THERE AND AWAY

Paektu is accessible only from May to September with any degree of reliability, and for most of the winter it is not accessible at all from the DPRK side.

Most visitors coming to Paektu from within the DPRK come by plane to the rudimentary Samjiyon airport, flying in from Pyongyang or Orang. Pyongyang to Paektu by prop takes one hour 40 minutes, by jet (in an other-era Tupolev 134), it takes 50 minutes.

Often the charter flight would be part of a bigger package taking in Chilbosan as well, the plane hopping over to Orang airport on the east side. The costs of a charter depend on the route taken and the size of the party, and by extension the size of the plane required. Trips by helicopter have been made in the past.

There may one day be more scheduled Pyongyang–Paektu flights if a plan goes ahead to have Chinese tourists enter the DPRK through the mountain area and then fly on to the capital. However, this is still just a plan.

North Koreans travel to Paektu by train, which from Pyongyang can take around 36 hours. While the railway system is opening up for foreigners' use, Paektusan is not yet on the itinerary.

The Chinese side of Paektu is comparatively more easily accessible (from China, naturally) and there are various means to do this under your own steam or on tours (see page 245). Note you still can't access the DPRK from China or vice versa anywhere around Paektusan.

 WHERE TO STAY

The **Pegaebong Hotel** (*130 rooms;* **$$$– $$**) is a large Swiss-style hotel at the base of Pegae peak 2km from Samjiyon town. From here it is a 90-minute or so drive to Paektu. This airy and spacious hotel has been spruced up and there's a corridor bar upstairs.

WHAT TO SEE AND DO

Getting to the mountain requires a drive that in itself makes the whole trip worthwhile: an ascent to the spiritual spring of Korea in a landscape like that at the beginning of the world.

Coming straight from the airport takes 90 minutes by a bus arranged by the tour operator, first through a tunnel of trees, then around the hour mark the trees thin out and then it's a glorious shallow ascending sweep of barren hills and rock, not so many centuries cooled since pouring out from the earth.

From a distance you see where the funicular railway ascends the mountain, ending close to a massive inscription by Kim Jong Il. There's a funicular railway that goes up to the rim of the caldera, costing €10 for a round trip (which should be already paid for), or it's a 30-minute hike to the rim. At the higher funicular terminus, time constraints on tours may mean there is the choice of hiking further up to the thorns of the crown, or going down to the water's edge of Lake Chon, the steep scree-ridden hillsides streaked with dark reds, browns, yellows and greys, all contrasting with the bluest water. Going down, one can hike or to save time visitors can take the Newton's Cradle cable cars for €5 each way. Going up, left from the terminus, past a large stone propaganda placard, affords greater views at the end of what's around a 15-minute hike, but those views are at risk of being obscured by passing clouds and beware any gusts taking you over the little chain fences. Bad visibility and high winds near big drops means punters beware and take care! But when all the glory of the crown and the lake are in view, it's utterly stunning, it's breathtaking to be in so remote, so beautiful a place where a new world is born from the land on the edge of the world.

Paektusan is the crown of the Paektu range, which loosk like a third-degree burn of rock with Chilbo at the southern end, so, like Chilbo, Paektu has many spas that, according to local sources, are 'full of ion'. Paektu Spa is 73°C, Paegam Spa is on Lake Chon's northern shore, mild at 46°C, while Jangbaek Spa, nearly boiling at up to 82°C, is 850m from Jangbaek Falls. A double rainbow often appears in front of Sangmujigae Peak (2,626m). The Paektu area can be seen as rectangular, moated in by the Yalu or Amnok River, the Tuman River and the Sobaek stream running south from the edge of the Tuman.

A very bumpy 24km drive downhill and through the trees is the Amnok River gorge at Chongun Rock, or '1,000 soldier rock', an incredible gulley of pillars, clefts and buttresses like some naturally sculpted cathedral. The road continues to barrel along through tight foliage hugging the hillsides of innumerable and beautiful valleys, until, with everyone suitably disorientated, you arrive in the midst of signposts here and there for the **Paektu secret camps**, starting with **Paektu Secret Camp No 1** hidden up Sobaeksu Valley, and shielded by steep-sided hills and peaks. This was, officially, Kim Il Sung's headquarters from 1936 to 1943, where he lived and held meetings with anti-Japanese guerrilla units and was the biggest of four camps in the area, but it was so secret that following the war the camp was lost and as soldiers who fought there died off, it was not rediscovered until 1986.

Here stands the house where the Great Leader expanded the Party and conducted the strategy of liberation. In Kim Jong Il's house of birth are toys made by soldiers and swaddling blankets made from donated uniforms. With its weapons' repair shop, hospital and publishing house among other buildings, this was evidently a veritable camp to hide out in. Putting to one side ideas that Kim Il Sung was actually based in Manchuria during that time, and going on to wondering if the good condition of the huts must be more than a miracle, as former editions of this book cynically thought... well it's not a miracle: they are mostly rebuilds as the guides admit. One of the first exhibits is the remains of a hearth, housed in a glass case, indicating whatever the origins of what was found here; it was indeed in a right state.

The camp is in the Sobaeksu Valley area, and the Sobaek stream runs through the camp, which has a few points from which visitors can drink its waters. All around are screened-off trees bearing slogans like 'our nation is the greatest nation in the world that gave birth to General Kim Il Sung' and 'Successor to General Kim Il Sung was born in Mount Paektu', written by Korean soldiers during the anti-Japanese struggle. More and more of these slogans are being discovered and preserved all the time in the valley. One interesting site is the house where Kim Jong Il was born, according to official lore, which conflicts with the version believed by the rest of the world that he was born in Khabarovsk. Word is that Kim Jong Il's birth was marked by a bright sunrise promising the completion of the revolutionary cause of Juche started by President Kim Il Sung, the glory of Korea and a source of greatest joy to the Korean people. Inheriting the blood of a patriotic and revolutionary family and receiving the soul of Mount Paektu, Kim Jong Il grew up to the sound of gunfire in the flames of the anti-Japanese war and the blizzards of Mount Paektu as his lullabies. Other revolutionary sites are pointed out by guides with local literature to regale you with, but the area's natural beauty makes it all worth it, including the 1,797m Kim Jong Il Peak, that sits exactly 216m behind his birth house (16 February (2/16) was Kim Jong Il's birthday! Now that's a miracle.). It was renamed in 1988 from its former moniker of General Peak, with the Dear Leader's name on it in massive, 100-tonne, red characters, 7m by 6.5m, that took months to install.

Another site in the environs of the camp is **Mount Kom** (Komsan), or 'bear mountain', a round, bulky mass covered in moss that staggers up to 1,860m. Four kilometres from Kom is Sonosan Secret Camp, adjacent to the Hyongie (brothers) Falls, two ribbons of water cascading side by side in summer and held frozen in winter. A kilometre away are Paektu Falls and the refined, three-tiered Sagimum Falls. Paektu Bridge and a restaurant are 5km northeast of here.

Moving on from the camps, and rampaging for 45 minutes along dusty roads walled with pine and birch trees in close steep hillsides and through pretty, shaded villages gets you to the **Rimyongsu Falls** (formerly Ei Myun Su), speedily seeping out of the crevices of basalt cliffs. This is one site of some 45 spots along a 20km band where this phenomenon is noted, and with the water temperature never below 4°C it doesn't freeze. There's an artificial lake and a pavilion from which to

In Korea's revolutionary history, Lake Samji is an epicentre of great significance, particularly for the Battle of Musan Area in May 1939 that was a spiritual turning point (if not an outright military victory) in the Korean People's Revolutionary Army's war against the Japanese – or rather, that's how it's told. Kim Il Sung at the time was commanding the 6th division of partisans, 2nd army, part of the 1st route army, ie: he was a general among many (although he was also by that point of the war one of the few commanders still alive). Those taking up arms in the name of a free Korea came in all colours politically, but they're not part of the revolutionary narrative we have today.

What Musan marked was the end of what would later be called the 'Arduous March', the *first* Arduous March. This was a period of crucial importance for Koreans to learn the appalling harshness of the times in which the first major blows against Japanese imperialism were struck, the fighters who led these assaults, and the quality of the people, their patriotism and revolutionary fervour that the times forever instilled in them. So far so florid, but for outsiders the first Arduous March must be looked at as the time that forged Kim Il Sung's traits of utter relentlessness applied to any given task, the tenacity of his decisions whatever the outcome, his dominating personality, his demands for loyalty (with his love for those who gave it, and violent sorrow for those who didn't), and more broadly how propaganda, arms – and starvation – could become defining facets of the DPRK.

In short, while there had been many periods during the 1930s when the fortunes of Korea's guerrilla forces were seriously low, the freezing winter of 1938/39 was the most perilous time, 'our bitterest time of trial in the entire history of the anti-Japanese armed struggle', Kim Il Sung wrote, with a department of ghost-writers, in his biography *With the Century*. The various units of the KPRA had been losing men hand over fist to constant Japanese harrying attrition attacks. They were isolated, dispersed, low on food and supplies, and all the worse that their battles with the Japanese had taken place not in the homeland but in Manchuria, their blood being repeatedly and futilely spilt on foreign soil.

Meanwhile, rebel forces and the civilian population were still suffering from the violent expurgation of all resistance cells, revolutionary and otherwise, by raids carried out Japanese forces in autumn 1937, leading to hundreds of operatives and innocent civilians being arrested and executed. The crackdown was in retaliation for what the Japanese called the 'Hyesan incident', or when Kim Il Sung's forces had destroyed Japanese installations and killed police officers in Pochonbo town, Hyesan that June.

By late 1938 morale among the soldiers and civilians had never been lower, compounded by Japanese lies that resistance was spent, lies propagated in newspapers and radio, a media machine that Kim Il Sung cursed for the impotence of his counter-measures, writing: 'Simply scattering a handbill could easily cost the life of a patriot. An underground worker had to risk his life to go into Korea with a knapsackful of leaflets.' Meanwhile his own force was holed up in the town of Nanpaizi, with the Japanese about to attack with everything from machine guns to poison gas.

He could have sought to slip his soldiers out, and sit out the winter somewhere in safety. Instead, he chose to take the battle into Korea: 'Advancing into the homeland and shooting off our guns there was the best way to declare that the KPRA was still very much alive and to expose the enemy's propaganda lie that the KPRA had been destroyed. The sound of our gunshots would help set the underground organisations back on their feet.' That would involve a six-day march from Nanpaizi to the nearby town of Beidandingzi, but in these wintery conditions of three-foot snow drifts, it would take an appalling, epic 110 days, 'because we had to fight the enemy every single step of the way!', against ground and air units.

His predictions of ending up eating tree bark proved optimistic. They went from eating two meals of gruel a day to one, eating raw horsemeat, fox millet and ultimately just snow. 'Hunger and emaciation piled on top of the cold – and we had to fight several battles a day without rest or sleep. The hardships were beyond description,' he wrote. But it was a campaign Kim Il Sung hardily brought upon his force: 'If we had slipped out of Nanpaizi, as we had done for previous expeditions, we would not have gone through such severe troubles. However, it was impossible for us to do this. We had to let our gunshots be heard right from the start.'

He also tells of many tearful partings by comrades and their sacrifices for his safety. 'When I was fighting in the mountains, I felt sorriest to see my comrades-in-arms unable to eat their fill, suffering all kinds of problems and unable to get married at their most marriageable age.' Kim defines men by their toughness, and depending on them 'to be a man', and in stark contrast to those he loves, he finds himself throughout the winter and into spring to be affronted by discovering former comrades who prove weak in character, surrender and tell the Japanese where Kim's forces are hiding.

Physically and spiritually, the trek was 'such an unprecedented ordeal that it is beyond comparison with any other expeditions in terms of duration and misery' and 'was indescribably arduous, so it finally came to be known as the Arduous March'. Its lifelong impact on him is evident as he waxes lyrical throughout the autobiography he wrote in the very early 1990s, asserting: 'No matter how much I might describe the hardships we suffered during the Arduous March, you who have not experienced it cannot imagine what it was like.'

But whoever wasn't killed by this, learned from it, tempering Korea's forces into becoming tough as steel, mettle they showed when taking battle to the Japanese around Musan in May, and winning handsomely. 'Workers, peasants and other people of other strata joined the anti-Japanese revolution with a firm faith that a new day of national liberation would be sure to come as long as there was the KPRA.'

For all the years thereafter, Kim never showed loyalty to any others like those he fought with in those years of frozen hell. 'Men of Paektu' is an expression still in use that fuses Paektu's spiritual and mythical significance for Koreans with the generation of revolutionaries that came from those days to rule the DPRK for decades. However, those on the wrong end of even just a suggestion of disloyalty would suffer harshly and sometimes without end, with relatives and friends included. More so, expectations were never lowered about what people were expected to endure. Finally one wonders how Kim Jong Il might have sought in the 1990s, when the country was isolated, starving and surrounded, to inspire his countrymen and be a man in the eyes of his dead father, by having his own Arduous March.

take pictures of the tidy houses of the local village. Around 30km from the Secret Camp No 1, and a dozen kilometres or a half-hour drive from the Rimyongsu Falls, is **Lake Samji**, or **Samjiyon**. The tranquillity of this location is all the more affecting considering the violence that went on in these parts in the 1930s and 1940s, and the natural beauty of Paektusan aside, one might wonder what is so special about this vast tract of forested mountainscapes that urges the Koreans to build such almighty monuments here and bring visitors so far, so remotely to see them.

The first monument to go up was the **Samjiyon Grand Monument**, dedicated in 1979 by Kim Jong Il upon the 40th anniversary of the major battle fought near here in 1939. The battle was heralded as a great victory for morale with Korean fighters proving able to defeat the Japanese on Korean soil, although the victory was in that sense more symbolic than marking any great strategic gain in the war. The monument is centred on a 15m-tall statue of the Great Leader in his youthful guerrilla days, clasping binoculars, ready for battle, against the backdrop of Mount Paektu. To his right is a 50m-tall statue of the Juche flame and the revolutionary monument; to his left, a group surrounding the 'trumpeter of the advance'.

Amid the lot are groups of soldiers and Koreans in various states of readiness for battle and other worthy causes, like 'Reverence', 'Advance', 'Camping' and 'Water of Motherland'.

The lake is adjacent to Samjiyon town, notable for its nicely proportioned villas and gaudy-coloured roofs, and it's near here you'll probably stay at the **Pagaebong hotel**. You won't be able to refuse a visit to the town's **revolutionary museum**, full of Musan battle memorabilia and other relics from fighting the Japanese, and being somewhat kitsch for having been built as a great big log cabin. There's also the **Paektu Museum** which has various maps of interesting things in the area, and the bright red-roofed **Schoolchildren's Palace**, fronted by a massive model of a Korean tiger (true to scale, do you think?) and where a somewhat militarised show may be put on. Samjiyon is also a skiing village: www.skiresort.info reports there are 2km of slopes, most easy, some intermediate, that descend from 1,608m in altitude to 1,364m, with two ski lifts. Feel free to enquire about them.

Some 40km due east of Mount Paektu, next to the Tuman River border with China, is the town of Taehongdan 대홍단, and near there is another vast forest-clearing memorial to the Musan battle, the **Monument to the Victorious Battle of the Musan Area**. Here, next to a great bayoneted rifle muzzle is a bronze statue of the young Great Leader, coat billowing in the cordite winds of war as he points his forces into battle. Bronze reliefs of Kim Jong Suk amid several other guerrillas engaging the Japanese in fierce fighting contrast with images of the bounteous legacy of their sacrifice, with one bronze relief called 'joy of potatoes'. In 2000 the Dear Leader visited the much smaller monument previously at this site since 1969, and ordered a massive replacement stressing the value of victory through arms. And it is vast, an 11,000m^2 space, with the rifle obelisk touching 40m in height. The guide may undertake to sing the local song 'The Vast Expanse of Taehongdan', with the words carved out at the monument. Another museum, the **Taehong Museum**, celebrates all things Paektu. The area's also known for its blueberries.

Meanwhile, around 40km south of Samjiyon but on the Amnok River border is the city of Hyesan 혜산, worth visiting for another China/DPRK comparison that's also a favourite for visitors to Dandong (see page 256). Apart from its sclerotic lumber, paper and textile industries, and being a hub for copper mining, it's the best base for seeing **Pochonbo** 보천보, Hyesan-ri. The town has the remains of a Ri dynasty castle, but is better known in DPRK folklore as the location of a successful KPRA attack on the Japanese on 4 June 1937, when 200 fighters attacked and burned a Japanese police substation and various imperial installations and later ambushed and killed a contingent of Japanese police, looting them of weapons. As Kim told it, they followed up by pasting 'proclamations' and posters all over town and he told cheering crowds, 'let's fight for the liberation of the country' before spiriting away and carrying out a similar assault two days later. It was daring and delivered a good psychological boost to guerrilla forces, and earned a still young Kim great kudos. But it wasn't without consequence. The attack was what the Japanese would call the 'Hyesan incident' (see box, page 248) and led to a massive manhunt for Kim's forces and crackdown on any suspected resistance. A more modern homage is the top DPRK popular beat combo, Pochonbo Electronic Ensemble, which is named after the city's eponymous battle. Look out for their works in any of the gift shops you come across.

FOLLOW BRADT

For the latest news, special offers and competitions, subscribe to the Bradt newsletter via the website www.bradtguides.com and follow Bradt on:

- f www.facebook.com/BradtTravelGuides
- @BradtGuides
- @bradtguides
- pinterest.com/bradtguides

11

12

The Border with China and Beyond

For a map of the region see pages 224–5.

SINUIJU 신의주

40.1°N, 124.4°E; on the Amnok/Yalu River, Sinuiju is the capital of North Pyongan Province, DPRK border city

For many travellers, the last (or first!) they see of the DPRK is at the border city of Sinuiju, through which the Pyongyang–Beijing train trundles, but it is now possible to visit the city and stay over. Sinuiju sits on the east bank of the Yalu ('Amnok' to Koreans) River, opposite China's thriving port-city of Dandong. A thick belt of fields divides Sinuiju in two and the city is surrounded by huge expanses of the flattest farmland. With a population of a third of a million, Sinuiju's substantially smaller than its Chinese neighbour, but has similar industries to Dandong, including paper milling, chemical production, aluminium, alcohol distillation and the processing of soya bean products. It is also of course the rail hub of the DPRK and China, and as the train from Pyongyang curves up from the south towards Sinuiju the contrast in fortunes between the two countries becomes clear, as the fields full of Korean farmers doing back-breaking work provide an enormous foreground against the skyscraping urban heights of Dandong. Nonetheless, despite some grand hopes for investment being dashed over the years, Sinuiju may no longer be left behind.

HISTORY Sinuiju was formerly known as Ai-Chiu, a border fortress and 'gate to old Korea' from before the Ri. The drain sluices of its thick granite walls provided the routes for early missionaries to sneak into the city and the country beyond. It's been the capital of North Pyongan Province since 1923, taking over from Uiju 16km upriver. Following the outbreak of the Korean War in July 1950, US commander General MacArthur decided that the flow of troops and supplies from Manchuria into North Korea had to be cut. In November a series of raids by B-29 heavy bombers pounded bridges all along the Yalu, mainly hammering Sinuiju Bridge. As Chinese MiG jet fighters soared up to intercept the bombers and their jet escorts, Sinuiju earned the dubious distinction of hosting the world's first jet-to-jet combat. Sinuiju briefly became the DPRK capital in October 1950, as Kim Il Sung bestowed that status on the city when Pyongyang was briefly lost to United Nations forces. Much was levelled during the war, and was rebuilt afterwards to make the city into a not inconsiderable industrial base. Former Japanese factories were rebuilt and machinery works, ironworks, bearings, electrical, chemical and defence-related works were added by successive multi-year economic plans in the 1960s and 1970s.

While the world of watchers across the water viewed the place as being in some permanent state of inactivity, as the US Korea Institute at SAIS (*www.38north.org*) points out this view belied the city's considerable industrial base and its importance was indicated by the Dear Leader's frequent visits to factories there.

A big shift in the city's business came in the early 1990s, however, when China and Russia gave up barter and demanded cash. The new game in town became currency dealing, led by numerous trading companies, established and run primarily by military departments in the front line for priority to get foreign currency.

Senior DPRK traders were noted for their overcoats of dog 'fur' and secondhand bicycles while flour and medicinal herbs were traded for metals and used cars. Border towns are obvious targets for free enterprise, and in 2002 Sinuiju was announced to become a Special Economic Zone (SEZ), being heralded as the 'Hong Kong of the North', specialising in trade, distribution, light industries, tourism and finance. Unfortunately, virtually upon the announcement, the Chinese-Dutch entrepreneur Yang Bin set to organise the scheme was done for tax evasion, among other things, and both sides of the river pretty much shelved the plan.

In 2006 the Nautilus Institute described a 'change in the air' around Sinuiju, as the city's trading-port status rejuvenated. Several thousand resident Sinuiju families were being moved out of the city and their homes surrendered to trading companies and currency dealers, headed by big Pyongyang business types, many with familial or other ties to China that could be capitalised upon to attract the latter's high-rolling moneymen.

Those well-connected North Koreans certified as 'foreign traders' have the freest rein to do business and leave and re-enter the DPRK, and Sinuiju and Dandong (where the DPRK's currency Korea Trade Bank has a branch) are the cities to where many (mainly men despite communist emancipation) 'commute' practically on a daily basis. As a result there are possibly more North Koreans to be seen in Dandong than in any other place outside DPRK.

The city is also a major wholesale market trading point in wares from clothing to mobile phones and computers, and a substantial part of China's exports to the DPRK go via Sinuiju. The markets took a hammering from the 2009 currency re-evaluation, but survived and revived, as they did after torrential rains hit North Phyongyan in the summer of 2010. The rains killed hundreds and displaced tens of thousands of people in Sinuiju, bursting rivers and dykes, damaging villages and farms, and leading to relief efforts from the KPA and aid from the ROK and US. The city's major trading venue, the centrally located Chaehu market, was knocked down and replaced with a park in 2012, but the market itself was simply moved to an even bigger venue just a little way further out of town.

Scores of trucks are seen crossing the narrow road/rail Sino–Korean Friendship Bridge every day, ferrying goods in and out, but that's soon to be joined by a massive suspension road bridge being built some 8km (as the crow flies) south-southwest of central Sinuiju. Broadly speaking, the new connection should serve traffic coming from developments in the two huge river islands of Wihwa (to the city's north) and Hwanggumphyong (to the city's south) that comprise different parts of Sinuiju's Special Economic Zone. In June 2011, China and the DPRK held ground-breaking ceremonies on those pitches to herald the recommencement of the SEZ's development, and the new bridge suggests that they're serious.

As it is, there have been reports of amusements for traders in Sinuiju including intranet cafés, karaoke, saunas and massage – not that the average Western tourist has yet seen much of these entertainments, but the city is opening up. It may no longer be the case that the best place to 'see' Sinuiju is from Dandong opposite (see *On the waterfront*, page 260).

GETTING THERE AND AWAY One route is to do a day trip into Sinuiju from Dandong (see page 256), coming over by bus. The other way of visiting, only by

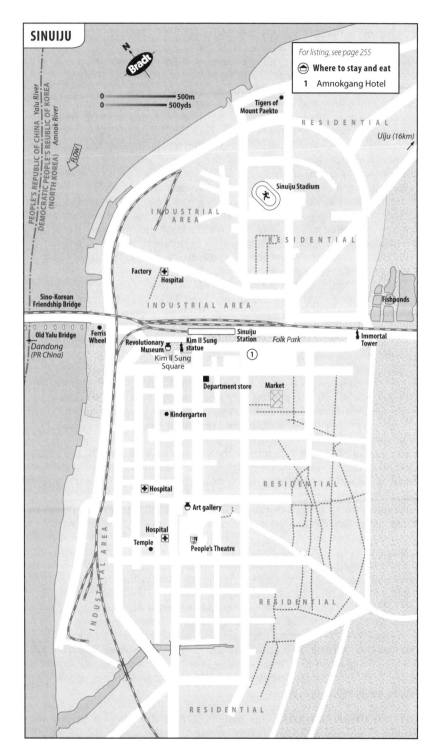

SINUIJU

For listing, see page 255

⊖ **Where to stay and eat**
1   Amnokgang Hotel

N

Bradt

Tigers of
Mount Paekto

RESIDENTIAL

Uiju (16km)

0 _____ 500m
0 _____ 500yds

PEOPLE'S REPUBLIC OF CHINA *Yalu River*
DEMOCRATIC PEOPLE'S REUBLIC OF KOREA
(NORTH KOREA) *Amnok River*

FLOW

Sinuiju Stadium

INDUSTRIAL
AREA

RESIDENTIAL

Factory
Hospital

INDUSTRIAL AREA

Fishponds

Sino-Korean
Friendship Bridge

Old Yalu Bridge   Ferris
                   Wheel

*Dandong
(PR China)*

Sinuiju
Station   *Folk Park*

Revolutionary   Kim Il Sung
Museum   statue

Immortal
Tower

Kim Il Sung
Square

Department store   Market

Kindergarten

Hospital

Art gallery

Hospital
Temple
People's Theatre

RESIDENTIAL

RESIDENTIAL

RESIDENTIAL

pre-arrangement, is to alight from the Beijing–Pyongyang train (or go Pyongyang–Beijing) and make a one-day tour, or stay over one night. But this *must* be pre-arranged – don't just get off at Sinuiju.

Restrictions One-day trips from Dandong to Sinuiju run from Tuesday to Sunday. Day trips to Sinuiju are not as relaxed as for the rest of the DPRK, ie: don't bring laptops, iPads, mobile phones or religious literature into Sinuiju. US and Japanese visitors are also not allowed into the city, let alone to stay over. US travellers are not allowed on the train going through, either.

For those passing through on the train, a large chunk of the 24 hours of the journey either way between Beijing and Pyongyang is spent in the cross-over points of Dandong and Sinuiju, particularly at Sinuiju, and the whole caboodle of going through customs and passports on each side – with officers boarding the train, you don't get off – can take about four hours. Delays of up to 36 hours on the DPRK side have been reported, but these are very rare, and it is for the most part a very orderly system (for more information, see page 258).

Otherwise, to get a real contrast with the DPRK, quite a few people like to spend a day or so in Dandong just across the river in China.

WHERE TO STAY The **Amnokgang Hotel ($$)**, next to the railway station, is the only accommodation available in Sinuiju; it's basic but serviceable.

WHAT TO SEE AND DO Being a border town, many of Sinuiju's inhabitants are 'privileged', but not necessarily trusted to 'wander into China', as local literature puts it. A lot of Sinuiju is fenced off with barbed wire so the locals can't enter, let alone foreigners. In terms of tourism, the traffic is largely one-way with foreigners (overwhelmingly Chinese) coming in on blue, border-area-only one-day passes to do some business or just have a look and go back across the bridge, although this scheme has been intermittently revoked. Other foreigners, albeit facing tighter restrictions, can make the same short tours, the highlight of which is Sinuiju's **central square** next to the railway station and its statue of a youthful **Kim Il Sung**, in something of a forceful mode, as he would have looked when he came in 1945 to put down a substantial student riot. One half of the square is clean and bright, and you can photograph it. The other half is dirty, derelict, and in the past has been seen to be full of beggars, quite an admission, and couldn't be photographed. Behind the statue is the obligatory **revolutionary museum**. Going in the opposite direction from the square runs the **Sinuiju Folk Park** where you can play golf, do some shooting, engage in archery or some swinging – as in there are swings – or circulate among locals promenading or holding court on worldly matters.

Down the main road running southwest of the statue is one of Sinuiju's **kindergartens**, known for training children on unicycles for the Mass Games, and which puts on a strong variety show with skits involving kids dressed as commandos taking on ROK and US soldiers, or wearing T-shirts adorned with tanks made from sequins. Further along this same stretch is an impressive **art gallery**.

Sinuiju's list of sites with flags planted on the summit of 'Things of Interest to Tourists' continues to grow, including an impressive **triptych of mosaics**, the 'Tigers of Mount Paektu' depicting Kim Il Sung, Kim Jong Il and Kim Jong Suk, and put up for the 100th anniversary of the Great Leader's birth in 2012. The **Sinuiju History Museum**, full of artefacts and art from the locale, has things stretching

In April 2004, over 100 people were killed and thousands injured in a massive explosion on board a train at Ryongchon station, 20km from Sinuiju. The blast caused a stir worldwide as it was believed that the train carrying Kim Jong Il back from a visit to China had passed through that station just hours beforehand. Was the blast a failed assassination attempt? KCNA belatedly reported the blast as an accident as a result of 'an electrical contact caused by carelessness during the shunting of wagons loaded with ammonium nitrate fertiliser'. The trouble is, fertiliser and electricity have long been in pretty short supply in the DPRK, and for the two to combine so disastrously could also be considered as something of a rare mischance.

Some sources from within the DPRK's security apparatus purportedly treated the incident as an assassination attempt, with the trigger being a mobile phone – then a rarity in the country – and to know the timing of the Dear Leader's movements would suggest a high-level plot indeed. ROK reports posited that the trains were carrying petrol and liquefied gas from China, ironically as gifts for the departing Kim Jong Il, that subsequently collided and blew up. Or maybe KCNA's version is the right one: it was an accident, possibly not helped in being prevented by the kerfuffle of pressures falling upon the local rail infrastructure and timetable as Kim Jong Il's train passed through. We just don't know.

back to Neolithic Korea through the Koryo and Koguryo up to the Ri. The **People's Theatre** and a **temple** have also made claims to such heights in the past, but neither is on any current tour itinerary.

UIJU 의주 In the past, it's been known for visitors to Sinuiju to also go to the city of Uiju, 16km northeast along the Amnok. It was first known as Ryongman, meaning 'a river bend with dragons', but the city's history is largely steeped in battling invaders from every direction, mostly from China. From Koguryo a fort existed here and the city never lost its military significance. Peaceful trade links over the river made Uiju prosperous in times of peace, and it was the provincial capital from 1907 to 1923, when Sinuiju took over. The **Uiju Revolution Museum** is devoted to Kim Il Sung's father, Hyong Jik. Two hundred metres away is the Uiju Nam Gate, which originates from Koryo times. Another site, 1km north of here, is **Thongounjong Pleasure Ground**, home to numerous pavilions that date from the Koryo when the area's hills marked it for defensive purposes. Sites like the Thongung Pavilion (1117) were part of the walled city of Uiju. Literature comments on the presence of a waterfall and hot springs but says not where.

DANDONG 丹 *With thanks to the team at Dandong Xpat (http://dandongxpat.com)*

40.1°N, 124.3°E; in Liaoning Province, China. Dandong is the border city on the River Yalu facing the DPRK city of Sinuiju; formerly called Andong; population 2.93 million

From Sinuiju, the train carriages are batted across the bridge into Dandong, a city with two major tourist features for the Chinese: first, it's China's only city right on a national border, and a natural border at that; second, and far more alluring, the country across the river is the DPRK. It's mostly Chinese tourists that make the day trip into Sinuiju, and for everyone unable or unwilling to get over there, there are still many means to get within metres of the world's most secretive, inaccessible country. For those Chinese in their 40s and older, there is the added poignancy of seeing a land so close that so resembled their own country only a generation ago, and for many years there was the heartbreaking ability to watch the DPRK's appalling famine strike only a few hundred metres away.

The difference between the two cities' fortunes is painfully obvious. Dandong's commercial towers reflect sunlight onto Sinuiju's smokeless chimneystacks. At night the Chinese side is a jungle of neon, the Korean side, darkness. In winter, the river can scarcely freeze on Dandong's side as its warm waste waters pour into the river, while Sinuiju remains behind its shore-long barrage of ice, perfectly marking the mid-river border of China and the DPRK.

HISTORY Now the largest city in east Liaoning, Dandong was until the 1960s known as Andong. With the town recorded as under Zhou dynasty administration in the 6th century BC, Andong was built by the timber trade, becoming a major trading centre from the wood floated downriver. In 1903 the Qing dynasty proclaimed it a free trade port. Rapid growth from 1907 followed the railway link-up to northeast China, and further from 1911 when the bridge into Korea was completed. British and Danish traders were instrumental in developing Andong in the first two decades of the 20th century, with the British setting up the Chinese imperial customs service. The Japanese industrialised it during their occupation in the 1930s and '40s, and the neat grid layout around the station is the 'Manchukuo' Japanese quarter of town, so called from Japan's colonial name for Manchuria.

Prior to Japanese domination, the US had also built up a substantial diplomatic presence in Andong, reflecting the city's strategic location between China and Korea. By then a major rail and river communications and supply link to North Korea, its significance to the US was later expressed by bombing heavily both Andong and Sinuiju after China's intervention in the Korean War. When the bridge was damaged, Korean and Chinese forces valiantly connected the banks with pontoon bridges. It was also from Andong's Langtou airfield (now Dandong's airport) that Chinese and DPRK MiG fighter jets operated and shot down many US air force planes during the Korean War, in a stretch of airspace known to the UN forces as 'MiG Alley'. Today, Dandong is a flourishing industrial area, best known among the Chinese for its production of silks and ShuGuang (formerly HuangHai) coaches seen all over northern China's roads, as well as wood processing, paper, rubber, chemicals, ginseng and tussah, and is a major and growing port for the river and coastal trade. It is also rising up fast in its financial sector.

With this new growth has come the contrived need to dispense with the old, and since this book was first written in 2003, the old Chinese-town part of the city, especially the area towards the river, has been mostly demolished (akin to the wholesale demolition of Beijing's old *hutong* areas), with monotonous brassy towers replacing old-world charm. High-rises and higher have spread along almost the entire length of the city's riverfront, the modern walled city, but it is still a pleasant and interesting enough place to visit.

GETTING THERE AND AWAY

By air Dandong Langtou airport (DDG) is located 12km southwest of central Dandong down G201 road. It's an old-school concrete and glass airport with a charming botanical display at the luggage carousel (a new airport's due in 2014). Served by Air China among many of the larger Chinese airlines, connecting with Beijing, Qingdao, Shanghai, Macau, Guangzhou, Xi'an, Chengdu and Shenzhen, albeit not all of them every day. Beijing to Dandong takes one hour 45 minutes and can cost from CNY550 to CNY850 one-way, plus CNY170 in taxes and fees.

By rail Beijing–Dandong train numbers 2251/2253 leave Beijing daily at 12.13, arriving 21 hours 37 minutes later at Dandong station, CNY131–398. Coming back, 2258/2255 leaves Dandong at 13.10 arriving in Beijing 22 hours three minutes later.

There are also the international services K27 Beijing–Pyongyang via Dandong and K28 coming back, which are much shorter but still go overnight through China. K27 leaves Beijing at 13.10 and arrives 13 hours 50 minutes later in Dandong. K28 leaves Dandong at 18.31 and comes back to Beijing 14 hours later, CNY142–399 (see also page 87).

By bus The long-distance bus station is at 98 Shiwei Lu, with connections to Beijing (approx 11hrs; CNY220), Shenyang (approx 3hrs; CNY100) and Dalian (approx 4hrs; CNY100).

TRAVEL AGENCIES The CITS and KITC in Dandong are very good at making the arrangements to cross into the DPRK, if you're going to catch the train from Dandong to Pyongyang. But if that's what you're going to Dandong for, you need to get the ball rolling at least two weeks beforehand (unless you sort out the papers from Beijing or elsewhere), initiated by phone/fax. Never forget that the visa process in the DPRK is not as simple and straightforward as it is in other countries.

CITS 2nd Flr, Mudanfeng Hotel (adjacent to Dandong railway station); ✆+86 415 213 2237/214 0145; www.ddcits.com
Dandong Chosun Travel Service Jiangcheng Dajie 15, Dandong, Liaoning 118000; ✆+86 415

2300133/6; m +86 134 700 0218/9; f +86 415 216 0867; e ddcts@163.com; www.ddcts.com. Also offers tours to the DPRK.
KITC Xian Qian Rd, Yuan Bao District, Dandong; ✆+86 415 281 2542/0457; f +86 415 281 8438

GETTING AROUND All buses for the town and beyond go from the square in front of the railway station. Taxis kerb-crawl the streets for CNY5 minimum fare (nowhere in town will cost over CNY10 to get to so don't pay more) and pedi-cabs for half that.

 WHERE TO STAY There are now several international-standard hotels in town.

🏠 **Crowne Plaza Dandong** 158 Binjiang Middle Rd, Zhenxing District, Dandong 118002; ✆+86 415 318 9999. Tremendous views of the DPRK from this towering 5-star hotel. $$$$
🏠 **Mudanfeng Hotel** 3 Liujin Street, Dandong; ✆ +86 415 213 2196. $$$
🏠 **Zhong Lian Hotel** 62 Binjiang Middle Rd, Zhengxing District, Dandong 118000; ✆+86 415 233 3333. Next to the river & giving amazing

views of the blown-up bridge & the DPRK, with binoculars provided. ATM, Wi-Fi & AC. $$
🏠 **Dandong International Hotel** 88 Xian St, Dandong 118000; ✆+86 415 213 7788; f +86 415 214 6644. $
🏠 **Yalu River Guesthouse** 87 Jiuwel Rd, Dandong 118000; ✆+86 415 212 5901; ✆+86 415 212 6180. $

WHERE TO EAT AND DRINK There are now innumerable restaurants and coffee shops scattered across the grid of streets running north and northeast of the station. Along the boardwalk that runs southwest of the bridges are lined many cafés and very good Chinese and Korean eateries. One that receives regular praise is Peter's

Temple, Buddhist Nunnery

Lutheran church (Danish 1930)

Great Wall, Jilin

Motorway, Benxi, Shenyang

Catholic church ✝

0 ———— 500m
0 ———— 500yds

N

Phoenix Mountain

Korean Protestant church ✝

Pedestrianised shopping centre

People's Park (Renmin Gongyuan)

Mosque ☾

SHAN SHANG JIE

YALU YAN JIE

QI JIN JIE

LIU WU JIE

Coffee shop

Supermarket

PLA Complex (former Danish legation) ●

✉ ④

③

Central Square

Mao statue

Boat trips

Sinuiju (DPRK)

Dandong station

Bus stop

② CITS office

Sino-Korean Friendship Bridge

Old Yalu Bridge

SHAN SHANG JIE

⑤

Boat trips

Culture Square

Museum to Commemorate US Aggression

Memorial to Resist America & Aid Korea

FLOW

PEOPLE'S REPUBLIC OF CHINA Yalu River
DEMOCRATIC PEOPLE'S REPUBLIC OF KOREA (NORTH KOREA) Amnok River

Parade ground

For listings, see pages 258 & 260

⌂ **Where to stay and eat**

1 Dandong International
2 Mudanfeng
3 Peter's Coffee House
4 Yalu River Guesthouse
5 Zhong Lian

Off map
   Crowne Plaza Dandong

Crowne Plaza Dandong, Dandong Langtou Airport ↓ (16km)

DANDONG

Coffee House, on the waterfront about 1km northwest of the Friendship Bridge (*103 Bingjiang Rd, Dandong, Liaoning, 118000;* ☎ *+86 415 216 841*). While not really a place to eat, the Real Love nightclub with its live floor show is another venue to seek out and enjoy.

WHAT TO SEE AND DO Dandong is an unusually doable city, compared with other northern Chinese cities, and is quite clean and human in scale (its 800,000 urban population is villagesque compared with other Chinese conurbations). Many sights relate to the border, Chinese–Korean relations and communism. Arriving by train or bus, the first thing you see in the new station square is Mao Tse-tung's statue, now in pragmatic salute to the city's bustling capitalism.

The station and square are on the southern side of the 'Manchukuo' town, and in this grid of streets fenced in by the railway are most of the hotels, bars and amenities. The higgledy-piggledy streets north of here are the old Chinese-built town.

From the station square, which has been doubled in size of late, buses (1, 2, 4, 5) can be caught southwest up to the **Memorial to Resist America and Aid Korea**. This huge white column, 53m tall in reference to the year 1953, when combat operations during the Korean War abated, is highly visible to most people in Dandong and pointedly to anyone in Sinuiju. It reminds everyone, Koreans especially, of China's contribution during the Korean War. After paying a yuan to enter the Jinjiang hill park where the tower is, at its base you find the **Museum to Commemorate US Aggression** (⊕ *08.30–16.00 Tue–Sun; free*), an impressive series of halls full of the war: bombs, tanks, fighter planes, wreckage, maps, documents, photos of decapitated POWs, etc. One hall has an extraordinary 360° diorama where you're surrounded by communist liberators fighting up a hill towards you. The museum tells the story of the war from the Chinese point of view and makes for an interesting comparison with Pyongyang's own excellent war museum, and for Westerners how 'well' the United Nations comes out of it all, but only if you can read Chinese or Korean! A brand-new pedestrianised shopping square now sits on the eastern end of Qi Jin Jie, stretching north, with an underground shopping complex planned for 2014.

From the monument follow the Shan Shang Jie road and railway northeast until on the left appears a **PLA complex** with peculiar Danish 'gingerbread' detailing. Adjacent to that is the entrance to 'People's Park', with pleasant walks and steep ridges to get views of the town and the DPRK. On the park's north side is a Korean **Protestant church**, built in the 1990s by the South Korean Church and packs in 2,000 worshippers, Chinese style. Further north just off Shan Shang are two more churches, one **Catholic** built by American missionaries, and one **Lutheran**, built by the Danes in the 1910s. Tucked into a small valley leading away from this area are a small temple and a Buddhist nunnery.

The main old 'Chinese town' in the northeast section of the city has been or is undergoing wholesale demolition, a real swizz, as some modernists with money don't appreciate the things that make cities good, leaving only a few 'showpiece' buildings and for the time being a lot of dust, building sites and urban flux in this part of town.

On the waterfront Of the two bridges beginning from Dandong's shores, only the Sino–Korean Friendship road/railway bridge makes it all the way across. The Old Yalu Bridge, a stone's hurl south of the rail bridge, was bombed during the Korean War (first hit in 1950 but it held together until early 1951). The Chinese half of the Old Yalu still stands, as a monument to 'American aggression'; on the Korean side only stone bridge stumps protrude from the waters, like furious stelae. For a fee of CNY30, you can walk out along this bullet- and shrapnel-scarred bridge until its girders gnarl to nowhere. In summer here is a mini-café; in winter you can try to lob snowballs onto Korea's frozen riverside (meanwhile, a massive new bridge is being built south of the city, planned for 2015).

If this isn't close enough, in fair season from the Yalu River Park and operating from piers north and south of the Old Bridge are slow boats, some with dragonheads and tails or speedboats that, for CNY50–60, take you to the river's midway 'border', if not closer to the DPRK shore. In this, Sinuiju has joined the game, and occasionally boats filled with well-heeled North Koreans waving, and jolly martial music blaring out, can now be seen pootling over towards the Chinese side and back. Otherwise river traffic from the Sinuiju side is also increasing, with what appear to be commuter boats ferrying work units or travellers up and down the DPRK riverfront. Although Sinuiju is behind a large dyke-type wall, you might see, like many others do, parties of schoolchildren in white shirts and red neckerchiefs trotting gaily along the Sinuiju bank behind groups of fishermen and youthful soldiers. From the outside, Sinuiju is changing, glacially. New dock railheads and a high-profile residence have been built, and a waterslide has joined the city's own sad landmark, a Ferris wheel that's not turned in all the years it's been there. Save for the floodlights on the Great Leader's statue, the town remains much in darkness at night.

For Dandong, south of the Old Bridge is a development zone, and from the southern end's Culture Square this is a pleasant place to amble along at dusk, with all Dandong people out strolling, playing, enjoying the breeze, doing tai chi and open-air calligraphy, playing chess and fishing, as well as an abundance of dancers and musicians. A new boardwalk now runs 3km north of the bridge to over 5km south, and along the boardwalk are many little Chinese businesses and excellent restaurants run by Koreans (look out for one restaurant graced by a poster of the *Mona Lisa* with a great big dope plant). Many Koreans are living and working in Dandong in this way. You can also pick up DPRK stamps, trinkets and Kim Il Sung badges here (the latter being of debatable authenticity, though). The square is often used for promotional events and is very popular with wedding parties, which are worth seeing: dresses of bright turquoise and a palanquin on hand to give the couple a ride, with an accompanying traditional band and MC. Further downstream along the Dandong riverfront, for a few years was moored a muddy island a casino boat, set up by an enterprising Korean for Chinese gamblers. This somewhat infamous floating den of iniquity has now gone, and the island it was moored at has been converted into a gated community of sorts with plans for all manner of amusements for the well moneyed. The island is faced by growing estates of detached houses and gardens where the Chinese middle classes are building their own suburbia, with all the lawn sprinklers and Tupperware that goes with it.

AROUND DANDONG Lying 52km northwest of Dandong, just outside Fengcheng, is the stunning **Phoenix Mountain** (Fenghuangshan) set in its own small **reserve** (⊕ *08.00–17.00; admission CNY50*). Taoist worshippers come here to pray for relief from their illnesses, for the God of Longevity occupies the mountain's west ridge. Every 28 April a 'Medicine King Meeting' is held at one of the temples but, in company with former T'ang and Yuan emperors who pocked the mountain with their own tributes of temples and pagodas, the mountain's scenery and serenity are worth taking in anyway. Take the slow train from Dandong (1hr).

Within Dandong's boundaries is the Baishilazi Natural Protection Area, a large reserve committed to protecting China's deciduous broadleaf forests; it is both a natural botanic garden and a zoo. Also of note are the Dagu Mountain with groups of ancient temple structures, the Qingshan gully with natural waterfalls, and to the southwest of Dandong is Dagushan granite outcropping; with a well-preserved temple upon it and with surrounding sites including another temple it makes for a good day's excursion from town.

SOUTH FROM DANDONG

For more border-related points, go south of Dandong, following the Yalu to the coast, to Donggang town on the Chinese side. There's not much beyond a container park and a permanent yurt, but here the River Yalu splits around little islands, property of the DPRK. A few kilometres further west along the coast is Dalu Island, a 'pearl on the Yellow Sea', and a splendid natural retreat of caves as well as the Camel Peak. It also offers the chance to splash lazily in Moon Bay. It has a bizarre collection of buildings, from T'ang temples to a Danish church and a British lighthouse. There's also the tomb of Deng Shichang, a Chinese captain killed in 1894 as the Japanese fleet sank the Chinese fleet *en route* to 'rescuing' Korea from the Tonghak. Ferries run to Dalu (CNY80–100).

FROM DANDONG TO SOUTH KOREA Ferries run from Dandong to the ROK port of Incheon, the primary port serving Seoul. The South Korean ferry runs from Dandong (Dandong Hangun Terminal) to Incheon (Incheon Port International Ferry Terminal 1 – Yeonan Budu) every Tuesday, Wednesday and Sunday at 15.00. From Incheon to Dandong it runs Monday, Wednesday, Friday, leaving at 17.00.

For reservations and information, call the Dandong information office (⋏ +86 415 316 2165). The Incheon office is ⋏+82 32 891 3322, and the Seoul office is ⋏+82 2 713 5522 (English, Chinese), or look up www.dandongferry.co.kr (in Korean) or try www.visitkorea.or.kr/intro.html. Costs for one-way travel are first-class, two-berth cabin US$215 per person; second-class four-berth cabin US$160 per person

The Chinese ferry goes from Dandong overnight to Incheon, leaving Dandong at 16.00 on Tuesday, Thursday and Sunday each week and arrives in Incheon the next morning at 09.00. Economy class, o/w CNY990 (⋏ *+86 415 315 2666;* f *+86 315 6131;* www.ddfcl.com.cn (in Chinese)).

NORTH FROM DANDONG

North along the Yalu from Dandong is the town of Changdianhekou, unremarkable except for its own rail terminus, but 3km north of here is the Taipingwan hydroelectric dam. Halfway across the dam is a rusted, padlocked metal gate, another border with the DPRK, and noticeable along the DPRK bank are regular sentry points. It's possible to get a speedboat up and down on this reservoir.

The Yalu is not a deep river, and in summer this natural border becomes especially shallow, a fatal flaw for a natural national border. Many small islands surface in the shallows, that are technically the DPRK if you're considering going and standing on them. A well-known point for this is the 'One Step Crossing' that is a short trek downhill from the Tiger Mountain Great Wall. The mountain is where China's Great Wall begins, and its good views into the DPRK make it a great attraction. One Italian journalist made the 'One Step Crossing', reached an exposed island, where he stood and he was being hailed by a DPRK guard to come across, an 'invite' which he accepted! The Italian wrote later he was well fed and asked questions for a few days before being sent to drift back into China (far easier than fiddling with visas at controlled border points). Great for japes, though I would not recommend you try it yourself!

In the regions running northeast from Dandong along the Yalu, the Korean influence becomes more and more marked. In Jilin and Heliongjiang provinces live 1.8 million ethnic Koreans, 800,000 of whom live in the Yanbian Autonomous Prefecture, a triangular enclave forming the last section of China's border with the DPRK.

From the southeast of Liaoning Province all the way to Changbaishan are entire Korean villages, visible in the shop signs, bilingual road signs, Korean forms of dress, the density of Korean Protestant churches and the highly conscious bilingualism of the locals. Korean communities grow in rural and urban concentration the closer to Korea you are. (Unfortunately, Korea's division manifests itself in the peninsula's diasporas, and in Beijing the distinction between the ROK and DPRK communities is clearly defined.)

HISTORY Tides of migration have ebbed and flowed from China into Korea and back for millennia. Some tribes or groups were nomadic, touring the lands before arbitrary borders were defined in search of new lands of plenty when previous habitats were lacking, natural disasters destroyed their crops or ill treatment posed some kind of threat. They then either resumed their livelihoods elsewhere or formed military forces to resist and possibly oust their homeland rulers. Sometimes, people were given in tribute from one state to another, or were stolen by foreign raiding parties.

The area came under Koguryo control from the late 400s as Koguryo united the Puyo people and ruled all the way up to the Amur River for 2½ centuries. Following the division of Koguryo into separate states from the late 600s, a former Koguryo general formed an army with the Malgal tribe and led a mass migration into Manchuria, settling around today's Jilin and founding the new state of Palhae in 713. This soon expanded to take over the northern remnants of Koguryo to combine them with gains made in Manchuria. The state reached its pinnacle in the first half of the 9th century under King Seon, when Palhae stretched from the Yellow Sea to the Sea of Japan, and from Chongjin in today's Korea up to Yanji, with its capital in today's Chongchun. However, the state was only as stable as its neighbours allowed it to be, and Palhae wasn't exempt from the warring that brought down the T'ang dynasty, succumbing to the Khitan in 926. Those of the ruling classes that could escape to their more common kin in the new Koryo state did so. The Koreans joined with the Malgal people and assimilated into Manchurian life, eventually helping found the Jurchen.

Later Koreans were just taken. In 1254, the Mongols returned from Koryo with a booty of 26,000 Koreans. Many returned over the years, and many migrated back, so in 1464, 30,000 Koreans were recorded as living in Liaodong, the Chinese peninsula west of today's Sinuiju. The 1627 and 1637 Manchu raids on Korea enslaved tens of thousands. Some Korean families somehow earned freemen status and attained minor nobility under the Manchus, but these were the exception.

From 1677, an area one thousand *li* north of Changbaishan was declared off-limits by the Qing dynasty that also established a buffer zone just north of the Yalu and Tuman rivers (the li unit of measurement varied over time, but at that point was roughly 600m). Any interlopers were thrown back south of the rivers to the Ri, who built half a dozen garrisons to prevent any concerted invasion from the north.

Nonetheless, people continued to migrate across the rivers in fair seasons, dressing down and cutting their top-knots to appear more Chinese as they escaped the harsh life of northern Korea. For two centuries this continued until a string of

12

natural disasters in northern Korea caused a sudden upsurge in migration away from famine. From 1865 the Qing officially allowed Koreans to live and farm in Manchuria and later Dunwha, where Korean farmers pioneered and prospered on the land. Immigration to Manchuria eased as trade with Ri was established, and by 1894 there were 20,000 in Yanbian alone.

It's from those decades of migration that the current Korean population's cultural origins are thought to source. Earlier waves and pockets of Koreans saw their own way of life drowned in the sea of Han Chinese culture. The circumstances of their arrival, often destitute and starving, prevented them reaching any position of wealth and influence to defend their culture. As well as happenstance and convenience, their new rulers demanded the migrants' assimilation, to turn them from obstructive aliens into trusty clans people. The Yuan rulers established a governor-general office to rule these people from Koryo, as did the Ming. Migrants arriving in early Qing Manchuria were dispersed far and wide, and it wasn't until the late Qing era that Korean culture was given serious toleration.

Migration from Korea into China rose dramatically during imperial Japan's rule of Korea and the coloniser's attempts to smother Korea's culture in the 20th century. That, and the impoverishment of Korea's peasants, saw migrants into Manchuria surpass 450,000 in number in 1920 to reach 2.1 million by 1945. But while many had fled the Japanese, many more were sent there by Japan, with Koreans viewed as Japan's great but subservient brethren and entrusted with securing and populating Manchuria for their Japanese masters. However, the scale of the landscape and the sheer numbers of Koreans living there allowed for great resistance. Many of the disparate political and military movements that were collectively the Korean National Liberation Movement were based in Manchuria throughout Japan's rule, aiding and abetting Chinese resistance against the Japanese; and thousands of Koreans volunteered for the communist forces in China's civil war of 1946–49, engaging in fighting and liberating cities like Changchun and Jilin.

This assistance to the communist victory was in return for Chinese help in Korea's own struggle against the Japanese and later in the Korean War. Long-term training and support, ideological and material, were also provided by the Soviet Union at this time, where Kim Il Sung refined his leadership skills. The extreme conditions of guerrilla warfare in this part of the world imbued toughness in its veterans that would serve them well.

The roads in this area pass a landscape of forested hills, gulleys and peaks. From Dandong to Tonghua on route 201 is Huanren town, where there's an odd little theme park. From there you can take a powerboat to the adjacent lake that stretches over the Liaoning/Jilin border to an artists' colony where Chinese artists go and commune with nature, living in a tiny valley in which sit little Gothic-style timber houses. Visitors are welcome to stop off to visit, see their works and hang around for a bizarre but relaxing sojourn. Further along the way is Huadian, a town on a river where you're almost compelled to stop and try the local fish restaurants.

TONGHUA 通 *41.3°N, 126°E; 40km from DPRK border, Jilin Province, China.*
This sprawling provincial town hangs onto the lower slopes of the Longgang mountain range, with parts over 1,500m in altitude. It doesn't serve up any great treats for the visitor and is mainly useful for its proximity to Ji'an.

Getting there and away
By rail There is an overnight train (number K429) to Tonghua from Beijing departing at 11.10, taking 19 hours 15 minutes, costing CNY136–411 for a hard

seat–soft top bunk. Coming back the K430/K7430 leaves at 16.40 and arrives in Beijing 17 hours and 19 minutes later.

The Dandong–Tonghua K7378/7379 leaves at 14.42 and arrives 12 hours 11 minutes later, and costs CNY76–234. The Tonghua–Dandong train K7380/K7377 leaves at 01.19 and takes 12 hours 19 minutes.

By bus Buses from Dandong bus station take about ten hours to get to Tonghua. Buses 80 and 94 leave Dandong bus station at 06.30 and 08.50. At Ji'an the bus to Tonghua from the long-distance bus station takes two hours and costs about CNY15.

By taxi Tonghua to Ji'an takes an hour by taxi.

Where to stay The **Shiraton Hotel** (*1777 Tuanjie Rd;* **$**) has standard doubles from CNY250 up to CNY511 for a deluxe suite. Breakfast is extra.

JI'AN 集安 *41.10°N, 126.05°E; China/DPRK border, Jilin Province, China.*
This is a small, bilingual city of 100,000, stashed in the mountains flanking the Yalu, but is rich in its ancient history and its tourist industry thrives on ROK tourists coming to what was the capital of the Koguryo Empire. It was established by the Q in 221BC, and noted sights include the **Tianxiang Memorial**, the **Bailuzhou Institute** or the **Xiyang Palace**. Ten thousand ancient tombs and other historical sites are around the city, although many are barred to non-Chinese. One to note is the General's Tomb, also known as that of King Kwanggato, the 19th king of Koguryo who reigned from 391-413AD. His exploits are noted in detail on a 7m-tall stele erected in 414, and the tomb itself is massive, with a 75m square base and 11m in height, and apparently inspired the design of the reconstructed tomb of the mythical King Tangun, outside Pyongyang.

Aside from the small **Ji'an Museum** of Koguryo things, the town's main draw is the view of the DPRK over the river, compared with which Ji'an's slightly run-down look appears more favourable. From Ji'an station a train runs to the DPRK, for which there is little chance you can get on, but following the tracks to the very sturdy-girdered Ji'an Bridge is one viewing point for those coming in and out of the DPRK. Border guards and railway workers may be amenable to some fee allowing you to get very close to the dividing border line on the bridge (look out for trains steaming over it, however). The risk's up to you.

Getting there and away
By train Four overnight trains leave daily from Beijing West station for Ji'an, taking from 15 to 19 hours and costing CNY198. One eight-hour train goes from Baihe to Ji'an and back every day for around CNY64/98.

By bus Two buses leave Dandong in the morning for Ji'an at 07.30 and 09.20 (6hrs; CNY72). Three buses go from Shenyang to Ji'an at 06.20, 11.20 and 14.55 (6hrs; CNY75). From Tonghua buses go every two hours from morning to late afternoon (2hrs; CNY25).

Where to stay The **Hong Kong City Holiday Hotel** (*22 Liming South Rd, Ji'an 134200;* **$**) is well located and has a much nicer interior than its grey concrete exterior suggests. A discounted standard room is around CNY368/night, and a business room runs CNY418/night.

CHANGBAISHAN 長白山 NATURE RESERVE   42°N, 128°E; China/DPRK border,
southeast of Jilin Province.

This is China's largest nature reserve at over 200,000ha of virgin forest, a 78km by 53km area across three counties, and is a UNESCO World Biosphere Protection Zone. It is home to the rare Manchurian tiger, sikas, sables, snow leopards and wild ginseng, and as the ground rises up from 500m above sea level to over 2,000m, the forests between the clearings turn from coniferous through birch, Korean and Scots pine, Japanese yew, spruce, stunted fir and then tundra. Bioreserve though it be, there are many lumber lorries coming in the opposite way to tourist buses.

The transformation of the landscape forms the backdrop as you plough skywards, towards the heart of the reserve where sits Changbaishan, with 'Changbai' meaning 'eternally white' and 'shan', like in Korean, meaning 'mountain'. Changbaishan is of course known to the Koreans as Mount Paektu or Paektusan, and the Korean name 'white-topped mountain' is in effect the same. This crown of volcanic rock surrounds a piercingly clear round lake in its caldera, the Tian Chi Lake (meaning 'heavenly lake') or Lake Chon to the Koreans.

There are two entrances to the reserve, one on the northern slope (⊕ 07.00–18.00), about 20km by road from Baihe, and the other on the western slope (⊕ 07.00–16.00), for which the nearest town of access is Songjianghe about 40 minutes' drive away. The two entrances are some 100km apart so for a one-day trip it's one or the other.

To get into the reserve costs foreigners CNY100 (students pay less), then it's another CNY25 to access Tian Chi Lake. Transport between the entrance and the lake is another add-on (and unavoidable as it's over ten miles). Buses are CNY45 and 4x4s are CNY80–100 to assail the hairpin bends to the volcano's summit, where the views are terrific if no clouds are in the way.

Going by the northern slope passes one of the largest 'underground forests' in the area. A result of all the volcanic activity in the region has left numerous craters of varying sizes, the most obvious being Tian Chi itself, and there are many not filled with water but with trees that are referred to as 'underground' or 'below ground' forests. The largest is 60m deep and about 3,000m wide, and is big enough to discern three ranges of trees, from broadleafs down to conifers, including Korean pine. You can walk around one that is about 12km from the entrance.

On Changbaishan's north side are also many hot springs, identifiable from the hot, steamy air that wafts from them all year. The waters are supposed to be of great medicinal benefit, and some pools can be entered, but be careful as they're mostly over 60°C, with an extreme measured at 82°C. They're hot enough to boil eggs and corn if you're peckish.

The Deep Green pool is as it sounds, with an 80ft waterfall, but the prize waterfall is the 68m Changbai Waterfall that flows out of Tian Chi, making it highest volcanic waterfall in the world. Taking the path past this waterfall is scenic but dangerous enough to entail another charge of 'insurance' and a hard hat to walk up steps sheltered with metal sheet. There's not so much to see on the western slope. Changbaishan Canyon (Changbaishan Daxiagu), compared with the Grand Canyon, is only 70km and born out of volcanic events and soil erosion, and it is not dissimilar to the 1,000 soldier gorge on the DPRK side. Scaling up the western side to the lake means ascending about 1,000 stairs.

Whichever way one comes, the view of Tian Chi is magnificent to behold. High winds may be blowing between the sharp peaks stabbing the sky round Tian Chi, but the lake itself will be mirror flat. Many Koreans wade into the scarcely thawed water and sing songs, while the Chinese take pictures. There are also a hundred-odd little towers of piled stones, impromptu pagodas that tourists build. The mountain's significance to Koreans, and proximity to Yanbian Province, means there is an obvious Korean presence around Changbaishan despite it being in China.

Many of the tourist buses are Korean-made, and filled with Koreans, while there are also Daewoo and Hyundai billboards. Hackles have been raised over the mountain's 'ownership'. Although China and the DPRK agreed in the early 1960s to 'co-own' Paektu, with the latter controlling just over half of the site, Koreans suspect China is wheedling to take a greater hold of the mountain by various economic, cultural and historically revisionist moves and growing tourism by expanding Fusong and Changchun airports. The latter airport was built for the 2007 Winter Asian Games, held at Changchun and prompting China to place a lit torch on Changbaishan, irritating South Koreans enough for its athletes to brandish signs saying 'Paektu is ours'. In the longer term, tourists would be coming to see what could become a UNESCO World Geopark and World Heritage Site, if China has its way. This would be much to the irritation of Koreans, as such a listing implies the mountain is China's property and thus they are allowed to list it their way.

Although the lake's half-Chinese, half-DPRK, there's no sign of the border at all in the crater, and it's not obvious outside of it either – no great electric fences or 'LANDMINE' placards about. Once you're free of the crater, it's a landscape (or moonscape) of moorlands well scored with paths, but be very careful where you stray. One Bristol chap wandered off and came across a hut where he went to ask directions to the nearest Chinese village. The DPRK border guards inside took him to the nearest DPRK village, where he wasn't badly treated for the two months of haggling the authorities took to get him out.

Getting there and away One way to get to Tian Chi is to book a three-day tour through CITS in Jilin (✆ *+86 432 244 3442;* f *+86 432 245 6786*) for all transport and accommodation up to and around the lake.

Getting to Baihe

By bus Jilin to Baihe 白合 takes seven hours and costs CNY50. Yanji to Baihe takes 3½ hours and costs CNY45–50; seven services run daily. Dunhua to Baihe takes four hours; there are six buses a day starting at 07.45. There's also a direct bus from Yanji to Changbaishan that takes 4½ hours. Going to the northern slope involves going to Baihe first, and from Baihe railway station buses go to Changbaishan from 06.00 in the morning to midday, and the last one leaves the park at 16.00.

By train Six trains run daily from Baihe to Tonghua, taking around six hours, costing around CNY24 one-way. There is a single eight-hour Baihe-Ji'an train journey and three 14-hour trains run from Baihe to Shenyang (06.46, 17.35 and 19.10) for CNY51–99. There are seven daily two-hour trains from Baihe to Songjianghe.

By car From Tonghua and Yanji it's possible to hire drivers who will take you to Changbaishan in one-day missions (from CNY300–500) but from any further places you would have to account for their accommodation. You can get a taxi from Baihe to the park entrance for around CNY60.

Getting around There are ferries going from Donghae in the ROK to Vladivostok, Russia, from where travellers can press on into China. The summer schedule from March to November leaves Sundays at 14.00 from Donghae, arriving in

Vladivostok at 13.00 on Monday, which comes back from Vladivostok at 14.00 on Wednesday to arrive in Donghae at 10.00 on Thursday. The winter schedule runs December to February, leaving Donghae at 14.00 Monday and arriving in Vladivostok at 15.00 on Tuesday, going back 14.00 on Wednesday from

Vladivostok and arriving at 12.00 on Thursday at Donghae. Ticket prices range from US$205 economy one-way or US$335 economy return, up to US$3,185 return in the presidential suite. There no longer seem to be tours that go by ferry from the ROK port of Sokcho to Russia's Zarubino, with passengers then taking the bus via Hunchun in China to Changbaishan (all requiring Chinese and Russian visas). The website www.dongchunferry.co.kr is moribund.

🛳 **DBS Ferry** Seoul: ☎ +82 2 548 5557/5502; f +82 2 548 5503; Donghae: ☎ +82 33 531 5611; f +82 33 531 5612/3; e dbsferry@dbsferry.com. www.dbsferry.co.kr/eng; ⏰ 09.30–17.00 Mon–Fri

YANBIAN KOREAN AUTONOMOUS PREFECTURE 延┌朝┌族自治州 연변 조선족 자치주
43°08'N, 129°11'E; Northeast part of the China/DPRK border, Jilin Province, China.
Changbaishan sits just on the southernmost corner of Yanbian Autonomous Prefecture (Yonbyon to Koreans). This triangular area on the DPRK's border is home to over half of China's Koreans, who make up half the population, as they have for a century. This population density has meant that Yanbian's Koreans have been able to defend their ethnicity as a coherent community by being more powerful politically and economically, hence China's communist government recognises the Koreans as a distinct nationality, ethnically separate from the dominant Han Chinese. From 1949, Han Chinese began to repopulate the area, in the cities of Tonghua, Wangqing and Yanji. The Korean nationality is the 12th largest of China's 56 minorities, although it makes up under 0.2% of the total population. In Yanbian Chinese and Korean languages are used at varying levels in local government and are taught in schools.

History For centuries up to the late 1800s, Yanbian was off-limits, kept by the Ming and Qing as an exclusive reserve of primeval forests and virgin land used as royal hunting grounds. The region was only officially to come under cultivation from the 1880s, although many migrants, including Koreans, had surreptitiously begun to till the land before this. It was the Koreans who became most noted for their skills in turning huge tracts of apparently useless land over to wet-field agricultural use. Their reputation for changing this wild frontier into usable paddyfields was something on which the Japanese wished to capitalise when they forcibly populated Manchaca with Koreans. Complicit in Japanese suppression of Korean culture from 1910 onwards were the Chinese warlords who filled the post-Qing power vacuum at the time – although even the Qing hadn't been overtly tolerant of Korean culture.

In that second decade of the 20th century, Yanbian became a centre of anti-Japanese resistance, and 20 towns recorded disturbances during the 1919 March 1 Movement, formulating the first coherent civilian response to Japan's occupation of Korea. In 1920 major battles were fought between the Japanese and forces of the Korean provisional government (based in Shanghai). A Korean division wiped out a smaller Japanese force in June, and lost 1,000 troops in heavy fighting around Chung-san-ri (northwest of Changbaishan) in October 1920. Japanese forces retaliated by burning 2,500 homes and schools and killed or imprisoned over 10,000 Koreans in the Yanbian area. Thousands of skirmishes occurred in the 1920s, and small groups later formed into anti-Japanese guerrillas or worker-peasant righteous armies, accruing 12,000 Korean troops in Yanbian by 1932. The Northeast Anti-Japanese United Army (NEAJUA) soon formed, the main resistance force among a myriad of other units that sprung up across Manchuria and the Sino–Soviet border. Many stayed on after 1945 to fight Chiang-Kai Shek's forces, and by 1949 some 14,000 Koreans had died fighting for the Chinese communists. The People's Republic of China established the Yanbian Autonomous Prefecture in September 1952, which remained a backwater for decades as Koreans and Chinese settled into reconstructing their agrarian lives.

Since the early 1990s, three groups of Koreans have been migrating back to the region. One group is of business investors from the ROK, keen to plough hundreds of millions into the area as a centre of Korean industry and commerce in China's industrial northeast and on Russia's border. ROK-supported businesses have grown since China recognised the ROK in 1992, and the average wage in Yanbian is higher than the Chinese national average. Much of their investment caters to the second group from the ROK, tourists. The third group is another migration of Koreans, this time refugees from the DPRK in the wake of the country's agricultural collapse in the 1990s. Hundreds of thousands are estimated to be hiding in China, some finding luck by being taken in by sympathetic homes and given shelter and waged work, others falling prey to trafficking networks, forced marriages and what is in effect slavery. Any DPRK refugees in China are in a real bind, whether they're eking out a living with other Koreans, or *en route* to refuge in other lands, because the Chinese security services forcibly repatriate these illegal immigrants back to the DPRK, from where they only may have sought to escape poverty, but may return to face prison or worse. The plight of DPRK refugees in China came to the world's attention by a steadily rising stream of refugees storming foreign embassies in Beijing from 2000, particularly in the run-up to the 2002 World Cup being hosted in the ROK. This raised tensions between the two Koreas and caused great political embarrassment for the Chinese government. The Chinese took the side of the DPRK (it would be difficult for them not to) and there were incidents of Chinese troops 'invading' embassies with some violence to retrieve refugees. The barbed wire that now bedecks Beijing's diplomatic quarter is one very visible result of this hard-line policy, barbed wire that the DPRK Embassy also put up as if to stop refugees invading its embassy.

For more information on the plight of refugees and what they are escaping, search for North Korea under the United Nations High Commission for Refugees (*www.unhcr.org*), Amnesty International (*www.amnesty.org*) or the Human Rights Watch (*www.hrw.org*).

Yanji 延吉 *42.5˚N, 129.25˚E; Jilin Province, China.*

The capital of Yanbian is Yanji, a small city of 350,000 people of whom 60% are ethnic Koreans, as seen in the bilingual street signs. The Chinese minority speak less Korean, but Koreans typically speak both languages. Investment from ROK businesses into industry and tourism has been pouring into the prosperous-looking city, with wide roads, lots of glass and steel and shopping malls, but there's really not much to keep visitors here. There are hundreds of Chinese–foreign joint ventures in Yanji.

It's easy to get whole-body massages and facials that go on for hours for only CNY50, and Yanji is full of good cafés, Korean restaurants and to that end dog restaurants. The Xishichang market is the main place for wares ranging from cheap clothing to dog meat. There is a zoo and the Yanxijie amusement park on the river.

In very early September is the Korean folk festival, that exhibits folk arts in painting, dress and food, but also folk customs in song and dance, with competitions such as wrestling, see-sawing and swinging that date back centuries in Korea. But this all takes place at the end of the season when Changbaishan is easily accessible, so time it well. The Tuman River International Art Festival of Yanbian Prefecture is another festival that you should ask China International Travel Service (*www. cits.net*) about as well as the Bingchuan beer festival that comes around in summer.

Getting there and away No special permits are needed for the Yanbian Prefecture. Yanji is the nearest big Chinese city to Changbaishan.

By air Yanji airport is 5km southwest of the city. Flights from Beijing to Yanji (YNJ) take two hours and cost around £125 plus £5 tax one-way (Air China), and Yanji connects to most major Chinese cities. Yanji also connects to Incheon airport (ICN) in the ROK, 2½ hours' flight time, with Air China, Korea Air and Asiana Air, the lower end being around £350 return.

By rail The daily Beijing–Yanji trains (K215 from Beijing railway station 北京火ㄷ站 to Tumen) go daily at 13.10, taking up to 24 hours, prices ranging from CNY171 for a hard seat up to CNY516 for a top soft bunk. Five trains go from Shenyang to Yanji, taking between 11 hours (CNY102) and 15 hours (CNY62). There is a mini-bus that goes from Yanji station at 05.00 to make the five-hour drive to Changbaishan, costing CNY290 for a return.

Where to stay

Home Inn 2562 Changbaishan West Rd; +86 433 280 5599. One of the very serviceable Home Inn chains & located on the main road running through the south side of the city. **$$$–$$**

Yanbian Baishan Hotel 66 Youyi Rd; +86 433 258 1111. 4-star hotel in central Yanji, 3km from the airport. **$**

Yanbian Sung Bo Wenzhou Hotel 350 Jiefang Rd, Yanji 133000. **$**

Where to eat
There are a lot of Korean barbecue restaurants, cold-noodle restaurants and dog-meat restaurants in the northern centre of the city.

Appendix 1

LANGUAGE

The Korean language, part of the Altaic family of languages, developed in its modern form from the language of the Silla and some Mandarin and Japanese. Korea's longstanding use of Chinese characters in writing changed from the 15th century when a phonetic script called Hangul was developed with 17 consonants and 11 vowel sounds represented in very simple characters that could construct all of the linguistic syllables (since reduced from 28 to 24 characters). Hangul's simplicity allowed it to spread with relative ease beyond the elite and this is the script in use across Korea today.

Like Japanese, Korean traditionally had different grammar and vocabulary for addressing people of different ages, genders and social status, but after 1945, the Communists expunged the language of many of these nuances, many foreign and borrowed words and all writing in Chinese form.

North Korea's isolation has left it with a somewhat olde-worlde, 1940s form of the language, devoid of any modern slang whatsoever. The DPRK 'dialect' uses Pyongyang as its standard, spoken with a harsher tone than Korean in the south.

GENERAL

Hello	Annyong haseyo	It's too expensive	Nomu pissayo
Goodbye	Annyonghi kyeseyo	I'd like to buy…	…issoyu
Good morning/		Where is…?	…i odi issoyu?
afternoon/evening	Annyonghasimnikga	Excuse me	Yobosio
How are you?	Pyonanhasimnikga?	I don't understand	Modaradurossoyu
My name is (I am)		What street is this?	Yogin musun
John	Jega John imnida		gorimnikga?
Yes	Ye	I'm going to	Nanun Pyongyang-e
No	Aniyo	Pyongyang	gamnida
Please	Juseyu	doctor	uisa-sonsaengnim
Thank you	Gomapsumnida	hospital	byong-uon
How much is this…?	Iga olma eyo…?		

TRANSPORT

airport	konghang	Take me to…	…e kajuseyo
bus	bosu	Turn right	Oruntchoguro kaseyo
bus station	bosu tominol	Turn left	Wentchoguro kaseyo
bus stop	bosu chongnyujang	Go straight on	Dokparo kaseyo
metro	chihachol	How much to go	…kaji kanund olma
railway station	kichayok	to…?	eyo?
taxi	taegsi	Stop here	Yogiso seuojusibsio

271

hospital	*pyongwon*
pharmacy	*yakkuk*
embassy	*taesagwan*
doctor	*wisa-sonsaengnim*
Help me	*Towajuseyo!*
Call the police	*Kyongchal pulojuseyo*
Call a doctor	*Wisa pulojuseyo!*
It hurts here	*Apayo*

What street is this?	*Yogin musun gorimnikga?*	What station is this?	*Yogiga mosun yogeyo?*
Where can I buy a ticket?	*Pyo odiso salsu issoyo?*	Does this bus go to…?	*Ibosu… e kayu?*
Does this train go to…?	*Ichiga… e kayu?*	How long is the tour?	*Yohang hanund omana kollyoyo?*

HOTELS AND RESTAURANTS

hotel	*hotel*	Please give me…	*…jom jusipsio*
restaurant	*shiktang*	Please give me some tea	*Cha jom jusipsio*
toilet	*hwajangshil*	I don't eat pork/egg/meat	*Nanun doejigogi/ dalgyal/gogi an mogsumnida*
I'm hungry	*Che paegopun*		
I'm thirsty	*Che mongmarun*		
I'm tired	*Che pigonhan*		
Please show me the menu	*Sigsa annaepyo jusibsio*	Cheers!	*Konbae!*

FOOD

beans	*kong*	omelette	*dalgyalsam*
beef	*sogogi*	onion	*pa*
bread	*bang*	pork	*doaejigogi*
butter	*bada*	potatoes	*gamja*
carrot	*hongdangmu*	rice	*bab*
chicken	*dakgogi*	salad	*saengchae*
cucumber	*o-I*	soup	*gug*
egg	*dalgyal*	soya	*ganjang*
fish	*saengson*	spinach	*sigumchi*
fish soup	*saengson-gug*	tomato	*domado*
meat	*gogi*	vegetables	*yacha*

DRINKS

beer	*maegju*	milk	*uyu*
coffee	*kopi*	water (soda water)	*saida*
tea	*cha*		

OTHER USEFUL WORDS

post office	*ucheguk*	bank	*unhaeng*
department store	*pakwajom*		

TIME

What time is it now?	*Jigum myosimnikga?*	minute	*ban*
What time does		3 o'clock	*Se si*
(it)…	*Mun onje*	03.05	*se si da ban*
open/close/leave/	*yoroyo/tadoyo/*	03.15	*se si sibo ban*
arrive?	*donayo/tochakayo?*		

DAYS OF THE WEEK

Monday	*Wolyoil*	Friday	*Kumyoil*
Tuesday	*Hwayoil*	Saturday	*T'oyoil*
Wednesday	*Swuyoil*	Sunday	*Ilyoil*
Thursday	*Mokyoil*		

MONTHS

January	*Iluol*	July	*Chil-uol*
February	*I-uol*	August	*Pal-uol*
March	*Sam-uol*	September	*Gu-uol*
April	*Sa-uol*	October	*Si-uol*
May	*O-uol*	November	*Sibil-uol*
June	*Yu-uol*	December	*Sibi-uol*

NUMBERS

1	*hana*	30	*sorun*
2	*dul*	40	*mahun*
3	*sed*	50	*suin*
4	*ned*	60	*yesun*
5	*dasod*	70	*irun*
6	*yosod*	80	*yodun*
7	*ilgop*	90	*hun*
8	*yodol*	100	*baeg*
9	*ahop*	200	*I + baeg*
10	*yol*	1,000	*chon*
11	*yol + hana*	10,000	*baeg + man*
20	*sumul*	half	*ban*

SOME USEFUL PHRASES

What a fast Chollima speed!	*Cholima-sogdoimnida!*
Fancy abolishing taxation!	*Segumul opsaedani!*
President Kim Il Sung is	*Kim Il Sung jusongimun chamuro*
really the greatest communist	*uidaehan gongsanjuitusaisimyo*
fighter and a true revolutionary	*jinjonghan hyongmyongga isimnida*
Long live the Juche idea!	*Juche sasang-manse!*
Korea must be identified independently	*Josunun jajujoguro tong-il haeya hamnida*
Yankees are wolves in human shape	*Yankingum in gane tarul sun sungnyang-ida*

Appendix 2

FURTHER INFORMATION

The Korean Publications Exchange Association (*PO Box 222, Pyongyang;* ☏ *850 2 18111 (8842);* ✆ *850 2 381 4632/4416/4427*) welcomes orders from and exchange with foreign friends and overseas Korean compatriots.

BOOKS Many of the contemporary titles listed below are available through booksellers or can be found on www.amazon.co.uk or www.amazon.com. Older titles could be obtained through Probsthain's (*41 Great Russell St, London WC1B 3PE,* ☏ *020 7636 1096*), a specialist bookshop on east Asia, or the School of Oriental and African Studies (SOAS) (☏ *020 7637 2388; www.soas.ac.uk*). A comprehensive list of DPRK publications in Western languages can be obtained from the Korean Publications Exchange Association (see details above).

Contemporary DPRK

Abt, Felix *A Capitalist in North Korea: My Seven Years in the Hermit Kingdom* Tuttle Publishing, 2014, ASIN B00APO647E. Abt's seven years in the DPRK allowed him to see a very different country from the one normally portrayed, and have great adventures on the way. Meeting hundreds of high-ranking officials and ordinary Koreans, he helped set up the Pyongyang Business School among other ventures, and notes how young Koreans are signing up to study business – if only UN sanctions got out the way.

Cha, Victor *The Impossible State: North Korea, Past and Future* Vintage, 2012. By the National Security Council's director for Asian affairs. A neocon insider offers his sharp, catty view of how Seoul and Washington tried so hard to deal with Pyongyang.

Choi, Sung-Chul *Human Rights and North Korea* Institute of Unification Policy, Hanyang University, 1999, ISBN 89-86763-05-2.

Chol-Hwan, Kang, co-written with Rigoulot, Pierre *Aquariums of Pyongyang: Ten Years in the North Korean Gulag* Perseus Press, 2001, ISBN 1-903985-05-6. Kang's personal, chilling account of his life in a DPRK prison camp.

Cornell, Erik *North Korea under Communism* Routledge, 2002, ISBN 0700716971.

Cumings, Bruce *Korea's Place in the Sun* W W Norton & Co, 1998, ISBN 0-3933-168-15. A comprehensive history of Korea focusing mainly on the tumultuous last century and the origins of both sides' political economies.

Cumings, Bruce *North Korea: Another Country* The New Press; reprint 2004, ISBN-10: 1-565849-40-X. Cumings is one of the finest analysts and writers on the DPRK and its place in the world, and in this he charts the far deeper connections and battles going on between it, its neighbours and arch-nemesis the US than the rest of the world is commonly told.

Cumings, Bruce and Hoepli-Phalon, Nancy L (eds) *Divided Korea: United Future?* Headline Series, 1995, ISBN 0-8712-416-41.

Demick, Barbara. *Nothing to Envy: Ordinary Lives in North Korea* Granta Books, 2009, ISBN-10: 1-847081-41-X. A beautifully written account of the lives of North Koreans who survived the 1990s famine.

Everard, John *Only Beautiful, Please: A British Diplomat in North Asia* Pacific Research Center, 2012, ISBN-10: 1-931368-25-2. Everard, ex-UK ambassador to the DPRK, gives a somewhat undiplomatic take on the regime.

Grangereau, Philippe *Au Pays du Grand Mensonge: voyage en Corée du Nord* Le Serpent de Mer, 2001, ISBN 2-913490-05-0.

Harden, Blaine *Escape from Camp 14* Pan, 2013, ISBN-10: 0330519549. Shin Dong Hyuk was born in a gulag, and his mother and brother were executed after he informed on them. After a childhood full of hunger, abuse and torture, he escaped in 2005.

Harrison, Selig S *Korean Endgame: A Strategy for Reunification and US Disengagement* Princeton University Press, 2002, ISBN 0-691-09604-X 448. Harrison argues that the North is not about to collapse and the path to permanent peace on the peninsula is being obstructed by US policy.

Hayashi, Kazunobu and Komaki, Teruo (eds) *Kim Jong-Il's North Korea: An Arduous March* Institute of Developing Economies, Tokyo, 1997. Accessible accounts of the DPRK's economic woes.

Henderson, Gregory *Korea: The Politics of the Vortex* Harvard University Press, 1968.

Hunter, Helen-Louise *Kim Il Sung's North Korea* 1999, Library of Congress No 98-24560, ISBN 0-275-96296-2. Easy-to-read section-by-section account of life in the DPRK, from school to army to workers, based on declassified CIA reports from defectors.

Kang, Kyok *This is Paradise!* Little, Brown, 2007, ISBN-10: 0-316729-66-3. This book goes into uncomfortable depth detailing how life in the DPRK is anything but.

Kongdan Oh, Kongdan and Hassig, Ralph C *North Korea through the Looking Glass* Brookings Institution Press, 2000, ISBN 0-8157-6435-9. A must-read dissection of modern North Korea and how its society and economy have come to be.

Krause, Lawrence B and Cumings, Bruce *Korea's Economic Role in East Asia – The Great Game on the Korean Peninsula – Japanese Colonialism in Korea: A Comparative Perspective* James Lilley, 1997, ISBN 0-9653935-18.

Lankov, Andrei *The Real North Korea: Life and Politics in the Failed Stalinist Utopia* Oxford University Press (USA), 2013, ISBN-10: 0199964297. By the Russian professor of history at Seoul's Koomkin University.

Natsios, Andrew S *The Great North Korean Famine* United States Institute of Peace, 2002, ISBN 1-929223-33-1. In-depth coverage of the collapse of DPRK's agriculture.

Noland, Marcus and Bergsten, C *Avoiding the Apocalypse: The Future of the Two Koreas* Institute for International Economics, 2000, ISBN 0-881-322784. A droll and accessible yet broad account of the complex socioeconomic and security issues facing the North and the South.

Ok, Tae Hwan and Lee, Hong Yung *Prospects for Change in North Korea* Regents of the University of California & Research Institute for National Unification, Seoul, 1994, ISBN 1-55729-045-8.

Scalapino, Robert (ed) *North Korea Today* Frederick A Praeger, 1963, Library of Congress No 63-20152. A readable overview of the post-war DPRK reconstruction and rebirth.

Scalapino, Robert and Lee, Chong Sik *Communism in Korea* vols 1 & 2, University of California Press, 1972.

Smith, Hazel *Hungry for Peace* United States Institute of Peace Press, 2005, Library of Congress Control No 2005936704. A fascinating update on the ongoing issue of the DPRK's agricultural situation and its wider ramifications for the state's society and policies at home and abroad.

Suh, Dae-Sook and Lee, Chae-Jin (eds) *North Korea after Kim Il Sung* Lynne Reiner Publishers, 1998, ISBN 1-55587-763-X. A broad selection of essays on the DPRK's economic, military, political and foreign prospects.

Appendix 2 FURTHER INFORMATION

A2

Jin Sung, Jang *Dear Leader* Rider (UK) and Simon & Schuster (US), 2014. Jang Jin Sung, former poet laureate and chief propagandist under Kim Jong Il, defected to South Korea in 2004. *Dear Leader* is his fascinating and searing memoir detailing court life, his disillusion with the regime and his escape.

Korean history

Hatada, Takashi *A History of Korea* American Bibliographical Center, Clio Press, 1969, LCCCN 69-20450. A very economics-oriented take on Korean history but with some good passages, when not bogged down in detail.

Henthorn, William E *A History of Korea* Free Press, 1971, LCCCN 75-143511.

Maidment, Richard and Mackerras, Colin (eds) *Culture and Society in the Asia Pacific* Routledge, 1998, ISBN 0-415-17278-0.

Suh, Dae-Sook and Schultz, Edward J (eds) *Koreans in China* Center for Korean Studies, University of Hawaii 96822, 1988, ISBN 0-917536-18-5.

Tennant, Roger *A History of Korea* Kegan Paul International, 1996, ISBN 0-7103-0532-X. An enjoyably readable history of Korea.

Pyongyang Pingpong Diplomacy – What Achieved and Not Achieved Korea Herald, Kwanghuamun, PO Box 523, Seoul, ROK, 1979. Collection of largely speculative articles about what the 1979 Pyongyang Ping-Pong Tournament was to achieve. More interesting for how universally cynical Western journalists can be.

Language Bear in mind that neither of the following teach the nuances of 'North' Korean:

Kim, In-Seok *Colloquial Korean* Routledge, 1996, ISBN 0-415-10804-7.

Vincent, Mark and Yeon, Jaehoon *Teach Yourself Korean* Teach Yourself Books, 1997.

The Leaders

Armstrong, Charles *Tyranny of the Weak* Cornell University, 2013, ASIN B00E6TIEUE. From the Korean War to the collapse of the USSR in 1991, this book shows how the DPRK has, against great odds, dealt with the outside world to maximum advantage, its 'self reliance' enabling resistance to pressure to change from enemies and allies alike.

Baek, Jo Song *The Leadership Philosophy of Kim Jong Il* Foreign Languages Publishing House, Pyongyang, Korea Juche 88, 1999.

Buzo, Adrian *The Guerilla Dynasty* Westview Press, 1999, ISBN 0-8133-3659-7. This is the Pyongyangologists' guide to the DPRK, a masterpiece of inference.

Kim Chang Ha *The Immortal Juche Idea* Pyongyang Foreign Languages Publishing House, Pyongyang, 1984.

Kim Il Sung, *Kim Il Sung: Works* Foreign Languages Publishing House, 1996. The 39 volumes by the Great Man are the clearest DPRK-produced texts, for it is himself and his ideas in his own words.

Lankov, Andrei *From Stalin to Kim Il Sung: The Formation of North Korea 1945–1960* Rutgers University Press, 2002, ISBN 0-8135-3117-9. This charts in detail the first decades of North Korea when Kim Il Sung's power was forged to be absolute. This has a complete biography of Kim Il Sung to his death in 1994.

Suh, Dae Sook *Kim Il Sung: North Korean Leader* Columbia University Press, 1995, ISBN-10: 0231065736. Charting the gulf between the propaganda for and against the Great Leader from both sides, this is a great book on DPRK's first leader. Essential reading.

The True Story of Kim Jong Il The Institute for South–North Korea Studies, Korea Herald Inc, 1993, OCLC 28479091. Scandalous in every sense, this ROK publication is worth reading for its extreme view of the DPRK.

North Korean-published guides Few of the following publications can be found easily outside of the DPRK except in some university libraries, but contact the Korean Publications Exchange Association (*PO Box 222, Pyongyang, DPRK,* ☏ *+850 2 381 4632*).

Hyok, Hwang Bong and Ryol, Kim Jong *Korea Tour: A Land of Morning Calm, a Land of Attractions* National Tourism Administration Juche 86, 1997. Irritatingly vague at times.

Ju, Pang Hwan and Hyok, Hwang Bong *A Sightseeing Guide to Korea* National Tourism Administration, Foreign Languages Publishing House, 1991

Korea Tour National Tourism Administration, Pyongyang, 1998. One of the more recent guides with more factual details.

Kaesong/Mt Paektu/Mt Myohyang/Kumgang Tourist Advertisement and Information Agency, Songuja-dong, Mangyongdae, Pyongyang. Well-written guides to their respective areas, with good maps and details on routes and pockets of interest.

Pyongyang Review Foreign Languages Publishing House, Pyongyang, 1995. A dry mini-encyclopaedia on Pyongyang.

Overview of Korean culture

Hoare, James and Pares, Susan *Korea: An Introduction* Kegan Paul International Ltd, 1988, ISBN 0-7103-0299-1. A rounded and enjoyable introduction to the history and culture of the peninsula.

Hoare, James and Pares, Susan *Korea* World Bibliographical Series vol 204, 2000, ISBN 1-85109-246-3.

Howard, Keith, Pares, Susan and English, Tessa *Korea People, Country and Culture* SOAS, 1996, ISBN 0-7286-0266. A highly accessible breakdown of the major facets of Korean life.

Lee, Hyangjin *Contemporary Korean Cinema* Manchester University Press, 2000, ISBN 0-7190-6007-9. This thesis discusses cinema on both sides of Korea and details what's been shown at the Pyongyang Odeon.

Meuser, Philipp *Architectural and Cultural Guide: Pyongyang* Dom Publishers, 2012, ISBN-10: 3869221879. A two-volume guide by architect Philipp Meuser looking at the rebirth and rise of Pyongyang, what the building styles say and their use in symbolising the power of the cult over the individual.

Revolutionary Operas SOAS, London, DKN 782-387-559. A collection of operas produced through the lens of Juche.

Overviews of North Korea

Belke, Thomas J *Juche: A Christian's Study* Living Sacrifice Book Company, 1999, ISBN-10: 0882643290. This is a religious dissection of Juche but is far more readable than its title suggests, with lots of eyewitness accounts of what life is like in the North.

Crane, Charlie *Welcome to Pyongyang* Chris Boot, 2007, ISBN-10: 19057-120-49. A large-leafed series of fine photographs of Pyongyang.

Harrold, Michael *Comrades and Strangers: Behind the Closed Doors of North Korea* Wiley, 2004, ISBN 0-470-86976-3. A young Englishman lands a job in North Korea in 1986 and ends up staying for over seven years. It's a charming, insightful account of a life and love in the capital.

Lankov, Dr Andrei *Pyongyang and Its People: Notes of a Soviet Student* A very good read.

Phyo, Jon Won, Gang, An Chol and Su, Ri Pom *Panorama of Korea* Foreign Languages Publishing House, 1998.

Shuhachi, Inoue *Modern Korean and Kim Jong Il* Yuzankaku, 1984.

Springer, Chris *Pyongyang: The Hidden History of the North Korean Capital* Entente Br, 2003, ISBN 93 00 8104 0. This is a slightly odd book, with the appearance and at times written style of a classic DPRK-produced guidebook, but with a decidedly sharper commentary and some interesting nuggets of information.

Juche 88, 1999 Very similar in scope to *Pyongyang Review* and filled with maps and pictures to break up a fact-filled but dry text.

Travelogues from the early 19th and 20th centuries

Allen, Horace N *Things Korean* Fleming H Revell Co, 1908.

Bergman, Sten *In Korean Wilds and Villages* Travel Book Club, 1938. A somewhat pro-Japanese travelogue of this ornithologist's expedition around Korea shortly before World War II.

Bishop, Isabella Bird *Korea and Her Neighbours* Yonsei University Press, Seoul, reprint 1970. An interesting and warm account of missionary life in the late 19th century, if not a little heavy on the salvation angle.

Carles, W R *Life in Corea* Macmillan and Co, 1888. Quite a dull book for someone with such access to top-drawer chicanery.

Cavendish, Captain A E J *Korea and the Sacred White Mountain* George Philip & Son, 1894. A dour account of one man's hunting holiday, but useful to understand how the West saw Korea.

Griffis, William Elliot *Corea The Hermit Nation* Charles Scribner's Sons, New York, first published 1882, Scribner 1897. Of the accounts by early venturers to Korea, Griffis's is by far the most comprehensive, detailed and respectful.

Jaisohn, Philip *My Days in Korea and Other Essays* Institute for Modern Korea Studies, Yonsei University, 1999, ISBN 89-7141-497-9-03900. Jaisohn's works give a highly intelligent but personal insight into Korea's history from the run-up to Japanese colonialism, Japanese rule and the post-World War II division.

Sihanouk, Norodom *The Democratic People's Republic of Korea* Foreign Languages Publishing House, Pyongyang, 1980. The King of Cambodia gets a very nice tour of the country and dutifully records everything he was told.

Underwood, L H, MD *Fifteen Years among the Top-Knots* American Tract Society, 1904. American Lillian Underwood came to Korea as a young woman and became a physician to the Queen. Her memoir of this insight into the royal court was published in 1904.

War

Baldwin, Frank (ed) *Without Parallel: The Korean–American Relationship Since 1945* New York, Pantheon Books, 1974.

Becker, Jasper *Rogue Regime: Kim Jong-il and the Looming Threat of North Korea* Oxford University Press, 2006, ISBN-13 978 0 19 530891 4. Does what it says on the tin with a bit less accuracy.

Hastings, Max *The Korean War* Pan Macmillan, 1993, ISBN 0-333-59153-4. Well-written account of the conflict but virtually bereft of any Korean civilian or North Korean accounts.

Kirkbride, Major Wayne A *Panmunjom: Facts about the Korean DMZ* Hollym International Corp, USA, 1985, ISBN 0-930878-42-6.

Stone, I F *The Hidden History of the Korean War* Monthly Review Press, 1952, ASIN B0000CI9SA.

Vatcher, William H, Jr *Panmunjom* Frederick A Praeger Inc, 1958, LCCCN 58-7887. Hyperbole and vitriol at the armistice talks. A really bad-tempered book by someone evidently too close to the action.

A Practical Business Guide on the Democratic People's Republic of Korea European Union Chamber of Commerce in Korea, 1998, www.eucck.org.

MAGAZINES There are four magazines of interest: *Democratic People's Republic of Korea, Foreign Trade in the DPRK, Korea Business News Bulletin* and *Korea Today*.

WEBSITES Both Yahoo! and Google have free news tracker-alert gizmos that email you any and every DPRK-related headline you wish to receive.

Blogs and individuals

americaninnorthkorea.com By self-styled international adventurer and tour leader, Joseph Ferris III.

http://dandongxpat.com Written by expats living in the Chinese border city of Dandong, this chatty blog is subtitled 'the Gateway to North Korea' and provides a unique perspective on the DPRK.

www.korea-vision.com The website of Dr Leonid A Petrov, a noted Korea observer, writer and researcher at the Australian National University College of Asia and the Pacific.

www.a-capitalist-in-north-korea.com Felix Abt is a serial entrepreneur and investor in new markets including North Korea where he is a shareholder in several joint ventures.

http://thenorthkoreablog.com By two Californians, Jordan Harbinger and Gabriel Mizrahi, who've been infatuated with the DPRK since visiting in 2011.

www.retrodprk.com A kind of 'Ostalgie' site of images of the DPRK from the 1950 to the 1980s, run by Chris Graper.

Current affairs and think tanks

http://38north.org A readily accessible but detailed DPRK-focused site, covering all matters from mobile phones to nukes. It's an adjunct of the US–Korea Institute at the Paul H Nitze School of Advanced International Studies (SAIS), Johns Hopkins University, with its website www.uskoreainstitute.org.

http://blog.keia.org/ The Peninsula blog is a project of the Korea Economic Institute and is a forum for discussing foreign policy, economic, and social issues on the Korean peninsula.

http://goodfriendsusa.blogspot.co.uk Going for nearly a decade, the North Korea Today weekly newsletter published by Good Friends seeks to deliver 'the voices of North Korean people'.

http://nkleadershipwatch.wordpress.com This highly regarded site focuses on the DPRK's leadership, government, military and political institutes and culture.

north-korea.narod.ru/pyongyang_watch.htm Pyongyang Watch, a very well-sourced site for current affairs and a somewhat more academic tone.

www.asianresearch.org Association for Asian Research that seeks to educate the American public with in-depth analysis of Asia.

www.cfr.org Council on Foreign Relations is a forum giving the big guns in Western analysis a platform on the world's order. Can sign up to the Foreign Affairs newsletters.

www.fas.org Federation of American Scientists reports on the DPRK in a security context.

www.iaea.org International Atomic Energy Agency. Details of the situation regarding the DPRK's nuclear programmes.

www.koreasociety.org New York-based group that holds conferences on Korean political and business affairs, cultural and art tours, and issues affecting Koreans.

www.nautilus.org An informative website for the Institute for Security and Sustainability, a California-based think tank that focuses much on the DPRK and the broader region.

www.nbr.org The National Bureau on Asian Research, a US-based group organisation that fields analysis on all Asia's relations with the US. A portal is www.accessasia.org.

www.ncnk.org The US-based National Committee on North Korea is a coalition of former diplomats and experts on Korea working to promote understanding and engagement with the DPRK, covering all aspects from food to weapons.

www.piie.com The Peterson Institute for International Economics. Non-partisan institute dedicated to studying international economics, including the dynamics of east Asia.

www.sinonk.com Sino–NK collates Sinologists and Koreanists documenting and analysing the dynamics and ties between China and the DPRK.

www.wilsoncenter.org/program/north-korea-international-documentation-project The North Korea International Documentation Project disseminates declassified documents about the DPRK from former communist allies et al, for scholars and policymakers.

DRPK friendly sites

http://juche.v.wol.ne.jp/en.htm Tokyo-based International Institute of the Juche Idea, with the study of the philosophy of the Great and Dear Leaders available in Japanese, English, French and Spanish.

http://ndfsk.dyndns.org National Democratic Front of South Korea Unification Party and into abolition of US colonial rule in South Korea.

www.chongryon.com News and views of the General Association of Korean Residents in Japan, in Japanese.

www.hiddenhistory.info/Links.htm Collection of links compiled by Chris Springer about the DPRK.

www.korea-dpr.com The Korean Friendship Association's page, which is claimed to be the primary website for the DPRK, for business, travel, engagement and culture, and incorporating the Juche Idea Study Group of England.

www.ournation-school.com Kim Il Sung Open University website dedicated mostly to Juche.

Diaspora

http://londonkoreanlinks.net/ Covering Korean things in London since 2006.

www.kancc.org Korean American National Co-ordinating Council providing information for Korean Americans.

Economy

http://eba.nosotek.com The European Business Association, operating since 2005, works to help broach relations and foster investment into the DPRK from European companies.

www.kbc-global.com The very handsome website of the Korean Business Consultants company, working to bring understanding and investment to the DPRK.

www.nkeconwatch.com North Korea Economy Watch. A very well-organised archive of news and features from many sources about the DPRK and the changes it's undergoing, maintained and strung together by Curtis Melvin.

www.northkoreatech.org Technology-focused blog covering developments in the country's IT industry, media, cyber warfare, space programmes and iPads!

www.uktradeinvest.gov.uk Homepage for the UK's department of trade, investment and exports.

Education and engagement

https://sites.google.com/site/nzdprksociety/Home The New Zealand–DPRK Society works to increase engagement and understanding between the two countries.

www.cankor.ca A Canadian education and engagement resource seeking peaceful alternatives to the region's conflicts and refuting stereotypes from the Western media.

www.chosonexchange.org Choson Exchange is a Singaporean non-profit organisation focused on providing top-quality training in business, economic policy and law to young North Koreans.

www.dprkorea.org.nz DPR–Korea New Zealand is an NGO aimed at promoting diplomatic, cultural and economic ties between the DPRK and New Zealand.

www.pyongyangproject.org A self-sustaining group working in the DPRK and Yanbian in education and development, providing scholarships, training and humanitarian assistance for North Koreans.

Government and diplomacy

http://kp.china-embassy.org/eng The Chinese Embassy in Pyongyang's website, which among other things has information about PRC–DPRK cultural exchanges.

www.china.org.cn/international/six-party/node_1202851.htm This is the official Chinese state portal for information and coverage of the Six-Party Talks, working to resolve the DPRK's nuclear programme.

www.mofa.go.jp/policy/other/bluebook/index.html Japan's ministry of foreign affairs annually publishes a Diplomatic Bluebook that summarises the country's foreign policy.

www.swedenabroad.com/en-GB/Embassies/Pyongyang/ This gives information about Sweden's embassy in Pyongyang.

www.unikorea.go.kr Homepage for the ROK's Ministry of Unification.

Humanitarian/aid

http://greentreekorea.org/ The Green Tree Charity Foundation sends food et al to North Korea's disabled.

http://kp.one.un.org The UN's umbrella site for its work in the DPRK.

www.cureblindness.org The Tilganga Institute of Ophthalmology under the Himalayan Training Program trains North Korean providers and surgical teams in improving eye care.

www.engagedprk.org Engage DPRK is an excellent online resource mapping all of the development, humanitarian, business and education projects in the DPRK that have been, and are, run by outside organisations since 1995.

www.fao.org The UN's Food and Agriculture Organisation ranks alongside the WFP in terms of reach and involvement in rehabilitating the DPRK's agricultural base.

www.goodneighbors.org Humanitarian NGO with projects in the DPRK.

www.handicap-international.us/north_korea Supports the Korean Federation for the Protection of the Disabled (KFPD), assisted by the Kadoorie Charitable Foundation www.lucwesd.org/Enasp/AmaiAbout.asp?ID=25 in producing prostheses.

www.hollows.org.au/our-work/north-korea The Fred Hollows Foundation focuses on cataract surgery.

www.kccc.org Korea Campus Crusade for Christ but the chapter at www.kcccla.com is in English.

www.lovethechildren.org Love North Korean Children is a small UK-based NGO working to provide food and cooking facilities for orphanages across the DPRK.

Some groups are Christian in orientation, but are *not* proselytising.

www.mercycorps.org/countries/northkorea Mercy Corps has supplied fish and fruit trees for farm projects in the DPRK.

www.reah.org Reah is a Church-backed umbrella organisation for humanitarian works in the DPRK, with its Reah International mission of 'empowering the people of the DPRK one project at a time'.

www.thelighthousefoundation.com Lighthouse Foundation.

www.together-hamhung.org/ TOGETHER Hamhung e.V is a German NGO working on educational and vocational training for the deaf and blind.

www.unicef.org/dprk The UN Children's Fund has an extensive programme in-country covering education, health, nutrition and water sanitation.

www.un.org Home page of the United Nations, which has been involved with the DPRK in peace and war, from sending troops there in 1950 to dealing with its famine and nuclear projects.

www.wfp.org The UN's World Food Programme, working in the DPRK since the 1990s and with perhaps the most comprehensive, up-to-date information on the country's food situation.

www.wheatmissionnk.org Wheat Mission ministries, works with orphanages, operates bread and noodle factories in Pyongyang and beyond, and has a medical force working with the North Korean Medical Association.

www.who.int/countries/prk/en/ The World Health Organisation's work in the DPRK.

Human rights

en.nknet.org Network for North Korean Democracy and Human Rights, set up in 1999, and the creators of NK Daily and Radio Free Chosun (*www.rfchosun.org*).

www.amnesty.org Amnesty International does not have a presence in the DPRK but has several publications available about conditions there.

www.eahrnk.org European Alliance for Human Rights in North Korea (EAHRNK) set up in 2013, young activists, journalists and academics.

www.hrnk.org The US Committee For Human Rights in North Korea has a selection of excellent publications detailing the set up of the security and incarceration apparatuses within the DPRK. Includes information about the plight of worshippers in the DPRK. Has several publications for free download.

www.hrw.org/nkorea Human Rights Watch (hitherto known as Helsinki Watch) is a US-based global NGO set up to protect human rights.

www.jayu.ca This Canada-based venture hosts a film festival and has guest speakers all working to educate about human rights in the DPRK.

www.libertyinnorthkorea.org This organisation works on the ground to prise refugees out from China before they are caught and repatriated.

www.northkoreacampaignuk.org A UK-based grass-roots organisation concerning human rights.

www.stopnkcrimes.org The International Coalition to Stop Crimes against Humanity in North Korea (ICNK) seeks a UN Commission of Inquiry into the DPRK's human rights abuses, raising awareness through hearings, in parliaments and cultural exhibitions.

News

http://38north.org A detailed but readily accessible DPRK-focused site, covering all matters from mobile phones to nukes.

http://english.chosun.com ROK-based news agency, Chosun Ilbo.

http://english.yonhapnews.co.kr Yonhap is the ROK's largest news organisation and is publicly funded. Its DPRK-specific news is at http://english.yonhapnews.co.kr/northkorea/index.html.

http://iis-db.stanford.edu/pubs/24593/Zellweger_Disabilities_DPRK_web.pdf Kathi Zellweger's report from early 2014 for the Asia Pacific Research Center at Stanford looks at the position of disabled people in North Korea and charts the efforts and impacts that outside NGOs can have on their plight.

http://nkleadershipwatch.wordpress.com This highly regarded site focuses on the DPRK's leadership, government, military and political institutes and culture.

www.dailynk.com/english The Daily NK is a ROK-based news and features outlet, focusing on their neighbour to the north.

www.kcna.kp The website of Korea Central News Agency, the DPRK's official online daily news output, giving Pyongyang's perspective amid much furious, florid and flowery language, and a key resource for Pyongyang watchers, although its archive was deleted en masse in 2013. A slower backup site is www.kcna.co.jp.

www.koreatimes.co.kr ROK-oriented news outlet of the *Korea Times*.

www.naenara.com.kp/en 'Naenara', or 'my country' in Korean. The DPRK's most frequent English-language publications, namely the *Pyongyang Times*, *Korea*, *Korea Today* and *Foreign Trade*, which are excellent publications to get the look, feel and themes of the state's output and outlook, are all accessible online from here.

www.newfocusintl.com New Focus International is edited and run by former refugees from the DPRK, providing news based on North Korean insights and well-placed sources in the diplomatic and business sectors and the Sino–DPRK borders.

www.nknews.org A London-based real-time subscription news agency, solely focused on the DPRK, with a growing array of experts and Koreans providing insight.

www.ohchr.org/en/hrbodies/hrc/coidprk/pages/commissioninquiryonhrindprk.aspx See the report by the UN Commission of Inquiry, which produced a damning account of North Korea's human rights position in March 2014.

www.rfa.org Radio Free Asia is a highly esteemed online multi-media print, audio and TV outlet for news and features about Asia, with an extensive section on the DPRK.

www.rodong.rep.kp/ko/ The Central Committee of the Korean Worker's Party's new publication is *Rodung Sinmun*, available online here, with many articles in English.

www.uriminzokkiri.com A somewhat pro-DPRK news website with news and views in Korean, English, Russian, Chinese and Japanese, albeit with not all articles promptly translated into every language.

www.vok.rep.kp Shortwave radio station Voice of Korea can be listened to online.

Religion
www.nkmissions.com An umbrella organisation for missions to the DPRK.

ROK NGOs There are scores of NGOs in the ROK of humanitarian, religious and political origin involved in projects in the DPRK. The ten NGOs listed below have been randomly selected to show the diversity of such groups. The 'Korea NGO Council for Cooperation with North Korea' is an overarching group with 56 members, with an available online list being here: www.ncnk.org/resources/briefing-papers/all-briefing-papers/ROK_NGO_Issue_Brief.pdf.

www.goat4north.net Supplies goats to the DPRK.

www.icf.or.kr International Corn Foundation doing work since 1998 on famine relief by way of developing 'super corn' and various techniques to increase yields.

www.jts.or.kr Join Together Society. A development and aid agency working across Asia.

www.kfhi.or.kr Food for the Hungry International has projects in agriculture, education, general and emergency aid.

www.kltm.org Korea Living Together Movement covers various humanitarian, agricultural and development projects.

www.kuninet.or.kr The Korean Unification Network.

www.nkhumanrights.or.kr Citizens' Alliance for North Korean Human Rights, a ROK-based organisation providing help and assistance for refugees, particularly those in the ROK.

www.okfriend.org 'Okedongmu' society has set up various children-oriented nutrition, medical and educational projects.

www.pck.or.kr The Presbyterian Church of Korea.

www.sc.or.kr The Korean chapter of Save the Children

www.won.or.kr Won Buddhism Movement for Showing Grace is involved in humanitarian and medical projects.

Tourism and general travel
https://www.cia.gov/library/publications/the-world-factbook/index.html CIA.

www.exploreworldwide.com Adventure tourism company Explore Worldwide includes the DPRK amid its bevy of destinations.

www.fco.gov.uk British Foreign and Commonwealth Office for the British Government's view on travel to the DPRK.

www.korea.net A broad 'gateway' to all things Korean, somewhat southern-centric.

www.koryogroup.com Website for the pioneering Beijing-based Koryo Tours company, taking tours in the DPRK since 1993, with links and blog.

www.pyongyang-travel.com A Germany-based travel company with a website in English, German and Norwegian.

www.regent-holidays.co.uk UK-based firm that's been running tours to the further-flung parts of the world for 40 years.

www.state.gov US Department of State's website where general information and travel warnings about the DPRK can be found.

www.visitkorea.or.kr General website for South Korean tourism.

www.vnc.nl/northkorea Netherlands-based VNC Asia Travel goes to the DPRK.

Index

INDEX OF ADVERTISERS